THE MIDDLE WAY
The Emergence of Modern Religious Trends in
Nineteenth-Century Judaism

VOLUME TWO

STUDIES IN ORTHODOX JUDAISM

SERIES EDITOR
Marc B. Shapiro *(University of Scranton, Scranton, Pennsylvania)*

EDITORIAL BOARD:
Alan Brill *(Seton Hall University, South Orange, New Jersey)*
Benjamin Brown *(Hebrew University, Jerusalem)*
David Ellenson *(Hebrew Union College, New York)*
Adam S. Ferziger *(Bar-Ilan University, Ramat Gan)*
Miri Freud-Kandel *(University of Oxford, Oxford)*
Jeffrey Gurock *(Yeshiva University, New York)*
Shlomo Tikoshinski *(Jerusalem)*

THE MIDDLE WAY

The Emergence of Modern Religious Trends in Nineteenth-Century Judaism

Responses to Modernity in the Philosophy of
Z. H. Chajes, S. R. Hirsch,
AND S.D. Luzzatto

Ephraim Chamiel

VOLUME TWO

EDITOR: Dr. Asael Abelman
TRANSLATOR: Dr. Jeffrey Green

Library of Congress Cataloging-in-Publication Data:
A catalog record for this title is available from the Library of Congress.
Copyright © 2014 Academic Studies Press
All rights reserved

Vol. I:
ISBN 978-1-61811-407-5 (hardback)
ISBN 978-1-6181-409-9 (electronic)

Vol. II:
ISBN 978-1-61811-408-2 (hardback)
ISBN 978-1-6181-410-5 (electronic)

Cover design by Ivan Grave
On the cover:
"The Return of the Jewish Volunteer from the Wars of Liberation to His Family Still Living According to Old Customs", by Moritz Daniel Oppenheim (1833-34).

Published by Academic Studies Press in 2014.
28 Montfern Avenue
Brighton, MA 02135, USA
press@academicstudiespress.com
www.academicstudiespress.com

Contents

VOLUME ONE

Preface   *xi*
Preface to the English Edition   *xvii*
Translator's Note   *xix*

INTRODUCTION:
THE NEW MIDDLE WAY AND ITS PROPONENTS   2

CHAPTER ONE:
BIBLE CRITICISM AND THE BIBLICAL REVOLUTION   59

CHAPTER TWO:
RELIGIOUS REFORM: THE REFORM MOVEMENT AND THE HISTORICAL POSITIVE SCHOOL   158

CHAPTER THREE:
HASKALA, WISSENSCHAFT DES JUDENTUMS, AND THE INCLUSION OF SECULAR STUDIES IN EDUCATION   344

VOLUME TWO

CHAPTER FOUR:
EMANCIPATION, THE SPIRITUALIZATION OF REDEMPTION AND THE NEUTRALIZATION OF THE LAND OF ISRAEL

The Emancipation	1
Models of the Relation to the Land of Israel, to Exile, and to Redemption in Judaism	2
The Realists: The Land of Israel as a Focus for a Physical Attraction in History	3
The Utopians: The Land of Israel Is Distant, Outside of History	4
Exile as the Jewish Mission to the Nations	5
Judah Halevi	6
Maimonides	6
Nachmanides	7
Mendelssohn's Position	7
The Radical Neutralizing Position	13
Chajes's Response	15
Emancipation	16
The Arguments against Giving Rights to the Jews	16
Universalism	20
The Accusation of Dual Loyalty and the Neutralizing Response	25
The Reason for the Revelation to the Jewish People	32
The Mission and Progress	35
Hirsch's Response	38
Universalism and Humanity	38
Emancipation	43
The Arguments Against Giving Rights to the Jews and Dual Loyalty	46
The Neutralization of the Return to Zion and the Land of Israel	47
The Status of the Land of Israel According to Judaism	50

The Land of Israel has no Essential Sanctity	55
Why the Land of Israel Was Chosen	57
The Torah is Above Place and Time	61
Idealization of the Diaspora	63
Neutralization of the Temple	68
The Efforts of Rabbi Kalischer to Enlist Hirsch in Support of Settling the Land	72
Progress	75
The Reason for the Revelation to the Jewish People	78
The Mission	82
An Active Mission	87
The Image of the Messianic Future	89
Luzzatto's Response	99
Universalism and Humanity	99
Emancipation	103
The Accusation of Dual Loyalty, Neutralization of the Return to Zion, and the Messianic Future	105
Why the Land of Israel was Chosen	107
Progress and Mission	108
The Excellence of the Jewish People	111
The Passive Mission	114
The Turning Point	116
Summary	126

CHAPTER FIVE:
ATTITUDE TOWARD THE OTHER: IMPROVEMENT IN THE STATUS OF WOMEN

The Status of Women in Judaism: Background	128
The Position of the Haskala Movement	133
The Reform Position	135
The Traditional Religious Response: The Men of the Middle on the Status of Women	138
Chajes's Response	139
The Status of Women in the Framework of the Purpose of Man	140
Teaching Torah to Women	145
The Tension in the Middle Position: The Status of Women in the Synagogue	147
The Tension in the Middle Position: Women's Wigs	149
Hirsch's Response	152
Revolution: Women are Superior to Men	153
Woman in the Sources	166

    Education of Girls   *171*
    Personal Status   *175*
    Permissiveness and Modesty   *176*
Summary   *181*
Luzzatto's Response   *181*
    The Status of Women   *182*
    Permissiveness and Natural Morality   *191*
Summary   *198*

CHAPTER SIX:
THE RELATION TO THE OTHER: RELIGIOUS TOLERANCE

Background   *201*
Mendelssohn's Position   *213*
The Reform Response   *221*
The Traditional Religious Response: The Men of the
    Middle on Christianity and Islam   *223*
Chajes's Response   *224*
    The Difficult History   *225*
    The Damascus Blood Libel   *229*
    The Status of Christianity and Islam in Judaism   *231*
    The Present Situation and Hopes for the Future   *234*
    Summary   *237*
Hirsch's Response   *238*
    The Dreadful Past and the Wonderful Present   *240*
    The Figure of Jesus   *245*
    Original Sin: A Pagan Dogma   *249*
    Some Criticism   *253*
    Christianity as a Religion of Death: The Ultimate Source
        of Ritual Impurity, and the Place of Religious Leaders   *256*
    Monasticism and Asceticism   *264*
    The Importance of the Practical Commandments
        and their Place in the Religion   *269*
    The Status of Islam   *273*
    Summary   *275*
Luzzatto's Response   *277*
    The Status of Christianity   *278*
    Jewish Tolerance for Other Religions   *283*
Summary   *290*

Summary
   Chajes: The Talmudist and Rationalist, and
      the Restrictive Identicality Approach   295
   Hirsch: The Romantic Educator and the Position
      of Neo-Fundamentalist Identicality   299
   Luzzatto: The Romantic Scholar and
      the Position of Dual Truth   304

Epilogue
   Torah from Sinai and Halakha from Heaven   310
   Religious Fanaticism   312
   Universalism and Secular Studies   312
   The Combination and Contradiction of
      Revelation and Reason   313
   The Status of Women   313
   The Literal Meaning of the Bible   314
   The Attitude toward the Weak in Society   314
   Influence in the Twentieth Century   315
   Today   316

Appendices
   Appendix to Chapter One: Who is a *Ger*?   319

Appendix to Chapter Two: Illustration and Comparative Table for Clarification
   The Middle Trend   327

Appendix to Chapter Three: The Importance of the Study of History
   Introduction   331
   Chajes   332
   Hirsch   337
   Luzzatto   342

Bibliography
   Primary Sources   346
   Secondary Sources   351

Index
   Index of Subjects   369
   Index of Names   393

CHAPTER FOUR

Emancipation, the Spiritualization of Redemption, and the Neutralization of the Land of Israel

THE EMANCIPATION

A central modern phenomenon with which the Orthodox rabbis had to struggle was emancipation, which was granted to the Jews in one state after another in Europe. Generally, the Edict of Tolerance issued by the Austrian emperor Joseph II in 1781 is seen as the beginning of Emancipation. The process then gained impetus from the French Revolution, the Napoleonic wars, and the Revolutions of 1848.

Emancipation had important and critical effects on the Jews. The traditional religious scholars of the middle way examined the matter meticulously and found both positive and negative influences. On the one hand, the Jews were exposed to important sources of culture and allowed to engage in new professional fields, enabling them to take part increasingly in social, economic, academic, and political life, and many saw this as the beginning of the messianic age. On the other hand, there was great apprehension that the new openness might entice Jews to lose their bearings and convert, forgetting their uniqueness and special mission.

Indeed, in the wake of Emancipation and Haskala came acculturation and secularization, the desire to integrate into the non-Jewish world and even to assimilate and blend in. Universalistic and pluralistic ideologies of society and politics developed among the Jews, calling for reform of the Halakha, diminishing Jewish particularism, and rejecting the ideas of a personal messiah and of national redemption in the Land of Israel. These positions sought to spiritualize the idea of redemption and combine it with the redemption of Europe and of humanity, according to the natural, universal religion of reason or purified Christianity, and to neutralize the idea of the Land of Israel as an actual, physical place to which people yearned to return. According to this new approach, Zion was in Europe, and full emancipation among the nations of reason was redemption.

In contrast to the aforementioned influence, which distanced the Land of Israel from the minds of the people, there was also another alternative, bringing it closer, which was also opened up by Emancipation. Jews were now free to move from place to place, and the shifting of awareness to the Land of Israel as a realistic option became possible. Should this possibility be rejected or encouraged? Was it beneficial or dangerous?

Being post-Haskala thinkers, who had internalized important parts of the ideas of the Haskala movement, the modern but traditionally religious men of the middle way embraced equality of rights and universalism, and the neutralization of the Land of Israel. However, they had to consolidate an ideology that would justify Jewish particularism, preserve the Halakha and messianic hopes, and explain the need for Judaism and the role of the Jewish people among the nations in the new situation, and which would resolve the issue of dual loyalty. The status of the Land of Israel as a focus of attraction, at a time when the goods of Europe, both material and spiritual, were available to the Jews in the Diaspora, was therefore a central question that reverberated in the air.

MODELS OF THE RELATION TO THE LAND OF ISRAEL, TO EXILE, AND TO REDEMPTION IN JUDAISM

To understand the attitude toward the Land of Israel in Jewish thought in Europe during the first half of the nineteenth century, I will briefly summarize the positions taken on this subject in the history of this thought. In four articles, Aviezer Ravitzky[1] analyzed the theories on this subject, and these opinions can be laid out as follows:

THE REALISTS: THE LAND OF ISRAEL AS A FOCUS FOR A PHYSICAL ATTRACTION IN HISTORY

1. Those yearning for the homeland

Attraction for the purpose of fulfilling the commandments that can only be performed in the land—the Tosafists of France.
Attraction to the sanctity of the land, a special land in essence, climate, and geography, the only place where there is prophecy and perfection is possible in observing the commandments—Judah Halevi.

Attraction for political actualization—the Land was chosen at the beginning of human and Jewish history as the only place where an independent Jewish monarchy is possible, and where redemption will take place.

The expected future will unfold in three stages. First, the rebirth in the world of a Jewish state according to the Torah; second, the adoption by the nations of belief in the One God; and third, full spiritual and social reform of humanity. Only the third stage is Utopian and meta-historical—Maimonides.

2. Those Fearful of Sanctity

Only a select minority is worthy of living in the Land of Israel— Maharam of Rothenburg [Rabbi Meir ben Baruch of Rothenburg] and Hashla [Isaiah Horowitz, know by the name of his most important book, *Shnei Luḥot Habrit*].

---

[1] "'Hatsivi Lakh Tsiunim' Letsion: Gilgulo Shel Ra'ayon," in idem, *Al Da'at Hamaqom* (Jerusalem, 1991), 34-74; "'Kefi Koaḥ Haadam': Yemot Hamashiaḥ Bemishnat Harambam," in ibid., 74-105; "'Shelo Ya'alu Baḥoma": 'Al Rishuman Shel Shlosh Hashevu'ot Betoledot Yisrael," appendix to *Haqets Hamegule Umedinat Yisrael* (Tel Aviv, 1993); "Erets Ḥemda Veharada: Hayaḥas Hadu-Erki Leerets-Yisrael Bimqorot Yisrael," in *Erets Yisrael Bahagut Hayehudit Haḥadasha*, ed. idem (Jerusalem, 1998), 1-41. Referred to below respectively as "Tsiunim," "Hamashiaḥ," "Haqets," and "ḥemda."

The land has essential, mystical qualities; it is connected to the divine world and draws influence from it. It is the only place where observing the commandments has essential inner value. It is a religious duty for anyone who is capable of dealing with its sanctity to move there—Nachmanides.

THE UTOPIANS: THE LAND OF ISRAEL IS DISTANT, OUTSIDE OF HISTORY

1. Those Yearning for the Land

Kabbalists and mystics who sever themselves from the land because of fear of sin, awe of its sanctity, and the prohibition against "forcing the end" (the "Three Oaths" of BT Ketubot 111a)—Rabbi Isaac of Acre, Rabbi Ezra and Rabbi Azriel, Ḥasiduti Ashkenaz, Abraham Galante, the Maharal of Prague, the major Hasidic rabbis, Jonathan Eybeschutz.[2]

---

2   These are the references to Ravitzky, according to the date of publication, as listed in the previous note: the Tosafists—1993, 283; 1998, 19. Judah Halevi—1991, 46; 1998, 290. Maimonides—1991, 75-82; 1993, 282; 1998, 21. Maharam—1998, 5. Hashlah—1993, 297; 1998, 7. Nachmanides—1991, 42; 1993, 287. Philo—1998, 15. Meiri—1998, 15. Samuel Jaffe—1993, 292. Emden—1993, 299. Mendelssohn—1993, 301. Isaac of Acre—1998, 15. Rabbi Ezra and Rabbi Azriel—1993, 282. Ḥasidei Ashkenaz—1993, 284. Galante—1993, 293. Maharal—1991, 61; 1993, 294. The Major Hasidic rabbis—1993, 301; 1998, 15. Eybeschutz—1991, 64; 1993, 300; 1998, 23. On Judah Halevi and Maimonides, see also E. Schweid, *Moledet Veerets Ye'uda* (Tel Aviv, 1979), 59-78, and on the kabbalists and Nachmanides, 79-82. On the mystical, neutralizing position of the kabbalists versus that of Nachmanides, see M. Idel, "'Al Erets-Yisrael Bamaḥashava Hamistit Shel Yemei-Habeinayim," in *Erets Yisrael Bahagut Hayehudit Biyemei Habeinayim*, ed. A Ravitsky et al. (Jerusalem, 1991), 193-215. On the position of Nachmanides versus the neutralizing positions of Rabbi Ezra and Rabbi Azriel, see H. Pedaya, "Erets-Shel-Ruaḥ Veerets Mamash: R. 'Ezra, R. 'Azriel Veharamban," in ibid., 233-90. On the qualities of the Land according to Nachmanides, see Halbertal, *Haramban*, 173-75, 230-32, 260-65. According to his comprehensive explanation, the Land of Israel possesses a cosmic link with the Divine Presence [Shekhina], and it also possesses its own qualities and essences. As a result, in an ontological, non-voluntary fashion, liberation from the rule of inert nature takes place, and it is in a constant state of hidden miracles, with which the righteous is privileged, and the sinner is punished because of it by being driven out of the land. On the position of Judah Halevi, see also Guttmann, *Hapilosofia*, 120. On Maimonides's position, see S. Rosenberg, *Be'iqvot Hakuzari* (Jerusalem, 1991), 252; I. Twersky, "Erets-Yisrael Vegalut Bemishnato Shel

2. The Neutralizers

Philosophers and scholars who strengthened consciousness of exile and Jewish historical passivity.

Within history there are physical or spiritual substitutes for the Land of Israel: a person's body or intelligence, his present location, the community, *Kneset Yisrael* [the Jewish collective], the Torah, the human spirit, or the world. The spiritual substitute for the Land of Israel makes it possible to achieve religious fulfillment and moral and religious perfection even outside of the Land of Israel. Those who take this view are likely to refer to the Three Oaths, and they seek to strengthen Jewish life in the Diaspora and to encourage communities in difficult times or to maintain their achievements—Philo, Meiri, Samuel Jaffe, Jacob Emden, Mendelssohn.[3]

Below I show how the modern religious thinkers fit into this model.

EXILE AS THE JEWISH MISSION TO THE NATIONS

The idea of the mission or destiny of the Jewish people being the reason for the exile and part of God's plan in history is not a new one. In the early nineteenth century, after the French Revolution and the

---

Harambam," in *Erets Yisrael Bahagut Hayehudit Biyemei Habeinayim*, 90-123; A. Funkenstein, *Tadmit Vetoda'a Historit Bayahadut Uvisvivata Hatarbutit* (Tel Aviv, 1991), 103-56. On the mission according to Judah Halevi and the parable of the grain, see Rosenberg, *Hakuzari*, 87-88. On Judah Halevi's attitude toward the special merit of the Land and the people and the attitude toward exile and living in actual Zion, see ibid., 317-320. On the meaning of exile and Jewish passivity and activism in the course of history, see Funkenstein, *Tadmit*, 232-42. Compare the opinions on Maimonides and Nachmanides mentioned above to that of M. Z. Nehorai, "Erets-Yisrael Betoratam Shel Harambam Veharamban," in *Erets Yisrael Bahagut Hayehudit Biyemei Habeinayim*, 123-38, and on Judah Halevi, to the opinion of Y. Silman, "Artsiuta Shel Erets-Yisrael Besefer Hakuzari," in *Erets Yisrael Bahagut Hayehudit Biyemei Habeinayim*, 77-90. Naturally the model presented here is general and does not go into the nuances between the various positions. A different model is offered by Schwartz, *Hara'ayon*, regarding the medieval thinkers. He distinguishes between the apocalyptic messianism of Sa'adia Gaon (28-38) and the personal, naturalistic messianism of Maimonides (69-89). Judah Halevi (55-69) is one of those who led the process from the Geonim to Maimonides, and there are motives of both kinds of messianism in his work.

3 On the neutralizing philosophers, see Ravitzky, *Haqets*, 292, 299, 301; "Ḥemda," 15.

beginning of Emancipation, when it seemed as if, finally, humanity had truly embraced ethical monotheism and progress was clearly emerging, the idea moved to the center of the arena. However, this idea had already existed among medieval thinkers:

Judah Halevi

In the *Kuzari* 4:23, the Rabbi says:

> God has a secret and wise design concerning us, which should be compared to the wisdom hidden in the seed which falls into the ground, where it undergoes an external transformation into earth, water and dirt, without leaving a trace for him who looks down upon it. It is, however, the seed itself which transforms earth and water into its own substance, carries it from one stage to another, until it refines the elements and transfers them into something like itself, casting off husks, leaves, etc., and allowing the pure core to appear, capable of bearing the Divine Influence. The original seed produced the tree bearing fruit resembling that from which it had been produced. In the same manner, so it is with the religion of Moses. All the religions that have come after it are, in truth, being transformed to be like it, even though outwardly they reject it. These religions [Christianity and Islam] are thus only a preparation for the awaited Messiah who is the fruit. And all of them, when they acknowledge this, will come to be his fruit, and the tree will be one. Then they will exalt the root. Then they will revere the origin which they formerly dispersed, as we have observed concerning the words: "Behold My servant prospers."

Maimonides

In *Mishneh Torah*, Hilkhot Melakhim, the end of chapter 11 (in the uncensored Venice and Amsterdam editions), Maimonides explains who the Messiah is and speaks of two false messiahs who nevertheless were chosen by Providence to spread the principles of Judaism in the world: Jesus and Muhammad. Jesus was executed by a rabbinical court after causing the loss of Jewish lives and the dispersal of Jews and misleading the world, as if the Torah had been replaced and one should worship a different god:

Nevertheless, the thoughts of the Creator of the world are not within the power of man to comprehend, for His ways are not our ways, nor are His thoughts, our thoughts. Ultimately, all the deeds of Jesus of Nazareth and that Ishmaelite who arose after him will only serve to prepare the way for Mashiach's coming and the improvement of the entire world, motivating the nations to serve God together as Tzephaniah 3:9 states: "I will transform the peoples to a purer language that they all will call upon the name of God and serve Him with one purpose." How will this come about? The entire world has already become filled with the mention of Mashiach, Torah, and mitzvot. These matters have been spread to the furthermost islands to many stubborn-hearted nations. They discuss these matters and the mitzvot of the Torah, saying: "These mitzvot were true, but were already negated in the present age and are not applicable for all time." Others say: "These mitzvot contain secret matters and are not to be understood to their external [literal] meaning. The Mashiach has already come and revealed these secrets." When the true Messianic king will arise and prove successful, his position becoming exalted and uplifted, they will all return and realize that their ancestors endowed them with a false heritage and their prophets and ancestors caused them to err.

[Trans. Rabbi Eliyahu Touger, available online: http://www.chabad.org/library/article_cdo/aid/682956/jewish/mishneh-torah.htm]

Nachmanides

In his sermon "Torat Hashem Temima" [The Torah of God is Perfect], which he gave following the Barcelona Dispute, Nachmanides used the words of Maimonides to clarify his position on this subject and copied them almost verbatim, except for the sentence, "the improvement of the entire world, motivating the nations to serve God together," and the quotation from Zephaniah 3:9. He apparently omitted these because it seemed excessive to him to share the worship of God with other religions, and he preferred Maimonides's following remarks, which clearly imply that they are erroneous.

MENDELSSOHN'S POSITION

Mendelssohn's views stand in the background of nineteenth-century trends in Judaism. His point of departure was philosophical, rationalist, and universalist, according to which, by means of reason, which was the common property of all human beings, it was possible to reach the eternal metaphysical truths that every person needed in order to attain happiness and moral and intellectual perfection. The man who maintained this position was a proud, religious Jew, who observed the commandments and believed in the revelation to the Jewish people and in their messianic hopes, and he had to struggle with two cardinal questions, which are raised in his writing. These questions preoccupied all the Jewish thinkers of the nineteenth century.

The first question, raised in his *Jerusalem*,[4] is: how can Mendelssohn, if indeed this is his view, continue to believe in Revelation, for which there was no need? Alternatively, "If, therefore, mankind must be corrupt and miserable without revelation, why has the far greater part of mankind lived without *true revelation* from time immemorial?"[5] Mendelssohn answers this question as follows:

> I believe that Judaism knows of no revealed religion in the sense in which Christians understand this term. The Israelites possess a divine *legislation*—laws, commandments, ordinances, rules of life, instruction in the will of God as to how they should conduct themselves in order to attain temporal and eternal felicity. Propositions and prescriptions of this kind were revealed to them by Moses in a miraculous and supernatural manner, but no doctrinal opinions, no saving truths, no universal propositions of reason.[6]

Here Mendelssohn makes the famous distinction between eternal metaphysical truths, whose source is in the divine intelligence, or God's will, and founded on reason, and temporary historical truths that are connected to time and place, and based on the senses, experience, and reliable tradition. The powers of human reason are sufficient to prove the eternal truths demanded for human happiness. What was conveyed to the Jews on Mount Sinai were particular historical truths for the Jewish people regarding their removal from Egypt by God, who had

---

4   See Moses Mendelssohn, *Jerusalem*, trans. Allan Arkush (Hanover, 1983), 89-100, 126-28.
5   Ibid., 94
6   Ibid., 89-90.

made a covenant with them, and a practical legal constitution to be observed in their land to assure their success. These truths were ratified with signs and wonders. These laws, founded upon eternal truths, recall and summon everyone to these truths, but are not supposed to teach or prove them. The Jewish people cannot free itself from the covenant and the constitution except "if it pleases the Supreme Lawgiver to make known to us His will on this matter, to make it known in as clear a voice, in as public a manner, and as far beyond all doubt and ambiguity as He did when He gave the law itself."[7]

The second question is that of the dual loyalty of the Jews in the Diaspora, both to the law of the state where they are subjects and to the law of the Torah, in which they believe. Mendelssohn gives Jesus's answer to this question:

> Adapt yourselves to the morals and the constitution of the land to which you have been removed; but hold fast to the religion of your fathers too. Bear both burdens as well as you can! It is true that on the one hand the burden of civil life is made heavier for you because of the religion to which you remain faithful, and, on the other hand, the climate and the times make the observance of your religious laws in some respects more irksome than they are. Nevertheless persevere; remain unflinchingly at the post which Providence assigned to you, and endure everything that happens to you as your lawgiver foretold long ago.[8]

However, the question is deeper. Mendelssohn relates to the questions raised by Professor Johann David Michaelis, who doubted that it was possible for the enemies of Christianity to be enlightened humans, but was prepared to consider according certain rights to the Jews. He also relates to the liberal German intellectual Christian Dohm, who proposed in his book *Ueber die Bürgerliche Verbesserung der Juden* [On the Civil Improvement of the Jews] changing the attitude of the authorities toward them, to recognize them as human beings and to allow them to become citizens, so that they could improve their morality and their physical condition and contribute to society. As impediments he

---

7   Ibid., 133.
8   Ibid.

presented, on the one hand, the poor status of the Jews and their low ethical level—for in Dohm's opinion they were cheaters and thieves—and, on the other hand, the contradiction between the loyalty to the state demanded of a German citizen and the aspiration of the Jews to return to the Land of Israel and establish their own sovereign state there.

Regarding the first problem, Mendelssohn counsels caution making comparisons with the rest of the citizens, both because one must take into account the more serious ethical sins of which the Jews are not guilty, and because the comparison must be made only between merchants and peddlers, and not with the entire population. Moreover, one must remember that the Jew chooses this profession because of poverty and need and not by free will. Indeed, among the Jews there are many receivers of stolen goods, but most of them change their ways as soon as they have made enough money to purchase the right of protection.[9]

Regarding the contradiction of dual loyalty, Mendelssohn writes:

> The hoped-for return to Palestine, which troubles Herr M. [Michaelis] so much, has no influence on our conduct as citizens. This is confirmed by experience wherever Jews are tolerated. In part, human nature accounts for it—only the enthusiast would not love the soil on which he thrives. And he who holds contradictory religious opinions reserves them for church and prayer. In part, also, the precaution of our sages accounts for it—the Talmud forbids us *even to think* of a return [to Palestine] by force [i.e., to attempt Redemption through human effort]. Without the miracles and signs mentioned in the Scripture, we must not take the smallest step in the direction of forcing a return and a restoration of our nation. The Sages expressed this prohibition in a somewhat mystical yet captivating way, using the verses from the Song of Songs (Song of Songs, 2:7 and 3:5): I charge you, O daughters of Jerusalem,/ By the gazelles, and by the hinds of the field,/ That you stir not up, nor awake love,/ Till it please.[10]

---

9   Cited in Paul Mendes-Flohr and Jehuda Reinharz, eds., *The Jew in the Modern World: A Documentary History* (Oxford, 1995), 48. On the attitudes of Dohm and Michaelis and Mendelssohn's response, see Katz, *Hayetsia*, 61-72, 92-95.

10 Mendes-Flohr and Reinharz, *The Jew in the Modern World*, 48-49. Interestingly, in 1770 Mendelssohn corresponded with the Baron von Lynar, who presented himself

Settling in the Land of Israel is a matter for the end of days. It is utopian and miraculous, neutralized and thus removed from real history, and its place in the present time is only in synagogues and not in the real world. In the real world, the Three Oaths remain in force, forbidding any active measure to bring on the end and achieve actual settlement in the Land of Israel.[11]

---

as an anonymous admirer, and he asked Mendelssohn's opinion about the idea of establishing a Jewish state in the Land of Israel. Mendelssohn rejected the proposal with cautious diplomatic courtesy—without entering into a theological or ideological dispute—with practical arguments regarding character traits that the Jews had acquired during thousands of years of exile and suffering, giving rise to a passivity and lack of energy, the dispersal of the Jews and the lack of unity among them, and the huge investment that would be required, and the political situation that was necessary but impossible. See "Letter to 'a Man of Rank'" in *Moses Mendelssohn: Writings on Judaism, Christianity, and the Bible*, ed. M.Gottlieb (Waltham, MA, 2011), 37-38. On Mendelssohn's a priori neutralizing approach, on the one hand, and on his response to the baron's proposal, on the other, see Ravitzky, *Haqets*, 24-25. Ravitzky does not decide what Mendelssohn's "real" attitude was, but in any event he presents it as an ideology of passivity. While it is possible that Mendelssohn's answer to the arguments of the Gentiles was apologetic, in my opinion his answer to the baron showed cautious, practical diplomacy, appropriate to a practical proposal from a practical man. Mendelssohn's reply to Michaelis is ideological, and represents his deep opinion, which was passive from the start. W. Z. Harvey, "Moshe Mendelssohn 'Al Erets-Yisrael," in *Erets Yisrael Bahagut Hayehudit Ba'et Heḥadasha*, ed. A Ravitzky (Jerusalem, 1998), 301-12, presents both positions in detail and reaches the logical conclusion that his real opinion was practical and not neutralizing. The argument is that in a polemical situation you are likely to employ apologetics. In my opinion, it is difficult to accuse Mendelssohn, the straight-laced rationalist, of such apologetics. Another source on the subject, which Harvey himself cites on 309-10, is his commentary, *Habeur*, on Lev. 26:39, which fits in with the neutralizing position of awaiting a miracle. Harvey himself explains this passage in that way. Interestingly, Harvey regards the printing of Mendelssohn's paraphrase of "Tsion Halo Tishali" ["Zion, Will You Not Ask," a hymn by Judah Halevi] in a prospectus for *Habeur*, as a demonstration of Mendelssohn's practical position that the final step of rehabilitating the nation within history will be the establishment of a Jewish state in the Land of Israel. M. R. Niehoff, "Targumo Shel Moshe Mendelssohn Le'Tsion Halo Tishali' Shel R. Yehuda Halevi," in *Erets Yisrael Bahagut Hayehudit Ba'et Heḥadasha*, 313-25, analyzes the paraphrase in detail and in depth, proving that the absolute neutralization of the Land of Israel is conspicuous throughout the poem. Harvey himself, who seems to disagree with Niehoff (and me), drew Niehoff's attention to the poem and reviewed her article before it was published. See also Katz, *Hayetsia*, 66, who tends toward neutralization.

11 This fits in with Ravitzky's model regarding the Three Oaths as a seismograph, according to which every time real traces of the land emerge, the oaths appear (see

To the best of my knowledge, this is the first time that the motif of the three oaths emerges from the inner Jewish dialogue between those in favor of immigration and those opposed to it, and serves as an argument for Jewish loyalty in a dispute with non-Jews. Mendelssohn concludes his remarks by advocating the universal principle of separation of religion and state: "I think, moreover, the laws should not take into account personal convictions at all. Laws should take their inevitable course, proscribing whatever is not beneficial to the general good. When personal convictions conflict with the laws it is up to the individual to resolve this problem on his own. If then the fatherland is to be defended, everybody who is called upon to do so must comply. In such cases, men usually know how to modify their convictions and to adjust them to their civic duty."[12]

Because reason is a constant factor, which does not change in the course of history, Mendelssohn does not accept Lessing's position regarding progress and the education of mankind throughout history. Lessing's view enables him to argue that Christianity succeeded Judaism and therefore is superior to it and represents an advanced stage in the education of mankind. Mendelssohn rejects the thesis of progress, so he can deny this argument.[13] According to him, examination of human history refutes the theory:

> Progress is for the individual man, who is destined by Providence to spend part of his eternity here on earth. Everyone goes through life in his own way.... But it does not seem to have been the purpose of Providence that mankind as a whole advance steadily here below and perfect itself in the course of time. This, at least, is not so well settled nor by any means so necessary for the vindication of God's Providence as one is in the habit of thinking.... As far as the human race as a whole is concerned, you will find no steady progress in its development that brings it ever closer to perfection. Rather do we see the human race in its totality slightly oscillate; it never took a few steps forward without soon afterwards, and with redoubled speed, sliding

---

Haqets, 280). Of course, Chajes, Hirsch, and Luzzatto, who also bring up the argument about the oaths, also fit into this model.
12 Mendes-Flohr and Reinharz, *The Jew in the Modern World*, 49.
13 See E. Schweid, *Bein Ortodoqsia Lehumanism Dati* (Jerusalem, 1977), 136-38; Feiner, *Haskala*, 67-68.

back to its previous position.... Mankind continually fluctuates within fixed limits, while maintaining, on the whole, about the same degree of morality in all periods—the same amount of religion and irreligion, of virtue and vice, of felicity and misery; the same result if one compares like with like.[14]

Mendelssohn adopts the idea of the mission of the Jews. It turns out that mankind does not always make proper use of reason, and the existence of the Jewish people among them, who keep the laws of the Torah, makes possible the preservation of truths:

> The forefathers of our nation, Abraham, Isaac, and Jacob, remained faithful to the Eternal, and sought to preserve among their families and descendants pure concepts of religion, far removed from all idolatry. And now their descendants were chosen by Providence to be a *priestly nation*; that is, a nation which, through its establishment and constitution, through its laws, actions, vicissitudes, and changes, was continually to call attention to sound and unadulterated ideas of God and his attributes. It was incessantly to teach, to proclaim, and to endeavor to preserve these ideas among the nations, by means of its mere existence, as it were.[15]

A paradoxical question necessarily arises: if there is no progress, and humanity remains more or less as it was, what is the mission of the Jewish people in its two thousand years of exile? Conversely, if the Jews do in fact succeed in their mission during the exile, then there is progress! There is no alternative but to state that according to Mendelssohn, the mission of the Jews is static and not developmental: it is to preserve truths within history for a utopian future.

THE RADICAL NEUTRALIZING POSITION

Between the time of Mendelssohn and that of Chajes, Hirsch, and Luzzatto, nearly fifty years passed. During those five decades, many changes took place, mainly in Western Europe. The supremacy of reason as the means for knowing metaphysical truths was limited by Kant. Emancipation spread in Europe as a result of the French Revolution

---

14 Mendelssohn, *Jerusalem*, 96-97.
15 Ibid., 118.

and Napoleon's conquests. Secularization and the Enlightenment became widespread, and assimilation and Reform won over the Jews and eroded their communities, with the cooperation of the authorities, who wanted a strong central government. On the one hand, humanity seemed more advanced, ethical, and enlightened, while on the other hand there was a need to rehabilitate traditional Judaism.

Very soon, however, movement in the positive direction in Europe was blocked. The liberal Jews after Mendelssohn, who wanted to identify with universal values, to integrate into Europe, and to provide Judaism with a decent burial, were astonished by the change of atmosphere in Europe.

Universal rationalism gave way to particularist, chauvinistic romanticism, which gained momentum with the reaction after Napoleon's defeat. The hope of the members of the Verein für Cultur und Wissenschaft der Juden to integrate into the general civil society of Germany, bearing with them the Jewish values that were worthy of preservation, was disappointed, as was the proposal by Friedländer, to be attached to the Protestant church under certain conditions. Having no alternative, the men of the Verein developed an ideology of far-reaching reform from within. According to this ideology, the written Torah and the Oral Law were human creations, connected to the ancient times and places where they were written—the Land of Israel and Babylonia. Therefore, the Halakha had to be corrected according to the needs of the new time and to be adapted to modern Europe.

This ideology was meant to assure that, on the one hand, the average Jew would not abandon his Judaism and culture, claiming they were outmoded and unattractive, and, on the other, the Jews would be accepted as new Jews in the bosom of modern Europe. The reforms could achieve this by purifying Judaism of the cult of the past, of irrational beliefs that were out of date, and of the connection with Zion, and thus the Jews could be attracted to a new Judaism, and would be cleared of the accusation of dual loyalty.

This claim against the old Judaism, which until then had served those non-Jews who were opposed to granting emancipation to the Jews, now became an argument of the Reform in the internal dialogue within Judaism. The Reform Jews developed a radical doctrine of mission: on the day of Redemption, the New Judaism would become the world religion of Europe, and the other religions would unite with it.

As early as 1812, David Friedländer published a pamphlet in which he outlined changes in the lives of the Jews and also called for the purification and rectification of everything that characterized the Jews as foreign. Among other things, he recommended removing from the prayer book any mention of the desire to return to Zion, the advent of a personal Messiah, the rebuilding of the Temple, and the renewal of the sacrificial cult. This was done in the Reform Temple in Seesen from 1810 on, in Berlin starting in 1817, and in Hamburg beginning in 1818.[16] The Reform Jews who strove for total integration were radical neutralizers, and they effected full, universal spiritualization of the yearning for Zion. They argued: we have no interest in returning to Zion, neither real nor utopian; rather we want to be redeemed here in Europe.

CHAJES'S RESPONSE

As I have shown, although Chajes regarded himself as a rationalist, his unconscious absorption of the atmosphere of romantic idealism and his fundamentalism caused him to acknowledge the limits of reason. Hence he adopted, unlike Mendelssohn, a position according to which revelation was required as a standard for reason, which cannot always attain complete truth on its own.

This position reopened the question of why only the Jewish people were privileged with revelation, and Chajes addressed it. However, having internalized Haskala, with regard to the connection with the Land of Israel, the mission of the Jews, and universalism, Chajes leaned in the direction of Mendelssohn. Like Hirsch and Luzzatto, he wished to maintain and even to improve the achievements made by the Jews in their countries of residence, and encouragement of return to the actual Zion endangered these achievements. It should also be remembered that Chajes passed away before the appearance of the precursors of

---

16 Meyer, *Reform*, 44-47, 53-59; Rotenstreich, *Hamaḥashava*, 128-40.

Zionism in Europe—Alkalai and Kalischer—began to act and spread their appeal for settlement in the Land of Israel during the 1860s. From where he lived in Galicia, any practical thought about the Land of Israel was entirely irrelevant.

Emancipation

Chajes approved of the emancipation in Europe and hoped that in the Austro-Hungarian Empire as well the situation would improve and the Jews would receive more rights than they had so far attained. In his work against Reform, "Minḥat Qenaot," he wrote:

> It cannot be denied that God benefited His people in their political status, relieved them of the harsh servitude imposed upon them by their enemies, and thank the blessed God at this time we hear of no forced conversions, murders, loss, and expulsion at all, as we suffered in ancient days in Germany and Spain and France and Portugal and Naples and Sicily, and on the contrary in our generation everyone speaks honorably of us, and in the states of France, Italy, Holland, Belgium, and most of the states of Germany, the residents of the country are seen with no difference at all, and also in the Empire of Austria and in Britain there is hope, that the government will no longer make a difference between us and the rest of the residents of the state.[17]

The Arguments against Giving Rights to the Jews

Chajes was therefore aware of the relatively favorable situation of the Jews of Europe in his time, and says so elsewhere in almost exactly the same words.[18] However, from time to time people argue that the Jews are unworthy of emancipation, and Chajes addresses this issue in "Derush Nikhbad" [Respectable Sermon] at the beginning of his book 'Ateret Zvi, published in 1841. He lists three models of antisemitism, the first two of which were mentioned by Maimonides in the third Epistle of Yemen, and the third of which is a new, contemporary type.

The first model is national and political hatred of the Jews' bodies and strength. The second model is religious hatred of the Torah. The

---

17 Chajes, "Minḥat Qenaot," 984.
18 Chajes, 'Ateret Zvi, 453.

third model is racial, antisemitic hatred of the supposedly corrupt and treacherous character of the Jews. This kind of hatred on the part of antisemites is expressed every time decent and honest Gentiles advocate granting freedom and civil rights to the Jews in any of the various institutions of the state, since the Jews bear the burden of duties like any other citizen:

> Immediately Satan dances among them, and the opponents arrive with strange arguments, saying about us, "a people that shall dwell alone" (Num. 23:9), "and they have nothing in common with us" (ref. to Judges 18:7), the members of that nation regard themselves as sojourners, and they cling to their view that this land is not theirs, and their eyes gaze and are borne up to another place, and in addition to all this, they say of us that this nation is not yet ripe in manners and morals, and they will not walk together over time like the other subjects of the state, and besides this they also say, look at the flaw that clings to the traits of their spirit, and the morale of the Jewish people is very bad, they are lovers of idleness and their occupation is solely with commerce, peddlers who go about in the towns and villages, taking interest, to suck on the plenty of many nations, acting in cunning because they look only for lucre, rushing to get rich. And they add more and more strange arguments to strike out at us with various plots, exposing us to humiliation and slander, to justify their actions against us in broad daylight.[19]

These arguments are identical to those of Michaelis as presented by Mendelssohn. Chajes's answer is similar in principle to that of Mendelssohn, but it is more detailed and comprehensive:

> Indeed those who go deeply into the pure Torah of God, and who understand matters of the Oral Law, and who investigate the history of the nation with a penetrating eye, they are aware and know that not only to kings and ministers are we commanded by the Torah and again in the prophets and triply in the Oral Law to give honor, and to pray for their welfare, but also to every person, no matter who he may be, we were commanded to conduct ourselves with them with love and mercy, and all good virtues, merciful and bashful and compassionate. This has been found with us forever both regarding the individual and also regarding the generality, and we do not bear hatred at any time. Our way is only to be forbearing and to forgive....

---

19 Ibid., 355.

And he who looks deeply will see that our ancestors were only shepherds, and the sons have inherited the deeds of the fathers. In the land of their dwelling they knew no commerce and property, only pasture and working the land was all their planning and regard. They succeeded and bore fruit in that way, and the entire essence of the Torah of Moses comes only to strengthen the behavior of our ancestors, to distance them from commerce and property. It was forbidden to them by God to give and take interest and usury and usufruct, without which commerce is impossible.... And there are many more teachings of the Sages that guided us [to engage] only in matters of crafts and working the soil and cattle and flocks. In all the occupations of the Tannaim and the Amoraim we have found only working the field and vineyard.... Indeed after that, as much time passed, and we were driven from downfall to downfall, pursuit without letup, and we did not find rest for our weary souls. The residents of the land did not allow us to have a foothold in their state, and they prevented us from joining their estate in every manner of craft and public service, and nothing remained except commerce and lending. What could they do to preserve their souls, and the soul of the miserable members of their household? They were required to cling to their new way, strange to them, for more than two thousand years, and the nations forced us to do everything that we did, and because of them the evil of a few matters was caused.... For we are thought of as aliens in the land, and we have no part or estate in all the occupations related to settling and holding the land, and we are exposed at every moment to every mischance and misfortune—and they said (Yevamot 63a), "Disasters only come to the world for Israel," meaning that in every sorrowful occasion upon which the misfortune comes from *midat hadin* [the severity of God], if a whip falls suddenly, the residents of the country say that it happened because of Israel, that they threw poison into the wells. If fire breaks out from God and burns down an entire city, behold, the Jewish people caused it. They constantly attributed everything that went wrong to the reviled sect of Jacob who hear their curse and do not reply.... And the splendid scholar Krug wrote in his essay on saving the Jewish people, even if we assume and decide that the Jews do some cunning things in business dealings—which is still not confirmed, and [when] honest and innocent people among those residents are asked, whose hearts were not swayed by hatred of the religion, and who do not give a heedful ear to the prejudice whose foundation is in the days of darkness, then they bring words out of their heart, that there is no one more fit and worthy in commerce than a Hebrew merchant, who does not to rush to get rich, and satisfies himself with little, and is not ardent with rage of fornication and other sensual appetites, such as drunkenness and gluttony, and a small amount is regarded as large by them, and because of that they do not raise the price—and while the Jews stood like a thorn in their eyes, here we have seen that in the hour of war, cunning is something permitted and acceptable for the weak, to overcome his enemies. Experience has shown to our eyes in our times, that in those states and regions where the yoke upon us was lightened, and those states took a step in our favor, then we stepped twenty steps upward, and France, and Holland, and North America, and some of the regions of Germany prove this: and thus we whose pleasant fate it is to be under the rule of Austria, a kingdom of mercy toward all the nations who take shelter in its shadow, behold we have seen that we have improved our ways greatly.... And deficiency does not cling to our law, perish the thought, only the length of exile and the weight of the yoke have caused matters to be spoiled with us.... And thank God we are still outstanding among the nations, in wisdom and wealth and good virtues, and this has stood by us that we clung to the perfect Torah of God.... Because in the matter of the third hatred, for the flaws they impute against us, that they [supposedly] have clung to us by nature, the prophet said[:] This is the estate of the servants of God and their righteousness is from me, spoke the Lord, because after what happened to them from the persecutions and the various exiles, they still shine in splendor of virtues and knowledge. This is a sign and wonder of the honesty of their path, and it testifies to their root, that they are the community of Jeshurun, a place in His estate, worthy to be called by the name of servants of God. Their righteousness was caused by His exalted Providence, by their cleaving and endeavors in the ways of the Torah forever: ... And our hope is firmly set in the Rock of Israel and His sanctity, that the days will come, and they will not be distant, when no outcry will be heard anymore and no outburst among the nations and various people, because of hatred of the religion. They will all know together that the name of God was called upon us, and they will not be evil and will not destroy the mount of My sanctity, for the earth will fill with knowledge of God as the waters cover the sea [Is. 11:9].[20]

As sources for the argument about the attitude of respect and love that the Jews are commanded to adopt toward the nations and their kings, he cites the following in comments to the essay:

---

20 Ibid., 255-58.

> Midrash Shemot ch. 7: "and He ordered them to Pharaoh, king of Egypt, and the Holy One said to them, treat him with respect," and thus he did, as it is said, "all these servants of yours will come down to me," and he did not say it about Pharaoh, and see (BT Zevaḥim 102a) (and BT Menaḥot 98a) "the veneration of kings must never be a light thing in your eyes." From the prophets, Jer. 29 "Ask for the welfare of the city and pray for it"; from the Oral Law: Ethics of the Fathers, ch. 3, "Pray for the welfare of the kingdom."[21]

Chajes therefore rejects the racist argument about the particularly low moral standards of the Jews and claims that their morality is good, and that circumstances caused their decline. The Jews had always worked as shepherds and farmers. Exile and persecution forced them to deal in commerce and money-lending for interest, and to scheme, because they were not permitted to settle on the land or to engage in any other profession. This scheming is understandable in the situation of struggle for existence against enemies who always regarded the Jew as a scapegoat. Jews are free of all sensual corruption and are commanded to honor and love those who grant them protection, and this is according to the Torah, the observance of which shaped their pure character; and the day will come when they will be recognized by all the nations.

Universalism

One can find decided expressions of universalism in Chajes's writings:

> In the Bible[:] This is the book of the generations of man on the day that God created man, in the likeness of God He made him (Gen. 5:1). Man is honored only on account of the beginning of intellection in him. (See *Guide of the Perplexed*, pt. 1, ch. 1 and ch. 2.) That

---

21 See ibid., 255, notes. As was customary with preachers, Chajes is selective in his quotations. The Gemara in BT Zevaḥim 102a does present this opinion of Rabbi Yoḥanan and Rabbi Yanai, which represents a submissive and obedient attitude toward authority, which was apparently more accepted in the Beit Midrash. However, the oppositional, proud attitude of Resh Lakish is also presented there, regarding God's instructions about how to behave toward the ruler Pharaoh. Resh Lakish apparently brought this attitude toward the evil enemy to the Beit Midrash from his experience as a robber in the practical world: Moses did not hesitate, "he slapped him and left," and this is according to God's instruction as to how to behave toward Pharaoh and not to fear: "He is evil, and you should be impudent to him."

because of this it is said that He created him in the image of God. And as for souls, all the souls are quarried from the same place. United. And they have a single soul in regard to intellection. The intellectual soul that is in them, and in this respect it is a duty for man to love his fellow with essential love because of the unity of the soul, and this is a greater principle than "you must love your fellow like yourself (Lev. 19:18)."[22]

Chajes adopts Maimonides's universalism and states that rational human beings are equal, according to the phrase, "in the image of God He created him," from which is derived the obligation to love everyone who was created in the image of God. This is a supreme, universal duty, higher than the commandment of the Torah to love one's fellow. Elsewhere, Chajes stretches the literal meaning of the Midrash, "you are called man," to make it fit his universalistic ideology:

> You are called man—we see in this that the intention is not to exclude the other nations from the category of man, only the Sages came to interpret it that every time in the Torah and the Holy Scriptures just the word "man" is mentioned, it meant only the children of Israel, as in all the books and laws of religion that are unique to a single nation, everywhere that it is mentioned without qualification. For when a person is obligated or warned of such and such, the intention is only to those people who are required to listen to the voice of these commands. Thus in the Torah and the prophets, everywhere "son of man" is mentioned by itself, the intention is to the Jews, because only to them were their words preached, except for a place where they explicitly prophesy to the nations, and this is obvious.[23]

---

22 Chajes, *Ḥidushim Vehagahot Lashas*, Shabbat, fol. 31a. Chajes explains the opinion of Ben Azai here, in dispute with Rabbi Akiva (Bereshit Rabba 24:7), that the verse 'This is the book of the generations of man' (Gen. 5:1) is a more inclusive principle than "love your fellow as yourself."

23 Ibid., Yevamot 61a. On this see A. Sagi, *Yahadut: Bein Dat Lemusar* (Tel Aviv, 1998), 178. There he discusses the various approaches within Judaism toward the difference between Jews and Gentiles, and he distinguishes between the ontological and the restrictive in relation to the words of Rabbi Shimon bar Yoḥai, "You are called man," and he correctly counts Chajes among the restrictive. It should be pointed out that both Luzzatto (*Meḥqerei Hayahadut*, I, 161) and Hirsch (on Lev. 1:2) should also be included in the restrictive category. Sagi states on page 180 that "the restrictive tendency is especially notable among rabbis of the modern period, who were exposed to human reality outside of Jewish society." I add another

In an essay entitled "Tiferet Leyisrael" [Glory to Israel], published in *'Ateret Zvi*, which was about the struggle concerning the Damascus Blood Libel, Chajes wrote at length about the universalism of the Torah and the Halakha in relation to Gentiles. He begins with quotations from the *Ethics of the Fathers*:

> "Do not be contemptuous of any person" (4:3), [not] even a pagan from their day, as it implies, and they said: "Hatred of creatures [i.e. people] removes a person from the world" (2:11). The Mishnah uses the word "*briyot*" [creatures], meaning all humans in general and in particular. As long as they have not harmed us, it is forbidden to hate them, and they said, "Precious is man, for he was created in the Image" (3:14), as it is said, 'God created man in His image' (Gen. 1:27). The intention is to all types of people, since at the time of creation, only one man was created, and all the separate nations and peoples emerged from him, see the commentary of Tosfot Yom Tov there. And the prophet also proclaimed and spoke publicly: "Do we not all have one father who created us, why should one man betray his brother?" (Malachi 2)... Maimonides spoke about this at length (commentary on the Mishnah, Kelim 2:7), and see the pleasantness of his language there, how he repeated and tripled many times that the duty incumbent upon us is to behave toward them with honesty of measures and weights.... And our Sages of blessed memory commanded us to increase peace with every person, even worshipers of stars and constellations in the market (BT Berakhot 17b).... Because our nation is a wise and perfect one, behaving at all times with love and brotherhood and affection, with the circumcised and the uncircumcised, and the archetype of all these statements is the prayer of King Solomon of blessed memory, upon whom the spirit of prophecy descended, and the spirit of wisdom and knowledge, and he said in his prayer, "and also to the stranger who is not from your nation, Israel, etc.," and if he comes to pray in this house, and You shall hear from heaven, your abode, and you shall do everything that the stranger calls upon you (1 Kings 8:41-43).... And the more so that they behaved with love and affection with the other nations in whose shadow they took refuge, as it is said, "seek the peace of the city to which I have exiled you and pray for it to God, because its peace will be your peace" (Jer. 29:7), and Zedekiah, the king of Judah, was

---

reason: in the modern period for the first time the Gentiles granted emancipation to the Jews. Someone who accepts this offer gladly and seeks to strengthen and develop it cannot adopt the theory that there is an ontological difference between Jews and Gentiles.

punished because he violated his covenant with Nebuchadnezzar, that he had sworn to him. It is said that he did what was evil in the eyes of God, and he also rebelled against King Nebuchadnezzar, to whom he had sworn by God (2 Chron. 36:12-13). The Mishnah said, pray for the welfare of the kingdom, that is, the ruling nation, whatever the nature of its rule might be, and see also Midrash Kohelet, s.v. "I [say]: keep the king's counsels," the Holy One said, I conjure you, that if the monarchy passes harsh decrees, do not rebel against it in any matter that it decrees against you, but keep the king's counsel, in everything they tell you [to do]. They said [BT Ketubot 111a]: the Holy One made Israel swear three oaths in exile, "One, that Israel shall not go up [all together as if surrounded] as a wall; the second ... that they shall not rebel against the nations of the world," and now, if we see the decency of their behavior toward worshipers of stars who sacrificed to Ba'al, and who did not believe in the existence of God and His unity, nor in Providence and reward and punishment, ever the more so toward Christians, who believe in religion and in Torah from heaven, and the existence of God, and recompense in the next world, and in the other fundamentals of faith, without doubt the laws of resident stranger [גר תושב] apply to them. Those who observe the seven [Noahide] commandments because they were commanded to by God, through Moses, they are like the righteous of the nations, and they have a part in the world to come, as the Halakha states for us (Maimonides, ch. 3 of Hilkhot Teshuva and ch. 11 of Hilkhot 'Edut and ch. 8 of Hilkhot Melakhim), that the righteous of the nations have a part in the world to come, also Christians who observe the seven [Noahide] commandments and believe in the Torah of Moses that came from the mouth of God to Moses, and who believe in the existence of God, even though they join another matter to their worship. The Ran [Rabbi Nissim of Gerona] and Rabbenu Yeruḥam wrote, in the name of the Tosafot (Bekhorot 2b), cited in Rema [Rabbi Moses Isserles], Oraḥ Ḥayim no. 156, that Gentiles were not prohibited from combining other entities with God: and the seven commandments are the totality of the natural laws. Both the Christians and the Ishmaelites discuss them in their places of judgment, and they also supervise with a sharp eye to see they are obeyed, such as incest, spilling of blood, courts, blessing God, stealing, and they are very particular about punishing transgressors, and even about eating part of a living animal they have a hint in the words of their apostle Paul, who warned them not to eat from strangled animals, and also the Ishmaelites are not idolators, see Yore De'a no. 124. Also they are careful about the seven commandments and also warned against any eating of pork and eating of blood and carrion, and also what was not slaughtered while facing Mecca is not acceptable, see Yore De'a 4:7, see Koran, Sura two, called "Cow," and Sura five called "Table," and everyone who observes the seven commandments because he was commanded in the Torah by God through the hand of Moses, behold he is a resident alien among us, and see also what our rabbi Maimonides wrote, ch. 12 in Hilkhot Melakhim (Vienna printing) and see the *Kuzari*, pt. 4, no. 23, who [Halevi] wrote, "These religions [Christianity and Islam] are thus only a preparation for the awaited Messiah who is the fruit. And all of them, when they acknowledge this, will come to be his fruit, and the tree will be one. Then they will exalt the root." And from all that has been explained you will be wise and know correctly the roots of our holy Torah, how distant it is from us to cause pain even to unspeaking animals, and ever the more so to our brethren, ourselves and our flesh, who were created in the image and figure, and the Meiri wrote, as cited in Shita Mequbetset (Baba Qama 112b), "and in the matter of any ruling regarding the nations who are bound by the ways of the religions and worshipers of God in whatever way, even though their belief is far from our belief, they are not in this category, but they are entirely like Jews in every matter like returning a lost item to them and also if they erred, you have to return [the money they lost on account of] their error to them," and in all other things without any distinction at all, and the more so [not] to murder them [like the Damascus Blood Libel], and especially the mild children, who never tasted the taste of sin, and they did nothing evil. Why should their soul be taken from them? Who knows what will be their end? Perhaps they will grow into a splendid vine and be among those decent people, the righteous of the nations, who shine today upon the House of Israel in their splendor and stand as a shelter and hiding place for us, as in the kingdom of our lord the Emperor Ferdinand. Happy are his servants and happy are his officials, the consul from Damascus and the General Consul of Alexandria, and the honest and innocent, from the states of Britain, who were merciful to a scattered flock, and bring succor to us in times of trouble. Our eyes are raised to God who redeems Israel with eternal redemption, for those volunteers in the nation of the lord, the great minister of the Jews the honorable Moses Montefiore, from the capital city of London, and the great sage Herr Cremieux from the capital city of Paris. May they carry out their plan in the manner of emissaries to perform commandments who will not be harmed, and may iniquity shut its mouth, and for all the children of Israel may there be light in all of their dwellings.[24]

---

24 Chajes, *'Ateret Zvi*, 488-91.

Chajes employs verses from the Bible, citations from the Mishnah and Midrash, Halakhic rulings, the Three Oaths, and the writings of Judah Halevi, Maimonides, and the Meiri about Christians and Muslims in order to argue against the Damascus Blood Libel. These sources prove to anyone who doubts the morality of the Jewish people—the universalism of its laws and its warm relation toward any human being who was created in God's image. This attitude is to be applied according to the principle of *qal vaḥomer* [a fortiori] or *lo kol sheken* [ever the more so] to those among whom the Jews have taken shelter during the exile. The Jews were sworn not to rebel against them; they have the Halakhic status of "Resident alien [גר תושב, *ger toshav*]" because they believe in God and His revelation, in which the Torah was given to Moses, including the seven Noahide commandments, and they are a stage toward redemption.

The Accusation of Dual Loyalty and the Neutralizing Response

As stated above, in the second decade of the century, the accusation of dual loyalty began to be voiced not only by Gentiles but also among the Jews themselves, particularly the Reform Jews, who used the accusation against those who observed the tradition, in seeking to negate the connection with Zion completely. They argued that this connection was a sword in the hand of those who opposed granting emancipation to the Jews, and it must be nullified and denied to assure integration into Europe. Chajes raises the question with all his vehemence both outwardly, toward Gentiles, and inwardly.

In addenda to the essay "Torat Neviim Divrei Qabala," written in 1837, he responded to the arguments of the Gentiles that the Jews had dual loyalty, and that their aspirations for the Land of Israel were in fact rebellion against the government and betrayal of the fatherland. This was the essay that concluded his book *Torat Neviim* [The Teaching of the Prophets], published for the first time in 1835.

First Chajes mentions the punishment of Zedekiah, Jeremiah's injunction to seek the peace of the city, the Midrash on obeying the king's word, and the Three Oaths, which were also cited above—all of which argue for obedience to the Gentile rulers and their nations. He adds:

> Never has there been heard about us a hint of reproach in this respect, that our hands were raised to join those who plot against the ruling nation ... and such a thought never occurred to us ourselves, and it will not do so. For this is a legacy from our ancestors, not to rebel against the ruler, unless the Lord sends His angel before us, to take us out by miracles beyond the ordinary. Then, too the ruler and the minister must admit and proclaim that God is just, and the hand of God did this, and thus will be the future redemption, which we expect and hope for in every moment, then, God willing, all of the human race will rise up to heights such that in no way will there be a need or memory of rebellion... Indeed, before the advent of the hoped for man, far be it from us to raise a hand against a king and violate his law.[25]

With these words, Chajes is taking Mendelssohn's path and neutralizing return to the Land of Israel by making it a miraculous Utopian event, supernatural and beyond history, in which all the nations will attain the exalted peak, even though he is loyal to the tradition that the end of history is likely to come at any moment, and that it must be looked forward to. In another passage in the seventh chapter of *Darkhei Hahoraa* [The Ways of Ruling], of 1842, Chajes tries to maneuver between the concrete traditions found in some sayings of the Sages about an independent Jewish monarchy in the Land of Israel and the neutralization of this reality:

> You must know that our brethren, the Children of Israel, are notable today among the nations in two ways: On the one hand, they have a particular religion and are separate in the roots of their belief from other religious people; on the other, they are also separate, as they were a particular nation in ancient times, with a separate language and particular customs, when they lived in the lands of Judah and Israel, and in the future, soon in our day, as we expect. In addition to the correct hope that the Temple will be rebuilt and prophecy and the Great Court will be restored in Israel, and the great court of the Jews will restore the glory and splendor of the Torah, and observing all the commandments in their original force, we also hope and yearn

---

25 Chajes, *Torat Neviim*, 177.

for the return of the Jewish people to be an independent kingdom, in the Land of Israel, which belonged to our ancestors, and is our inheritance…. And the Sages instructed us that there will be a future redemption, as there was with the Second Temple, the Temple was built first, and then the monarchy returned under the Hasmoneans. And only because there is no possibility of restoring the Temple, lacking prophets, who have to testify to the place of the Temple and the altar, and other things that have been forgotten…. And now, when no prophet or seer is among us, behold among us the principle and root in faith is that Elijah of blessed memory, who according to our true tradition is still living in the secret abodes of heaven, and he is the prophet who was living at the time of the prophets, will precede the Messiah, and he will restore the great court, and he will testify with the power of prophecy which is within him about things that were hidden and forgotten over a long time: behold in our exile, we maintain the Torah and the commandments, in part because we are members of a particular religion, we cling to the faith of our ancestors. On the other hand, since we are in exile today and have ceased being a separate nation, and we have been commanded by the Sages that while we are still submissive under whatever nation there might be, we must to place the load on our shoulder, to bear the yoke that is placed upon us and listen at all times to the governor, whatever he commands, and the fate of the nation and the government where we live must be our lot as well, for better or worse, to be joyful with their joys, to take part in their grief, nevertheless the Sages imposed a duty upon us, also to keep a memory and a sign of the return of the monarchy and the nation, and in addition to the necessity of using the Hebrew language in prayers, in the Priestly Blessing and the like, they have also been commanded to learn the holy tongue, and this is both so that they will have something to mark them among the nations, and to strengthen the cords of love and brotherhood among them and so that they can easily recognize one another…. To summarize: the commandments help us and assist us, in relation to the purity of the religion alone in spiritual life, and the customs that are practiced mainly publicly and openly in the synagogue or at the time of weddings and on festivals, they maintain the nation in external life alone, to keep the memory for days that will come, the days of the messiah, that the kingdom will return to us in the future in the land of our fathers.[26]

---

26   Chajes, *Darkhei Hahoraa*, 239-40. On Chajes's connection with Kalischer regarding the offering of sacrifices in Jerusalem in the present, and on the letters that were suspected of being forgeries on Chajes's opposition to Kalischer's activity, see I. D. Beit Halevi, *Ḥayut*, 71-74, and Hershkovitz, *Maharats*, 229-32; Rotenberg,

The tone of this passage is closer to the formulations of Maimonides. Chajes vacillates here between a description of the events of Jewish uprising, ostensibly within history, as it appears in some teachings of the Sages and in the philosophy of Maimonides, and a utopian event, when Elijah the Prophet, who is in heaven, will come down to us and renew prophecy by revealing hidden things in a supernatural way, as a prelude to the future advent of the Messiah.

Chajes presents a realistic vision combined as it were with a Utopian one, in contrast to harsh daily reality, in which the Jews are subject to an earthly government. However, it should be noticed that, unlike his usual practice, Chajes does not quote Maimonides at all, though he discusses the topic at length, nor does he seek to read him differently, in his own way. Chajes's words are more reminiscent of Mendelssohn's neutralizing voice, calling to bear the yoke. There is no possibility of bridging the realistic, historical position of Maimonides in chapter 12:1 of Hilkhot Melakhim—"Do not presume that in the Messianic age any facet of the world's nature will change or there will be innovations in the work of creation. Rather, the world will continue according to its pattern"—and Chajes's neutralizing, miraculous, supernatural position.

Maimonides does mention the prophet who will come not to perform miraculous deeds, but only "to inspire Israel to be upright and prepare their hearts ... [to] establish peace within the world" (12:2). The subject is only raised incidentally, and it relates to the words of the Sages on these matters as legends that are not binding. Chajes, like neutralizers before him, does not answer the paradoxical question that arises from his words: what need will the Jewish people have for their land in the supernatural end of days? If all nations and human beings attain the height of spirituality and unity, what is the point of having the Jewish people live in their land? What can this add for them?[27]

Ḥayut, 136, discusses this passage at length and concludes that Chajes—via his student Abraham Krochmal—influenced the national Zionism of Smolenskin. In my opinion, actual Zionism is very limited in Chajes.

27 See Ravitzky, "Hamashiaḥ," 67-68.

Chajes responds with great vehemence to the internal arguments of the Reform Jews regarding dual loyalty in his essay "Minḥat Qenaot," which he began to write in 1845, after the rabbinical conference in Frankfurt. He completed it only in 1849, and it was published a year later:

> These conference people do not intend to benefit the general public, to retain the people in the Jewish religion, so they should not turn their backs to us. If as they say they select the minority that holds the majority [i.e. they retain the essentials], in order to correct the sinners, then why did they decide to hold prayers in the German language? And perish the thought that they should mention in prayer the matter of the messiah, the revival of the dead, the restoration of the Temple service, the flourishing of the kingdom of David. But how can these beliefs harm those who spend their time in the vanities of the world? For the essence of their intention is to make things easier.... These people might claim that the reason that they removed certain matters from the prayers is so that the government will not be angry at us, saying, "This nation lives among us, and we inundate them with everything good, yet their eyes look to the land of their fathers, and they are to be thought of as temporary residents in the land where they live." But [the Reform Jews justify themselves by saying that] they do not intend to deny the principles of faith, but there is no substance to this apology, certainly because without doubt the Sages set these things in the prayers, and they change things that are the foundations of the religion. Without doubt they do it by reason of heresy, and what they say, that they do it all because of fear of the government, behold all the kings and ministers know that our yearning for the land where our fathers lived is strong. Nevertheless they do not think badly of us. In France, Holland, Belgium, and the like, we are thought of as residents of the land, with no difference from the other residents of the state, and we heard no reproach or challenge to us in that respect, because the members of our nation pray there every day for the restoration of the Temple service and the kingdom of the House of David. Experience has shown the opposite. Even though they pray for future redemption, nevertheless in every government service they show a strong effort for the good of the state, and they are faithful to their masters, in every aspect and respect, in that we were also ordered by the prophet: "seek the peace of the city to which I have exiled you, and they prayed for it to God, etc.," and also the Sages in the Mishnah say, "Pray for the safety of the kingdom." The ministers of officers of the state of Holland have given strong testimony, that the

children of Israel are faithful and submissive at all times to the orders of their state, and they do not mingle with conspirators and rebels, and they also testified of them that they are brave soldiers and know how to win in war, as against the French in the fortress of Antwerp in the year 5591 [1831]. We saw that when the order went forth in Prussia, that they were not forcing the children of Israel to give their sons to the army, [the Jews] thought that matter was a great shame, and the whole Jewish people from the end made their request, to go as one man, as friends freely to the army in war. All the nations know our way in this respect, and therefore they do not accuse us in that respect, and in vain the new people [Reform Jews] will labor to flatter them, in that they show that they have removed belief in the Messiah and the restoration of the Temple worship from their prayers. Experience has also shown that they do not cure the wound by so doing, to contradict the slander of the adversaries. But on the contrary in those nations where they did not rise up against rabbis and preachers to uproot matters of Torah, the people love us and give us the legal status of residents and citizens of the country, as in France and North America and Holland, and our brothers the Sons of Israel still behave correctly there according to the religion of the Torah, and in our time [the Jews of] Belgium and Canada, even if they are not perfect in [observing] the commandments, nevertheless they are firm in matters of faith, and their thought is desirable in any event, which is not the same of some of our brothers the children of Israel in Germany. They set out first to destroy matters of religion, and what was their reward? All the accusations against us arose only in Germany, and all the hatreds and plots to harm us came only from them. Look and see their situation in the states of Bavaria and Saxony and Prussia—before the days of March 5608 [the Revolution of 1848]—even though the preachers tried to flatter them and to permit marriage with them and show them in the wording of the prayers that they do not place it upon their hearts to believe in the advent of the Messiah and the restoration of the kingdom of the House of David, and only the land of Germany is the land of their abode, where they were born and there they will end and there they will die. Nevertheless their political status is very bad, and not only do they not attain the desired goal that way, their status is only worsened from time to time, as has become evident to us by the behavior of the kingdom of Prussia from the year 5573 [1803] to 5607 [1847].[28]

---

28 Chajes, "Minḥat Qenaot," 927-31.

That is to say, the Reform claim that they were saving the people from irreligion by modifying the law and giving up certain dogmas was a lie, and the true reason for their action was the desire to make life easier for themselves and to throw off the yoke of Halakha. The claim regarding assuaging the anger of the Gentiles was also a falsehood: the true motivation was denial that the Torah and the Halakha were from heaven, and flattery to find favor and integrate. The desire for Zion is a prayer for Utopian future redemption, and the Gentiles know that. Experience shows that they find no fault with it, and that the Jews participate in every national task with the nations among whom they live. Actually, in places where the Jews remained loyal to their faith, the Gentiles did less harm to them.

Chajes was cautious in phrasing his claims, to avoid appearing to be neutralizing in cooperation with the Reform Jews, but he certainly went beyond hinting that the Gentiles knew the difference between a religious function and a practical functions, in which there was full cooperation of the Jews in every civil obligation, in accepting civil law, and even in military service—participation and excellence in wars. Chajes was not aware of the deeply rooted antisemitism of the German people and advanced the preposterous argument that the reason for the hostility was the dishonesty of flattery. As if in the other countries of Europe, where the Jews did not try to flatter and resemble the Gentiles in their beliefs and opinions, they received respect, and their rights were honored, whereas in Germany, where Reform was active, the Jews were oppressed. It is more likely that antisemitic Germany feared signs of closeness to the Jews and responded with hostility.

Interestingly, Chajes's claim that the Jews were loyal to the government and never rebelled against it took on a further dimension in his book *Imrei Bina* [Words of Wisdom], published in 1848. There, Chajes presented a renewed and current appeal on this matter:

> We have been commanded by the prophets and the Sages to seek the peace of the government, beneath whose shadow we are sheltered, and to pray to God for it, and especially not to be in connection with rebels.... And especially the danger, which is very threatening, before rebels, who have made themselves liable to the penalty of

death, and the man whose hand is with the plotters is in danger of death at all times, endangering his soul always and regarded as a suicide.[29]

The Reason for the Revelation to the Jewish People

I now return to the question to which Chajes owes an answer, which is why only the Jews were privileged with revelation. Chajes related this question in the introduction to his first book, *Torat Neviim*, of 1835. Surprisingly, Chajes employs an exceptional argument while using a familiar motif from Aggadic Midrash (which, in his view, is from Sinai), whose original purpose was different, to compel the Gentiles to keep heteronomous law and ethics to a minimum:

> And this is one of the aspects of the religion, that the Torah that was given to our master Moses, may he rest in peace, is only the portion and lot of the Children of Israel alone, nevertheless the Merciful One, the Ruler of the entire world, did not leave the human race without Torah or instruction in the honest virtues that are needed and necessary to perfect a group of people in the value of their mutual status, and because of this he gave to Adam and also to Noah certain commandments necessary for private human life and for their settling and movement, and these the Sages included in the seven commandments of Noah, the second general father and progenitor of the human race after the Flood, and the details of these seven general laws multiplied, as is necessary by the nature of all things, that they increase at all times, and their branches and roots extended from a single principle for example laws, one commandment and the details grew greatly.[30]

That is to say, the rest of humanity also was granted a revelation that enabled it to receive the necessary divine instructions, and there was no discrimination in favor of the Jews on that score. Chajes does not write this explicitly, but the wording he uses, "branches and roots extended from a single principle," could hint that in this revelation as well, as in the revelation at Sinai, words were actually conveyed, but some details

---

29 Chajes, *Imrei Bina*, 943.
30 Chajes, *Torat Neviim*, 5-6.

were only potential and were actualized like the branches and roots of a single trunk in the course of the rational activity of the nations.

Chajes repeats this idea later on, and leaves less room for speculation:

> And this general benefit was not for the Children of Israel alone, for the divine religion to teach people how to behave was given to all the human race, and Adam and Noah were ordered to keep many commandments, which are called the Noahide commandments, and these commandments encompass all the natural and necessary commandments for the behavior of the human race, and these are what we spoke of: that the Holy One saw that according to the nature that was stamped into the creatures, there is a necessity for a leader and legislator, and the laws of reason are not enough. Therefore from the beginning of creation, God endowed the human race with Torah from heaven, to guide its steps, so that his steps will be steady between the many opinions that twist and grow about every matter of study and intellect. Indeed, the blessed seed of the children of Abraham, Isaac, and Jacob was added to them, whom the Blessed Name loved and gave them one more reward than to other mortals. The Sages said that the Holy One wanted to privilege Israel, and therefore He gave them much Torah and many commandments. See [Maimonides's] commentary on the Mishnah at the end of Makot. The essence of the matter is that by means of Torah from heaven, our legs were grounded, without fear of terrifying blows that may stand against the laws of reason and say that they stray from the path. But now by means of the Torah of God, which is with us, our feet tread in a straight path and track, leading to the house of God.[31]

That is to say, all the nations received divine revelation of the Torah from heaven, including all the details of natural religion that reason cannot attain fully, and it enables them to cope with problems and contradictions which reason is incapable of resolving, and to find the correct path in it. All of these things are included in the seven Noahide commandments, but the Jews received an additional portion of commandments because of God's love for them and His desire to increase their reward.

---

31 Ibid., 9.

Is it possible to argue that the revelation at Sinai was therefore solely particular? Chajes's answer to this question is negative, for two reasons. The first of these is that the revelation at Sinai gave the first revelation obligatory force for the nations as well, to reward them with eternal life of the soul, according to Maimonides's approach, in total contrast to Mendelssohn, who stated that Maimonides's position has no basis in the Talmud:

> And now also it will be explained what Maimonides wrote in Hilkhot Melakhim Umilḥamot, 8:11: "Anyone who accepts upon himself the fulfillment of these seven mitzvot and is precise in their observance is considered one of 'the pious among the Gentiles' and will merit a share in the world to come. This applies only when he accepts them and fulfills them because the Holy One, blessed be He, commanded them in the Torah and informed us through Moses, our teacher, that Noah's descendants had been commanded to fulfill them previously. However, if he fulfills them out of intellectual conviction, he is not a resident alien, nor of 'the pious among the Gentiles,' nor of their wise men." Our rabbi's reason for this is hidden from us.... But Maimonides follows his own method in this, as well, as we have seen: had they not been commanded by the Lord at Mara, the seven commandments would not be obligatory to us, and this is true of the sons of Noah as well, that they would not be binding on them. For Israel before God endowed them with the beloved Torah, had the status of Noahides, and the seven commandments of the sons of Noah are only binding on them as well not because Adam and Noah were commanded, but only because they were commanded by our master Moses. See Maimonides, 8:6[10] of Hilkhot Melakhim: "By the same regard, Moses was commanded by the Almighty to compel all the inhabitants of the world to accept the commandments given to Noah's descendants." That is, Adam and Noah were truly commanded to keep the commandments, but this was just a good practice for them, for it still had not became a permanent law for them, to find transgressors guilty, because a man had not yet been sent to them to tell them that it was a commandment of God, only by our teacher Moses, for he was the first emissary, as I have explained. Just as our teacher Moses was the first emissary to Israel regarding the 613 commandments, so, too, Moses was the emissary to impose the seven commandments on everyone in the whole world. Just as Israel must believe in all the commandments, which our teacher Moses spoke from the mouth of the Almighty ... the same applies to the descendants of Noah, because

our teacher Moses was the emissary to them to command them from the mouth of God about the seven commandments, and to impose them, certainly they must also believe that Moses our master pronounced them from the mouth of God, and not from his own mouth, and a person who observes them from intellectual conviction denies the mission of Moses our master.[32]

The Mission and Progress

The second reason for the universal need for the revelation at Sinai is the doctrine of the destiny of the Jews and their mission to the nations, which is immediately combined with the idea of human progress. Chajes did not negate the idea of progress, as Mendelssohn did, since he did not believe in a linear history of all the nations. Such a view would have confirmed Lessing's claim of the superiority of Christianity, which succeeded Judaism.

Chajes, we assume, adopted the parallel version of history proposed by Krochmal, that the eternal Jewish people and their Torah move in parallel with world history, in which there is progress. The Jewish people is the compass sent to the nations to guide and counsel them on their path. According to Chajes, the seven Noahide commandments are not sufficient to maintain the nations on the high spiritual level required from humanity, which seeks salvation. Only the presence among the Gentiles of the nation that observes the commandments of the broad revelation every day can advance them to this end. This intention of God also explains the exile of the Jews. Here are Chajes's words on the subject of exile and mission in the introduction to *Shut Moharats*, published in 1850:

> Since we have come to inquire into the prime reason why the Lord did this to the chosen people, who did not do well in their political situation, and even in the land of their dwelling they did not succeed.

---

32 Ibid., 66-67. See also the note on a correction of the words of Maimonides regarding their wise men, אלא [*ela*, rather] rather than לא [*lo*, nor of]. On Mendelssohn's opinion, see Open Letter to Deacon Lavater of Zurich, available at http://www.germanhistorydocs.ghi-dc.org/pdf/eng/15__TheJews__Doc.2__English.pdf, 4. In the original Hebrew, Chajes's references to the *Mishneh Torah* are erroneous.

And what is this great fury, that they were forced to go into exile and to sing a song of the Lord on alien soil? Arguments of this kind give power and strength to our opponents, to say of the children of Israel, they are scattered on the mountains like sheep with no shepherd, abandoned to chance and misfortune. But, if the main purpose of the children of Israel was to perfect their political situation alone, it would be proper for them to ask, where is their splendor and glory, and also in the land of their dwelling, a land of mountains and hills, and small quantity [i.e. not a big, fertile country], also there they did not find repose due to their bad nature, and they are not fit for rule because of the hatred and hostility among them. But when we look with an open eye, we quickly discover that from the beginning God consecrated us as a kingdom of priests ... and just as the Priests and Levites, the servants of God, had no part of the land, only God was their portion and inheritance, and they are teachers and instructors of the nation, so, too, all the Jewish people in general, they are priests to the nations to teach them true knowledge, and the marvelous and terrible dispersion of the children of Israel teaches wisdom to the nations about the reality of a spiritual essence, which gives existence to everything that is, and is not a body and is not a force in a body, and also they believe in the possibility of prophecy and Torah from heaven, and in reward and punishment, and in the other principles of the Torah of Moses, and the Torah of Moses and the stories of the patriarchs are known to the ends of the settled world, and all of this is caused by us, and our holy Torah, which we bore with us in all the lands of our dispersion, was a light before them to prepare a moral path for them. In this respect with the perfection of knowledge and virtues we have fulfilled our purpose and the obligation that was placed on us in every manner, and our government, the government of knowledge and intelligibles, is spread out over most parts of the settled world. For this the prophets destined us not with strength and not with power but with my spirit, said the Lord of hosts (Zechariah 4:6). Our rule over the nations will not be by strength and power [but] only by the spirit of God, and the seed that we sow in silence by the dispersal of the Jewish people gave fruit above to perfect the whole world in the kingdom of God, and in God we shall place our trust that days will come when they, too, will again believe in the simple unity, and nation will not lift up sword against nation in vengeance on matters of faith, and the earth will be filled with knowledge of God as water covers the sea, and now the arguments of our enemies and accusers will pass away completely, because since God gave us the mission to be teachers and priests to all nations, we therefore needed to go into exile to complete the task demanded of us.... And the secret of this thing was also seen by the *Kuzari* in the fourth chapter, no. 23.... And even more you should see the pleasant words of Maimonides in the end of ch. 11 of Hilkhot Melakhim (which I copied from the venerable old Venice printing, which were omitted from [other] editions of Maimonides, and I copy them here).... Behold you see that also the opinion of Torah greats, that these nations and religions are means for preparation and the perfection of all who dwell on earth in the kingdom of God, and to prepare them so they will be worthy of receiving the purity of religion and the aspect of true unity.[33]

Chajes spiritualizes the function of the nation. The function of Israel and its government is not in the political and economic realm, but in the spiritual realm. Therefore there is no foundation to the words of the antisemites that the poor political and economic state of the Jews, who have no land, supposedly shows that they are not worthy of any function, and that the fact that they lost the land that had been theirs, which was small and largely infertile, allegedly proves that they are no longer the chosen people.

Chajes does not speak of the exile as a punishment at all. The people were sent into exile because they were intended by God to teach the nations in a passive and quiet manner about the eternal, ethical, perfect truths, which were revealed to them at Sinai, and that the spirit is preferable to material power. This task is gradually achieved because the nation bears the Torah with it to every corner of its Diaspora. Indeed, a portion of the task has already been accomplished, as Judah Halevi and Maimonides said. Today's religions believe in an abstract God, the Creator, who looks down and rewards or punishes, who revealed Himself and delivered His teachings directly to Moses, His prophet. All of this is preparation for anticipated progress, when the task of the nation is fulfilled, and the nations accept ethical and unified monotheism, without the admixture of alien factors in the divinity, and then the world will be perfected in the kingdom of God. Chajes does

---

33 Chajes, *Shut Maharats*, 607-8. On the mission of the Jews in Krochmal, see *MONH"Z*, 37-38. It should be noted that Chajes, like Hirsch, also speaks about "the portable Torah," which the Jewish people bears with them on their journey of mission to the nations, which is in fact the Jewish spiritual kingdom in all parts of the civilized world. See note 58 below.

not dwell at all upon the experience of the nation in their land in antiquity, which was an effort to maintain a nation with political power and economic independence, which did not succeed, because it was not appropriate to the nation's mission. He merely hints that the Land of Israel was chosen particularly because it is not fertile, and it is appropriate for a nation whose task is to flourish in the spiritual, not the material realm, and it must be satisfied with little. As the nation chosen to bring the world correct theological views and ethics, like the Priests in the Jewish people, who did not receive land and an estate, it ultimately finds itself without an estate and in exile. This is a unique phenomenon among the nations, both marvelous and terrible.

HIRSCH'S RESPONSE
Background

As a romantic fundamentalist who had internalized Haskala, Hirsch vacillated between neutralization of the Land of Israel, following Mendelssohn, and the rabbinic tradition, which speaks explicitly and in detail about the return of the Jews to their land, and about the establishment of a politically and institutionally independent monarchy. On the one hand, the Land of Israel was distant, not relevant, and it separated the Jews from all the good things that the new and enlightened Europe could offer them, and there was an urgent need to oppose Reform ideology resolutely, and to argue that the Torah was from heaven, and that it was eternal, beyond time and place—claims that reinforce neutralization. On the other hand, in the Torah and the Sages the return to Zion has concrete meaning for any fundamentalist. Hence, it was impossible to agree to complete neutralization of the return to Zion, even at the end of days, as the Reform Jews held. This would contradict what was given to us in the tradition.

Universalism and Humanity

Hirsch fully embraces the importance of the individual and the universalism that flows from it, which were the basis of Mendelssohn's approach. However, unlike Mendelssohn, who regarded the Torah as a particular constitution that was most suitable to the criteria of reason, Hirsch, like Chajes, regarded it as a universal law that would occupy the heart of all humanity.

Against the attackers of Judaism, who saw the Torah as a coercive, autocratic theological law, Hirsch usually emphasizes democracy and freedom of will, respect for humanity, equality of the rights of the individual and his importance as the center of existence—all of which the Torah advocates, and the other nations have learned from the Torah and will do so in the future. These values underlie the Jewish community:

> The perception of mankind as one united family in which all members are equal had its origins in Judaism. Judaism was the first to recognize that, regardless of their differences in tendencies, talents, and intellectual and moral development, all men have one Father, that their essence as human beings reflects the image of God and that they all have a portion in the Divine love which educates them for the objectives common to all human civilizations—the attainment of happiness and peace.[34]

Even in the Jewish state, for which the Torah is preparing the nation, and which is meant to be a model state, every ethical person will receive full rights, equality, freedom, personal freedom, and happiness, in democratic fashion:

> *Complete equality of the native-born and the stranger is a basic characteristic of Jewish Law. In Jewish law, the homeland does not grant human rights; rather human rights grant the homeland! Jewish law does not distinguish between human rights and citizens' rights. Whoever accepted upon himself the moral laws of humanity—*שבע מצוות בני נח [the seven Noahide commandments]—*could claim the right of domicile in Judea.*[35]

This is because ultimately the Torah is intended for all humanity, which will accept the ethics of Judaism:

---

34 Hirsch, *Writings*, VII, 266.
35 Hirsch on Ex. 1:14. Italics in source.

At this time, upon the establishment of the Jewish nation, it is declared that the establishment of this nation is not just for the sake of the descendants of Avraham [sic], those redeemed from Egypt and their posterity. The events that transpired from the days of Avraham until the redemption from Egypt transpired for the benefit of all mankind. Any man can make this past his own, and enter the circle of the redeemed. In God's state, what matters is not lineage or connection to the homeland, but only one's inner life, one's humanity. One who is born a Jew forfeits his title if he becomes a בן נכר [ben nekhar], a pagan, estranged from his people. Conversely, one who is born a pagan attains equal rights as soon as he and his family join God's covenant with Israel. Moreover, the Jewish state is ready to grant the right of domicile, with all the attendant civil rights, to any *man*, even if he does *not* become a Jew, as long as he becomes a גר תושב [*ger toshav*, resident alien] and accepts upon himself the obligations emanating from his vocation as a human being.³⁶

These principles were determined even during the Exodus from Egypt, when the nation came into being, and they are based on the image of God in every human being:

> He had chosen them to proclaim the eternal freedom, the undying God-like nobility, and the kinship of God which are the birthright of individual man.³⁷
>
> The Jews ... restored the lost consciousness of the one Father of all mankind, of the equal rights and the equal status of children of God inherent in all men. From the hands of those liberated from Egypt, mankind received the book which confirms and seals the rights, the freedom, and the God-like dignity of every human soul.... It is their teachings and their example which offer equally to the black slave on the plantation and to the European intellectual at his desk a basis for hope and confidence.³⁸

---

36 Hirsch on Ex. 12:48. This is a clear message from Hirsch to his readers, students of the Torah, that the relation of the Torah to an ethical Gentile (גר תושב) is better than the relation the Jews were then receiving in Germany and in Europe in general. The Jewish mission to humanity is gradually to bring the ethics of the Torah to it. Cf. Chertok, *Qanqan*, 38-44.
37 *Writings*, I, 73.
38 Ibid., 76.

These are the relations between the individual and the institutions of society and government that should prevail, according to Judaism, relations that mankind will one day adopt:

> The home is the palladium of the state, not vice versa. The home does not exist for the state; the state exists for the benefit of the home. The prince is here to serve his people, and the purpose of citizenship is to serve the needs of the individual citizen. The prince derives his power and his functions, and the completion of his personality, from his people, and citizenship derives its purpose and its functions, and the perfection of its institutions, from the individuals who are the citizens. The community exists solely for the sake of its individual members, to provide a channel for concerted effort through which every individual can aspire to human perfection in the purest, fullest measure. The flowering of individual life is the sole basis and criterion for the life of the community. Only the individual can endow his community with a firm foundation and true meaning....
>
> The time will come when the nations, too, will respect and protect the human quality in man. The lessons of history will teach them that the state can find stability and purpose only through the greatest possible human perfection of its citizens. Political scientists will increasingly turn their attention to developing the human element within the state to its highest potential. Henceforth only that state will be considered superior which can claim to have reached this goal.... Israel's name among the nations will rise. Then the Jewish nation will shine forth in all its unique splendor, that nation which the merciful Father has sent among men over thousands of years as messengers of a Law providing the most perfect solution for the human condition.[39]

That is to say, the individual and his happiness are the purpose, and the state is the mean. Totalitarianism and the supremacy of the state are unacceptable. The public administration must also act democratically for the good of the community and not for its own benefit:

> It is not the rabbinate or the board of trustees but the community itself that is the focal point of all Jewish communal life. It is from the community that all religious authority must emanate.... Judaism

---

39 Ibid., II, 302-3. See also Hirsch on Deut. 24:5. Hirsch absolutely rejected the idea of the state as an end in itself (fascism) and regarded the Tower of Babel as a symbol of this idea. See his commentary on Gen. 11:4.

has no "hierarchical authority" that can impose regulations on the community, or appoint religious functionaries against the community's will or even without consulting the community. Our Sages teach us,... "One does not appoint a trustee for the community without first having obtained the free-willed consent of the community" [BT Berakhot 55].... The Sages further teach us,... "Any ordinance enacted by the religious authorities but not accepted by the majority of the community has no binding authority under the Law" [JT Shabbat 81:4].... God offered His holy Law to the entire community for their free-willed acceptance.... None of these obligations had been imposed upon them from the outside. Whatever had become part of their religious duties could be nothing else than that which their ancestors had already recognized as being in character with the spirit of Judaism and hence conducive to the accomplishment of Judaism's lofty mission.[40]

The right to freedom and happiness and the obligation to contribute to the benefit of the community with one's abilities and talents belong to every ethical person, according to Judaism:

Judaism believes that a truly viable state cannot be founded solely on collective power or individual need; it must be based on a sense of duty shared by all and on a universal respect for human rights.[41]

Judaism does not lay exclusive claim to happiness and glory. Decried because of its supposed particularism, it is just this Judaism which teaches that any righteous person of any nation can attain, and is entitled to, a life of bliss and happiness.[42]

Human rights and dignity are the basis of the entire system of the commandments of the Torah. In Parashat Misphatim [Ex. 21-24] the Torah begins to present the commandments in detail. It begins with laws applying to a Hebrew who had stolen and was sold into slavery, and a Hebrew bondwoman whose impoverished father sold her so he could survive, and states how one is to behave toward them. In his explanation of why these two marginal and unattractive laws were chosen for the beginning of Parashat Mishpatim, Hirsch says:

---

40 Ibid., 23-25, in "The Character of the Jewish Community"; see also *Horeb*, vol. 2, 452-59.
41 *Writings* VII, 270, and also see *Horeb*, vol. 2, 452-59.
42 *Writings* VIII, 7.

God's Law, the Torah, wants to instill in us the principles of justice and humanity, on the basis of which it commands us to respect human rights.... Crime and poverty—these are the two factors that generally tend to lower a person's dignity to the ground. *The Torah places the criminal and the child of abject poverty at the head of its laws concerning personal rights. By so doing, it demonstrates the importance it attaches to human dignity and the manner in which it seeks to safeguard this dignity, right down to the very lowest rung of society.*[43]

Emancipation

Hirsch was aware of the spread of emancipation in Europe and regarded it as a sign of human progress toward redemption, and, in principle, he accepted it gladly:

Just as it is our duty to endeavor to obtain those material possessions which are the fundamental condition of life, so also is it the duty of every one to take advantage of every alleviation and improvement of his condition open to him in a righteous way; for the more means, the more opportunity is given to him to fulfill his mission in its broadest sense; and no less than of the individual it is the duty of the community to obtain for all its members the opportunities and privileges of citizenship and liberty. Do I consider it desirable? I bless emancipation, when I see how the excess of oppression drove Israel away from human intercourse, prevented the cultivation of the mind, limited the free development of the noble sides of character, and compelled many individuals to enter, for the sake of self-support, upon paths which, to be sure, men filled with the true spirit of Judaism would have shunned even in the extremest necessity.... I rejoice when I perceive that in this concession of emancipation, regard for the inborn rights of men to live as equals among equals, and the principle that whosoever bears the seal of a child of God, unto whom belongs the earth, shall be willingly acknowledged by all as [a] brother, freely acknowledged without force or compulsion, but purely through the power of their inner truth and demand, as a natural consequence, the sacrifice of the base passions, love of self and gain. I welcome this sacrifice, wherever it is offered, as the dawn of a reviving humanity in mankind, as a preliminary step to the universal recognition of God as the only Lord and Father, of all human beings as the children of the All-One, and consequently brethren, and of the earth as soil

---

43 Hirsch on Ex. 21:2,11.

common to all, and bestowed upon them by God to be administered in accordance with His will.... I bless it, if Israel does not regard emancipation as the goal of its task, but only as a new condition of its mission, and as a new trial, much severer than the trial of oppression; but I should grieve if Israel understood itself so little, and had so little comprehension of its own spirit that it would welcome emancipation as the end of Galuth, and the highest goal of its historic mission. If Israel regards this glorious concession merely as a means of securing a greater degree of comfort in life, and greater opportunities for the acquisition of wealth and enjoyments, it would show that Israel had not comprehended the spirit of its own Law, nor learnt aught from the Galuth. But sorrowfully, indeed, would I mourn, if Israel should so far forget itself as to deem emancipation—increased room for the acquisition of gain and pleasure through freedom from unjust oppression—not too dearly purchased through capricious curtailment of the Torah, capricious abandonment of the chief element of our vitality. We must become Jews, Jews in the true sense of the word, permitting the spirit of the Law to pervade our entire being, accepting it as the fountain of life spiritual and ethical; then will Judaism gladly welcome emancipation as affording a greater opportunity for the fulfillment of its task, the realization of a noble and ideal life.[44]

The fact that Jews are accepted today as equals requires them even more to preserve their Judaism:

> The merciful Father of mankind has, in our days, stirred up the spirit of righteousness and humanity in the world, a spirit that has opened the gates of the ghettos and introduced the sons of authentic Judaism into the sphere of European civilization as equal citizens. Could the Jew, under these new conditions, find a loftier task than to preserve his ancestral heritage beneath the light of justice and religious freedom, even as he did during the centuries of darkness and under the oppression he suffered in a world of error and delusion?[45]

---

44 Hirsch, *Nineteen Letters*, 164-68.
45 *Writings*, VI, 21-22, in "The Character of the Jewish Community." Use of the term "humanity" rather than "humanism" is consistent with the distinction made by Rosenberg, *Hakuzari*, 43. R. Horwitz, "Yaḥaso Shel Shimshon Refael Hirsch Leerets-Yisrael," in *Erets Yisrael Bahagut Hayehudit Haḥadasha*, ed. A. Ravitzky, 456, inaccurately speaks of Hirsch's "humanism." On the emancipation in Hirsch's writings, see Breuer, *'Eda*, 79-80.

In itself the emancipation is positive. It reflects the progress of mankind toward more justice and humanity, which was advocated by the Torah of Israel from time immemorial, and it enables the Jew to accomplish his mission under improved physical conditions. However, it is also a challenge. Will the Jew fulfill his mission, or will he regard the emancipation and a life of affluence as a goal, as, in Hirsch's opinion, the Reform movement did, exploiting the opportunity to throw off the yoke of Torah and betray the nation's purpose.

Over the course of his life, Hirsch sometimes was disillusioned from his optimism. One hears prophecies of doom from him, as from one who prophesies without knowing what he foresees. He witnessed, on the one hand, an abiding hatred of the Jews, which was liable to undo all the achievements of emancipation, and on the other hand, the pursuit of wealth and pleasure that had penetrated Jewish society, and he was apprehensive lest this be the undoing of the Jews in the Diaspora, just as they stumbled in their own land:

> O, you deluded ones! Look at the society which is now freely open to you. Look around on the great marketplace of life. Has the race of Hamans died out completely with him and his ten sons? Could you not find someone from the Rhine to the Oder, from the Volga to the Danube who is capable of being his successor? Be sober and observe. Indeed the horizon of the Jew may well become somber; sultry clouds hang in the German sky. Even in our own Jewish circles indications for gloom are apparent. No one is secure.[46]
>
> When, after all these centuries of spiritual wandering, the Israel of today is again faced with the challenge of שמנת עבית כשית ["you waxed fat, you grew thick, you became gross"], will history have to repeat itself by recording (again) the ancient tragic refrain וישמן ישורון ויבעט ... ויטש אלו-ה עשהו וינבל צור ישעתו ["But Jeshurun waxed fat, and

---

46 *Writings*, VIII, 247, in "Sober Thoughts on the Joy of Purim." Professor Shalom Rosenberg has told me that he believes that in his old age, seeing the rise of antisemitism, Hirsch changed his positive attitude toward the emancipation and all that it brought with it. This is a very likely supposition. The quotations presented here are from the eighth volume of Hirsch's collected writings, which, according to the introduction to the volume, were published in *Jeschurun* between 1854 and 1867. In Rosenberg's view, they were apparently written toward the end of that period.

kicked ... and he forsook God who made him, and condemned the Rock of his salvation," Deut. 32:15].[47]

The Arguments Against Giving Rights to the Jews and Dual Loyalty

Hirsch responded to arguments about the low ethical level of the Jews and their dual loyalty in a manner similar to that of Mendelssohn and Chajes:

> [If the] Jews in European countries became strangers to agriculture ... the fault lay solely with the hostile attitude of the nations and people that either categorically forbade Jews to acquire land or else subjected land purchase and ownership by Jews to such severe restrictions as to make it virtually impossible for Jews to become farmers.... Jews did not enjoy equal rights and equal protection under the law with their non-Jewish neighbors and had to live in constant fear of being driven from hearth and home.... Jews were forced to concentrate on acquiring movable goods that they could take with them wherever they might be forced to flee, and to cultivate skills with which they could make a living for themselves and their families, no matter where they might find themselves.[48]

That is to say, the Gentiles among whom they lived are to be blamed for the low moral state of the Jews, as they discriminated against them and permitted them to engage only in dubious professions.

The issue of the Jews' loyalty to the authorities concerned Hirsch, and he reverted to it frequently. He quoted the same verses and Midrashim that Chajes cited, also basing his argument on Jeremiah:

> The Jews pledged to honor and obey the governmental institutions and the laws of the country into which their exile had led them. At the outset of their wanderings they had received the directive: ... not to rebel against the authorities, to respect their laws [the law of the kingdom is law].... The Jew put at the ruler's disposal his possessions, property, earthly fortunes, even his blood, but drew a

---

47 Ibid., 294, in the essay "האזינו [Haazinu] and Our Time," published in *Jeschurun* (July 1868).
48 *Writings*, VII, 223.

line when it came to religion.... It was left to a modern-day Haman to attempt to break this loyalty and readiness for self-sacrifice by distorting the meaning of [the law of the kingdom is law] ... to the effect that the Jews were obliged to submit to the command of their respective rulers ... their religion as well.... [The Jews] were loyal, obedient, faithful, even ready for self-sacrifice for the ruler—as long as it did not directly violate the Divine Law.... "Promote the welfare of the city to which I have exiled you" (Jer. 29:7).... They joined them gladly in all their endeavors and worked to promote every undertaking necessary for the prosperity and welfare of the community. They contributed immensely to the growth of states and nations and in particular to the development of domestic and world trade.[49]

The reviled Talmud educated the Jews in loyalty:

> The Talmud bids the Jews to give firm and loyal support to the ruling authorities in times of revolution and upheaval. Furthermore, the Talmud has taught the Jews to maintain and demonstrate good will toward their fellow citizens of other faiths, regardless of whether such good will, justice and humanity are reciprocated. It is the Talmud that has taught the Jews to endure abuse and brutality without ever yielding to the impulse to repay their foes measure for measure.[50]

The Neutralization of the Return to Zion and the Land of Israel

We find that the passivity demanded of the Jew in the Diaspora is not expressed only in obedience, loyalty, and assistance to the ruler, but also in passivity regarding the promised return to the Land of Israel:

> [The Fast of Gedaliah] warns us against the folly that in the *Galuth* Israel must wrest its independence by its own efforts, as if in its wanderings through its age-old wilderness it was thrown back solely upon itself and therefore had solely of itself to free itself, as far as it could, from the chains of suffering that held it in thrall.[51]

---

49 Ibid., II, 389-91.
50 Ibid., VII, 213.
51 Hirsch, *Horeb*, vol. 1, 145.

The oaths by which the Jews were bound are also enlisted on behalf of the argument:

> Not in order to shine as a nation among nations do we raise our prayers and hopes for a reunion in our land, but in order to find a soil for the better fulfillment of our spiritual vocation in that reunion and in the land which was promised, and given, and again promised for our observance of the Torah. But this very vocation obliges us, until God shall call us back to the Holy Land, to live and to work as patriots wherever He has placed us, to collect all the physical, material and spiritual forces and all that is noble in Israel to further the weal of the nations which have given us shelter.... It forbids us to strive for the reunion or the possession of the land by any but spiritual means. Our Sages say God imposed three vows when He sent Israel into the wilderness: (1) that the children of Israel shall never seek to re-establish their nation by themselves; (2) that they shall never be disloyal to the nations which have given them shelter; (3) that these nations shall not oppress them excessively (*Kethuboth*, 111a). The fulfillment of the first two vows is confirmed in the pages of history; about the third the nations concerned must judge themselves.[52]

The prayers formulated in the Talmud connect the Jews' return to their land to the redemption of all mankind, and this fact might be misleading, as if this was something given to us. Those who think that Hirsch changed his mind in old age and drew even slightly close to the Hovevei Zion movement should see an essay that he wrote in 1884 on "Talmudic Judaism and Society," in which he repeats his earlier arguments, stating:

> The Talmud incorporated into our daily prayers the assurance of our ultimate return to the land of our fathers and the restoration of the Temple in order that the Law of God may then be carried out in its entirety upon the soil of the Promised Land, which this Law has claimed as its own from time immemorial. This restoration will come hand in hand with the dawn of the Kingdom of God on earth, which will bring everlasting peace to the whole world, because at that time all mankind will recognize God and unite to worship Him by living a life of duty, justice and mercy.
> According to that same Talmud which proclaims this promise and those hopes as fundamental components of Jewish belief, any

---

52 Ibid., vol. 2, 461.

> self-willed attempt on the part of its adherents to return to the Land would be an act of criminal rebellion against the Will of God; the Jews must leave the fulfillment of the Divine promise to the Will of God, Who alone can sound the call for their ingathering. Until that time, the Jews are expected to endure their exile patiently in the lands to which they have been scattered, to love those lands as their fatherlands, to promote the welfare of those countries, and to conduct themselves as loyal subjects to their fellow citizens, even as Jeremiah (29:1-7) bade them do when they were exiled to Babylonia.... The Talmud ... regards any evasion of government-imposed taxes or customs duties as outright theft....
>
> The Talmud teaches us that non-Jews who recognize and worship the God of heaven and earth as proclaimed in the Bible, and who fully accept the fundamental rules incumbent upon all men, such as the prohibitions against murder, theft and adultery, etc., are to be placed on an equal level with Jews when it comes to our performing the duties all men owe to one another. They are entitled to look to us not merely for justice but also for active charity and compassion. (Maimonides, Laws of Kings 10:12)[53]

In the Grace after Meals as well, the benediction, "the Good and the Beneficent" includes a reference to this subject:

> One addition [to the Grace after Meals] was made by the Sages. When, during the reign of Hadrian, the rebellion led by Bar Kochba proved to be a disastrous error, it became necessary to warn Jews of all generations not to repeat this attempt. For not by their own power and by the might of their own hand should they attempt to restore Israel's crown to its former glory; rather, they should entrust their national future solely to Divine Providence.[54]

Hirsch uses the three oaths to refute the accusation of dual loyalty and to justify the neutralization of the Land of Israel in the present time—for all generations. Although the prayer book contains expressions of yearning for Zion, this is a yearning for an event given over to God, that is, a neutralized, meta-historical, utopian event, which we are forbidden by oath to advance by human initiative. This event is connected to eternal peace, acceptance of the kingdom of God by all

---

53 *Writings*, VII, 224-25.
54 Hirsch on Deut. 8:10. On the neutralization of the return to Zion in Hirsch, see Breuer, '*Eda*, 80.

of humanity, which will be united in worshiping Him. Then the Jewish people can once again observe the Torah in its entirety, which is possible only in the Land of Israel. But, until then, within history, we are sworn to be loyal to our hosts and to participate fully in the flourishing of our homeland with all the means available to us, like any local citizen.

The Status of the Land of Israel According to Judaism

This connection, within history, to a land and state other than the Land of Israel does not, in Hirsch's opinion, present any problem in principle from the point of view of Judaism:

> The former independent state life of Israel was not even then the essence or purpose of our national existence but was only a means of fulfilling our spiritual mission.
>
> Land and soil were never Israel's bond of union, but only the common task of the Torah; therefore, it still forms a united body, though separated from a national soil; nor does this unity lose its reality, though Israel accepts everywhere the citizenship of the nations amongst which it is dispersed. This coherence of sympathy, this spiritual union, which may be designated by the Hebrew terms עם ['am] and גוי [goy], but not by the expression "nation," unless we are able to separate from the term the concept of common territory and political power, is the only communal band we possess, or ever expect to possess, until the great day shall arrive when the Almighty shall see fit, in His inscrutable wisdom, to unite again His scattered servants in one land, and the Torah shall be the guiding principle of a state, an exemplar of the meaning of Divine Revelation and the mission of humanity.
>
> For this future, which is promised us in the glorious predictions of the inspired prophets, whom God raised up for our ancestors, we hope and pray; but actively to accelerate its coming [would be] sin, and is prohibited to us.[55]

This implies that the Land of Israel never had essential value or particular virtue in itself, but it served as a technical instrument for the people to observe the Torah. In the situation of exile, the Land of

---

55 Hirsch, *Nineteen Letters*, 161-62. See also *Writings*, VI, 35, in "The Character of the Jewish Community."

Israel is not crucial and will only become so with the advent of miraculous redemption at the end of history, when the people will return to their land.

Hirsch differentiates in principle between the importance of a homeland for the Gentiles and its importance in the lives of the Jews:

> It was not God's Will that the Children of Israel should become a nation in the land that was destined for them and develop into a nation in accordance with the conditions and influences of that land. Rather, unlike all the other nations, they *became a nation before they possessed a land*.... What other nations receive from the soil of their land, Israel receives from its relationship with God. The emergence and existence of other nations are rooted in the soil of their land. They prevail over the land and conquer it, and by cultivating it and developing it, they turn it into the basis for the development of their society. At the same time, they are subject to the climatic influence of their land. The climatic conditions of the land determine the physical, intellectual, moral, and social development of their culture. They therefore come to deify what they consider to be the forces that shape their culture; they come to worship these factors as gods on whom their national prosperity depends. Not so Israel. Israel is to *bring into its land its physical, intellectual, moral, and social culture already fashioned by God.* Israel is not to subordinate itself and its national life to the land; instead, it must make the land subordinate to itself and to its national life as fashioned by God.
>
> Thus, through its very national existence, through its national life and national prosperity, Israel shall proclaim that God is the sole true Power and that He alone is the Source of the welfare of all nations.[56]

The center of the life of other nations is their land. It is the foundational narrative from which all the powers and culture of the nation

---

56 Hirsch on Deut. 32:9. See also his commentary on Gen. 12:2-3; Ex. 6:7. The myth of the homeland as the earth mother can be found in Plato (*Republic*, Book III) as a noble falsehood that assures the existence of the state, whose subjects as soldiers sacrifice their life for it. Mircea Eliade, the scholar of religion, showed that this myth exists in many cultures. Hirsch states here that in Judaism, God and His word as revealed in the Torah are the narrative that establishes the nation's historical memory and not the land, and only observance of the ethics of the Torah and its commandments guarantee possession of the land. Plato would certainly say regarding these claims that the noble falsehood had been replaced but this had not improved in Judaism.

develop. The nation enslaves itself to the land, and it makes its forces into gods. For the Jewish people, God is the source of their virtues, and they bring their virtues into the land from outside it, subjecting the land to themselves. God's will is central to their life, and the land is an instrument for applying it.

This fundamental difference explains several historical phenomena and clarifies certain elements of the nature and substance of the Torah, the Jewish people, and the relations between them:

A. Israel is to be fully constituted as a nation even *before* it receives a land of its own. Hence, its existence as a nation is not contingent upon possession of a land; rather, its possession of a land is contingent upon the faithful fulfillment of its task as a nation.[57]

B. You are the only nation in the world that possessed laws before it possessed a land of its own.... You ... became a nation through the Torah, and you received a land for [the sake of observing] the Torah.... Your lawgiver, the man from whose hands you received your Law, *has never even seen your land*, never set foot on it. He merely *transmitted* to you the Law, *and his grave in the wilderness is the Divine seal on the Law that he, the lawgiver, transmitted; his grave attests that this Law is eternal and immutable*. The laws of the Torah are absolute, whereas you and your land are conditional. The laws of the Torah do not change in accordance with changes in your fortunes or in the fortunes of your land. Rather, your fortunes and the fortunes of your land change in accordance with the extent to which you are faithful to the laws of the Torah. With the Torah in your arms, you now stand on the border of the land you are to enter, in order that you may there observe the Torah in its entirety. With the Torah in your arms, you will be temporarily exiled from the Land, but again and again you will stand as a nation whose whole purpose is to live for the observance of the Torah. Thus shall you await the moment when you will be able once again to enter the Land, which was given to you so that you may observe the

---

57 Hirsch on Ex. 6:8.

Torah in its entirety. You are the people of the Torah, not the people of the Land; the land is the Land of your Torah, and without Torah the land is not the Land of Israel.[58]

C. This Divine Law has remained the only bond that ties the sons of Israel together in [their] greatest dispersion. It has remained the only ground, the only property upon which the sons of Israel stand.[59]

D. The [carrying poles] of the Ark symbolize the destiny and the mission of carrying the Ark and its contents beyond the precincts of its present standing place, if this becomes necessary. The command that the poles must never be removed from the Ark establishes from the outset and for all time to come the truth that *this Torah and its mission are not confined to the soil on which the Sanctuary and the Temple once stood.* The constant presence of the [poles] testifies that God's Torah is not bound to or dependent on any particular place.... *Israel's Table and Israel's Menorah—the fullness of its material life and the flowering of its spiritual life—are bound to the soil of the Holy Land; Israel's Torah is not.*[60]

E. Possession of its land, like freedom and independence, is not an asset that Israel owes to its own power and prowess. Rather, only by observing God's commandments did Israel gain and retain its land.[61]

F. Israel cannot possess God's land without God's Torah, for the Land was given to Israel thanks only to the covenant established by their forefather, a covenant that is none other than [the covenant of the Torah]. The Land and the prosperity guaranteed by it

---

58 Hirsch on Deut. 4:5. See also Deut. 27:18-19. This is Heine's idea (based on the opposite of this idea in Spinoza, see Yovel, *Spinoza*, 204-6) about the Torah as the portable homeland of the Jewish people. See also Viner, *Hadat*, 105; Ravitzky, "Tsiunim," 70, and another source that he cites from Hirsch on Deut. 11:18. See also Hirsch, *Nineteen Letters*, 76: "The Torah, the fulfillment of the Divine will, was to be its soil and country, and aim"; and *Writings* VI, 37: "There has always been only one national territory to protect and defend, and that national territory is the תורה [torah]." See also the following citations.
59 *Writings*, I, 122.
60 Hirsch on Ex. 25:12-15.
61 Hirsch on Lev. 2: 11-12. See also on Deut. 17:14.

must be subordinate to this covenant, as the means are subordinate to the end. To have the Land without the Torah—that would be the surest way to Israel's downfall. Israel would be lost and would be erased from the Divine record of the history of nations if, like the other nations, it were to regard a land of its own, and the prosperity to be gained from that land, as the one supreme goal, compared to which spiritual and moral concerns have no intrinsic value but serve only as a means to an end.... In this conception, only right and morality have intrinsic value. Right and morality are not valued because they can yield and ensure material prosperity; rather, material prosperity has meaning only insofar as it helps attain right and morality—humanity in the truest sense of the word.[62]

G. For other nations, material independence and material prosperity constitute the main objective—almost the sole objective—of their national unity. Yet, for the Jewish nation, precisely this objective is of secondary import. To be sure, God watches over the national welfare, just as He watches over the welfare of each individual.... Not only our personalities and destinies belong to God, but our material welfare, too, depends solely on Him.... [Material welfare is mentioned] only as a secondary consideration ... because the nation of Israel, as such, has neither national might nor national possessions.[63]

We may learn from this that the special connection between the Jewish people and its land, which is subject to the will of God, implies that during the process of God's establishment of the nation, He intended to accord small importance to the land for the existence of the nation. The nation was created and consolidated outside of its land, it received its constitution before it had a land, its legislator never saw the land, and it did not acquire its land by its own power but as a reward for keeping the commandments and for the purpose of keeping its ethical laws there.

---

62 Hirsch on Deut. 16:9.
63 Hirsch on Lev. 2:1.

Different principles are at work in the life of the Jewish people than in that of other nations: their spiritual Torah unites them, and in their state, material affluence and political and military power are subordinate to ethics, justice, and humanity. The Torah is eternal, and the fate of the nation and their dwelling in the land change according to the degree to which they keep the Torah. Therefore, in the future as well, the return to the land will not be by physical power but as a reward for keeping the commandments, and it is entirely in the hands of God. The people must take no active initiative on this matter. Israel is the nation of the Torah, not of the land.

The Land of Israel has no Essential Sanctity

Just as the Jews are the nation of the Torah, so, too, is the Land of Israel the land of the Torah. The Jewish people was chosen as the nation most appropriate for keeping the Torah in the land most appropriate to God's plan for history. Before developing this topic, I wish to show how far Hirsch was from attributing uniqueness and essential sanctity to the Land of Israel. In his words we find denial of all independent sanctity to times, places, and objects. Sanctification of certain objects and places makes the rest of existence valueless:

> The sanctification of certain persons, things, times, or places can lead to the pernicious idea that it suffices if holiness and sanctification are limited to these persons, things, times, and places. People imagine that, through the consecration of these things, the tribute has been paid, and that the demands of holiness for everything else have been bought off. All other persons and things, days and hours are left to the lower aspirations of life. It is clear how such a notion, to which the main object is the consecration of the few, can lead to the decline of holiness and the dismissal of morality from all the other aspects of human life.[64]

Hirsch is clearly arguing mainly against the Reform movement here, for like Christianity, Reform Judaism sanctified only what took place within its houses of prayer and secularized daily life. However, Hirsch

---

64 Hirsch on Ex. 13:3.

goes on to say that the specific sanctification of material things is liable to become mystical idolatry:

> [Sanctity] resides in an object only for as long as the object is a means to a מצוה [*mitzvah*] that is to be performed; but once the mitzvah has been completed, the object loses its sanctity. Thus Judaism opposes the superstitions of heathen mysticism, which ascribes magical powers to sanctified objects. Sanctified objects are a means in the service of an idea—and this idea alone is holy. Only so long as they serve as a means of expressing this idea do they partake of its holiness. The sanctity conveyed to them is not tangible and does not attach to them forever.[65]

Hirsch attributes two grave dangers to the positions of Judah Halevi and Nachmanides. The first is degeneration into mysticism, which pollutes the sanctity of the spiritual idea and attributes divinity to matter. Second is antinomianism and the breaking down of the barrier of observance of the commandments. If the commandments have real value only in the Land of Israel, and sanctity is restricted to a certain place, then in other places all bonds are loosed. Removal of the Torah from every area of life and restricting it to times of ritual and to the temple alone, like the Christians—which is what the Reform movement sought to do—will lead quickly to moral degeneration as well.[66]

Thus the reduction of the importance of the Land of Israel to the level of an instrument, without which the people can still maintain a complete life and carry out their mission in full, also has a philosophical background. By adopting this perspective, Hirsch rejects the neo-Platonic and kabbalistic conception regarding the intrinsic sanctity of places, and he accepts the instrumental, functional approach of Maimonides, that the sanctity of a place or object is temporary, as long as they are used for religious activity that is sanctified by the commandments of God in the Torah.

---

65 Hirsch on Lev. 6:20. See also Lev. 23:3. On Hirsch's disagreement with Judah Halevi about the special virtues of the Land of Israel, see Breuer, *'Eda*, 65.

66 See Ravitzky, "Tsiunim," 50-60, on the antinomianism that grew up on the margins of Jewish history following the methods of Rashi and Nachmanides. Is Reform a continuation in that direction?

At the same time, we must emphasize that Hirsch also disagrees with Maimonides, who believed that the land was a necessary instrument for the Jewish people to fulfill their mission, so that their return to it would be within history. As I show below, Hirsch believed that the Jewish people was more successful in carrying out its mission in the Diaspora, without the Land and its temptations. The distance from here to complete or partial neutralization of the meaning of the sanctity of the Land and the Temple, and to according inner, universal, spiritual meaning to them, is not great.

Why the Land of Israel Was Chosen

Now we may return to the matter of the Land of Israel as the land of the Torah. Hirsch argues that the Land was chosen to be the land of the Jewish people for historical reasons and not because of its intrinsic uniqueness:

> Whereas God chose this place [Beit-El] and made it a starting point for the salvation of the entire human race, beforehand nothing of note had been noticed in this place.[67]
>
> Although the land of Canaan at the time was occupied by the descendants of Cham, the most corrupt tribe among the Noachides [sic], we find living in the land also מלכי צדק מלך שלם [Melchizedek King of Shalem] who, according to tradition, was none other than Shem, Noach's son (*Nedarim* 32b). Thus, in the land of Canaan we still find alive the people who retained the knowledge of God in its purest form. We have another tradition that Mount Moriah, where Avraham performed the עקדה [*'aqeda*, the Binding] and where later the altar and the Sanctuary were built, was also the place where Noach and Hevel brought their offerings (see *Bereshis Rabbah* 34:9). And, according to our Sages, it was from there, the place of כפרה [*kapara*, atonement]—i.e., from the place where man is constantly reborn spiritually and morally—that the dust was taken to form the body of the first man (ibid. 14:8).
>
> In light of the foregoing, we suggest: Avraham fled from Chaldea because he stood there alone with his convictions and because the Chaldean kings and priests felt threatened by him. It was only natural, then, that he moved toward the place where men once were

---

67 Hirsch on Gen. 28:19.

close to God. He longed for this land because of its history and perhaps also because of its physical nature.[68]

Here Hirsch adopts Maimonides's position in the *Guide of the Perplexed*, part 3, chapter 45, where it is explained that Abraham chose the place mainly because of its history.

Hirsch writes of the physical nature of the land: what is its meaning and importance? As a fundamentalist, he could not ignore the verses in the Bible and the many Midrashim regarding the uniqueness of the Land of Israel above all other lands, in addition to its historical past. To explain this, Hirsch made a special move—the Land has no essential, mystical sanctity, but there is an entirely different matter here. By nature the Land is not fertile, and its abundance comes by virtue of the Torah:

> Just as the people of Israel are by nature an intractable, "stiff-necked" people who, by the power of the Torah alone, became God's people, so, too, the Land, by nature, was hard and unfruitful, subject to famine, and only through the power of the Torah did it became a land of abundance and blessing.... Land and people are intimately connected; neither can blossom without the other.[69]

Aside from its infertility, the Land also has political drawbacks, and it is possible to survive there only by observing the Torah:

> In the land promised to [Abraham] as the future homeland of his people, the first trial he faced was *famine*, and the second was *war*! The land does not, *by its very nature*, provide *material* prosperity and *political* independence. In both these respects, the land of Israel is the antithesis of Egypt. The land is dependent on heaven for its fertility, and its political position is one of dependence; it cannot offer resistance to a foreign invader. *In and of itself, the land of Israel is prone to famine and political dependence.* Since it is situated at the crossroads where Europe, Asia, and Africa meet, all the major wars that have shaken the world have inflicted severe damage upon it.

---

68 Ibid., 12:5. See also on Deut. 12:9. The spelling of the biblical names and the inclusion of Hebrew in the text is from the quoted source.
69 Gen. 26:1.

But *precisely for this reason it was chosen*. Had Israel built a holy life on this land, no foe would have dared to approach its borders. Three times each year the borders of the land would have been left undefended and vulnerable, yet no one would have covetingly touched the land (see *Shemos* 34:24). All the מלכויות [*malkhuyot*, kingdoms] of the world would have fought one another and passed near Israel's land, but no sword would have entered the most prosperous yet most defenseless of lands—וחרב לא תעבור בארצכם [*Veḥerev lo ta'avor beartsekhem*, and the sword shall not pass through your land] (*Vayikra* 26:6). Then all the nations of the world would have seen with their own eyes: "God is there!" God is the stronghold of Zion; His deliverance stands in place of wall and bulwark: ["God in her palaces hath made Himself known for a stronghold," Ps. 48:4], ["walls and bulwarks doth He appoint for salvation," Is. 26:1]. All the prophets' promises for the future would have been fulfilled thousands of years ago, Zion would have shone forth as a light unto the nations, and the peoples would have said: "Let us go with you, for we have seen that God is with you" (*Zecharyah* 8:23).

To the people of Israel, who are destined to live in the environs of the ruins of Sedom and Amorah, the events described in these verses serve as a warning: if there is no countervailing moral force, abundance and luxury are the natural enemies of freedom. Only if they devote themselves to the Torah with all their might will the people of Israel enjoy freedom and independence in this land. A rich land "flowing with milk and honey" tends to produce a population of weaklings. Only submission to the yoke of the Torah guarantees freedom and independence. Every field in Eretz Yisrael should bear the imprint of the Torah's reign (כלאים [*kilayim*, forbidden mixture of crops]), and this applies with special stringency to viniculture, the cultivation of the plant most symbolic of plenty and luxury (כלאי הכרם, איסור הנאה [*kilei hakerem*, mixed crops of the vineyard; *issur hanaah*, prohibition against enjoying]). Everywhere, and at all times, let this warning be heard: only on the basis of the Torah will Israel flourish; if it throws off the yoke of the Torah, Israel will go to physical and social ruin.[70]

The Jewish people and their land, connected with the Torah, are signs of the redemption of all humanity:

This is the relationship that exists between man's behavior and the earth as a whole. But God has established a much closer relationship

---

70 Ibid., 14:1. Biblical quotations in square brackets substituted for Hebrew in source.

between Israel and its land. For both have been chosen to be instruments for the moral rebirth of mankind. Just as the people is "God's people," so its land is "God's land"—and He calls it ארצי [*artsi*, my land] and נחלתי [*naḥalati*, my estate] (*Yirmeyahu* 2:7 and many other places).

All of humanity and the whole earth are destined to be God's; they, too, will be dedicated exclusively to the performance of His Will. But for this purpose of educating mankind, the foundation stone was set in the midst of this people and this land.

From the time that Abraham was chosen and the land was chosen for him, the Land of Israel has not tolerated the corruption of its inhabitants.... A population that is socially and morally corrupt has no future on this Land.[71]

The Land of Israel was not chosen because of its distinct, inherent excellence, but precisely because of its climatic sensitivity—the dependence of agriculture on rain, and its strategic weakness—being a crossroads open to any intruder. The People of Israel dwell in a land that has no economic or political security, and there is a practical difficulty in maintaining a prosperous state there. The divine plan was to prove that the Jewish People, who obey the will of God and His ethics, embodied in the commandments of the Torah, is protected economically and politically, and thereby it serves as an example for imitation by all of humanity. Existence in the Land is supernatural and not merely physical. The Land of Israel possesses theological and educational merit connected with the ethical nature of existence.

The epithet "flowing with milk and honey" is not necessarily a virtue, and as a sole purpose in itself it is even dangerous. In contrast to those who view the verse, "a land which the LORD thy God careth for; the eyes of the LORD thy God are always upon it, from the beginning of the year even unto the end of the year" (Deut. 11:12), as praise for the land, which promotes physical existence (such as Sa'adia Gaon, Rashi, Nachmanides in his first commentary, and Abraham Ibn Ezra), Hirsch believes that this verse presents the educational value of the land, which derives from its physical and political weakness and its dependence on Providence, which demands

---

71 Hirsch on Lev. 18:24-28.

the observance of the commandments (and thereby he is taking the path of Rabbi Samuel ben Meir, Nachmanides in his literal commentary on the Bible, Ḥizquni, and Sforno).[72]

Hirsch emphasizes that this merit is earned, not inherent. The fact that the land spits out corrupt populations is not an inherit quality but one determined only after Abraham and his country were chosen by God for their mission in the divine plan. The Jewish people is that nation of the Torah, and their land is that land of the Torah. These are two instruments in the service of the Torah according to the divine plan, and both of them will evanesce if it is not obeyed. The Torah is the only eternal element, and it is the central axis, independent of any earthly matter such as a nation or a land, as is appropriate for something divine whose source is in heaven.

The Torah is Above Place and Time

The divine plan that was originally designated for the Jewish people and their land might have caused a serious theological error:

> God wished to rejuvenate mankind and to restore His Presence to man's realm. Toward this end He chose a land that was eminently suitable for this purpose, a land on which it would be possible for men living in accordance with God's Will to attain the highest degree of moral virtue. This land, however—at that time and later, too—was inhabited by people who became more and more corrupt, until finally they were deserving of nothing but destruction. Thus the Torah, too, was given in the wilderness, to teach us that the elevation of mankind is not tied to any particular time or place.... The character of a land inevitably has some effect on the character and qualities of the people who live on it, nevertheless, the Divine quality in man, the ability to attain closeness to God, are within the reach of every nation, in Lapland as in Greece. In Avraham's place of residence, רוצחים [*rotsḥim*, murderers], too, can reside; the same soil can bear a רוצח [*rotseaḥ*, murderer] next to a נביא [*navi*, prophet]. God's choice fell deliberately on a land seductive enough to corrupt its inhabitants so thoroughly that the very soil "spewed them out." This was the land on which he planted His people, who

---

72 See Hirsch on Ex. 3:8.

themselves are not the most tractable of peoples; one of their basic character traits is קשה עורף [*qshe oref,* stiff-necked].[73]

The idea that keeping the commandments of the Torah depends on time (antiquity) and place (the Land of Israel) is mistaken and to be rejected. It is possible and necessary to carry out the nation's mission everywhere, at all times. Reform Judaism made this theological error. Their goal was to reform the Halakha and adapt it to a modern people living in Europe under new social conditions, and for that purpose they adopted a new theology:

> Instead of making them more observant of the *mitzvos* [sic], the exile will loosen even more the ties that bind them to the Torah. They will view exile as a writ of release from the commandments... They will argue that the observance of the Torah is suited only for the conditions of Eretz Yisrael. They will persuade themselves that on foreign soil, amidst alien and even hostile conditions, the duty of self-preservation requires or at least excuses defection from the Torah.... This will be עונם [*'avonam*], the new iniquity of the Exile: conscious defection from the Torah, on grounds of altered circumstances ... the claim that conditions on foreign soil have changed.[74]

Such an effort is a grave iniquity, and it is opposed to the divine plan based on the eternal Torah, which is above place and time, and therefore it will not succeed:

> No one should ever imagine that the Torah should be adapted to changing times; on the contrary, each generation is entitled to a present and future only inasmuch as it accommodates itself to the Torah.... The Torah was not given to Israel so that the people should adapt it to the changing times or to suit the people's convenience. Rather, the Torah was given to Israel so that this nation should shape and adapt itself until it has elevated itself to the moral and spiritual heights of this Torah.[75]

---

73 Hirsch on Gen. 12:6-7. See also Hirsch, *Nineteen Letters,* 75-76.
74 Hirch on Lev. 26:39-41. Here and also on Deut. 15:22-23, he presents the event described in Ez. 20 as an example.
75 Hirsch on Ex. 32:1.

The failed effort to adapt the Torah to the present time and place is a failure of the generation, not of the Torah. The Torah expects the nation to adapt itself to it at all times, wherever it is.

Idealization of the Diaspora

Hirsch takes this theory to an extreme, which leads him, on the one hand, to regard the Diaspora in a favorable light, with major spiritual significance, and, on the other hand, to neutralize the return to the Land of Israel by situating it outside of history. The state of lacking a homeland has been part of the divine plan in history since the times of the Patriarchs. The nation was intentionally constituted outside of its homeland:

> In the wilderness it received the Torah, and thus in the wilderness, without land or soil, it became a nation. It became a body, whose soul was the Torah.... Its national existence, therefore, was neither dependent upon, nor conditioned by transitory things.[76]
>
> It was destined to become apparent that the existence of this nation is a second act of creation by God in history, and toward this end it was necessary that Israel become a nation only by way of גלות [exile] and גרות [homelessness], without a homeland. Had Israel, from the very beginning, dwelled in its own land, its creation would not have appeared as אצבע אלוקים [the finger of God] or as 'מעשה ה [an act of God].... "I wish to make of you a nation that will be a beacon to the nations, a nation to which the others need only look in order to become aware of their own tasks."[77]

The Jews sinned, and therefore they were exiled from their land. The nation's sin was precisely in the sensitive area of making a means into an end in itself. "Even the first leader of the nation, Moses, foretold that upon God's soil they would forget God; that, led astray by the example of the other nations, they would esteem only wealth and pleasure worthy of seeking, and would become oblivious to their mission."[78]

---

76 *Nineteen Letters*, 75-76.
77 Hirsch on Gen. 12:2-3. The source of the idea about the creation of the people of Israel appears in Judah Halevi. On this see Rosenberg, *Hakuzari*, 164.
78 *Nineteen Letters*, 79.

The reason for the first exile was preference for the land rather than the Torah as a basis for independence:

> Judah was sent into the Galuth because it prized land and soil as the bulwark of its freedom and belittled the Torah.... We can really be delivered only when the centuries of Galuth shall have taught us their lesson, which is that when we have assured our freedom and independence and recovered possession of the land which has been waiting for us for thousands of years we must use them purely in the service of God on the altar of the Torah.[79]

Veneration of the land and political independence was the downfall of the Jews every time they returned to the land:

> From time to time in the course of the centuries God allowed His people ever and anon to touch the earth again. He put it to the test to see whether it had become ripe for the external Torah-state on earth.... But ... as soon as it touches the soil and thinks that it has firm ground under its feet it runs the danger of abandoning the Divine Law and revering as gods, alongside of the Torah and of its God, the political independence, the social freedom and the civil rights which this soil provides. It runs the danger of devoting its life to them and finding room for the Torah only in its synagogues, committing afresh all the old sins which brought on it the חורבן [ḥurban], the destruction of its state and temple.[80]

The Jewish people, in contrast to the Gentiles, must concentrate on spiritual and ethical values and not on material prosperity:

> [The law of the nations] reflects the philosophy of an independent, prosperous national life becoming reality on it own soil and through its own resources. For Israel, supreme lex—the Law is the supreme factor in its existence.... As a result of its unconditional acceptance of this Law in its midst, Israel became a nation in the wilderness before it could call an inch of land and soil its own.... Israel is to concentrate on the spiritual and moral values of human existence in the face of a world wedded to land and soil.... The Jew is certainly not called upon to reject the benefits of his material resources. On the contrary, he should take advantage of all the opportunities that life has to offer, provided he remains in control and does not

---

79 *Writings*, I, 117.
80 Ibid., 285-86.

gradually succumb to the mindless pleasures of crass materialism. וישמן ישרון ויבעט [But Jeshurun waxed fat, and kicked, Deut. 32:15] has always been the historical fruit of excessive freedom, independence and prosperity. This is what happened to the people as it emerged from the desolation of the desert into the land of abundance and plenty. It did not take long before they turned away from God's Law and, following the example of the surrounding nations, embraced the idols of wealth and political power.[81]

Hirsch constantly winks with one eye to his own time and place, where, in his opinion, the Reform movement repeated the same error, abandoning the Torah when it seemed to them that they had flourished materially and politically. This is also what happened at the time of the downfall of the Hasmonean kingdom:

> The descendants of this Hasmonean family now began to use their swords, which had been unsheathed to save the Sanctuary and its Law, to gain political power and independence and to further the self-interest of their new royal dynasty. As a result, the Sanctuary and its holy Law were drawn into the whirlpool of political aspirations and became a tool in the hands of an ambitious dynasty. Thus the days of this Sanctuary were numbered....
> The Temple fell, and the people were taken into captivity. But the Shechinah joined them and accompanied them into captivity.... "I remain the Holy One among you, even without a city that would accept Me." (Hosea 11:9)[82]

This means that the repeated sin of the nation also has an entirely different consequence. Real return to Zion within history has been proven by historical experience to be dangerous. When all the commandments are kept there, the Land of Israel provides material abundance to its inhabitants. Within history one finds the phenomenon of "thou didst wax fat, thou didst grow thick, thou didst become gross" (Deut. 32:15), in which the nation fell prey to sensual corruption and accepted

---

81 Ibid., VIII, 293.
82 Ibid., II, 230-31. This verse was used by neutralizers, who found sanctity alternative to that of the land in the heart of the people or of the individual. See for example the words of the Kabbalist 'Azriel in H. Pedaya, "Erets-Shel-Ruah Veerets-Mamash: R. 'Ezra, R. 'Azriel Veharamban," in *Erets Yisrael Bahagut Hayehudit Biyemei Habeinayim*, 260-62.

other gods in addition to God as objects of veneration, and from there the way was short to a second destruction and exile.[83] For that reason, Hirsch sought additional meaning in exile, and he stated that exile was not only a punishment to correct the failings of the past. It should be seen as part of the divine plan, and therefore as a positive and blessed phenomenon:

> The Jewish people will be seed sown by God among the nations, and בעמים—in the midst of the societies of these nations—they should waken and promote a different view of the world and of life and of fulfilling life's purpose. For הפצה [dispersion] does not always bring destruction, also find the scattering [הפצה] of seed: וְהֵפִיץ קֶצַח (Yeshayahu 28:25 [he casts abroad black cumin]). When this decree was carried out, the name given to Israel in exile was יזרעאל (Hoshea 2:2), "seed sown by God."[84]

The loss of Jerusalem was for the best. The nation lost its material and political independence, but since then it has brought a new idea to the nations:

> When Jerusalem fell, Israel lost everything that is defined as power and majesty, political achievement and civic honor; it was separated from the political and ecclesiastical elements that uphold and protect the prosperity of nations.[85]
>
> The Jew does not mourn for his lost city.... For the lost sanctuary of the Torah, for the lost home of the majesty of God, for that the Jew mourns.[86]

---

83 See I. Heinemann, *Ta'amei Hamitsvot Besifrut Yisrael*, pt. 2 (Jerusalem, 1955), 158. Heinemann writes that Hirsch called the Land of Israel "a land that devours its inhabitants" for that reason. Ravitzky, "Ḥemda," 5-10, and nn. 21, 25, 28, quotes from Maharam [Meir of Rothenburg] and the Shlah [Isaiah Horowitz], also citing Heinemann's words in n. 21, and correcting him, since Hirsch was not the first to do so. Heinemann does not cite the source in Hirsch, and I could not locate it. This epithet for the land does indeed appear in *Shut Maharam*, ed. A. M. Bloch (Berlin, 1891), 5, and also in Isaiah Horowitz, *Shnei Luḥot Habrit* (Warsaw, 1863; photocopied edition, Jerusalem, 1963), 2, fol. 11a.
84 Hirsch on Deut. 4:27. Like Chajes, Hirsch uses the term "seed" used by Judah Halevi in the parable of the grain.
85 *Writings*, II, 302.
86 Ibid., I, 340.

> From the grave of Jerusalem and Zion, from the ruins of its happy statehood ... Israel went forth as the herald of this new world-conquering principle.[87]
>
> The people wanted to limit and restrict God to the narrow confines of the Temple.... The time came for the Divine judgment to liberate and redeem the Sanctuary of the Divine Law.... The beleaguered Sanctuary of God's Law which had become alienated from the people and estranged from the state, lay in ruins—free!
>
> For the destruction of the Sanctuary marked the beginning of the victorious march of the Divine Law through the centuries without bearers, without priests, without official power and force of arms.[88]

How glorious and fortunate is the nation in its exile and torments, while fulfilling the exalted mission of bringing ethical values to the Gentiles:

> Israel accomplished its task better in exile than in the full possession of good fortune.[89]
>
> Summon up, I pray you, before your mental vision, the picture of such an Israel, dwelling in freedom in the midst of the nations, and striving to attain unto its ideal, every son of Israel a respected and influential exemplar priest of righteousness and love, disseminating among the nations not specific Judaism, for proselytism is interdicted, but pure humanity. What a mighty impulse to progress, what a luminary and staff in the gloomy days of the Middle Ages had not Israel's sin and the insanity of the nations rendered such a Galuth impossible!... When Galuth will be comprehended and accepted as it should be, when in suffering the service of God and

---

87 Ibid., II, 302.
88 Ibid., 223.
89 *Nineteen Letters*, 82. Within history Hirsch preferred the blessed Diaspora, where the Jewish people fulfill their mission as the nation of the Torah, and he opposed rushing the end and violating the Halakha. Interestingly, we find refusal to see intrinsic value in the land later on (under Hirsch's influence?) in the writing of Rosenzweig and Leibowitz, too. Rosenzweig (Franz Rosenzweig, *The Star of Redemption*, trans. William W. Hallo [New York, 1970], 299-309, 334-35; note that there is some similarity in language to that of Hirsch in the *Nineteen Letters*) believed that the Jewish people does not have a task in history, that it lives in eternity, and it is unified by blood relationships—the nation itself. He was apprehensive about normalization. Leibowitz, who lived in the sovereign State of Israel, was afraid that the land, as "Holy Soil," would become a focus of idolatry and false messianism, and he regarded the Halakha as the factor that bound the Jews together as a nation.

His Torah will be understood as the only task of life, when even in misery God will be served, and external abundance esteemed only as a means of this service, then, perhaps, Israel will be ready for the greater temptations of prosperity and happiness in dispersion.[90]

This teaches us that in the situation that prevailed in the Land before the destruction of the Temple, when people's priorities were reversed, we should not regret the loss of a homeland of which we were unworthy. The Temple was released from its bonds and neutralized from them, and a new, far more preferable stage began, of true liberation from the bonds of material assets and political independence, of the Torah's and the spirit's march of triumph over matter, a period of happiness and grace. Indeed, this is full idealization of the exile.

Neutralization of the Temple

The way has been opened to the neutralization of the Temple itself. Hirsch's position—that places and objects have no sanctity of their own, if the Jews do not actually keep the commandments there—extends to the most sacred place of all:

> Every Israelitish house should, nevertheless, be a temple of true faith in God, of reverence and love for Him.... Every Jew should ... be a silent example and teacher of universal righteousness and universal love.... The dispersed of Israel should show themselves everywhere on earth the glorious priests of God and pure humanity.[91]
>
> The more Israel lost its political significance, the more did its Law become free from its alliance with an aristocracy that misused or betrayed that Law for the sake of its own interests. The more Israel's political fortunes waned, the more did the Law gain ground among the people.... By consecrating its homes anew every year, every succeeding generation was to advance further and further in the consecration of the Sanctuary of God until that day when the House of God's Sanctuary will be sustained by every household in Israel, by the entire "House of Jacob," a day when the ultimate, true Hanukkah can begin, marking Israel's arrival at the height of its

---

90 *Nineteen Letters*, 163-64. Hirsch might have found, paradoxically, support for his idealization of exile in the words of Judah Halevi, *Kuzari*, 3:12.
91 Ibid., 85-86.

goal.... The new, ultimate Hanukkah will be attained when the light tended in Israel's homes will triumph so that they may ignite the light of the Temple to become a true, everlasting נר תמיד [eternal light].⁹²

The Temple of God has been neutralized and replaced by the Jewish home, which has been charged with the mission of bringing the nation to the yearned-for height of its purpose. Exile has received a positive ideological aspect of educational value and is perceived as more significant than the ancient period of political independence. It has preference in the divine plan, whereas the physical Land of Israel and the Temple are far from the Jew's daily awareness and are relegated to the margins of his consciousness, to the unreal, messianic, and utopian end, and they are neutralized by local or abstract substitutes. The spiritualization of the Temple is clear in Hirsch's commentary on the verse, "And let them make Me a sanctuary, that I may dwell among them" (Ex. 25:8), where he exploits to the full the fact that the text does not say, "that I may dwell in it":

> The meaning of ושכנתי בתוכם [I will dwell among them] in our verse extends far beyond the Presence of God merely in the Temple. Its true meaning is the proximity of God in our midst, the fulfillment of the covenant between Him and Israel, which manifests itself in the prosperity of private and national life under His protection and by His blessing....
>
> מקדש [*miqdash*, temple] expresses the totality of the task we are to fulfill towards God; משכן [*mishkan*, tabernacle] expresses the fulfillment of the promises made to us by God in return for our fulfilling that task. מקדש signifies the consecration of all of our lives, both public and private, to the fulfillment of God's Torah. משכן signifies the promised presence of the Shechinah, manifesting itself in the prosperity of our private and national life under His protection and by His blessing.⁹³

---

92 *Writings*, II, 266-67 in the essay on Hanukkah. It should be noted that scholars disagree about Maimonides's position regarding the essential sanctity of Jerusalem and the Temple (Hilkhot Beit Habeḥira 6:16). Hirsch rejects this possibility completely. On the sanctuary that is in the Jew's heart and home, see also Hirsch on Psalm 30:1.
93 Hirsch on Ex. 25:3-8.

He states this even more clearly in his commentary on the verse, "Keep my Sabbaths and fear my sanctuary" (Lev. 19:30). Here Hirsch uses a Midrash to stand the literal meaning of the verse on its head:

> [And fear my sanctuary]: fear to violate the regimen of life that is learned in the Sanctuary of My Torah.... We must not turn reverence of the Sanctuary into fetishistic worship of the wood and stone. Rather ... just as our keeping the Sabbath holy is not directed to the day itself, but to God Who orders the institution of the Sabbath, so in honoring the Sanctuary our thoughts are not to be directed to it, but to God Who orders us to keep the Sanctuary holy. [BT Yevamot 6a-b].... This place, then, still constitutes an invisible bond between all those who observe "Torah and mitzvos" [sic]; for it connects and unites all who keep the Torah, for whose Sanctuary site this place is dedicated. Our precious memories of the past turn us toward there, and to this place are linked also our prayers and hopes for the future. The hopes for the future of all mankind, also, are linked to this place; for it is from there that salvation will come to the world, through the power of the Torah....
>
> The actual Sanctuary united the nation only within the narrow borders of Judea. But the abstract idea illumines the hearts of Judea's scattered sons; it unites them over the ruins of the Sanctuary, through the power of the eternal meaning of this place. It is the invisible bond between Israel's sons, who are scattered all over the earth.[94]

That is to say, one is not to fear the Temple itself, but rather separation from the Torah and the commandments, which the Holy One teaches, for there is no immanent sanctity in a specific object, place, or time. Their importance only lies in their enabling a connection between the dispersed parts of the nation and their uniting it in awareness of the covenant, which is connected in collective memory of the place, the object, and the time, in hope for the abstract spiritual redemption of the nation in its dispersion and of all humanity. The Temple and the Sanctuary have become symbols for something connected to our lives here and now. The substitute for the physical, limited Temple is the abstract idea of a way of life governed by the Torah, which is effective everywhere, and its consequences. Salvation

---

94 Hirsch on Lev. 19:30. See Maimonides, Hilkhot Beit Habeḥira, 7:1.

here is not actual, connected to a concrete place, or connected only to the Jewish people.

Hirsch neutralizes the Land in a radical manner. He is drawn to it neither physically nor spiritually. He does not even need a physical substitute. It is nothing but an instrument that served in a failed divine experiment. Its time has passed, and it will only return in a utopian future. Meanwhile, the instrument has been replaced by a superior abstract instrument. Hirsch therefore consciously rejects any possibility of fear of the holy place in itself, because it has no exceptional sanctity. We do not find in him the phenomenon of attraction to the holy land in theory and distancing from it in practice, which would ostensibly derive from his fear of approaching sanctity, lest harm should come to him. He simply does not need it anymore. It is liable to be destructive in its great beneficence, and he prefers exile, full of grace, in a beloved homeland. He neutralizes the Land of Israel and the Temple and replaces them with abstract ideas of living a Torah way of life, the Jewish home, or the Jew's heart.[95]

So long as the complete, final redemption has not yet come, in Hirsch there is more than a hint of the spiritualization of the commandment of possessing the Land, which Nachmanides placed among the positive commandments applicable at all times, in the context of the concrete land of Israel. On the verse, "Justice, justice shall you pursue, so that you may live and possess the land" (Deut. 16:20), Hirsch writes:

> Scripture uses the term "וירשת" ("and take possession") [from *yerusha*, ירושה], with reference to the political security that Israel will gain if it will honor and promote justice. From this we learn a

---

95 See the model in Ravitzky, "Ḥemda," 16-18, where he rejects received opinion and argues that an absolute distinction should be made between neutralization and distancing because of fear. Fear is an existential response connected in fact to the strong attraction of the sacred center, and it causes the distancing of most of the people or their absolute separation at this time. Neutralization, by contrast, is the ideological response of a person in exile who seeks a substitute and new horizons for the lost center. Such spiritualistic conceptions "made it possible for the Jews to attain religious fulfillment outside of the Holy Land, too, offering fulfillment and religious values beyond time and place as well." Hirsch's approach here exemplifies this model. Precisely because of his neutralization of the holy place, he consciously rejects any possibility of fear of the physical place.

> momentous truth: [Israel's] possession of the Land can be called into question at any time, and the Jewish state must take possession of the Land ever anew through the full realization of justice.[96]

Hirsch believes that the land and the state of the Jews are not necessary values in themselves, but instruments—which are liable to prove ephemeral—for attaining values. The people's dwelling in their land and state is a perpetual program of inheritance and depends on maintenance of justice and ethical law. Without them, the people are liable to be severed from their land, and the transitory instrument will be replaced by a better one, less tempting, outside the Land of Israel, so that the commandment to take possession continues, since it is valid at all times, but solely in a spiritual context, that of justice.

The Efforts of Rabbi Kalischer to Enlist Hirsch in Support of Settling the Land

The correspondence between Hirsch and Zvi Hirsch Kalischer (1795-1874) provides a good demonstration of Hirsch's separation from any essential connection with the Land of Israel in the present time. Kalischer addressed Hirsch directly several times as well as through intermediaries, in an effort to gain his support for settling the Land of Israel as a way to hasten redemption.

His first appeal was in 1862. Kalischer wrote to Hirsch asking him to speak to a member of his community, Baron Simon Wolff Rothschild, and ask him to make a contribution for the settlement of the Land of Israel, and to give him his book *Drishat Tsion*, which argued for the religious duty of immigrating to the Land of Israel extensively and publicly, as an awakening from below, to hasten the messianic vision. When no answer was forthcoming, he addressed him again, two years later, regarding what he regarded as the duty to promote settlement of the Land of Israel in the present, and asked him to publish information in Jeschurun about the organization established in Frankfurt on the Oder for this purpose.

---

96 Hirsch on Deut. 16:20.

According to Kalischer, redemption will come even without repentance, love of Zion will bring the nation to repent, and longing for the Land is the essence of repentance. Hirsch answered him in a letter stating that in his opinion settlement of the Land was not so great a commandment and obligation as Kalischer thought. In contrast to Kalischer's messianic writing in *Drishat Tsion*, in a mystical, kabbalistic vein, Hirsch wrote sarcastically:

> And I, in my poverty, who have no familiarity with hidden matters, nothing is good for me except to maintain the way paved by our ancient forebears, may they rest in peace, who had nothing before their eyes except to be fearful in all the efforts of our strength to correct our ways in the way of the Torah before our God and to remove obstacles from within us, and to expect redemption every day if we hear His voice. And they never placed it upon our shoulders to turn to the path of redemption by strengthening and correcting the Holy Land except by strengthening and improving our heart and our actions toward success.

Hirsch added that God could not possibly choose those who throw off the yoke as His agents to bring redemption (an allusion to Disraeli and Crémieux, whose rise to prominence was seen by Kalischer as a sign of redemption, though Hirsch did not consider them fitting). Indeed, in the framework of the commandment to donate to charity one must help the needy who are already in the Land of Israel, but the settlement of new areas in an organized way would create new obstacles of violating the Sabbath and violating commandments that depend on the Land.[97]

In 1869 Kalischer addressed Hirsch once again, through an intermediary, asking him to join in his efforts. Hirsch's response was: "Regarding the acquisition of the Holy Land, about which your excellency, may your light shine, commented to me, I will not conceal under my tongue that my soul is revolted by the whole matter, and according to my limited view, no benefit of good will come of it for the Torah and our destiny." He added again that it was wrong to join forces with the Alliance Israélite, which did not observe the commandments.

---

97 See Hirsch, *Shemesh Marpe*, 211. Hirsch's statements are based on BT Sanhedrin 97b-98a.

In 1872 another appeal came regarding the baron, and this went unanswered. Kalischer addressed Hirsch several more times and finally accused him of delaying redemption. In 1886 Hirsch wrote to Jacob Lifschitz, the secretary of Rabbi Spector of Kovna, in response to an appeal to him on this subject, reminding him that he had opposed the late Rabbi Kalischer's ideas absolutely, and he concluded: "I asked him to leave me alone on this matter, because what they think of as a great commandment, is no small transgression in my eyes."[98] His further letters on this matter[99] clearly show that he absolutely opposed settling the Land of Israel as a political program and public effort, though not settlement by separate groups or individuals who emigrated to the Land, for whom he even contributed and solicited contributions. In his view, the three oaths applied only to the community, not to the phrase "storm the walls." Hirsch believed that according to the Rebuke in the portion "Behuqotai" (Lev. 26:14-40), the land was largely barren, and for a long time it had not been flowing with milk and honey.

For example, in 1888 he opposed permitting the sale of real estate in the seventh year of the Shmita cycle, because this would be a public act of "storming the walls," and he published an appeal for financial support to farmers who were harmed. He also published an appeal in 1883 to support the settlers in Petah Tiqva, and he regarded the Land of Israel as an appropriate place for settling refugees fleeing the pogroms in Russia.

---

98 Ibid., 216. Hirsch is faithful here to his approach, according to which, just as the Exodus to freedom from Egypt was a new creation for the nation in a situation of absolute helplessness, from which only God could rescue them, so, too, the future redemption to political independence would come only by the hand of God and not by human initiative. See his commentary on Ex. 5:22-23, 6:1-3, 12:15, 12:17, 12:39, and Lev. 2:11-12, 7:12-14.

99 Ibid., 212-17. See also his letter of 1882 to his son-in-law Michael Levi, who was living in London, in which he tells him that he had sent money to help religious immigrants from Russia who wished to settle in the Land of Israel, and he thought it was important for them to earn a living from their own work—published by Breuer in *Hama'ayan* 3, no. 1-2 (1957): 49.

Progress

Following Yehuda Halevi and Jacob Emden, and in opposition to Mendelssohn, Hirsch accepted the idea of human progress with open arms. Gotthold Ephraim Lessing had been one of the first proponents of the idea, which was developed by the idealism of the nineteenth century in the thought of Kant, Hegel, and their students, regarding historical development toward the hoped-for redemption of mankind. The difference between the Jewish and Gentile thinkers was only in the content of salvation.

Naturally Hirsch's view was that the Jewish Torah, rather than purified Christianity under the aegis of a general state, would bring redemption to humanity. What kept Mendelssohn from accepting this theory no long troubled Hirsch. After Kant there was a vital need for revelation, because pure reason was no longer the instrument for attaining metaphysical truths. Hirsch was not afraid that, since Christianity came after Judaism, it had to be superior to it. Like Chajes, he adopted—apparently unaware—Krochmal's theory about the status of the Jewish nation, which bore Judaism with it, in parallel with the rest of the nations. Whereas they all arose and disappeared, the Jewish people will exist eternally. The Jewish people and their Torah are above history, and therefore outside of the developmental framework. Christianity is not, as Mendelssohn thought, a degeneration into irrational, idolatrous belief, which appeared despite Judaism, but rather human progress from paganism, which came under the influence of Judaism as it moved along a path separate from that of the nations. Regarding progress, Hirsch states:

> In our time ... much of that mania has already vanished ... much of that barbarism ha[s] disappeared.... A much more human civilization, a much more enlightened culture has surfaced. Respect for what is right and for the truth, for human dignity and freedom, have become rooted in the minds of men.[100]
>
> The justice and the love which the Jew finds on earth is a gauge of the progress of the human race, and his deliverance goes hand in

---

100 *Writings*, I, 132.

hand with the deliverance of the human race from injustice, selfishness, and the crass denial of God.[101]

Humanity does not acknowledge that it is in a process of redemption led by Judaism, and it is brought to it by Providence without knowing it:

> An eye that is open to God can see the גאולה [redemption] grow any day, at any time.... Nevertheless the ultimate redemption will take mankind by surprise. Because it expects salvation precisely from where it will never obtain it; because it is dazzled by material splendor, mankind pays no mind to the seeds of the spirit of God that grow quietly and modestly. Mankind will advance blindly toward its salvation.[102]

On the appearance of Jesus, Christianity, and the Christians, Hirsch says:

> The Jew is glad when he sees man increase his acceptance of truth and morality, and foresees for his fellow man the rise of a morning sun which will shed cloudless light upon all mankind. It occurs to him that a single seed from among the multitude of God's saplings was implanted into the lap of mankind some two thousand years ago—although not free of distortion and misrepresentation. Still, the seed has blossomed to benefit many.... Then he follows the slow progress the world will have made toward the realization of truth, love and justice for mankind—concepts which, knowingly or not, have been plucked from the Jewish Tree of Knowledge.[103]

First mankind was freed by monotheistic Christianity from crude idolatry:

> On the very eve of the exile, a branch left the parent tree, which was obliged to surrender largely the characteristics of the parent stem, in order to bring to the world, which had relapsed into polytheism, violence, immorality, and inhumanity, the tidings of the existence of the All-One and of the brotherhood of man and his

---

101 Ibid., II, 271.
102 Ibid., 258. Hirsch uses Judah Halevi's motif of the seed again here.
103 Ibid., VIII, 8. See previous note.

superiority to the beast, and to proclaim the deliverance of mankind from the bondage of wealth-and-lost worship. [Israel was] assisted greatly by this offshoot in rendering intelligible to the world the objects and purposes of [its] election.[104]

The consequences of the spread of Christianity are beneficial:

> The peoples in whose midst the Jews are now living have accepted the Jewish Bible of the Old Testament as a book of Divine revelation. They profess their belief in the God of heaven and earth as proclaimed by the Bible, and they acknowledge the sovereignty of Divine Providence in both this life and the next. Their acceptance of the practical duties incumbent upon all men by the Will of God distinguishes these nations from the heathen and idolatrous nations of the Talmudic era.... The peoples in whose midst we live today are regarded by the Talmud as the complete equals of the Jews and therefore entitled to our charity and compassion in every respect.... R. Ezekiel Landau, R. Elazar Fleckeles and R. Jacob Emden dealt extensively with this subject in their writings. R. Jacob Emden in particular emphasizes this in his commentary on Chapters of the Fathers 4:13: "We should consider Christians and Mohammedans as instruments that will help bring about the recognition of God by all men on earth."[105]

Indeed, this also applies to Muslims: "The existence of Christians and Mohammedans helped disseminate among the nations the awareness of God's existence, and introduced into the most distant lands the realization that there is a God Who rules the world, Who rewards and punishes, and Who has revealed Himself to men."[106]

Like Chajes, Hirsch discerned progress in history, and he believed that this progress was accelerating. Like Maimonides, Judah Halevi, Emden, and Chajes, and contrary to Mendelssohn, Hirsch believed that the nations would attain redemption only if they acknowledged the seven Noahide commandments as a divine decree conveyed by Moses at the revelation, that Christianity and Islam are testimony to this acceptance, and that their appearance was a stage in historical progress.

---

104 *Nineteen Letters*, 81.
105 *Writings*, VII, 226-27.
106 Ibid., 227.

The recognition of the Gentiles of what they learned from Judaism is not conscious, and mankind must go a long way in severing itself from the veneration of material assets and converting them into spiritual values, sanctification of sensuality, and recognition of the unity of the transcendent, abstract God. The nations will take this path without knowing it, and this is the "cunning of Providence," which Hirsch adopts in place of Hegel's "cunning of history," which, in certain senses, is deterministic.

The Jew joins the other citizens of the state as the first among equals in the process of redemption:

> The gates to non-Jewish civic life have been opened to us and the concerns of that civic life have become the concerns of Jewish citizens as well.... The better a Jew one is, the better a citizen he will be.... Every aspect of Jewish thought and Jewish conduct, if faithfully and honestly cultivated, will serve as a building brick for the increasingly evident progress toward the salvation of all mankind, and ... the Jewish man is, at the same time, the most complete citizen of the world.[107]

Here Hirsch refers us to the principle of the Jewish people's mission in exile among the nations, a principle that we have already seen in Mendelssohn, and which was also adopted by Reform thinkers. The Reform Jews developed a doctrine of mission divorced from the Halakha and connected solely to ethical monotheism. Hirsch expands the scope and sees Jewish law, the source of which is Torah from Sinai, as an entire system that teaches what God wants from mankind in the world, and which must be taught to all of humanity.[108]

The Reason for the Revelation to the Jewish People

Hirsch must answer Mendelssohn's question: why were the Jews the only ones to receive revelation? Mendelssohn's answer—that it was

---

107 Ibid., VI, 11.
108 On universalism, progress, and the idea of the Jewish mission among Reform thinkers and in the Wissenschaft des Judentums, see Rotenstreich, *Hamaḥashava*, 128-41, and Meyer, *Reform* on Steinheim, 67-70; Formstecher, 70-72; Samuel Hirsch, 72-73; Holdheim, 80-84; Fränkel, 84-89; and Geiger, 89-99. On the subject according to Hirsch, see Rotenstreich, *Hamaḥashava*, 116-119, 134.

possible to attain truth through reason, and that the particularity of the revelation was merely a historical truth—was not acceptable to Hirsch. Kant had taken reason down from its pedestal. Sensuality restricted the ability of reason, and certainly this was not a way to educate an entire public. Revelation and not reason was the standard for truth and morality. Hirsch therefore had to produce an answer of his own.

First, it must be emphasized that we find in Hirsch the answer that Chajes offered regarding the first revelation to all of humanity, in which they received the seven Noahide commandments. In his commentary on the Torah, Hirsch accepts the opinion of the Sages, that "the moral code of all mankind—the seven Noachide [sic] laws—was also given by Divine revelation."[109] This first revelation, to Adam in the Garden of Eden, is written in the second revelation at Sinai, and it is alluded to in the first commandment that he received: "And God commanded man, saying: from every tree of the garden you may surely eat."

The citation from the Talmud begins, "ויצו אלו הדינין" [and He commanded, these are the laws], and Hirsch goes on to elaborate: "This defines the essence of the first Noachide duty, [*dinin*] דינין: upholding the law and administering justice; enforcing the laws of morality in all realms of human society. (Parenthetically, let us note that hereby the state is given profound moral significance, surpassing the fiction of a 'social contract,' which is precipitated by necessity or expediency.)"

However, Hirsch, who sees the revelation at Sinai and the entire Torah as the key to human salvation, does not develop this answer, since he prefers the doctrine of mission. For the doctrine of mission to be a good answer to Mendelssohn's question, Hirsch must present its universalism in a manner consistent with the universalistic position he internalized from Haskala. For that purpose he entirely rejects Judah Halevi's position regarding the excellence of the Jews, which is expressed in the prophetic ability, giving them a status superior to that of the Gentiles. A man who desired emancipation and fought for it against reclusive romanticism, which develops into chauvinistic nationalism, cannot speak for the particular merit of the Jews.

---

109 Hirsch on Gen. 2:16, based on the opinion of Rabbi Yoḥanan in BT Sanhedrin 56b.

Judah Halevi's famous hierarchy of excellence—mineral, vegetable, animal, speaking, the Jews—is only acceptable to Hirsch until the final distinction. For him, what distinguishes ordinary humans from Jews, as in Maimonides, is only the giving of the Torah, which is explicitly merely temporary and technical, and not essential. The Jews only enjoy priority in time, as the first among equals in the divine plan to educate humanity, and thereby Hirsch removes the particular significance of the idea of chosenness in favor of universal meaning.

After the first revelation failed several times (the Garden of Eden, the Tower of Babel, the Flood), Providence decided to establish a nation from the seed of Abraham through a new creation, and to educate all mankind by means of it, according to the instruction of the Torah. First this was the nation in its land, and then a nation dispersed among the Gentiles:

> Hence, when God says בני בכרי ישראל [Israel is my firstborn son], this means: With Israel, the womb of humanity will be opened; with Israel, the dance will begin; all the people are obligated to join him as My sons. I come to you in your own name and in the name of all humanity. Israel is My first but not My only child; Israel is only the first people that I have won as Mine.... Israel is not the first in rank, but the first in time.[110]

In his commentary on the verse, "which a man shall do and live thereby" (Lev. 18:5), Hirsch writes:

> It does not say here אשר תעשו אותם ותחיו בהם [which you shall do and you will live thereby], but rather אשר יעשה אותם האדם וחי בהם [which a man shall do and live thereby]; and it does not say אדם [a person], but האדם [all men]. The inference is that Scripture here refers to anyone who exemplifies the spiritual and moral character implied by the term האדם (see Commentary, Bereshis 1:26)—an attainment that can be reached only through fulfillment of God's laws. Thus Toras Kohanim infers.... Even a non-Jew who keeps God's Law is the equal of a High Priest; for it says: "... which a man shall do and live thereby." ... We see, then, that life, the teaching, closeness to God, happiness, and well-being are attained through Torah and mitzvos not only by Israel; rather, any man who draws his world view and his

---

110 Hirsch on Ex. 4:22-23.

principles from the Torah, anyone who elevates himself to the heights of pure humanity by fulfilling the Torah's חוּקִים [*ḥuqim*, laws] and מִשְׁפָּטִים [*mishpatim*, judgments], is ensured of attaining the highest level of perfection and happiness in nearness to God.... The חוּקִים, which—from a spiritual and sensual standpoint—govern the life of the individual, and the מִשְׁפָּטִים, which govern the life of the society, are not designed to boost us to extraordinary, superhuman levels. Rather, they are designed to restore to us the same human level which was the original destiny, and remains the destiny, of man who was created in the image of God. The unfolding of this destiny began with the Jewish family of man, and will end with the whole of mankind. This is the whole purpose of God's guidance in history.[111]

This is a position explicitly contrary to the uniqueness of the Jews according to Judah Halevi. Even if we accept Eliezer Schweid's reading of Judah Halevi, according to which Jews are not superior to other people in reason or ethics, but only in the power of prophecy,[112] it is still impossible, in my opinion, to see Hirsch's position on chosenness as a development of Judah Halevi's opinion, as Rosenberg suggests, and I prefer the view of Mordecai Breuer.[113]

---

111 Hirsch on Lev. 18:4-5. See also Lev. 20:26. Note that Hirsch writes in terms of mankind's keeping the laws and judgments of the Torah, an important matter treated below.
112 See Schweid, *Moledet*, 59-60.
113 Breuer, *'Eda*, 65-66. On the uniqueness of the Jews according to Judah Halevi, see Guttmann, *Hapilosofia*, 119. Rosenberg addressed this subject at least twice. In S. Rosenberg, "Lev Usgula Ra'ayon Habeḥira Bemishnato Shel Rihal Uvapilosofia Hayehudit Haḥadasha," in *Mishnato Hahagutit Shel Rabi Yehuda Halevi*, ed. H. Schwartz (Jeruslem, 1978), 109-19, he presents Judah Halevi's position on the subject of chosenness as a dialectic. On the one hand, uniqueness—heart and shells—and on the other hand, mission—heart and organs. Both Hirsch and the young Luzzatto continued, according to Rosenberg, in the approach of Judah Halevi, in that they adopted his doctrine of mission. In Rosenberg, *Hakuzari*, 62-63, he states, without citing details, that Hirsch continued Judah Halevi's approach on the subject of chosenness. My opinion is that there is no need to see a dialectic here. Judah Halevi believed that the Jewish people was unique, and its uniqueness gave it responsibility and a mission for the rest of humanity. Hirsch and Luzzatto did not accept the uniqueness of being chosen, and therefore it is impossible to view them as continuing in the path of Judah Halevi. Although Hirsch accepted Judah Halevi's doctrine of mission, it was not from the point of departure of uniqueness. He regarded the Jews as being earlier in time, with the mission of bringing all of humanity to it. The young Luzzatto also believed, as Rosenberg

The Mission

The theory of the mission of the Jews was discussed at length in Hirsch's first book, the *Nineteen Letters*. This mission had two stages: the first stage, as a nation in its own land, and the second stage, as a nation in exile, dispersed among the Gentiles. The second stage was chosen after the failure of the first. Here is the account from the *Nineteen Letters*:

> In the wilderness it received the Torah, and thus in the wilderness, without land or soil, it became a nation. It became a body, whose soul was the Torah, and therefore could be truthfully called ... "a kingdom of priests," for as the priest in the midst of a single people was this nation to be in the midst of universal mankind, preserving the law of God, and practicing and fulfilling its holy precepts.... "Holy nation" was also to be its appellation, for through the fulfillment of the Divine law, it was to become holy, not participating in the worldly doings of other nations, but preaching the sacredness of humanity by the example of its life....
>
> It was to be a people in the midst of the people; as people it was to show the [other] people that God is the Source, and the Giver, of all blessing that to dedicate oneself to the fulfillment of His will means the attainment of all happiness that man can desire; that this sacred resolve is sufficient to give stability and security to human existence. It received, therefore, the blessings of a land and state-power, not, however, as end, but as means of carrying out the Torah, its possession and retention dependent, therefore, upon fulfillment thereof as [the] only condition. It was to be separate, even in happiness, from the nations in order that it might not learn of them to revere well-being and fortune as the goal of life, and, like them, sink into worship of wealth and lust....
>
> Only for a short time was Israel able to attain its ideal, the fulfillment of its mission in prosperity.... There came the time when, even in Israel, the prophet could lament—"As the number of thy cities were thy gods, O Judah." It became necessary to take away the abundance of earthly good, the wealth and the land, which had led it away from its mission; it was obliged to leave the happy soil which

---

states, in the doctrine of mission, but he dismissed it in his maturity. See below, note 167. Compare Rosenberg's view to that of Schwartz, *Hara'ayon*, 56-59, where he presents Judah Halevi's doctrine of chosenness and mission, and it seems that in his opinion there is no dialectic here, and also at the end of the process, the unique differences between Jews and Gentiles will not be blurred.

had seduced it from its allegiance to the Most High; nothing could be saved except the soul of its existence, the Torah; no other bond of unity should henceforth exist except "God and its mission," which are indestructible, because they are spiritual. Through the annihilation of Israel's state-life its mission did not cease, for that had been intended only as a means to an end. On the contrary, this destruction itself was part of its fate; so strangely commingled of divine and human elements, in exile and dispersion its mission was to be resumed in a different manner.... For its special office was to preserve itself pure from all sin and perversity, since "ה" was its God. Destruction and misfortune are therefore no less instructive for Israel than prosperity. The dispersion opened a new, great, and wide-extended field for the fulfillment of its mission....

The nation was scattered into the four quarters of the earth, unto all peoples and all zones, in order that in the dispersion it might better fulfill its mission....

On every side, states in all the glory of human power and pride disappeared from the face of the earth, while Israel, upheld only by its fidelity to God and His law, maintained successfully its existence.... With Israel's heart-blood is written on all the pages of history the doctrine that there is but one God, and that there are higher and better things for mankind than wealth and pleasure....

And now ... the scattered ones of Israel are tolerated, protected, even accepted as citizens, how beautiful, nay, how necessary [was] it that they should, in accordance with the permission of the nations, develop in peace and quietude all the grandeur of the Israel life. How beautiful it would be if Israel, obeying the word of its prophet, should attach itself closely to every state which has accepted its children in citizenship, and should seek to promote the welfare and the peace thereof.

If, though everywhere the habitations of men should cease to be the orchards in which are grown human fruit pleasing in the sight of God and man, every Israelitish house should nevertheless be a temple of true faith in God, of reverence and love for Him; if, though everywhere avarice, lust, and greed should become the motives of human actions, every Jew should still, in despite thereof, be a silent example and teacher of universal righteousness and universal love—if thus the dispersed of Israel should show themselves everywhere on earth, the glorious priests of God and pure humanity, O my Benjamin, if we were, if we would become what we should be—if our lives were a perfect reflection of our law—what a mighty engine we would constitute for propelling mankind to the final goal of all human education! More quietly, but more forcefully and profoundly, would it effect mankind than even our tragical record of sorrows, powerfully though this latter teaches the intervention of Providence in human affairs.

In the centuries of passion and scorn our mission was but imperfectly attainable, but the ages of mildness and justice, now begun, beckon us to that glorious goal; that every Jew and every Jewess should be in his or her own life a modest and unassuming priest or priestess of God and true humanity. When such an ideal and such a mission await us, can we still, my Benjamin, lament our fate?[114]

We learn from this that in his opinion the Jewish people received a homeland in order to use it to teach humanity that a people that lives in its land according to the ethics of the Torah is rewarded with plenty, and thus to plant in them admiration for the spirit and not idolatrous admiration of possessions and pleasures. This effort failed, because the nation sinned precisely in the most sensitive area, in the message it was supposed to convey to the Gentiles. Contrary to the mission entrusted to them, the well-fed nation turned its back on the spirit and venerated possessions. Exile came to them as a punishment and as a correction, but also to teach the Gentiles that they had erred in the object of their veneration, and most importantly to encourage them to perform their mission better. At first fulfilling their mission was slow and difficult, and it was attained by the actual existence of the nation for thousands

---

[114] *Nineteen Letters*, 75-86. Hirsch's position is based on Mendelssohn; however, most likely he heard a great deal about it from his rabbi, Ḥakham Bernays. On this see Horwitz, "Erets-Yisrael," 450 n. 5. On the sources of the doctrine of mission, see Rosenberg, *Hakuzari*, 309-10, and idem, "Galut," 174-81. According to him, the sources go back to the Apocrypha, Philo, and Josephus, and then, as we have noted, it appears in Judah Halevi and Maimonides. The significance and processes of the mission differ from thinker to thinker, but all of them emphatically advance the claim that the theory of punishment as an explanation for the exile is no longer sufficient, and Rosenberg notes the reasons for this. From a superficial survey of the various opinions, it appears that, the better the situation was for the Jews where they were living, the greater was the use of the idea of mission to bring out the positive nature of the exile and to neutralize the Land of Israel. See, for example, ibid., on the views of Rabbi Abraham, the son of Maimonides, Rabbi Baḥya ben Asher, Rabbi Ḥayim ben Betsalel, Rabbi Mordecai Dato, and the Maharsha [Rabbi Samuel Eliezer Edeles]. On the Jewish mission according to Hirsch, see Breuer, *'Eda*, 81-82.

of years of suffering and persecution, while it remained faithful to Torah and its values, while all the empires with material power fell one after the other.

Today, in the situation of increasing emancipation and enlightenment, it is possible to attain great achievements in the education of humanity to fear God, to love Him, to have faith in Him, and to love justice. These achievements will be attained if every Jewish home lives according to the commandments of the Torah and its morality and serves as a model for emulation by the Gentiles, among whom it acts in equality. Hirsch devotes an additional section to the state of the Jews during the first and second Temple periods. On the one hand, he emphasizes the sensitivity of the subject and its dangers, and on the other hand, he explains how the nation must act in the framework of its own state to fulfill its function of educating the Gentiles:

> The danger is very real that industry and politics [will] become the subject of man's worship, and God, Who is to be the beginning and end of all human endeavors, must be satisfied with a fragment of the incense-clouded feast.... Israel was to evolve a national life where science and art, industry and trade, man's ingenuity and power do not draw the veil over the human eye to prevent it from recognizing the presence of God.... Israel's main challenge is the building of a national political life in which all activities, be they insignificant or of vital importance, live up to the precepts of the Divine Will.[115]

When there was a Jewish kingdom, it was supposed to combine Torah with science, wisdom, politics, and the economy, and to educate

---

115 *Writings*, VIII, 212-13, in the essay, "The Jewish Sabbath." See also Hirsch on Ex. 25:21. Horwitz did not take note of his unifying position regarding the Jewish state, and stated only his position regarding the present state where he lived. See "Erets-Yisrael," 449. Hirsch expresses a similar opinion in his argument on the Jewish community as well. He speaks of the medieval period until 1848, when the religious and political authority of the community was in the hands of the same leaders, because this was the desire of the government. This situation enabled the authorities to exploit the Jews, who were deprived of rights, but it also permitted the effective and autonomous management of communal life. In his day, when the Jews were granted equal rights, but deprived of civil administration, the only hope was the separation of religion from the state, so the government would not intervene in the management of the community's religious life. See *Writings*, VI, 66-75.

humanity that in an ideal state there was no separation between religion and the state, and that only a combination of the divine will with human wisdom would lead to an optimal outcome. As we have shown, for Hirsch these two areas were identical and necessary for man's path to perfection, with the Torah being the yardstick. This is also true in the life of the model state that the Torah presents, and all the public Halakhot are directed toward this goal.

Importantly, Hirsch's position applies only to a Jewish state, both the ancient one and apparently also the future one. Until then, in existing states, where there are people of other religions and where Hirsch represents a minority religion, he, like Mendelssohn, believes that the civil state must be separated from all intervention in the religious life of the communities and their rituals, while it should have the monopoly on civil affairs.

In his other writings as well, Hirsch usually speaks of the Jewish people's mission in its dispersion, and on the content that they are supposed to teach the Gentiles:

> Recognition that the source of goodness in the world in every generation is God, who rules the world, and whoever knows Him and devotes himself to Him, will have the upper hand.[116]
>
> Education for justice and humanity, understanding that God wants the continued existence of the Jewish people.[117]
>
> Recognition of the miracle of the continued existence of the Jewish people as proof of the rule of God and His power, and understanding that the punishment of the Jewish people by exile from their land is proof of the divine principle of reward and punishment.[118]
>
> Recognition that the Jews are God's chosen people, led by Him in a supernatural manner, in spite of the powerful effort of mankind to destroy them.[119]
>
> Education of humanity to acknowledge God and knowledge and understanding of their function and duties.[120]

---

116 *Writings*, I, 86.
117 Ibid., 177.
118 Ibid., 371.
119 Ibid., II, 35.
120 Ibid., 387.

Transmission of the message of universal cooperation, preservation of the truths of revelation for the moral enlightenment of humanity.[121]

Victory of the unarmed spirit and morality over material power and the strength of the sword and violence.[122]

And, finally, the law of the Torah:

For two thousand years, the major share of all that is noble and good, true and gentle, belongs to the קול יעקב [the voice of Jacob], the Divine word which has penetrated the heart of mankind.... Most of the laws which govern the world today are based on the Jewish law.... Thus far mankind has adopted only a small portion, only an echo of Jacob's words. The Jewish nation still carries the major portion of the Law within itself, unrecognized by the world.... But there will come a time when that which the world now ridicules and mocks will become its salvation and redemption. It will then realize that the welfare of mankind resides in the Jewish law.[123]

Here Hirsch states explicitly that in the future the entire Torah will be adopted by all mankind, as discussed below.

An Active Mission

Does activity in the framework of the mission also require initiative on the part of the Jews? Hirsch, unlike Chajes, says yes. The Gentiles do not see that Providence is leading them to salvation, but the Jews must be aware of this, and they must not be content with quiet action that will do its part with the help of Providence. The Jew must be active, to help Providence and actualize it, and also to prepare for this. Progress and emancipation are signs that should encourage us to carry out this task.

In explaining the purpose of the destruction of the Temple and of the exile in Horeb, Hirsch expounds the idea of mission at length, and concludes that the exile is indeed a warning about the result of sin, but it is mainly:

---

121 Ibid., 392.
122 Ibid., 416.
123 Ibid., 393.

[to] become by its own example the beacon for the avowal of God ... to be a holy people and a kingdom of priests, bearer of the Divine scheme, and God's instrument.

Warning: Beware of the results of these sins of the fathers.

Admonition: To bring into effect the purpose of the Galuth, understood in its true objective within our own lifetime, and to help to bring it to realization within the lifetime of our brothers.[124]

Elsewhere he comes back to this matter, saying that in part the mission is conscious:

> Precisely, or so it seems to us, this point in history marks the beginning of the penetration of the Word of God, which had been entrusted to Israel, into the non-Jewish world. While millennia of Jewish history formed Israel to become ever more faithful messengers of this Word, Israel, knowingly but more often unknowingly, scattered upon its path the seeds of light from the Word of God, sowing them in the midst of mankind which one day, like Israel, is to be won for this Word. And even as Israel steadily matures toward its destiny, the seeds of light from the Word of God, scattered into the rest of mankind, will eventually act to prepare mankind for the same future.[125]

The Jewish people must be prepared to fulfill its mission:

> Now, at long last, the nations are beginning to get a glimmer of our vocation, which is to bring about the salvation of all mankind. Little by little, this realization is moving all mankind closer to the Jewish view of life and human destiny. The harvest of millennia of toil and trouble appears to be at hand, and we should be preparing to scatter the rich seed of Jewish wisdom and of the Jewish fulfillment of life's tasks into the waiting acre of mankind.
>
> Now that we are so close to our goal, should we suddenly turn our backs on our own mission? Should we suddenly brand God's wisdom as folly, devotion to Judaism as nonsense, and Jewish consecration as madness? Have we not been accepted by the rest of humanity in order to bring to all men the saving treasure of God's Law that was entrusted to our care, in order to draw all men to us

---

124 *Horeb*, vol. 1, 144.
125 *Writings*, II, 254-55.

into the Divine covenant that consecrates men to the priesthood of true humanity?[126]

The Image of the Messianic Future

What future is Hirsch preparing for us? Will the Gentiles adopt the entire Torah or only its theological and ethical truths? Will there be a need for a Jewish state in the messianic age, when humanity attains a peak of universal, moral togetherness which acknowledges the kingdom of God and His will, and, if so, what will be its purpose? We find that here, in the area of the unreal future, Hirsch is vague, oscillating between the tense extremes of his fundamentalist traditionalism and his ideological philosophy, which is influenced by the thinking of his generation. Hirsch endeavors to interpret the verses of the Rebuke in Behuqotai (Lev. 26:14-40) and to show from them that the punishment for sin and the bitter exile need not continue until the end of days. We are capable of turning them into a fortunate exile, if we observe the Torah in the Diaspora, and if we happily fulfill the function assigned to us to carry the message of God to the Gentiles. Hirsch distinguishes between the long way to salvation and rapid redemption, which will come in three stages. The long way to salvation is:

> בקרי [in opposition]: In all the events of world history—which do not appear at all to be directed toward the return of the exiles—I will walk with them. Their whole experience in the land of their enemies—with all the effects of this experience, which educate through suffering—and the whole course of the development of world history itself will ultimately lead to the result that the exiles will be ripe to return to independence. And the events of the history of the nations—the events themselves—will restore the exiles to their homeland. Thus, the whole long and extended exile "in the land of their enemies"—including all the old and new sins—in essence merely actualizes והבאתי אותם [and I will bring them]. God Who conceals Himself brings them home by long, roundabout paths; He brings them back to their ancient homeland and to their original, eternal mission.

---

126 Ibid., VII, 407.

או או [if then]: Or perhaps the other possibility for the future will come to pass. They will not continue the iniquity of their fathers, and will not augment it with new iniquity born of exile. Rather, אז, after all the crushing blows of the initial period of exile, the hearts of הנשארים בהם [those remaining of them], those who survive this difficult period, will be humbled. They will not "rot away in sins old and new"; rather, their hearts will be humbled before God, and will ceased to be "ערל" [uncircumcised] and recalcitrant toward Him (see Commentary, Bereshis 17:10).

ואז, and then—not only in the end of days—ירצו את עונם [they expiate their iniquity]: They will cheerfully accept their destiny in exile and gladly carry out their mission in exile, regarding this as ריצוי עונם [expiating their sin], a means of redressing the wrong of their past sins. Their destiny and mission will satisfy themselves and also "satisfy" the debt they have incurred. If this happens, the גלות [exile] will assume an entirely new form. Instead of being a grave of decay, exile will become ground for new fulfillment of Israel's God-ordained mission, fruitful soil for a גלות-life directed toward God and bound up with Him.[127]

That is to say: there are two paths to salvation. One is "in its time,"[128] a time long and full of suffering, in which sins are continued in exile, lengthening it and preventing miraculous redemption. God returns the Jews to their land naturally, with a hidden miracle, through prolonged and tortuous historical events. The end of days in this path, which is also beyond history, will come by the agency of God as though by itself, and no one will be aware of it until it happens. This is the only time that Hirsch speaks about a salvation that is not openly miraculous but rather is achieved by a hidden miracle, and this exception proves the rule. Hirsch does not conceal that this exception is not desirable, and he prefers the short path—"I will hasten it"—in which the Jews submit to God, refrain from further sins, and accept joyously the mission assigned to them. This path will be regarded as atonement for the sins the Jews committed in their land, and it will

---

127 Hirsch on Lev. 26:39-41.
128 See Lev. 26:44. Hirsch uses a rabbinic Midrash from BT Sanhedrin 98a, on the verse in Isaiah 60:22.

make possible a happy exile and not one in which they rot in the grave, like the first one.[129]

The short path in the development of the Jewish historical mission has three stages, which are described here as three covenants. The Covenant of Jacob is the time of bitter exile during which there will be expiation of sins through suffering, pogroms, and martyrdom. The Covenant of Isaac, which follows it, was in Hirsch's time, the time of dawn in the firmament of the nations. The Jewish people has begun to flourish on soil that had previously been alien soil, and their happiness will increase, and then they will suffer from the envy of the nations, who will vacillate between humanity and envy. The Jews will exploit their powers, which were enriched and liberated, to fulfill their function in the Diaspora, and they will observe the Torah in affluence, with more perfection and diversity. When they have withstood this trial, the Covenant of Abraham will come:

> Like Abraham, they will observe the Torah, which has been entrusted to them for the salvation of mankind, and they will actualize the full goodness and truth of the Torah in the midst of many peoples. Ultimately, the nations will tolerate and respect Israel—not even though they are the people of the God of Abraham, but because they are the people of the God of Abraham; because they know and observe God's Torah, which brings salvation to mankind.... They will overcome all the obstacles over which they stumbled while dwelling in their own land, and only then—והארץ אזכר [I will remember the Land]: When they have become "Abraham," I will restore them to

---

129 Horwitz, "Erets-Yisrael," 456, quotes the passage from Hirsch's remarks about the long and less desirable path, and she sees it, rather, as the short path to salvation that will be within history. In my opinion, examination of this passage must consider what is written after it about the preferred path, in which salvation will come faster and miraculously. It must be emphasized that according to Hirsch, even the undesirable path will only be actualized beyond history. It appears that Horwitz is following P. Rosenblit, "Bein Shnei 'Olamot," in *Torah 'Im Derekh Erets Hatenu'a Isheiha Ra'ayonteiha*, ed. M. Breuer (Ramat-Gan, 1987), 33-43, and idem, "Galut Veerets Yisrael 'Al Pi S.R Hirsch Uvnei Doro," in *Sefer Zikaron Lemordekhai Viser Pirqei Ma'as Vehagut*, ed. S. Schmidt (Kvutzat Yavne, 1981),160-69, in which he speaks about the duality that stood out in the attitude of Hirsch and his circle toward the Land of Israel, and he, too, cites this passage, in my opinion, erroneously.

> the land, so that they should fulfill their mission as the people of the Torah on the land of the Torah.
>
> We see then that [the Covenant of Jacob, the Covenant of Isaac, and the Covenant of Abraham] are the three stages in which they are to perform their task in the גלות [*galuth,* exile]. When they have gone through these three stages, their sin will be atoned for, and at the same time they will be ready to return forever to the land of their independence.
>
> (Verse 43) והארץ וגו' [and the land etc.]. When the people will be ready for their mission, the land, too, will be restored to its mission. For the mission of the land is to be the soil of Torah observance for God's people. But until the people are ready for this, the land will await them in desolation. The land will not be given to another people, and its soil will not promote the development of strangers. In its desolation it will atone for its Sabbaths—as long as the people in their exile must atone for their sin.[130]

Hirsch does not offer details about the final purpose of the Land, aside from its being a reward for atoning for sin. He uses phrases about the land of God for the people of God, but he does not give them substantial content. He does not say when the third stage will end and that there will be a return to the land, nor how we will know—if this is to be an actual event—that the time is ripe to return to the Land, despite the oath and despite the danger of dwelling in the land when everything is good.

Elsewhere Hirsch describes the narrowing of the gaps between Israel and the nations in the course of history. In its history the Jewish people discovers the One God who directs history, but there is something of a divine revelation in the people's actions as well, because it subjects its actions to the laws of God. In contrast, among the Gentiles, only their history contains something of a divine revelation, but their deeds do not testify to it. They act according to nature and are subject only to themselves, to their hearts' desires and impulses, and not according to the will of their Creator.

> But *this contrast diminishes more and more.* Under the influence of Israel's mission and under the influence of the example that Israel

---

130 Hirsch on Lev. 26:42-43. See also on Gen. 26:15.

quietly sets among the nations, this contrast becomes smaller and smaller.... The seventh day [of the Succot sacrifices] is the goal of the development of mankind and of Israel's mission for it, and on this day the contrast will cease to exist. Israel and all of mankind will be united in their acknowledgement of God and in the life-service of deeds....

However, as regards the historical guidance and their role in fulfilling the mission of mankind, the special standing of Israel amidst the nations will not be discontinued. For Israel and the nations differ in their historical development and in their ability to realize the purposes of mankind; hence Israel and the nations, the nations and Israel, will continue to be separate and distinct, even though they will be equal in their value. Both will be close to God in His direction of their history, and both will lead the world for the achievement of mankind's purposes, but they will continue to be seven *and another* seven כבשים [sheep], one and another איל [ram].

Nonetheless, they will be identical in rendering homage to God by fulfilling the commandments given to each respectively; the Sinaitic Teaching given to Israel, and the general Teaching given to mankind. *In rendering homage to God by doing His Will, Israel and mankind will become one.* The active life of all people will bear the stamp of faithfulness to moral duty, just like the active life of Israel.... וְהָיָה יְהוָה לְמֶלֶךְ, עַל-כָּל-הָאָרֶץ; בַּיּוֹם הַהוּא, יִהְיֶה יְהוָה אֶחָד--וּשְׁמוֹ אֶחָד ["And the LORD shall be King over all the earth; in that day shall the LORD be One, and His name one"] (Zechariah 14:9).[131]

Hirsch does not say when this unification will happen, nor does he give substantial content to the continued separation of the Jewish people in its land after Israel and the rest of humanity have united, and there will be identicality both in their history and in their action. The second path is none other than an idealization of the Diaspora.

Hirsch does not take the path of Maimonides, who completely condemns the exile, regarding its resulting persecution and troubles as the cause of the people's spiritual degradation, nor does he follow Judah Halevi, who sees the task of the exiled nation as serving God and bearing the sufferings of humanity, as a passive agent of its progress.

---

131 Hirsch on Num. 29:13. In his commentary on Psalms 25:4, he distinguishes between forbidden foods and sexual relations, which apply only to the Jews, whereas the laws of justice and truth, honesty and compassion, and the social obligations of the Torah will be observed by all mankind.

Hirsch certainly does not follow Nachmanides, who sees no real true, ideal value at all in keeping the commandments outside of the Land of Israel.

These three men yearned for Zion within history. Judah Halevi and Maimonides even fulfilled their dream of traveling to the Land of Israel, believing that it possessed inherent excellence. Hirsch's way is similar to that of Mendelssohn, presenting exile as a mission to the nations by providing a personal and public example of someone who draws upon two sources of culture. However, they do disagree about the connection and relation between these two sources, about human progress, and about actively pursuing the mission.

It is possible to read the passages quoted here about the stages of salvation as did Isaac Breuer[132]—a descendant of Hirsch's who became a messianic, Ultra-Orthodox Zionist—who interpreted them as expressing identification with the messianic Zionism that preceded Herzl.

It is also possible to read these passages as Pinḥas Rosenblit[133] and Rivka Horwitz[134] did. They were aware of Hirsch's reservations regarding the active return to Zion in his time, but they limited it only to his generation, and saw the future Hirsch described as the last stage in history. Thereby they tried to keep him within the consensus of those who yearn for Zion in reality.

These readings seem erroneous to me, warped by a Zionist conception, and I prefer the reading of Mordechai Breuer.[135] In my opinion, demonstrated above, the future Hirsch describes is utopian, beyond history. Within history the Land of Israel and the Temple are neutralized and replaced by the homeland in the Diaspora, by the Torah, and by the home and heart of every Jew.

The nation's sin will be atoned for only beyond history. Only then will the Jewish people be able to dwell in the Land of Israel, free

---

132 See Breuer, "Rashar," 16-21. Not surprisingly, this article does not contain even a single quotation from Hirsch.
133 See Rosenblit, "'Olamot," 37-38.
134 See Horwitz, "Erets-Yisrael," 455-456.
135 See Breuer, 'Eda, 79-81.

of all sensual seductions of abundance. Only beyond history will humanity be united, and God and His name will be One. In his essay "The Educational Value of Judaism," which for some reason was not published until 1937, Hirsch expressed some extraordinary ideas about Torah and science. This essay contains an important passage about universalism, the mission of the Jewish people, and the messianic future. It relates explicitly to the miraculous character of the end of days, when the wolf will dwell with the lamb, and eternal peace and brotherhood will reign, and he paraphrases the words of the prophets, taking them literally, without any allegory:

> The enlightenment of all the nations on earth was expressly named as the purpose of all the momentous events in the history of the Jewish people.... The gathering of all mankind around God was stated as the ultimate objective of the many sorrows that the Jewish people had to endure over the centuries of its history....
>
> The Prophets of Judaism, which has been so unjustly maligned as exclusivist, were the ones who portrayed as the ultimate goal of the history of the Jews, as well as of the rest of mankind, a future era in which all the nations will go to Mount Zion in order to receive the Word of God. On that day, all men will learn to break up their swords and spears and no longer lift up the sword against each other; they will no longer practice the arts of war but will walk, together with the House of Jacob, in the light of the Lord (Isaiah 2:3-4). In that future world, righteousness will gird the loins and faithfulness will gird the hips, the wolf will dwell together with the lamb and the leopard with the kid, evil and destruction will no longer be practiced, and the earth will be filled with the knowledge of God just as waters cover the bottom of the sea (Isaiah 11:5-9; Micah 4:1-4; Habakkuk 2:14). This will be a world in which God will pour out His spirit upon all flesh (Joel 3:1), the language of the nations will become pure, and they all will call upon the Name of the one, sole God and serve Him dutifully as with one voice (Zephaniah 3:9).[136]

Had Hirsch been referring to an event within history—in which the people does not have permission to take an active part, and which will happen when it is God's will—the question of course arises as to how

---

136 *Writings*, VII, 267. See also Hirsch on Gen. 22:17, 49:1-2, 11, 26, 27; Deut. 17:14. There it appears that the sheep and the wolf are taken as a parable, but there is no doubt that he refers to a utopian time.

and when we will know that it is His will. Horwitz asks this question[137] and offers no answer. According to my interpretation, the decision of Providence, at least that which Hirsch desires, will be accompanied by miraculous, supernatural actions, and the Jews will certainly recognize it.

Two subjects remain unclear from Hirsch's statements, and he apparently left them ambivalent and fuzzy on purpose, since he was caught in the tension between the universalism of the Haskala and fundamentalism, faithful to the tradition of the inerrant Bible and the Sages. These subjects are connected to the content and meaning of the people's dwelling in their land in a utopian situation, and what laws humanity will then observe.

In my opinion, like the Reform Jews, Hirsch was pleased to be rid of the need for a separate nation in its land, even beyond history, but,

---

137 Horwitz, "Erets-Yisrael," 453. Horwitz's article in general is a collection of quotations from Hirsch without order or method, which is why it contains contradictions and errors, and Hirsch appears to be an incoherent figure, whose position has "two faces" of a complex manner of thought, which enabled so many people to depend on it (464-65). On the one hand, a position that regards the Land of Israel as the center of Jewish existence (448, 451), which has uniqueness (459), "an approach similar to that of Judah Halevi" (458). On the other hand, a position that restricts the place of the Land in favor of the Diaspora (456), and states that its sanctity is not inherent (458). Horwitz does not distinguish between historical time and Utopian time in Hirsch's approach, and therefore she accepts Rosenblit's view that salvation will come within history, without a miracle (455), stating: "sometimes he regarded the return to Zion as more imminent" (456), while she also cites sources that show that salvation is deferred till the end of days and connected with the spiritual ascent of humanity (451). The passages that she cites to show that for Hirsch the Land of Israel possessed unique excellence (458-60) do not testify to the inherent excellence of the Land, but rather, as she herself says there, to the uniqueness that derives from the performance of the commandments of the Torah there, and its excellence depends on the morality of its inhabitants. Horwitz decided that Hirsch's position regarding the centrality of the Land is only "for his generation," (460) and that "Hirsch's relation to the actual Land of Israel is problematic" (463). In her opinion, Hirsch was also similar to Judah Halevi in regarding the Jewish people among the nations as like the heart among the other organs (461), and she did not notice that according to Hirsch, it is not the excellence of the nation, but a temporary situation. I seek to show that on the matter of the excellence of the nation and the Land, Hirsch is very far from Judah Halevi, nor is there a way to begin from his position and reach a messianic Zionist position like that of I. Breuer (464).

unlike the Reform movement, he wanted to believe that the entire Torah would be kept in full, as much as possible, by all of humanity. The tradition of the return to Zion, which is found in the Bible, and the Halakhic distinction between the commandments of "the Torah from Sinai," which were given only to the Jewish people, and the seven Noahide commandments, which the nations must observe (a distinction made by Hirsch as well, see the quotation above at n. 131), prevented him from saying so explicitly and forced him to cling to the tradition.

As I have shown above, very frequently Hirsch finds it difficult to keep within these limits, and sometimes his words imply that the entire Torah, or at least large parts of it, is the object of the mission. He also fails to provide content and meaning to the return of the Jewish people to their land, beyond history, aside from the possibility of observing all of the commandments that depend on the land, and he is content with general phrases. When the Jewish people succeeds in its mission at the end of days, it will thereby restore all of humanity to the Garden of Eden, as it was before the Original Sin, and this sin will be atoned, and the process of the education of mankind, which began with Abraham, will be complete.[138]

According to Hirsch, the utopian future is in the universal spirit of humanity, but it is entirely permeated by Torah Judaism and bound up with the return to Zion:

> The day will come when Jerusalem and Zion will rise again and nations will make pilgrimages to the mountain of God so they, too, may learn to know the ways of that Law and to walk in its paths.[139]

---

138 See Hirsch on Gen. 3:19, 22-24.
139 *Writings*, II, 303. This passage and others like it (see for example Hirsch on Gen. 26:15 and 32:30), emphasize the difference between Hirsch and Reform on the matter of the place of the Land of Israel in the Jewish religion. Therefore, I do not accept the opinion of Z. Levi, "Erets-Yisrael Bamaḥshava Hayehudit Begermania Mehirsch V'ad Rosenzweig," *Kivunim* 4 (1979): 54-67, that, in Hirsch, the real connection between Judaism and the Land of Israel was entirely severed, and the bond with it is not and never was an essential part of Jewish religious faith. Levi identifies Hirsch's approach with those of Geiger and Rosenzweig. In my opinion, Hirsch cannot repudiate the sources. Therefore, to avoid duality—he transferred the return of the people to its land to the messianic, non-real realm.

Not only Israel but all mankind will benefit from the educational and moral influence of those among Israel who sanctify their lives through faithful fulfillment of the Torah. They tacitly serve as a light to all mankind, as models showing how man's sacred calling is to be put into practice.... Through Israel they will all band together and form a single group to do God's Will and to fulfill His command.[140]

In passages cited above,[141] Hirsch states that the Gentiles of his time were defined as doing the will of God in their practical lives. Thus, mention of keeping the commandments here must refer to more than that, to the commandments of the Torah. In many of the passages that I cited, the word "Torah" is used in a general sense in the context of a message for humanity which the Jewish people bears.

On the basis of the foregoing analysis, I have reached the firm conclusion that Hirsch was by no means a harbinger of the return to Zion, and that he hoped ideologically that the Jewish people would succeed in imparting to all of humanity as many laws of the Torah as possible, for they reflect the best ethical norms.

---

140 Hirsch on Deut. 33:3. See also on Gen. 33:20, Ex. 32:15-17, and Num. 10:35-36. Luzzatto wrote in a letter that he loved and admired the author of the *Nineteen Letters* because of his Jewish national pride, which he bears with honor and in public, but he thought that his positions and opinions were too conservative and inappropriate to the spirit of the age, and therefore they could not influence the thinking and action of the generation. He read the *Nineteen Letters* and attacked the position of its author, which is also expressed in the source just cited, according to which the mission of mankind is to serve God according to the commandments of the Torah. "Since the explicit revelation is not a natural event, but entirely supernatural, it follows from this that obedience to it cannot be regarded as the natural fulfillment of man's mission; for this appears to be something irrefutable, that this perfection must be attainable without any external, supernatural condition. Furthermore, obedience to the explicit revelation cannot be considered as the universal mission of mankind, until a specific revelation (be it what it may) will be made known to all of mankind and becomes its full belief" (see Luzzatto, *Epistulario*, 214-18, in a letter to Abraham Randegger of Trieste, 1837). Dita Campagnano translated this letter for me and I later found a Hebrew translation in Luzzatto, *Peraqim*. Artom stresses in his introduction to the selected letters that, at the time he read them, Luzzatto apparently did not know the identity of the author of the *Nineteen Letters*, which was published under a pseudonym.

141 Notes 123, 126.

LUZZATTO'S RESPONSE
Background

Until the end of his thirties, Luzzatto, who was a religious romantic and, like Hirsch, had internalized Haskala, related to the Land of Israel, to the Gentiles, and to salvation similarly to both Chajes and Hirsch. All three based their views on Mendelssohn in their universal approach, in their opposition to an actual return to the Land, and in adopting the idea of mission. Luzzatto accepted the idea of human progress, like Chajes and Hirsch, in contrast to Mendelssohn, and he struggled with Mendelssohn's question about the Jews as the chosen people.

With Luzzatto as well, the universal idea is connected with that of the mission. It is an error to regard Judaism as particularistic. The Jewish people received revelation on behalf of all the nations, who are equal before the Creator. The reason for their choice was, according to Luzzatto, very prosaic: they chose Him. Luzzatto related to Mendelssohn's question about chosenness several times in his writings, and it is the point of departure for many of his discussions of the topic.

Universalism and Humanity

Luzzatto's universal view of Judaism was a matter of principle. The ethics of the Torah are based, as I have shown, on the principle of compassion, which is universal and anti-racist. The Jewish people never hated other nations because of their different beliefs, and the prophets never preached about punishment by Providence for different belief, but for moral corruption. The Jewish people does not keep the Torah for their own sake but for all of humanity. The compassion underlying Jewish morality is a heritage for all of humanity: "The compassion that Judaism recommends applies to the whole world. It is intended, as God's compassion, for all His creatures. No race is outside the law, because all human beings, according to the teaching of Judaism, are brothers, children of a single father, and they were all created in God's image."[142] God chose the Jews for the benefit of all the nations, as both Judah Halevi and Maimonides said:

> The intention of divine Providence in choosing this nation was not solely for the benefit of the nation, but for the benefit of all the nations.... For the God of Israel is not a particular and private god for them, but He is the God of all flesh, and all the nations are His children.... And R. Judah Halevi (*Kuzari* 4:23) believed that the dispersion of the Jews in exile is one of the secrets of Providence, which was for the benefit of all the nations—and this divine intention persists and advances slowly over the generations, and if someone should say that Christians are idol worshipers (according to Maimonides in Hilkhot Maakhalot Asurot 11:7, in old printings: "But the Christians are idol worshipers, and their wine is forbidden for enjoyment), we respond, that this is not the truth, and that it was Rashi's belief that they are not idol worshipers (Tur and Yoreh De'a, no. 148).[143]

Judaism is the only tolerant religion that acknowledges that all humans bear the image of God, and they are judged according to their deeds and not their faith:

> Behold some of the ancient Gentiles worshiped a special god, which their neighbors did not worship, and therefore they believed that this divinity watched over them and loved them, and it was distant from their neighbors and hated them because they worshiped a different god. Not like them was the portion of Jacob, for their God was the Maker of all, the God of all flesh, and His mercy was on all his creatures; if Israel was his eldest son, all the Gentiles were also his sons, and He never was angry at the nations for worshiping other gods, and the prophets never said that a certain nation would receive a punishment for the transgression of worshiping wood and stone, but for the transgression of robbery and abominations that they did, for which He did not forgive them. And other ancient nations were disgusted by nations other than themselves and hated them, because they did not reach their height in wisdom and art, and they were called "barbarians," and they were regarded as animals in

---

142 Luzzatto, *Ketavim*, vol. 1, 55, in "The Essence of Judaism." Artom apparently mistranslated here, writing "Jews" where we wrote "human beings." Cf. the quotation from Hirsch at note 38 above. Their positions and even their language are extremely similar.
143 Luzzatto, *Meḥqerei Hayahadut*, I, pt. 1, 10 n. 2, in the book *Yesodei Hatorah*.

their eyes, but the children of Israel and their patriarchs did not hate other nations, nor were they revolted by them.... Indeed the faith of Israel, on the matter of the difference between them and the other nations, is that the Hebrew regards all human beings as children of a single father, and all of them are in the image of God, and no person is judged because of his belief, but for his deeds; but he believes, that since all the nations were idol worshipers, and Abraham clung to a single God, the master of heaven and earth, God made a covenant with him to multiply his seed and to be their God (to show them His divinity by signs and wonders), and to give them the land of Canaan, and as a sign of this covenant, He commanded him and his seed regarding circumcision. And when God came to give them the Torah at the hands of Moses, he maintained and strengthened this faith in them, and He said to them, "If you will harken to My voice and keep My covenant, you shall be My treasured possession among all the peoples. Indeed, Mine is all the earth [and all the human race is precious for Me], and you will be to Me a kingdom of priests and a holy nation"; and for this intention, to carve this faith in their heart, he gave them the Torah and many commandments, so that all the masses among the Jews would be on the level of priests among the other nations, who were separate from the masses in their special commandments and laws, to sanctify them for their gods.[144]

Luzzatto rejects Maimonides's opinion regarding hostility toward anyone who does not accept the principles of Judaism, and he argues that Judaism was always universal and humane, cooperating with anyone who agreed to act morally. God chose the Jews after Abraham chose Him, rising above all the idol worshipers of his time, and God appointed them as priests to the nations and gave them the Torah so they could live a life of sanctity and fulfill their mission, preserving the truths of Judaism for all of humanity.

Several times, Luzzatto discusses the choice of the Jews and the reason why revelation was only given to them. This question, which had already been raised by Judah Halevi and Mendelssohn, was, according to Luzzatto, the one asked in his time by the deists, who denied revelation. Luzzatto does not accept Judah Halevi's answer based on the prophetic abilities of the Jews, because this idea of

---

144 Ibid., 30-32. On universalism in Luzzatto, the influence of Rousseau, and the similarity to Hirsch, see Slymovics, "Luzzatto," 113-14.

excellence is unacceptable to a man who had internalized Haslaka and universalism. He also ignores the first revelation to the sons of Noah, which was cited by Chajes and Hirsch. This is a revelation mentioned only by the Sages, whose words are not, according to Luzzatto, from Mount Sinai. He focuses on Mendelssohn's answer, using the idea of the mission, but, like Hirsch, he does not accept Mendelssohn's religious and liturgical particularism. He only accepts the first part of Mendelssohn's answer:

> The existence and reality of the Creator are truths of the type that revelation cannot teach us, so that whoever is not convinced by other reasons of the unity of the Creator has no reason to believe in the teachings of God; and even the immediate revelation of God cannot be authoritative for him, if he has already not been convinced about God's existence.... Therefore God cannot be revealed to many idol worshipers and pagans, who have not admitted the unity of the Creator, because revelation would not have been effective in enlightening their hearts. He could be revealed to Abram, who, even though he was born in a family of pagans (Josh. 24:2), discovered the truth of this matter; and afterward He could be revealed to the Israelites, who followed in the footsteps of their patriarch and clung to the worship of a single God. And that revelation of God to the Jewish people was beneficial not only to that nation, but it was also intended to preserve the highly valuable kernel of knowledge of the most fitting truths on earth, which in the future would become fruit for the good of the generality and to spread its fruit in the broadest possible lands, and to prepare in that way for the desired time, when they will bring happiness to the entire human race and knowledge of the true God and obedience to His laws.[145]

Luzzatto accepts the words of Mendelssohn in *Jerusalem*[146] regarding the uselessness of revelation for someone who has not attained knowledge of the single God and of Providence through his reason, but he does not accept the idea that happiness and humanity can be attained solely through reason. Happiness will be accorded to mankind through

---

145 Luzzatto, *Ketavim*, vol. 1, 99, in *Lessons in Dogmatic Theology*. See also Luzzatto's commentary on Ex. 20:3. Shavit apparently did not notice Luzzatto's discussion of these questions. See Shavit, *Hayavnut*, 164.
146 Mendelssohn, *Jerusalem*, 97-98.

the merit of Abraham, who knew and chose the one God, and only then did God choose him, and by virtue of his descendants—the Jewish people, who, because of their fidelity to the heritage of Abraham, received revelation and preserved its messages and ethics throughout history for all of humanity.

Like Chajes and Hirsch, Luzzatto also cites Judah Halevi's parable of the seed regarding the mission and progress from one degree to another, which the appearance of the monotheistic religions faithfully reflects. Similarly, he also refers to Maimonides, chapter 11 in Hilkhot Melakhim, in the uncensored Amsterdam edition of 1551.

Emancipation

Unlike Hirsch, who saw emancipation in a favorable light, though he was aware of its dangers, at first Luzzatto gave it a chance, but later he saw it negatively. At first he thought that progress was possible among the Gentiles in his day, because enlightenment would lead them to overcome past transgressions and gradually attain brotherhood among men.[147] However, as noted, his opinion changed later on.

Luzzatto noted that the assimilationists, and the Reform Jews and Bible critics, who were influenced by non-Jewish culture and whom he defined as rationalists and Atticists, wanted to resemble their neighbors rather than seeking the truth and loving their own people. In a letter to Jost of 1840, in which he expresses national sentiments, Luzzatto writes:

> When, dear scholars of Germany, when will God open your eyes? How long will you fail to see that by being drawn after the multitude, and allowing national pride to be extinguished, and the language of your ancestors to be forgotten from the mouth of your seed, and by allowing Atticism to grow stronger among us every day, and that as long as you permit your brethren to paint a picture of perfection in their imagination, as if it were only to become equal to their neighbors and to be important in their eyes, and your heart does not rise up in zeal for God and zeal for the truth and zeal of love for your brethren, to teach them that the good is not visible, but it is felt in the chambers of the heart, and that the success of our

---

147 See below, note 155.

> nation does not depend on emancipation, but on love of man for his fellow, and on our being joined in a bond of brotherhood like members of a single family, that this is our success, and this is decreased and lost in the shadow of emancipation, and as long as you say that "the lands of France and Belgium and Holland are precious lands for the children of Israel," of necessity the word of Malachi (2:9) will be fulfilled, and in the end all of the Scholars of Israel will have to be woodcutters and drawers of water.[148]

In the course of time, his negative view of emancipation grew ever stronger. In response to the extreme Reform positions regarding the radical spiritualization of redemption, which regard emancipation as the first stage in the yearned-for redemption of the Jews, and the dialectical unification with humanity, whose meaning is assimilation and integration, as the ultimate redemption, he sees this as a great danger for Judaism:

> For you surely know that every single nation living in a particular land can also exist without faith, but the children of Israel, who are dispersed in the four corners of the earth, would not have existed until today unless they had clung to their faith, and if perish the thought they should cease to believe in Torah from heaven, then surely they would cease to be a people, and the name of Israel would no longer be remembered, but it would happen to them what happens to the rivers that flow to the sea, and this is the final redemption in a few people's opinion, and its name is "fusion [assimilation]." And the Jewish scholarship, with which some scholars in Germany are occupied with in this generation, cannot persist.... And they also have a different intention, and it is to give the Jews grace and honor in the eyes of the Gentiles, and they raise up high a few of our ancestors, in order to rush the first redemption, which in their opinion is emancipation, and this scholarship will not abide, but it will be annulled, immediately with the arrival of redemption, or when these people die out, who learned the Torah in their childhood, and who believed in God and in Moses before they went to study—with Eichorn and his students.[149]

---

148 *Igrot Shadal*, 660. The verse in Malachi: "And I, in turn, have made you despicable and vile in the eyes of all the people, because you disregard My ways and show partiality to your rulings."

149 Ibid., 1367. On "fusion" as the final redemption, see also ibid., 1378. On emancipation see Klausner, *Hasifrut* II, 106-8, and Artom, "Mavo," 30-31, and the other sources they cite. Klausner and Artom failed to notice that there were two stages in

The Accusation of Dual Loyalty, Neutralization of the Return to Zion, and the Messianic Future

Luzzatto also dealt with the accusation of dual loyalty. Like Mendelssohn, Chajes, and Hirsch, he also neutralized the aspiration to return to Zion by placing it beyond history, viewing it as a utopian, miraculous event, in which it is forbidden for the Jewish people to participate actively according to the three oaths. Our loyalty to the government is not in doubt, and it is commanded to us in our sources, and our hopes are not for a political reality but for religious salvation, in which all the nations are included, taking joy in it, and its place is in houses of prayer. As early as 1835, he wrote about the redemption of the Jews as follows:

> That He will return us and gather us, and our arm will not redeem us, and not one of us will raise his hand or foot, only we will stand and see what He does.... And this is a great foundation, and it is worthy of being promulgated and known, that the ingathering for which we hope, will not be by power or by strength, but by the spirit of God, as in the days of our Exodus from Egypt, He will show us miracles.[150]

Elsewhere he expresses himself with great clarity:

> The hope for revival, belief in the coming of the Messiah, have been widely presented as proof of the anti-social character of the Jews and their opposition to patriotism. Since the Jews believe that the ancient prophecies will be fulfilled, [the Gentiles] wish to conclude that they do not see as their homeland any place except the Land of Israel, and that possession of that land is chief among their desires. This is a

---

Luzzatto's view on emancipation, on the purpose of the Jewish people and humanity, on progress, and on mission. Slymovics, "Luzzatto," also overlooked the stages and stated that Luzzatto, like Hirsch, saw emancipation positively. Baron, "Shadal," was correct in pointing out the influence of the 1848 revolution on Luzzatto on this matter. He shows that before it, he kept his distance from the German scholars who wished to sacrifice everything for liberation and emancipation and who wanted to resemble other citizens in every respect. During the revolution he was slightly swayed by expectations for the liberation of Italy in general and the Jews in particular and took a positive view of European culture, but disappointment with the failure of the revolution restored his earlier criticism and even exacerbated it. Note that Luzzatto hints that in his opinion, when the Jews live in their land and state, faith is less important.

150 Luzzatto, *Beit Haotsar, Lishka A* (Lemberg, 1847), fol. 9.

> dream that the facts refute every day. Everybody knows that in whatever country the Jews are allowed to own property, they buy land, till it, improve it, work it, enrich the soil, fields, gardens; they erect houses and palaces, open workshops, factories, and enterprises of all kinds. And these things are not done sneakily by men of little faith and the least loyal to their religion; rather by very many, very religious and very pious in the opinions and actions of Judaism. And this is not typical just of recent times, but this is how the Jews have always acted, even in the time of the ancient Sages. These facts, which are so well known, combined with even superficial knowledge of Jewish writings, show without a shadow of a doubt, that the hopes of the children of Israel are not political hopes, but religious aspirations—that the salvation they expect is not merely their material ingathering in the Land of Israel, but also renewal of the spirit of the human race, the smashing of swords, the end of all wars—because the establishment of the Jewish kingdom in the Land of Israel under the protection of great powers will not be fulfillment of the prophecy and of the hopes of the Jews—because they do not dream that they can bring the end with their own powers or their clever deeds, but at most by their prayers—for if the end comes, no one will regret it, for then a golden age of the family of nations will arise—and in any event the Jews have no homeland except the country where they were born or where they make their permanent dwelling.[151]

Luzzatto goes on to cite the prophecy of Jeremiah to the exiles in Babylonia, which was also quoted by Chajes and Hirsch, as well as the words of the Sages in BT Ketubot 110a: "That the Holy One made the Jews swear not to rebel against the nations of the world." The rebellions against the Romans were truly political and took place before the dispersion:

> However, after the general dispersion, the Jews soon were convinced that any rebellion would be in vain, and that their revival could only take place entirely supernaturally. The Jews were and always will be loyal to the nation that hosts them, because the Torah of Moses especially requires them to be grateful for the hospitality from which the Jews benefited in Egypt in the past, and it demands that any resentment because of the barbaric treatment from which they suffered there would be canceled out because of the feeling of gratitude for that one favor: "Do not abhor the Egyptian, because you were a stranger in his land" (Deut. 23:8).

---

151 Luzzatto, *Ketavim*, vol. 1, 65-67.

In the book that he devoted to the poetry of Judah Halevi, *Divan Yehuda Halevi*, Luzzatto does not refrain from criticizing Judah Halevi for calling for revenge against the Muslim oppressors in his poems. Luzzatto consoles himself that this is his attitude as a poet, whereas his attitude as a Torah scholar was entirely different. Here, too, we find a reflection of Luzzatto's position with respect to the accusation of dual loyalty and the neutralization of the Land of Israel:

> Judah Halevi is not innocent of imitating the war-loving Muslims who exterminate infidels. But the Jews, on the contrary, love peace, and their sole desire is to dwell beneath their vine and fig tree in security, and they never desired the other nations to convert to Judaism, because their Torah is a particular possession of theirs, the private heritage of the community of Jacob. And the poets of Israel never at any time extolled the excellence of heroism and revenge. They only prayed that God would redeem His nation from their oppressors, and they praised His name when they were saved from their enemies. And the future salvation that the prophets pictured was always a divine act, not with power and not with strength but with His spirit, and they describe the nations among whom the Jews are dispersed, as helping them to return to the land of their fathers.... And this is what the poet says here: "Give pain to the field of Edom and the field of the Arab, the house of your destroyers, destroy with anger." But these are words unworthy of a Jewish poet, and especially to a great Scholar in our Torah such as Rabbi Judah Halevi, but these are splendid words for a poem, in the manner of the poets of Ishmael, and perhaps he wrote them in his youth. For behold, at the end of the first chapter, the king says to the Rabbi: "If you had power you would slay your enemies," and the Rabbi answers: "Thou hast touched our weak spot, O King of the Khazars." If, perish the thought, it were the belief of the author that in the time of salvation it would be proper for the Jews to take revenge against the Gentiles, he would have tried to justify the act of killing the enemies, but he says that it is our weak spot.[152]

Why the Land of Israel Was Chosen

Like Hirsch, Luzzatto does not attribute extraordinary importance to the Land of Israel. According to Luzzatto, the Land of Israel was

---

152 Luzzatto, *Shirei Rihal*, 146.

chosen for the Jewish people for geographical reasons—because its physical borders make it easily defensible from external influences and also because it enables the fulfillment of its purpose, and not, as Hirsch believed, because of its weakness. However, the people's error in not driving out the idolators was its undoing. In the end, the exile was the idea of Providence—to be beneficial, because the Jewish people was exiled among the nations, and their purpose was implemented even better.

> And see, He gave them natural borders, the sea and the desert and the river so that they would be freed of all the worshipers of stars and constellations, and if they had not allowed aliens to remain among them, they would have stood secure in their land forever; but they rebelled against His word. In the end everything that happened was only what arose in His thought, blessed be He, for in that way the world was filled with knowledge of God.[153]

Progress and Mission

As a young man, Luzzatto accepted in principle the idea of human progress, combined with universalist concepts, the people as chosen, and its mission for salvation, the expectation of which was shared by Judaism and Christianity:

> Supernatural Providence is not viewed as being a special privilege for our people.... The God of the Jews is far from being national, as others have claimed; He is the God of heaven and earth, the father of all human beings.... Abraham abandoned belief in many gods, which was held by his relatives and everyone in his homeland, and he returned to the pure religion of the first patriarchs (Adam, Noah, and the others); therefore he was beloved by God, and who made him a promise and imposed commandments upon him; that is, God did not want his healthy knowledge to be lost, but rather for it to persevere for the benefit of the whole family of nations, and therefore he entrusted it to Abraham, Isaac, and Jacob and to the latter's progeny, and therefore he ensured that they would exist forever. This purpose of Judaism, intended for the benefit of all the nations, is clearly expressed by the prophets, when they herald the blessed age, when the nations will smash their swords into plowshares, when

---

153 Luzzatto on Ex. 23:31.

no nation shall lift sword against nation, and they will study war no more; because Torah will go forth from Zion, and the word of God from Jerusalem (Isaiah 2:2-4; Micah 4:1-2). This future, for which the Jews yearn, is the hope of everyone who believes in progress and the improvement of mankind, in which Judaism was the first to offer guidance. This is the kingdom of God, sanctification of His name. This is the daily aspiration of Jews and Christians. Of the former, as they say: "May His great name be increased and sanctified … and may His kingdom reign," and of the latter, "Our Father who art in heaven, hallowed be thy name, thy kingdom come."[154]

Education in the correct opinions can lead to repentance:

> The nations are capable, and they are even used to changing habits and principles with the passing of generations, for otherwise there could be no progress in human society. If so, if human progress is not only possible, but also exists, it is clear that one nation and many nations can be swayed for a certain time, because of their ignorance to lack tolerance, and pass away from progress into perverted actions, and they harm people; however, afterward, when they have been illuminated with healthy knowledge on matters of logic and religion, they can admit to their earlier errors, abhor them, reject them, and erase with good deeds all memory of earlier barbarity; as a result of this gradually mutual brotherhood will be forged between them and those who were their submissive slaves.[155]

Progress is therefore a process with which Luzzatto agrees. The Jewish people are responsible for it, and the laws of the Torah enable it to preserve its autonomous uniqueness in the Diaspora as well:

> For those laws, without motivating us to be less sincere or less merciful toward anyone, or to love all of humanity any less, tend to preserve for us a special existence within a religious association, which certainly is not a state within a state, but a smaller family within the large family of the society; and would we wish to give up this existence?... Would we willingly give up the honor of belonging to a nation, which has kept within itself for so long, within an entirely corrupted world, the doctrine of the unity of God and the doctrine of the unity of the human race, and the principles of healthy

---

154 Luzzatto, *Ketavim*, vol. 1, 50-51, in "The Essence of Judaism."
155 Ibid., 67, in "Love of Humanity in Judaism."

ethics? To the nation from which went forth those exalted truths to illuminate, little by little, the darkness of the universe?[156]

In an Italian letter to David Costantini of Trieste, which was written on November 23, 1837, Luzzatto responds to his questions. Among these was Question Seven, in which the inquirer wished to know whether the other nations would observe the Torah in the future. Luzzatto answers that the religion of Moses will never become the religion of all mankind. Only the basic principle—belief in a single God—will be the property of all humanity. The Jewish people were chosen to preserve this deposit, to disseminate it among all the nations. In answer to Question Eight he replies that the goal of knowing God is ethical—imparting the virtues of compassion, love of humanity, and justice.[157]

Like Judah Halevi, Maimonides, Chajes, and Hirsch, and contrary to Mendelssohn, Luzzatto acknowledged progress and saw it as a gradual process that took place in history. Like Hirsch, Luzzatto did not accept the supremacy of reason, and, like Krochmal, he did not believe that the history of the Jewish people was on the same path as that of the other nations, but that its existence was assured forever on a parallel track. Because of these assumptions, Luzzatto, unlike Mendelssohn, had no difficulty in accepting Lessing's opinion about progress.

One can learn his opinion regarding the uniqueness of Jewish history from a letter to Rapoport of 1860, in which he praises Rapoport for being a true scholar of Jewish history. Luzzatto wrote to him that his wisdom was the Jewish wisdom that had always existed, based on belief in God and on the divine source of the Torah and the prophets, and also on understanding

> the history of this special nation, whose history is also unique, and to understand, in all the times that it underwent, the war of the divine spirit, which is its heritage, against the human spirit, which enters it from outside, and how in every single generation the divine part overcame the human part, so that if at some time the human part

---

156 Ibid., 120, in "Lessons in Jewish-Ethical Theology."
157 See Luzzatto, *Peraqim*, 30-31.

triumphs in Israel (as it has now done in some opinions), immediately the nation will cease and be lost. And behold, this true Jewish wisdom, which will stand like the stars forever, is the wisdom with which you deal, and it will give life to its author and bring your name to distant generations, for praise and blessing.[158]

The Excellence of the Jewish People

Luzzatto, along with Hirsch, disagreed with Judah Halevi's view of Jewish excellence. The chosenness of the Jewish people was temporary, because they were more fitting for revelation, having maintained the tradition of Abraham, but they were only the first among equals. God blessed Abraham, through whom all the nations in the world are blessed, and this is the message to the nations of the world, that they should be blessed by Abraham and his seed.

> How will this be? By knowing the God of truth and walking in His ways, and abandoning false gods and the abominations of their worship; things that most of the nations have already learned from the community of Israel and the Torah of Moses:… that all the nations of the world might be blessed and happy, which is the final purpose. For indeed Abraham was chosen for the Jews, and the Jews were chosen for the whole human race; for all the world is His, and He desires the good of everyone, but we are a kingdom of priests and a holy nation, and therefore we are commanded by more commandments, as is fitting for the priests and for the holy ones who stand as a sign to the nations.… Truly the light of our Torah has already appeared, the Torah of compassion, in half of the world, since all the multitude of Christians and Muslims believe in it, and they worship a single God, and they observe the path of God to do charity and justice; and what else do they have? Will they observe 613 commandments? Why? After all, even in the future, they will not do more than the commandments of Succot, because the commandments were only given to the Jews, so that they would be a kingdom of priests and a holy nation; so what will happen in the future is nothing but the complete extirpation of false gods and idols.… Therefore if there is a true Torah of the God in the world, it is impossible for it to be other than the same Torah, from which its light emerged for

---

158 *Igrot Shadal*, 1367. Slymovics, "Luzzatto," 119, 125, did not take note of this early stage in Luzzatto, and states that Luzzatto opposed the idea of progress.

the entire world, not for just a single nation; and what is it? It is without doubt the Torah of Moses; because from it were born and upon it were founded all the other Torahs that maintain the unity of God, which have grown strong on earth, and sown in it the seed of truth, justice, and charity. And behold, when God gave His Torah to Israel, He did not intend it only for our benefit, but for the benefit of the human race in general; and why did He give it specifically to the children of Israel? Because the people of those generations were so deeply immersed in vanity, that their dim eyes could not receive the light of truth, and the Jews alone were worthy of receiving it, therefore He sowed the seed in them, which afterward brought forth a flower, and budded a bud, and filled the earth with the knowledge of God; therefore Israel is called My eldest son, because all the nations will also be sons of God, but Israel came first; and everyone who speaks of the unity of God and walks in His ways to do justice, and love, and compassion, is called a son of God, and he is our brother and our flesh.[159]

Thus we see that, unlike Hirsch, Luzzatto does not expect that the Gentiles will observe significant parts of the Torah. The task of the monotheistic religions from now on is to do away with paganism in the half of the world to which the light of the Torah has yet to come: the Far East, Africa, and parts of South America. In fact, the West was already prepared for salvation, and the process was continuing, although, as we have seen, it will only be completed with the return of the Jews to their land in a supernatural event beyond real history. Then all the nations will believe in one God, and they will behave with justice and right, and only the Jewish people will keep all the commandments of the Torah in their land.

Luzzatto's position against the excellence of the Jewish people can also be seen from another point of view: in his opinion, the idea of the mission of the Jewish people was not made public to the nations and was also kept secret from the Jewish masses, in order to tempt them to believe that they were indeed a nation with special qualities, and this was so that they would observe the Torah and maintain it for the benefit

---

159 Luzzatto, *Beit Haotsar, Lishka B* (Przemyśl,1848), 42-43, in the essay, "The Depths of the Language," on synonyms in Hebrew. Luzzatto also uses Judah Halevi's motif of the seed.

of all humanity. To the "hidden wisdom" of the divinity, which Judah Halevi attributes in the *Kuzari* to the fact that the idea of mission was not conveyed to the Gentiles, and that they go toward the Messiah at the end of days with blind eyes, Luzzatto adds the fact that the idea was also hidden from the Jews.

Judah Halevi could not have meant this, because in his opinion the Jews truly are a nation of particular excellence, and there was no reason to conceal the matter of their mission from them. However, Luzzatto, a universalist Maskil, cannot agree to this particular quality. He therefore argues that the cunning of Providence was also directed toward the Jewish people, who were told that they were ostensibly a special people, and that God chose them for that reason. In this way, it was assured that the Jewish people would remain faithful to the yoke of Torah and sustain it for the benefit of the nations, who would be made equal to the Jews, who preceded them in time but not in substance.

In his commentary on the second commandment, "You shall have no other gods before Me," Luzzatto explains the difference between idol worshipers and those who worship the One God. Regarding the former, each of the nations worships a different divinity, and there is hatred among them and separation from other nations:

> They believe they have no close relation with them, as if they were not human beings like them, and only those who believe in the One God know that we all have one father, and one God created us, and that all human beings are beloved of the Blessed One; and in truth only after the Torah of Moses was spread throughout the world did the nations begin to acknowledge that we are all brothers. Therefore, for all of these reasons, God wanted knowledge of His Unity to exist among the Jews, and He threatened them with all those threats, and expressed in exaggerated fashion, so that they would not worship other gods, and all of this was not solely for the benefit of the Jews, but for the benefit of the human race in general, because from Israel will the Torah go forth, and knowledge of the unity of God will spread from them little by little to all human beings, until in the end of days the world will be filled with knowledge of God; and how pleasant are the words of Judah Halevi (*Kuzari* 4:22), who said: "Besides this, God has a secret and wise design concerning us, which should be compared to the wisdom hidden in the seed which falls into the ground, where it undergoes an external transformation into

earth, water and dirt, without leaving a trace for him who looks down upon it. It is, however, the seed itself which transforms earth and water into its own substance.... In the same manner, so it is with the religion of Moses. All the religions that have come after it are, in truth, being transformed to be like it, even though outwardly they reject it." So you will understand this secret, which God could not state explicitly in the Torah, because its being publicized would thwart its intention, because the Jews would not have eschewed the idols of the ancient nations nor kept themselves from resembling them, if God had not brought them close to His worship in all the ways that He saw in His wisdom to bring them close. And now, too, this matter should not be explained to ignorant people.[160]

Luzzatto is consistent with his approach, arguing that the purpose of the Torah was not necessarily to convey pure, logical truth, but to make the Jewish people and all of humanity better, and that what the Torah says is meant to attain that purpose, in the ways that seem correct to Supreme Providence.

The Passive Mission

Another conclusion emerging from these words is that Luzzatto rejects any possibility of an initiative on the part of the Jewish people as part of their mission, because most of them are not even aware of it. He repeats this explicitly in an essay on the essence of Judaism. Thereby he rejects both the Reform position and that of Hirsch. He concludes this essay with a few sentences that are the essence of his position regarding the function of the Jewish people among the nations, and what it will be at the end of days:

> Judaism has two principal foundations, one of which is intended to mold the intellect of man, and the second his sensibility; that is, it tries to implant two principles, one theoretical, and one practical: Providence and compassion. Reason, which was educated for faith in Providence, learns not to be blinded by the success of the wicked and not to be disappointed by the sight of the suffering of the

---

160 Luzzatto, *Hamishtadel*, on Ex. 20:3. In my opinion, Rostowsky, *Shadal*, was wrong in stating that Luzzatto identified with Judah Halevi's idea of chosenness, that the Jewish people possessed some characteristics that differentiated it inherently from other nations. See also note 113 above.

righteous; not to trust in its power or cunning in order to commit injustice and in order to overcome the weak or the imprudent. Providence, according to Judaism, judges the whole world and gives reward or punishment to people's actions, people of every nation, of every race. Abraham, who, in his time was the sole chosen vessel capable of retaining and transmitting his healthy knowledge, was chosen by Providence for that task. Consequently, various commandments were imposed upon him and his descendants, to obey them and to prevent their assimilation into the corrupt world of pagans. Sensibility, for its part, which was educated in compassion, thereby acquires softness and love of humanity, a pleasant and beneficent character, which is the source of all virtues in the social area. Judaism contains a general, human part, and a particular, national part. The feeling of compassion and belief in Providence are, or could be, the common property of all humanity. The covenant of Abraham and the Torah of Moses are the particular property of the sons of Jacob. In the kingdom of heaven, which was heralded by the prophets, Judaism will be accepted by all the inhabitants of the world in its general part, but the national part will never be accepted by them. Judaism never prevented anyone who wished to enlist under its banner from joining it, but it neither hopes nor wishes to become a world religion. Modern culture, as everyone knows, is the offspring of Judaism and it should have included within it the whole general, human part of it. But we see that this has not been fully actualized, because the Gentiles, in accepting the elements of Judaism in Christianity, did not succeed in completely freeing themselves from their former intellectual and ethical habits. Therefore, we still await the perfection of the kingdom of the Almighty, for their swords have not yet been ground into plowshares for agriculture.[161] The kingdom of the Almighty will be established by the Almighty himself. Judaism does not have the task of spreading it. It is sufficient for it to preserve itself. It is sufficient for it to exist. "The purpose of the Lord might prosper by his servant's hand" (Is. 53:10), without the servant acting consciously, or even knowing about his influence. The nations, like individuals, obey the plan of Providence without knowing it, without wanting it, or even if they want exactly the opposite. "There are many devices in a man's heart; but the counsel of the Lord, that shall stand" (Prov. 19:21).[162]

---

[161] That is, the kingdom of faith in a single God and peace. See Luzzatto, *Ketavim*, vol. 1, 59, "Love of Humanity in Judaism."
[162] Luzzatto, *Ketavim*, vol. 1, 55-56, "The Essence of Judaism."

In the framework of its mission, Judaism plays only a passive role, limited to the general and human aspects of Judaism, to the principles of Providence, compassion, and belief in one God, and the principles of the ethics of the Torah and peace. The cunning of Providence leads the nations to their redemption with blind eyes. Judaism (unlike Christianity and Islam) is not interested in becoming a world religion, and this is also true in the opinion of most of the Reform thinkers, such as Steinheim, Formstecher, S. Hirsch, Holdheim, and Geiger regarding Judaism or what they left of it.[163] It will be sufficient for Judaism when everyone in the world observes some monotheistic religion, which will adopt Jewish ethics, and in any event the equal rights of all humans will be recognized, and peace among religions and nations will prevail in the world.

The Turning Point

As a mature adult, Luzzatto changed his position on the content of the mission of the Jewish people and the content of progress, moving toward reaction and seclusion. He sounds more religious-national and less universal. In my estimation, there are two reasons for this change. One was disappointment with Europe after the failure of the 1848 revolutions and the chauvinistic religious reaction that came in its wake.[164] The second reason was the betrayal—in Luzzatto's opinion—of the Reform Jews, whose universalist position regarding the Jewish mission and human progress and their expectation of a world natural religion—based on an idealist philosophy that was foreign to Judaism—threatened the continued independent existence of Judaism and the Jewish people.

Luzzatto abandoned the idea of progress in 1840, when he published his essay in French about the difference between "Judaism" and "Atticism," in which he noted that progress did not exist in the moral realm, but only in the intellectual area, where the mind invents things and makes discoveries, and it also enchants people. In the area of morality, a person can reach the peak or the valleys in every

---

163 See note 108 above.
164 See Artom, "Mavo," 39, and n. 46.

generation. Technological advance does not necessarily entail ethical improvement.

In the introduction to *Beit Haotsar* and *Hamishtadel*, from 1848, the same idea also appears, phrased differently: the power of thought is admired because of its innovations, in contrast to sentiment, which is held in contempt because it does not innovate. Perhaps Luzzatto then made the distinction between development on the personal level, which does not exist in the ethical area, and progress and emancipation, which are possible on the national level and in the ethical area as well.

At any rate, with the passage of time he also rejected this option. In a letter to Geiger of September 1849, after the failure of the revolution, Luzzatto expressed disappointment with it, and his words convey tacit mockery of the idea of progress. Luzzatto expresses himself harshly against the position of the assimilationists, who flatter the Gentiles and expect to be redeemed by emancipation, saying, "We are all Germans, we are all sons of the same culture and ethics":

> Not so, not so. Culture and morality, whose foundation is in Greek philosophy, which has no fruit but only flowers, have filled the face of Europe with a din of speakers in choruses, masses of writers of falsehoods, and the trumpet sounding of rebellion, and they have caused men to take up sword[s] against their brothers, and destruction of cities, and poverty and want, and finally, they gain strength and courage for despised absolutism, to fulfill the ancient proverb: the camel went to ask for horns, and the ears, which he had, were cut off. But we, the sect of Jacob, have another culture, a different morality, and from then we learn to say little and do much, and not to trust our arms, for not by strength will a man prevail, only by good deeds and honesty, and we will not place hope in anyone, and we will not expect the republic, and we will not look forward to kings of the earth, because the salvation of man is in vain; and we will not rise up against the kingdom, but we will pray for its welfare, for without fear of it, one man would eat his fellow alive, not in generations of ignorance alone, but in the generation of progress as well.[165]

---

165 *Epistolario* II, 570-71. The word "republic" was self-censored when it was published in Padua in 1890, and in its place the word "הקהל" [community] appears. See Klausner, *Hasifrut* II, 106 nn. 10-13. Luzzatto uses Judah Halevi's motif of fruits and flowers in his negative reference to Greek philosophy.

It appears that at that time Luzzatto still believed in the Jews' mission to the Gentiles. In another letter to Geiger of 1850, Luzzatto repeats his opposition to extreme universalism and the granting of autonomy to every single nationality in Europe, and to rebellion against the Austro-Hungarian empire (to which northern Italy belonged until 1866). However, he wishes to preserve the uniqueness and tradition of the Jewish nation and of the other nations within the empire, and to promote universal human brotherhood among the nationalities within the empire, while the Jewish nation has an important role in that area. As Luzzatto writes:

> Our dispersion among the Gentiles is not meant to make us forget our nationality, but rather it is so that we can teach the other nations, so that all the families of the earth will learn that it is a good thing for every nation and language to retain its good qualities and memories and to honor its fathers, but ultimately all the families are the sons of one father, and it is not worthy that Ephraim should envy Judah, or that Germans should afflict Slavs, and the demand for autonomy to every single family is an abomination, and if we are seduced by it, we will return to the character of pagans, among whom every nation was born from the belly of the earth and had a particular god. And the children of Israel were chosen for this, so that the world would know the unity of God and the unity of the human race, and that all the nations are brothers, and if "one people shall be stronger than the other people; and the elder shall serve the younger" (Gen. 25:23), this is not bad, but it is good for both of them, and nationality stays in its place, it is precious and honorable, without throwing off the yoke and rebelling.[166]

In a long letter from Luzzatto to the editor of *Hamagid*, Eliezer Liepman Silbermann of Lyck, Prussia (now Ełk, Poland) of 1858, we can find clear statements against the idea of mission. He responds to the book by the Reform writer Ludwig Philippson, *Die Entwicklung der Religiösen Idee im Judenthum, Christenthum und Islam*, which Luzzatto read in French translation and afterward in the original German. He is aware that this book is not exceptional and reflects the position of the authors of similar books, which had been published

---

166 *Epistolario* II, 584. See Klausner, *Hasifrut* II, 118.

earlier in German, but which had not come into his possession. The book asks why Judaism exists, and why the Jews remained Jewish. This question, according to Luzzatto, is not asked by Jews or Christians who believe in the prophecy of Moses, because for believing Jews, their existence is the will and commandment of God, and for Christians, Judaism exists because of the ignorance of the Jews, who do not understand that their time has passed. The question can only be asked by those who do not believe in the prophecy of Moses. Philippson's answer, as presented by Luzzatto, was:

> that Judaism must exist until the time comes when the whole world returns to faith in a single God, and all human beings will be courageous fearers of God, men of truth, who hate wealth and will no longer be slaves to masters, and there will be no rich and poor, and there will no longer be fights among people, and lies and robbery and injustice and deceit will not be seen or found anymore on the face of the earth; and until that thing happens, Judaism has not concluded its mission for the benefit of the human race, and it must exist further to fulfill the success of mankind. Surely these are good things to see and pleasant to the ear, but in truth they are merely vain consolations, for the holy writ has already been widespread in this world for many generations, and it spreads more and more from day to day, without the Jews helping this at all; and the[se words] will not be useful, and they will not save, because they are barren, founded on lies and falsehood. And if the spread of the holy writ has not been successful in eighteen hundred years to bring the human race to perfection, what good will the Jews do for this, especially those who do not believe in Torah from heaven? The author wishes to flatter those Jews, who are not Jews in their hearts, but disciples of Spinoza, and he raises them up as if they were the foundation of the world, and from them would sprout the salvation of the whole seed of man; but they themselves, and all the nations, know that this is a vain dream and vision, and no good fruit has come from this dream, but on the one hand it makes the nations continue to hate the Jews, because of their dreams and words, and on the other hand it makes the rebels and transgressors cling to their path, and they think that without any faith in Torah from heaven and with desecration of the Sabbath and the eating of carrion, they still have an advantage over all the nations of the world.... And aside from what I have said, that the existence of Judaism is necessary so that the human race can reach perfection in the way that the author and his comrades says

(that is, in a natural way, without signs and wonders) is a vain dream and vision, it is also a vain dream and vision that the human race will reach that perfection, which the author depicts in his book. That picture cannot exist, unless God changes the hearts of men, and man stops being man, and that is not progress, but it is a substantial change in human nature. Nor did the prophets say that this thing would be, and they only said that in the end of days God will dwell in Zion, and when there is a conflict between two nations, they will send emissaries to Jerusalem, and God (by means of His prophets) will judge between the nations, and thereby they will no longer have to go to war; for in the present time, when there is a conflict between individuals, they go to court and are judged, but when there is a conflict between two nations, there is no one to judge between them, and they have to make war, and after much killing, one raises his head, and the other bows his head and accepts the verdict; in the end of days, God will be king over the whole earth, and He will judge the universe with justice, because all the nations will believe in God and His prophets, and those in conflict will accept the judgment passed by the prophets of Jerusalem, and there will no longer be war between nation and nation. But between individuals quarrels and contention will not cease, there will still be slave and master, rich and poor. When it says He will judge among the nations, it seems clear that conflict and disagreement will not cease, nor will the wish to be raised higher than others, but they will not have to make war, because they will have a judge of truth who will adjudicate between them, and they will heed his voice, and they will obey his words. And as for the marvelous perfection that some later scholars say will be in the end of days, and the golden age painted by the poets of Greece, as if it were at the beginning of creation, it is the same dream. And a philosopher who does not want to mislead himself and others sees that what has been is what will be, and that progress is truly in technology and knowledge, but the human heart remains what it was; and if there is a change here, it will only be for the worse, because egoism grows stronger day by day, and Spinozian philosophy, which is seeking one's pleasure, is no longer a horror and "a proverb, a taunt and a curse" (Jer. 24:9), but it is for praise and splendor, also among many of the children of Israel, and also among a few of those who are called Ḥakhamim and rabbis. But the Jew who believes in what Moses said, "if you will be scattered, etc." (Deut. 30:4), and what Isaiah said, "the Lord's house shall be established" (Is. 2:2), and "Judge, etc." (Is. 11:4), and he does not deceive himself with vain dreams, that people will change and become like angels, and more so, he does not flatter himself in his heart to say that this great change will be done by him, and that the success of the human race depends on him, and he knows that these are nothing but lies and vain consolations, and the false prophets imagine them for their own pleasure. And the upshot of all this for us is that Judaism without belief in Torah from heaven, cannot abide, and everything that some of the scholars of Germany do to prettify it and find favor and grace in the eyes of the Jews and the nations, will only be good for breaking its strength and making it stink; but the Judaism that depends on faith in Torah from heaven will last all the days of the earth, and it does not have to clarify and explain why and for what it exists, but the Jews will preserve their Torah for generation after generation, because this is their duty. The unbelieving Jew, even though he does not await redemption and the ingathering of the exiles, and despite his changing his prayers to remove every mention of Jewish hopes, everybody knows that his heart is set only upon his own pleasure, and neither the king nor the nation can trust him. But the Jew who believes in Torah from heaven, he knows that the salvation he awaits will not come by strength and not by power but only with the spirit of God, and without any effort by the Jews themselves; and therefore he prays for the safety of the city in which he lives, and as he was commanded by Jeremiah (29:7), and as our rabbis commanded in saying (BT Ketubot 111) that the Holy One made them swear that they would never rebel against the nations of the world. A believing Jew does not mock the faith of the nations amongst whom he lives, and he does not try to weaken their faith, because he was never commanded to spread his faith in the world; and He does not glorify himself over his neighbors because of his faith in the unity of God, since truly their intention is to a single God; and such a person is beloved above and precious below and will find favor in the eyes of God and man.[167]

---

167 *Igrot Shadal*, 1332-36. See also the second introduction to *Yesodei Hatorah* of 1865, where he writes that despite all the technological inventions and scientific progress, there are still "wars, murders, thefts, and poverty and want and illness, and envy and hatred, and sighing and moaning, and untimely death." We find this idea about possible progress in technology but not in the area of ethics, where a person can decline from his status but not improve and advance himself from a moral point of view, and he will always remain human, in his letter to Halberstam in his Italian letters, *Pardes* 3. On this see Klausner, *Hasifrut* II, 105 n. 2. Klausner, ibid., 107-8, as well as Heinemann, failed to notice that Luzzatto gradually changed his position regarding emancipation, the mission, and progress, and he quotes only from later essays. See Heinman, *Ta'amei*, 62-68. Rosenberg sees Luzzatto's position on the chosenness of the Jews, like that of Hirsch, as a development of Judah Halevi's position. In my opinion, this is not possible, since Judah Halevi begins by assuming the excellence of the Jewish people. Rosenberg also cites the letter to Zilbeman, but he does not see it as a turning point regarding Luzzatto's position on the mission of

We find that Luzzatto has retracted all of the beautiful ideas he had held regarding the passive mission of the Jews to bring about the kingdom of God, the ethics of the Torah, and world peace, and in old age he in fact completely rejects the idea of the mission and accepts Mendelssohn's view, that human progress for the individual or the public on matters of sentiment and ethics does not exist. Indeed, the situation in this area has only deteriorated, and the anti-ethical views of Spinoza are spreading. Progress exists only in experimental and applied science and technology, but not in wisdom and morality. Whoever believes in Torah from heaven continues to maintain Judaism, because this is his duty, and not as a mission to improve the world. The end of days, too, when the Jews will miraculously return to their land, will not turn people into angels, and eternal peace and brotherhood among individuals and nations is a vain dream. In the Utopian end of days, the nations will accept the rule of God and they will bring their disputes before His representatives in Jerusalem, but the belligerent and egoistic nature of individuals and governments will not change. The idea of mission is flattery to traitors, according them importance, and the extreme neutralization of the miraculous return to Zion in a Utopian era, according to which we will all remain in the ideal Europe, is flattery and egotism that will be rejected by the authorities and the non-Jewish community. The believing, passive Jew, faithful to his present homeland, who obeys the command of Jeremiah, who is subject to the three oaths and does not try to make his religion into a world religion—he is the one who will succeed and find favor in everyone's eyes.

With all of these views, Luzzatto also gave up on his efforts to explain why revelation was vouchsafed to the Jewish people in particular, and the reason for their dispersal among the nations. This was simply God's will, and man must accept it and obey.

---

the Jews, but only as denying the Reform version of the mission. In my opinion, there is more than that here. See Rosenberg, *Hakuzari*, 63-64. Also, Levi, *Ḥadasha*, 46, states that Luzzatto shared the common view regarding the mission of the Jewish people. On Luzzatto's disappointment with the revolution, see Baron, "Shadal," 57.

Having shown that in old age as well Luzzatto clung to the neutralization of actual return to Zion by displacing it beyond history, I wish to discuss Artom's view, that Luzzatto can be seen as a precursor of Zionism. Artom offers a moderate interpretation of the quotation from Luzzatto's essay on "The Love of Humanity in Judaism," which I quoted above (note 161), and which states the opposite and appears to be a denial of the entire idea of an actual return to Zion, by viewing it not as an ideological principle but as a practical conclusion, stating that Luzzatto's words "perhaps express more lack of faith in the practical power of the tribes of Israel to act than rejection of the goal that had been desired for generations, with some concession—this cannot be denied—to the views of the generation."[168]

In my opinion, Artom is projecting his own thoughts, which is why he chose to distinguish between the practical and ideological side,[169] and he is willing to bend the proud Luzzatto, who opposed the trends to his right and left all his life, to the spirit of the generation, only in order not to see him as neutralizing the actual return to Zion. Artom apparently did not see the letter of 1858, and the sources from *Beit Haotsar* and *Divan Yehuda Halevi* that I cited above, and as proof of his opinion he offers two other letters, which, in his opinion, contradict Luzzatto's words in his essay.

The first letter was written to Joseph Almeda in 1839, and in it Luzzatto writes that "the renewal that we hope for will be political for the Jews and religious for the whole human race."[170] The second letter is to Abraham Albert Cohen, of 1854, in which he praises Cohen and the Alliance Israélite for acting on behalf of the Jews of the Land of Israel, and states that he looks forward to the growth of a generation in the Land of Israel that will devote itself to agriculture and physical labor, behave according to the commandments of the Torah, and be free of exploiting their fellow, and issue just verdicts from judges who will be educated in a yeshiva where Torah and the words of the Sages will be studied.

---

168 Artom, "Mavo," 38.
169 Harvey made a similar move regarding Mendelssohn's view. See note 10 above.
170 Artom, "Mavo," 37.

Artom's conclusion from these words is that Luzzatto was skeptical about the ability of the Jews of his generation to take political action, and also skeptical about the possibility that the great powers would help, "but he believed that the Jews must act to return to their land, to work in it, to support themselves from the labor of their hands, and to foster spirituality."[171]

One can add a third letter, of 1849, to Naḥman Nathan Coronel of Jerusalem, in which he also encourages initiatives

> to try to see that the Jews little by little return to the occupations of their ancestors and earn a living from the work of their hands, especially in working the land, which was the most precious of all the lands, and if they occupy themselves in working it [the land], then it, too, will little by little continue to give its strength to them and return to being as in ancient times a land flowing with milk and honey. And if the earth gives its produce, then the other trades will succeed among you, and they will enrich those who engage in them. But these are lengthy matters.[172]

It seems to me that my analysis enables us to resolve these contradictory statements. Artom did not distinguish between Luzzatto's words on the situation within history and his words about the utopian state. Clearly Luzzatto believed that at the end of days there would be a miraculous return to Zion, and then the Jews would rise again politically, and there would be spiritual redemption for humanity, and this is the meaning of his letter to Almeda. In contrast, in the present time, when loyalty to the three oaths and Jeremiah's command is in force, the people are ideologically prohibited from making an organized national effort to rush the end and the return to Zion, which, as noted, will

---

171 Ibid., 38. The letter to Cohen can be found in *Pardes* 3, 117-19. Artom, who did not see the letter of 1858, did not notice that in old age Luzzatto denied both progress and the Jewish mission, but he remained loyal to the neutralization of the Land of Israel. Interestingly, Weiner states, according to the letter to Cohen, that Luzzatto became a partisan of a special kind of Zionism in the last years of his life. This, too, is possible, but then one must see it as beginning at least in 1849, after the failure of the revolution, with the letter to Coronal. See Weiner, *Hadat*, 100.

172 *Igrot Shadal*, 1071.

come without our lifting a finger, as Luzzatto said in the essay and letter of 1858.

However, as in Hirsch, at this time there is no obstacle to individual immigration to the Land of Israel or to support for the Jewish community there, and observing the commandment of charity, or even to encouraging the Jews in the Land of Israel to live a life of labor and productivity rather than depend on contributions from abroad, and this is the meaning of the letters to Cohen and Coronal.

Klausner quotes Luzzatto's letters to Cohen and Coronal and ignores all the other statements in which the return to Zion is neutralized. While he is aware that in the atmosphere of the period, one cannot speak of Zionism in Luzzatto in our sense of the term, in his opinion there are hints in Luzzatto regarding the establishment of a certain spiritual or national-cultural center in the Land of Israel within history. To support this claim, he cites another source: a letter of response to the Reform rabbi Aaron Chorin regarding his essays "Tsir Neeman" [Faithful Messenger, Prov. 25:13] and "Igeret-Elasaf" [The Epistle of Elasaf], in which he made the messianic idea entirely spiritual. Luzzatto wrote to him, "The prophets speak very explicitly about a real and physical return of the children of Israel to the Land of Israel."

In my opinion, this quotation does not add much to Luzzatto's Zionism. It merely contradicts the argument of Chorin, whose position was identical to that of other Reform thinkers, who radicalized the neutralization, saying that in the end of days as well there would be no actual return to the Land. Luzzatto is speaking about the non-historical end of days here, and therein he is similar to Hirsch and different from Geiger and Philippson.[173]

---

173 See Klausner, *Hasifrut* II, 93 n. 47, 108-10, 114-15. In Klausner's opinion, Hirsch's positions regarding political redemption in the end of days were similar to those of Geiger and Graetz, who spiritualized it, as opposed to Luzzatto's view. I disagree with this opinion, for I have shown that Hirsch, like Luzzatto, speaks explicitly about the return to Zion in the end of days, because that is what the sources say. True, he might have been pleased to give up the idea, had that been possible.

SUMMARY

I have presented the opinions of three religious Jewish scholars who internalized many Haskala ideas. All three of them developed positions regarding the neutralization of the return to Zion and the Land of Israel by placing it beyond history, and regarding the task of the Jews in their Diaspora among the nations, on the basis of Mendelssohn's position. None of the three can be seen as a precursor of Zionism. All three of them disagreed with Mendelssohn regarding the sufficiency of reason, so that the mission receives increased importance for them—not only the preservation of knowledge for the nations, but also imparting and teaching it.

Chajes, who saw himself as a rationalist, accepted most of Mendelssohn's views, except in the matter of progress, and he emphasized that the mission is passive. Hirsch, the romantic, also disagreed with Mendelssohn in that he demanded of the Jews awareness and even activism in fulfilling their mission to humanity, and aspired to impart as much of the Torah as possible to the nations. Luzzatto, also a romantic, was similar to the first two men in his youth, but like Chajes he believed that the mission must be passive and restricted to limited areas. In his maturity, Luzzatto's views grew more extreme. He agreed with Mendelssohn about progress and related negatively to the emancipation, totally rejecting the idea of the mission.

Chajes and Hirsch fully reflect the idealist concepts of modernity, which seeks a meta-narrative for interpreting the world and history. It was clear to both of them that the divine plan in history was to bring about redemption in the world by means of the Torah and the Jewish people in their Diaspora, and they look forward to the return of the Jewish people to their land at the end of history. Luzzatto, in his later years, was the only one who anticipated postmodern thinking (as described by Gili Zevin in her book, *Dat Lelo Ashlaya* [Religion without Illusion]) with respect to the impossibility of using metaphysical arguments to describe history and nature, and the inability of human reason to understand and see the divine plan in history, because of the separate languages of distinct or contradictory areas—that of religion, and those of reason and science. Therefore, he rejected the ideas of progress and mission, and he was not afraid to negate the value of emancipation for the Jewish people. However, being firmly ensconced in romantic religious modernity, he was not willing to give up the idea of Utopian redemption, in which the Jewish people would return to their land.

CHAPTER FIVE

Attitude Toward the Other: Improvement in the Status of Women

THE STATUS OF WOMEN IN JUDAISM: BACKGROUND

Many books have been written about the status of women throughout history in general culture and in Judaism. For our purposes here, it is important to mention just a few of them.

Shulamith Shahar's book[1] provides a great deal of information about the status of women in the Middle Ages in the general Christian culture of Europe. So many legal restrictions were imposed on women that one is justified in speaking of a separate estate in the hierarchical society of the Middle Ages. Women had no part in government, the state, or society. They were not entitled to serve in any position as a government official, army officer, judge, attorney, or, of course, religious minister. According to the Church, women occupied the second place in creation, and her part in Original Sin was central.

Negative views of women and their character were widespread, too, in secular culture and law, according to which women were of

---

1 S. Shahar, *Haisha Betarbut Yemei Habeinayim—Hama'amad Harevi'i*, second revised edition (Tel Aviv, 1990), 19-27.

limited intelligence, frivolous, deceitful, and avaricious. Women could not take part in public meetings, nor could they serve as representatives in any public body. They also had inferior status in courts of law. They were usually not permitted to testify, and their legal rights were limited. A married woman was usually represented by her husband.

This attitude toward women of course influenced the status of women in Jewish culture and religion. The place of women in Judaism was also heavily influenced by the patriarchal, biblical tradition, as well as the Mishnah, the Talmud, and the Geonim. It should be noted that Christianity also drew upon these sources. In his book on Jewish women in the Middle Ages, Abraham Grossman describes the inferior status of women among the Jews as well as among the Christians and Muslims. Grossman cites many medieval Jewish sources about the preference for men in creation and in the story of the Garden of Eden, as well as their preference in the performing of the commandments. Among others, he cites Rabbi Abraham ben David, Rabbi Levi ben Gershon, Rabbi Baḥya, Rabbi Isaac 'Arama, Maimonides, and others. Along with these, he also cites quite a few sources in praise of women.[2]

---

2   See A. Grossman, *Hasidot Umordot: Nashim Yehudiot Beiropa Biyemei-Habeinayim* (Jerusalem, 2003), 23-63; in idem, *RASHI* (Jerusalem, 2006), 261-62, he presents a brief summary of interpretations of the verses on the creation of woman from Adam's rib, and her curse "And he will rule over you," during the Middle Ages. Grossman points out that Rabbi David Kimche, Nachmanides, and Baḥya ben Asher interpreted it as evidence of the husband's right to rule over his wife, whereas Rashi restricted this right to sexual relations. See also E. Baumgarten, *Imahot Veyeladim: Ḥayei Mishpaḥa Beashkenaz Biyemei Habeinayim* (Jerusalem, 2005), 41, 51-53, 133-39. According to her, during the Middle Ages the woman was regarded as a servant and producer of offspring, and preference was given to male children. Women were isolated from religious acts, and their place in the hierarchy was secondary. See also E. Westreich, *Temurot Bema'amad Haisha Bamishpat Ha'ivri: Masa' Bein Masorot* (Jerusalem, 2002), who discusses the status of woman in marriage from a legal point of view from the period of the Geonim through the regulations of Rabbenu Gershom Meor Hagola and their various implementations in Ashkenaz and Sepharad, including eighteenth-century Germany. Westreich traces the gradual progress toward making the status of woman in marriage equal to that of the man, and the reasons for it. See also T. Rosen, "Haobyekt Hamedaber: Vikuaḥ Bein Ish Veisha Bamaqama Shel Alḥarizi," *Biqoret Ufarshanut* 39 (Jerusalem, 2007): 97-124, in which the author analyzes the *Maqama* of Alḥarizi and presents abundant sources and scholarly literature on the status of women in the Middle Ages in the general and Jewish societies. Rosen's article shows that most

In modern scholarship, opinions are divided as to the attitude toward women in the Jewish tradition. Justice Menachem Elon,[3] writing from a Modern Orthodox man's point of view, asserts that the status of women in the tradition was positive, and that they were honored and respected, loved and viewed as companions. There was no discrimination against them, but rather beneficial distinction. Elon emphasizes that every time a blow was dealt to the status of women, the Halakhic authorities and community leaders struggled with the situation and solved the problem by compromise, new regulations, reasonable assumptions, and the like.

Elon adds, too, that until the end of the Geonic period the status of women was a uniform norm. After that, differences of opinion and custom arose among the various centers and communities because of the lack of a central, accepted leadership. This situation continued until the time of the modern Zionist movement and toward the establishment of the State of Israel. An important milestone in the legal status of women occurred during the emancipation, when the judicial autonomy of the Jewish community, including a significant part of family law, was abolished and transferred to the secular state.

Tamar Ross[4] believes, in contrast, from a modern, even postmodern religious woman's point of view, that in traditional Judaism as

---

writers expressed the misogynistic view that women have contemptible traits, and presented women as inferior. Very few women made their voices heard, and when they did, this was usually through the pen and mouth of a man. On misogyny during the Middle Ages, see also M. Kellner, "Sinat Nashim Pilosofit Biyemei Habeinayim: Haralbag Le'umat Harambam," in *Meromi Leyerushalayim. Sefer Zikaron Leyosef-Barukh Sermoneta*, ed. A Ravitzky (Jerusalem, 1998), 113-28. In his opinion, Ralbag [Rabbi Levi ben Gershom] hated women, was contemptuous of them, and regarded them as inferior and subordinate, meant to serve men, and as a dangerous snare. On the basis of the Aristotelian view of matter and form, Ralbag stated that women have inborn intellectual weakness, they were not created in God's image, and their status is between animals and male humans. In contrast, according to Kellner, Maimonides believed that women were not innately inferior intellectually to men, and that they were born in the image of God, like men. According to Maimonides, the inferiority of woman was merely social and halakhic.

3   See M. Elon, *Ma'amad Haisha Mishpat Veshiput, Masoret Utmura, 'Arakheiha Shel Medina Yehudit Vedemokratit* (Tel Aviv 2005), 20-40.
4   T. Ross, "Ortodoqsia, Nashim, Veshinui Hahalakha," in *Masa' El Hahalakha*, ed. E. Berholtz (Tel Aviv, 2003), 388-89, and idem, *Armon Hatora Mim'al La: 'Al*

well the conception of woman was hierarchical. Women were considered inferior, and they were subordinated to their husbands and removed from communal life. Ross is not enthusiastic about the expressions of fondness for women in the sources, alongside of which are also expressions of condemnation and lack of appreciation, since the words of praise are also spoken by men and reflect male interests. Ross also is dissatisfied with the Halakhic solutions offered in modern times, attempting to resolve the difficulties and tensions between the tradition and feminism.

From the point of view of a modern, secular woman, Rachel Elior[5] expresses the most severe and blunt criticism of the tradition. She lists, one by one, the expressions in the canonical literature of Judaism that determine the inferior status of women, reflecting discrimination and rejection, mockery and disdain, revulsion and fear of women. These expressions—spoken and written down by men—demonstrate control of women, the imposition of mastery, separation, exclusion, subjection, fear, and isolation between the sexes, all for the purpose of taming man's dangerous, demonic nature, and in the name of sexual modesty.

As I see it, among the many expressions in the canonical literature, it is possible to distinguish two schools. The leading school is that which speaks of the essential inferiority of women, excluding them, and connecting them directly and generally with witchcraft, seduction, prostitution, and many other contemptible traits. Along with this, there is a much smaller school which offers a considerable number of sayings in praise of women and their virtues. However, what ultimately determined the inferior status of women in the Jewish tradition were the Halakhic decisions according to which women have a different and lower status than men.

The Halakhic status of women is equal to that of slaves and children, who are not autonomous but subject to their master, father, or

---

Ortodoqsia Ufeminism (Tel Aviv, 2007), 50-105. See also Zivan, *Ashlaya*, 285-87, who presents a similar position.

5 R. Elior, "'Nokheḥot Nifqadot,' 'Teva' Domem,' Ve'alma Yafa Shein La 'Einayim': Lesheelat Nokheḥutan Vehadaratan Shel Nashim Beleshon Haqodesh, Badat Hayehudit, Uvametsiut Hayisraelit," *Alpayim* 20 (2000): 214-70.

husband. Consequently, women have different rights and duties from men. Usually they have no public status, they may not be appointed to public positions, they are not counted in the quorum necessary for public prayer, during prayers they must stay on the other side of a partition, and they are not called to read from the Torah because of "respect for the community."

Women are not eligible to give testimony, like the mentally defective and minors, and they are not required to observe those commandments that must be fulfilled at a certain time, and they may not be taught Torah. The personal status of a woman is limited. In youth she is under her father's authority, and after she has been acquired in marriage she is under her husband's authority, and her status derives from his. In many areas of personal status such as divorce, levirate marriage, and abandonment, the woman's position is problematic. In fact, these Halakhot ensured that women were kept apart from the canonical culture and from public discourse, and their voices were not heard. They had neither significance nor authority.

In addition to these Halakhot, there was also the biblical view, based on an ancient statement: "Thy desire shall be to thy husband, and he shall rule over thee" (Gen. 3:16), and accordingly women are not part of the history of humanity that must be remembered and retained.[6] It is commonly thought that women remained separate, discriminated against, and inferior in Halakhic Judaism, and only in the twentieth century has their status begun to improve. Following the work of Mordecai Breuer, Ross noted Hirsch's contribution to the improvement of the status of women, but she criticized it.[7]

I intend to develop Hirsch's position further and to present additional aspects of it, and the difficulties that it arouses, and also to show that in Germany the Reform movement and Hirsch were not the only ones who dealt with improvement of the status of women in the nineteenth century, but other thinkers from the middle trend were concerned with it, some conservatively and others in a daring and interesting way.

---

6 See Ross, *Armon*.
7 Ibid., 87-93, 101-5. See also the discussion of Hirsch's views below.

THE POSITION OF THE HASKALA MOVEMENT

The American and French Revolutions also brought the beginning of new thinking about the status of women. New conceptions of equality with the Other, who is not a white Christian male householder, led to change in the status of women. Matters developed slowly, and it was not until the second decade of the twentieth century that women received the right to vote in Western democracies.

Regarding Jewish society, it may be said that the fall of the walls of the ghetto, the opening of Western culture to the Jews, and emancipation led to discussions of the status of women in Jewish society as well. The sensitivity of the subject usually prevented vociferous public polemics, although beneath the surface the conversation was turbulent and disturbed various thinkers.

In their book, Tova Cohen and Shmuel Feiner[8] describe the status of women during the Haskala period in a fascinating manner. They show that despite talk about liberty, universalism, and equality, and the struggles against the rabbinate, the Halakhic tradition, and ignorance, the status of women did not change significantly, and among the Maskilim women continued to be almost entirely excluded. The boundaries of freedom and modernization of Haskala did not include them; the movement remained one of men.

Women's efforts to break through the impenetrable wall usually failed, and their situation was more problematic than that of women in non-Jewish society. Women were not viewed as equal partners, and they were thought of as inferior intellectually, so much so that intellectual, educated women were rejected and mocked. Women who read or wrote in Hebrew were regarded as amazing exceptions. Cohen and Feiner list several reasons for this situation.

---

8 T. Cohen and S. Feiner, *Qol 'Alma 'Ivriya: Kitvei Nashim Maskilot Bameah Hatsha' 'Esre* (Tel Aviv, 2006), 9-44. In addition to the comprehensive survey of the status of women in the Haskala period, the book is devoted to exceptional Jewish women who read and especially wrote their works in Hebrew, and to a description of their struggle, difficulties, courage, and despair.

A. The ancient, pseudo-scientific theory to which enlightened Christians adhered according to which the laws of nature since creation established the inferior status of women intellectually and socially and determined that their place was in the kitchen, the bedroom, and the nursery. Nature planted physical and mental weakness in women, as well as excessive romanticism and a tendency to sensual seduction and frivolity. Women were prevented from studying Torah, which was the central intellectual activity in Judaism over the generations, according to the ruling by Rabbi Eli'ezer Ben Horkenos (Mishnah Sotah, 3:4): "Rabbi Eliezer says: Whoever teaches his daughter Torah, it is as if he teaches her licentiousness." Similarly, women were prevented from learning Hebrew, which was regarded as a holy tongue. Thus they were denied access to the "father tongue," which was the key to Jewish culture, and they were forced to make do with Yiddish and the spoken language of the country, "the mother tongue."
B. The fact that girls were excluded from formal education until the late eighteenth century.
C. The separation between the male-public sphere and the female-private sphere, typical of all patriarchal societies, which in Judaism received special Halakhic and religious authority because of the severity of the laws of modesty: "All glorious is the king's daughter within the palace" (Ps. 45:14).

This situation continued in Eastern Europe throughout the nineteenth century, the century marked by the spread of Haskala there. In Western Europe, where idealistic romanticism replaced the Haskala movement at the beginning of the century, the situation was no better. On the contrary, as noted, the Haskala movement declined at the beginning of the nineteenth century, and the generation of the founding fathers of Haskala did not see fit to teach girls Hebrew and Judaism privately, as was done in Eastern and Central Europe.

In Germany, under Hirsch's inspiration, formal Jewish education for girls began to develop, and it included study of the Hebrew language, though at a low level. Because of the attention paid to Jewish girls in

Germany, exposing them to sermons in German in the synagogue on a high level, as well as to studies in the Bible and Judaism, also in German, they were better educated, more involved in the economy and society, and more observant religiously than their counterparts in the East.[9]

As a result, aside from important pioneering exceptions in Eastern and Central Europe, until the late nineteenth century we do not find women who committed their thoughts to writing in Hebrew and published them.

Cohen and Feiner present the views of Rousseau, Mendelssohn, and Kant,[10] who were liberal, progressive, and enlightened, but nonetheless denied the possibility that women were capable of deep study, abstraction, and philosophical thought, and made fun of women who tried their hand at it. These attitudes reflect the inner contradiction in European Enlightenment. Those Jewish women who could not accept their situation found other channels to fulfill their desires for modernization and education. In the West, in the late eighteenth century, they took part in the well-known salons, immersed themselves in secular European culture, and some of them converted to Christianity. In the East, women began to become acculturated, secularized, academic, and bourgeois, under the influence of the vernacular literature to which they were exposed instead of Hebrew letters, from which they were excluded. Ironically, this process dismayed both the rabbis and the Maskilim.

THE REFORM POSITION

As with other modern phenomena, the question of the status of women was first raised by the Reform movement, which placed it on the agenda of Jewish society. The Reform Jews severely criticized the discriminatory attitude toward women in the tradition, and took step after step forward in this matter.

---

9 See Breuer, *'Eda*, 82-84, 118, 239-44.
10 See Cohen and Feiner, *Alma*, 17-18. On the attitude of Mendelssohn and the enlightened culture of his time to the role and status of women, see Feiner, *Mendelssohn*, 57-58.

Michael Meyer describes these steps in his book, beginning with the synagogue that was in the home of Jacob Herz Beer in 1817 in Berlin, where there was apparently no partition between men and women, and confirmation ceremonies were held in the Temple to initiate girls.[11]

In establishing the prayers and sermons, the founders of the first Temple in Hamburg, which was opened in 1818, took the special needs of women into account. According to Zunz, the need for reform, particularly in prayer, arose among the women. The Reform temple did indeed attract a much higher percentage of women than the traditional prayers did, especially because the prayers and sermons were in German.[12] Aaron Chorin wrote the following as early as 1820: "Those barbaric days have passed, when the stronger half of humanity sought to rule over the more noble half, when placing woman on the same level as man was regarded a sin."[13]

The Reform movement taught Judaism to boys and girls together.[14] In an essay of 1837, Geiger proposed the abolition of the laws of levirate marriage and abandoned women, and the creation of full religious equality between the sexes, aside from distinctions derived from natural differences.[15] In the mid-1840s, Holdheim raised the matters of marriage and divorce for discussion, arguing that women did not have equal status in Halakha, that the laws on these matters were primitive, and that the correct solution was to transfer all the subjects of legislation, including personal status, to the state.[16]

In the Berlin synagogue established by Sigismund Stern in 1845, men and women sat as equals in the sanctuary, although seating was not mixed, and both men and women sang in the chorus.[17] At the second rabbinical assembly in Frankfurt, David Einhorn stated that

---

11 See volume 1, Chapter 3, note 71.
12 See Meyer, *Reform*, 43-45, 49, 56.
13 See M. Meyer, "'Elohei Avraham Vesara,' Ma'amad Haisha Bayahadut Halo Ortodoksit," in *Barukh She'asani Isha?*, ed. D. J. Ariel et al. (Tel Aviv, 1999), 179-88.
14 Ibid.
15 Ibid., 165.
16 Ibid., 102.
17 Ibid., 153. In 1846 a mixed chorus was also introduced in Millasz, Hungary (see Hershkowitz, *Maharats*, 332 n. 22).

women suffered from discrimination in that they were not permitted to be called up to the Torah, and he was chosen to join a committee that would offer proposals for making the status of women equal. In the third rabbinical assembly, which took place in Breslau in 1846, Einhorn presented a proposed marriage contract that would grant equal rights and privileges to both husband and wife, in the following words:

> The rabbinical assembly proclaims that women are equal to men in religious rights and obligations: women are required to keep commandments connected with specific times, as long as these commandments still have life and spirit for us; the phrase, "who has not made me a woman," will be removed from the prayers; girls will be required from childhood to take part in religious studies and public prayer.... And they will be counted in a quorum of ten; women, like men, are to be regarded as adults from the age of thirteen.[18]

It was also proposed to abolish the husband's right to cancel his wife's vows, and of the father to cancel those of his daughter. Einhorn's proposals were not discussed, because of lack of time, but they were supported by the majority of those present, and they reflect the importance and great interest of Reform in this matter.[19] Another step was taken by Isaac Meir Wise in 1851 in his synagogue in Albany, New York, when he introduced family seating for the first time.[20] In 1858, Einhorn presided over an egalitarian wedding for the first time, in Baltimore, Maryland, without a marriage contract. The bride and groom each gave rings to one another, and both of them repeated the marriage vow.[21]

---

18 D. Golinkin, *Ma'amad Haisha Bahalakha, Sheelot Utshuvot* (Jerusalem, 2007), 19. The source is from *Ve'idot Harabanim Begermania Bashanim 1844-1846* (Jerusalem, 1986), 65. Meyer, "Ma'amad," 180, cites in full the passage about removing the phrase from the morning prayers: "The prayers of men from now on will skip the blessing that is so humiliating to women, thanking God that He did not make me a woman."
19 See Meyer, *Reform*, 140, and 451 n. 75.
20 Ibid., 280.
21 Meyer, "Ma'amad."

Nevertheless, it should be emphasized that all the changes that were proposed and implemented regarded technical, Halakhic equality between men and women, especially in prayers and personal status. The goal of these changes was, on the one hand, to make the Temple as much like a church as possible, and, on the other hand, to do away with Halakhot that were inconsistent with the spirit of the age.[22] In contrast, nothing was done by the Reform movement during the nineteenth century to rectify the conception of woman's inferior intellectual and moral status, which was anchored in the pseudo-scientific theses about the laws of nature. Women did not receive important, leading functions, and no significant effort was made to teach girls Hebrew or Torah and Judaism in a deep way. Nineteenth-century Reform Judaism did not have high regard for these subjects.

THE TRADITIONAL RELIGIOUS RESPONSE: THE MEN OF THE MIDDLE ON THE STATUS OF WOMEN

The Orthodox completely rejected the positions and alterations of the Reform movement. Aside from the prohibition against changing the Halakha, which was given at Sinai, they bolstered the pseudo-scientific theory with religious belief in the essential difference between men and women, anchored in the creation of Adam and Eve by God, and this has metaphysical status. Women have functions defined by God and the Torah, and it is forbidden to change them.

The Orthodox believed there was no true problem with the status of women in Judaism, and the whole subject had been raised by the Reform movement out of the desire to throw off the yoke and surrender to sexual desire, and the effort to adhere to flawed Western

---

22 Cf. Breuer, *'Eda*, 115. It seems to me that Breuer exaggerated the extent and depth of the Reform changes, and he did not notice that in the main area of exclusion of women—Hebrew and Judaism—the Reform movement did very little. See Ross, *Armon*, 74. Ross tends to underrate even more than I the value of the Reform innovations, and she connects them only with the synagogue as an imitation of the church. However, I show that other subjects were discussed and treated, though women's essential inferiority remained intact.

culture and resemble it.²³ In contrast, the men of the middle trend faced a true problem. The more they tried to advance a combination of tradition and modernity, the more troublesome this subject became, and it demanded taking a stand. Here, too, we find tension within the position of the middle trend.

On the one hand, there were clear Halakhot, and a solid conservative, traditional position from time immemorial, and on the other hand, it was impossible for them to ignore the demands of European culture, which they had internalized: equal rights for all rational humans, even the Other. One may also assume as a matter of course that their wives and daughters, too, who had not been disturbed by their position in the past and did not feel discriminated against, were aware of the new winds blowing in the world and began to seek change as well.

CHAJES'S RESPONSE
Background

Cohen and Feiner describe the status of women in Galicia as follows:

> The establishment of a Maskilic center in Galicia during the first half of the nineteenth century did not bring about the development of Hebrew education for women. We do not encounter Hebrew women intellectuals in this region. Not even the important Hebrew Maskil, Joseph Perl, gave his daughter a Hebrew education.... Similarly, in the Maskilic School that Perl ran in Tarnopol (it opened in 1813) only the boys studied Bible and Hebrew, and the girls learned to read and write in Yiddish. Whether it was an effort not to irritate the large Hasidic community that struggled against the Maskilic School, or unconscious acceptance of something of the Hasidic attitude toward women, the Maskilim of Galicia deprived women of Hebrew education.²⁴

In addition to the poverty of the Jews, their isolation from the general society and culture, and the slow pace of modernization in Eastern

---
23 See Ross, "Nashim," 392. On the development and variety of conduct in the area of relations between the sexes, among the Orthodox as well, beginning with the last quarter of the nineteenth century, see Breuer, 'Eda, 23-25.
24 Cohen and Feiner, Alma, 43.

Europe, the influence of Hasidic religiosity was dominant there. The exclusion of women among the Maskilim in the east was therefore extreme, and Chajes, the Talmudic rationalist who was close to the Maskilim, also feared persecution by the Hasidim. He was no exception in this matter.

The Status of Women in the Framework of the Purpose of Man

Since he was distant physically and mentally from the centers of Reform, and was a classic fundamentalist, the status of women did not concern Chajes, and he relates to the subject only indirectly, while discussing other topics. In the introduction to *Darkhei Hahoraa*, he mainly discusses the purpose of man in the world, and from there he comes to a brief discussion of the status of women. At the beginning of this discussion, he states, without textual support and solely according to his opinion, that according to Maimonides, everything that exists in the sublunar world was created for the benefit of man.

Maimonides's statements in the *Guide of the Perplexed*, part 3, chapter 13, regarding the creation of heaven and earth as derivative from the wisdom of God and not for any known purpose, relate only to the world of the spheres, according to Chajes.[25] He goes on to state, according to R. Joseph Albo, *Sefer Ha'iqarim*, III, chapter 1, that the purpose of man's actions is "to picture the intelligible secrets in his soul and to know the truths as they are upon him, and his perfection is the emergence of what is within him by actualizing his potential, and this is enlightened knowledge."[26] Chajes immediately asks the logical question: since divine wisdom does not create anything for no reason or in vain,

> why did the Holy One, blessed be He, create those people who will not come to knowledge of the secret of God, and will not know the intelligibles and secrets hinted at in the Creation, and we see that most human beings are denuded of wisdom, and most of them flee from knowledge, and they pursue arrogance and the vanity of money

---

25 Chajes, *Darkhei Hahoraa*, 212 and the note there.
26 Ibid.

[cf. Ps. 40:5], and the wise man who disdains the vanities of the world is one among many, and one finds only one such in a generation.... And the answer to this is that these people were created to serve that one excellent person, who is the goal of creation, that if all human beings were to seek only the essence of wisdom, the perfection of the world would be ruined, because man lacks many things in nature and needs many things, to learn plowing and sowing and the work of building and carpentry and tailoring, and the years of Methuselah would not be enough for a single person to learn all the crafts that a person needs to live, and when will he have leisure to learn them? Therefore the essence of the goal is the excellent man, the precious possession, raised above the multitude of his brethren, who stands as a sign to all the world, and all his occupation will be only to meditate on the Torah and wisdom, and to understand the secrets of all created things, and the other people deal with the way of the earth [דרך ארץ] and trade, and their perfection depends on their helping this excellent man, and one man helps his fellow, just as the Sage gives merit to his community and nation, imparting to them what he has gathered in his hands of Torah and wisdom, and in the hours and minutes that he devoted to his God, the same is for the [members of the] nation who submit to his discipline and conduct themselves by his rule, and rush to do his will, their perfection is in their effort to help this excellent Sage and provide him with his daily bread, so that he will not be troubled in earning a living.[27]

Chajes adopts the rationalist, elitist position of Maimonides here, with respect to the purpose of human existence, which only a select minority is capable of achieving. Other people were created to supply all the needs of the excellent man, to enable him to engage tranquilly in his mission on their behalf, and consequently each of them also supplies the needs of his fellow, everyone in his own area.

Since without suppliers, the superior man cannot exist, they also achieve fulfillment and the satisfaction of their duties in the world by doing their job. This is on condition that the simple person "intends in all his actions and deeds, that all of his endeavors are to obey the commandment of his Creator to be a means to help the superior man, behold his reward is with him and his action lies before him, and it is

---

27 Ibid., 212-13. Interestingly, Chajes uses the concept "the way of the earth" in its classical sense—making a living—whereas Hirsch and Luzzatto use the term in new ways. On this, see Volume 1, Chapter 3, esp. n. 134.

worthy for him to say, for me the world was created, and he also turns to increase goodness for the human race."[28]

From here Chajes goes on to teach that the modern universal principle of equality is anchored in the tradition. He explains the meaning of a Midrash on Leviticus, Parashat Qdoshim (Lev. 19:1-20:27), on the verse "thou shalt love thy neighbor as thyself" (Lev. 19:18): Rabbi Akiva said this was the greatest principle of the Torah. Ben Azai said "this is the book of the generations of Adam as he was created" (based on Gen. 5:1), which is in Genesis, and it is the greatest principle. In Chajes's opinion, Rabbi Akiva's principle enables a person to honor those close to him more than those far away, just as he would save his head and heart by sacrificing his arm or leg. However, Ben Azai's principle requires us to honor all people equally, because they were all created in the image of God, with a soul from the same source and equal intellectual potential. Therefore, all humanity is one, and they have one soul, and in any event someone who does evil to another, whether he is close or distant, harms his own soul and essence. Here, too, Chajes directs his reader to the first two chapters of the *Guide of the Perplexed*, which speak about intellectual potential as the meaning of the image of God.

Now Chajes turns to the problematic subject of the status of women, and he twists and turns in order to deal with it. Chajes explains Malachi 2:15, a difficult verse which reads: "And not one has done so who had a lofty spirit! For what does the one seek? A seed given of God. Therefore take heed to your spirit, and let none betray the wife of his youth." For the purposes of his discussion, Chajes cites the discussion in Mishnah Sanhedrin 4:5, which states: "therefore man was created unique," "for the sake of peace among men," as well as the words of the prophet himself, who says before that, in verse 10: "Have we not all one father? Has not one God created us? Why do we betray one another?" The prophetic verses in Malachi refer to the phenomenon of taking foreign women along with the Jewish wife of one's youth, and the prophet attacks this as an abominable act that

---

28 Ibid., 214.

undermines the aspiration to bring a fitting seed into the world, the seed of God.

However, this does not prevent Chajes from changing the context and using these verses for a universal purpose and also for a discussion of the status of women. Chajes's explanation of the verse is that, although God created the man first and gave him intellectual skills and a lofty spirit, and He made the woman from the man's bone, so that she is inferior to him and possesses fewer capacities, this was necessary for the sake of peace among men, so that everyone would know that man was created unique, and therefore all human beings are of the seed of God and they must respect one another, but far be it from males to lord it over females for that reason and to betray their wives, who are also of the seed of God. Here are Chajes's words:

> *And not one has done so*, did not the Blessed Name make man unique, *who had a lofty spirit*? Only that the man is usually more capable and talented in matters that depend on wisdom and intelligence and spirit than the woman, who was made from his bone, to inform him that she was taken from man, and she is subordinate to him, and nevertheless she is his bone and his body. *For what does the one seek?* That is, why was man created unique in this manner? To announce that everyone is of the *seed of God* and the purpose of creation was only that the origin of man should be in this manner because of peace among men. Therefore *take heed to your spirit* from arrogance because of this advantage that he has in wisdom and spirit over women, because they, too, are of the seed of God, and therefore they must not *betray the wife of their youth*, and this is what we wanted to explain here.[29]

Chajes was subject to tension between the tradition and modernity. According to the tradition, as he understood it, man was created unique, and the woman was created from him. This creation is anchored metaphysically in nature, and the difference between man and woman is expressed in the spiritual and intellectual superiority of men over women. However, Haskala and modernity, which he internalized, required a universal relation of honor for all human beings, and fear

---

29 Ibid., 215-17.

and contempt for the growing phenomenon of sexual permissiveness and betrayal of wives. All of this occurred against the background of secularization, on the one hand, which removed God, the Creator of nature, and mankind from the real human world, and, on the other hand, the discriminatory attitude toward women against which the struggle began in the modern period.

Chajes tries to live in both worlds, and he enlists the words of the prophet to assist him, giving them an interpretation far from their literal meaning, and from the interpretations of most rabbinical commentators, aside from Rashi.[30] Although man is superior to woman in spirit and intelligence, and this is inherent from Creation, since man was created first and woman was created from him, this was done by God particularly for universal reasons, to teach us that we are all equal as His sons, for we were all born from Adam, who was created alone, and we are all of the seed of men. The prophet warns his listeners not to draw a mistaken practical conclusion from the order of creation and the metaphysical facts, that men are valued and women are less valued, and therefore to exploit this inferiority and betray one's wife. Woman, too, is regarded as of the divine seed, and she is a bone of the man's bone, and she has an equal right to respect and proper treatment, even if she is inferior in her spiritual and intellectual ability.

In his novellae on Tractate Yevamot 22b, there is an additional reference to the permissiveness of modern times. The Talmud states that if a man has a son, his wife is exempt from the duty of levirate marriage. Chajes writes that he heard something taught by

> the Gaon, Maharan [Maharatz?—R. Zvi Hirsch Levin] of blessed memory, the chief Dayan of the community of Berlin that for this reason, they have annulled the commandment of levirate marriage today even though the ruling of removing the shoe instead of levirate marriage is not a commandment. Nevertheless, in the recent times of an unworthy generation, perhaps the deceased brother has a son in any event. And therefore he violates the prohibition against marrying his brother's wife. And this reason is true and should be publicized.

---

30 According to the manuscripts, Rashi interprets "the seed of God" as referring to woman. See A. Grossman, *Rashi* (Jerusalem, 2006), 259-60.

That is to say, permissiveness makes it possible to justify the sweeping abolition of levirate marriages, even though in principle it is preferable to removal of the shoe. In modern times, since the generation is licentious, there is a likelihood that the deceased brother has a son from another woman, and therefore his brother is forbidden to marry his late brother's widow, removal of the shoe is preferable, and levirate marriage is abolished.

Teaching Torah to Women

In his novellae on Tractate Sotah 21b, Chajes discusses the Halakhot of Torah study for women. The commentary of Tosafot on this page presents the story of a "matron" who asked Rabbi Eli'ezer why the Jews were punished for the sin of the Golden Calf with three types of execution, even though they committed only one sin. Rabbi Eli'ezer answered her, "a woman is only wise with a spindle," meaning that he refused to teach her. His son Horkenos told him that because he refused to teach her a single thing from the Torah, he caused him damage of three hundred *kor* of tithes every year. It seems that this "matron" was very wealthy, and she used to give her tithes to Horkenos, and because of his father's insulting answer, she transferred her payments to someone else. The father answered that it would be better to burn the words of the Torah than to teach them to women.

Chajes actually uses this story to soften the prohibition. First he presents Maimonides's words in Hilkhot Talmud Torah 1:13, who states that the teaching in Mishnah Sotah 3:4, "Rabbi Eliezer states that anyone who teaches his daughter Torah is as though he were teaching her licentiousness," refers only to teaching the Oral Law. While a father should not teach his daughter the written Torah from the outset, if he did teach her, he has not taught her licentiousness.

Chajes then quotes *Turei Zahav*, Yore De'a, number 246, paragraph 4, who wrote that one must distinguish between teaching girls the literal meaning of the Bible, which everyone agrees is permissible even from the outset, and commentaries to resolve difficulties and contradictions in the Bible, and homilies on the written Torah, which is forbidden from the outset. Chajes explains that from the story in

Tosafot, it is possible to bring proof for *Turei Zahav:* Rabbi Eli'ezer was not critical because the "matron" knew the story about the sin of the Golden Calf and its punishment, but he only took care not to answer her and teach her the rationale of the Torah and resolve her difficulties, and this was because it is permitted to teach women the simple meaning of the written Torah, even from the outset.

Chajes goes on to explain that on this matter there is a difference between pagans and women, to the women's disfavor. He cites the words of Arieh Leib Ginzburg, the author of *Shaagat Arieh* in his book, *Turei Even*, in his novellae on on Tractate Ḥagiga 13a, where it says that it is forbidden to communicate words of Torah to pagans. He distinguishes there between study, which is forbidden, and answering questions asked by pagans, because one finds that the Sages often answered the questions of pagans about the Torah.

Chajes writes that in contrast to this:

> In the matter of Torah study for women, we have seen no differentiation, and even to answer their question about words of Torah is forbidden, for Rabbi Eli'ezer did not wish to answer the question that the "matron" asked, and it must be said that it is even permitted to answer the question of a pagan because of apprehension about hostility. But as for women, for fear of their frivolity it is forbidden in any matter.

That is to say, Chajes places universalism, relations with non-Jews, including non-Jewish women, high on his order of priorities: it is forbidden to teach them Torah but permitted to answer their questions about the Torah, to avoid hostility. In contrast, Jewish women are low in the order of priorities. Not only is it forbidden to teach them, but it is also forbidden to answer their questions beyond the literal meaning of Bible stories. Chajes is still worried about women's frivolity but not about domestic and communal tranquility. The equality and freedom of the modern age do not include women. To make his position clear, so that his readers would not mistakenly think that it was forbidden to teach Gentiles Torah at all, Chajes took care to teach that the content of Torah study for a Gentile was equal to the content of Torah study for Jewish women. Indeed, in his novellae on the tractate, 35b, he states, regarding the ruling in Ḥagiga, that it was forbidden to communicate Torah teachings to pagans, "The rabbis already distinguished between the Oral Law, which is forbidden, and the written Torah, which is permitted, and the main reason why they did not place the Oral Law in writing was so that the nations would not say 'we are Israelites.'"

The Tension in the Middle Position: The Status of Women in the Synagogue

Chajes was aware of the positions of the Reform Jews on the subject of the status of women. In his essay "Minḥat Qenaot," he lists the changes and reforms in religion that "the first Reform Jews, led by Friedländer in Berlin, maliciously committed." These included matters connected with women, in imitation of the Christians: "they conspired together about what way they could correct matters of the religion, to be fitting for the times, and women also took part in the practice, and the main thing was that the order might be acceptable in the eyes of Christians, too."[31] Later on he discusses specifically several Halakhot and prohibitions that are connected to restricting women in the synagogues, which the Reform movement abolished:

> However, what is practiced in the holy congregation of Hamburg and especially now in Berlin in the synagogue of the Reform, that men and women are together, behold they have maliciously acted with a high hand against the Torah, and we know what the Sages said (Succah 52a), that a great rule was made, men by themselves and women by themselves, and they still declined into frivolity, [so] they ordained that the men should be below and the women above, and they learned this from a Bible verse, as it is written, "and the land shall mourn, every family apart" (Zech. 12:12), men by themselves and women by themselves, and in a place of trouble, women by themselves, etc. in a place of rejoicing ever the more so, see there. And in the book, *Tsror Haḥayim*, he also was aroused from this Gemara against them, and see in *Sefer Ḥasidim*, who was precise in reading the Bible, where it is written "both young men and maidens, old men and children" (Ps. 148:12), he read closely, "maidens," to teach that it was forbidden for them to be together, and especially those women, we know they walk with their thigh[s] uncovered and

---

31 Chajes, "Minḥat Qenaot," 981 n.

with their hair uncovered, and all of these are nakedness, and it is forbidden to pray before them, see *Oraḥ Ḥayim* no. 65, and even if they are wearing thin clothes, so that the flesh is visible from them, it is forbidden to recite the Shema, and especially those standing near her who hear her voice, which is forbidden, and if there is truth in these Reformers, we do not even hear a still small voice from any of them, nevertheless, according to what we hear, they practice that women help sing in a chorus, and there is no greater wantonness than that, as we know from Sotah 48a, "If men sing and women answer them this is wantonness," and see *Shut Ḥavot Yair* no. 222, on the question about someone who ordered before his death that his daughter should say the orphans' kaddish for him, and he answered that it was worthy and correct for every proper and God-fearing woman, whether single or married, not to make her voice heard, when there is a man present, only to move her lips, so her voice is not heard, because perhaps the man who hears might be led to have a sexual thought that is a severe transgression, because she must be careful so that no man stumbles because of her, as they say (Sotah 22a), we have learned fear of sin from a virgin, etc., and do not respond to me from the verse, "and Deborah sang," because the matter is different. (End quote). And see what is said by the Gaon R. Ephraim Zalman Margolioth in his book, *Mate Ephraim* in the booklet *Elef Lamate* on the laws of Kaddish, that "and Deborah sang" is not that she herself made her voice heard and sang before the people, only she wrote the words of the poem and the rhetoric, and see *Sefer Eliahu Rabba*, no. 75, in any event those who act this way are transgressing a prohibition of the Torah every time, and they also do not fulfill the duty of praying.[32]

Thus we find that the innovations of Reform to the left draw Chajes backward to the classical ruling that interpreted the sources with severity, and he preserves every possible restriction, as though to declare that with respect to women, modernity and liberation had not penetrated his world. For that reason it was forbidden to seat men and women equally in the synagogue; it was forbidden for a woman to sing in a chorus with men or alongside them; it was also forbidden for her to raise her voice—not even to recite the kaddish for her father—next to a man; the hair, skin (through light clothing), and voice of a woman are nakedness, next to which it was forbidden for a man to pray; anyone

---

32 Chajes, "Minḥat Qenaot," 993 n.

who did not obey these Halakhot was transgressing prohibitions of the Torah and has not fulfilled the obligation of praying.

The Tension in the Middle Position: Women's Wigs

It appears to me that not only fear of the strengthening of Reform to his left, but also the pressure of the devout Hasidim, who breathed down his neck on his right, influenced Chajes to take a severe stand on certain matters. As noted, Chajes retracted his ruling regarding the delay of burial because of pressure from the Ḥatam Sofer, and the same thing happened on the matter of wigs, which he ruled against contrary to his natural inclination.

In *Shut Maharats* part 1, number 53, Chajes discusses a question he was asked about "women here who have recently begun to decorate their heads with wigs [*shaitl*]."[33] That is, are women permitted to adopt the new custom of covering their heads with a wig made of human or animal hair, when this hair is visible and not completely covered, though their own hair is not revealed?

In a detailed discussion, Chajes lays out the dispute among the Halakhic authorities on this question: *Shiltei Hagiborim, Darkhei Moshe* by R. Moses Isserles (Rema, רמ"א), *Magen Avraham, 'Ateret Zqenim*, the *Levush*, Maharam Alashqar, *Yeshuot Ya'aqov*, and others, from which it appears that it is permissible, in contrast to the *Zohar*, Mahari Mints, *Beer Sheva'*, and others, according to them it appears to be forbidden. Chajes quotes extensively from Alashqar, who rules according to R. Eliezer ben Joel Halevi, R. Mordechai ben Hillel, and R. Asher ben Jehiel: "It seems that there is no reason for apprehension here at all, because they were accustomed to revealing it, and even during recitation of the Shema, the rule that a woman's hair is nakedness applies only to hair that a woman is accustomed to covering, like a handbreadth etc., but something that is accustomed to being uncovered and one's heart is indifferent to it, it is permitted even during recitation of the Shema."[34]

---

33 Chajes, *Shut Maharats*, 584.
34 Ibid., 785.

Alashqar also writes (as Chajes quotes him):

> Everything is according to the customs and the places ... and as that man did not notice and did not feel that matter, since they were accustomed to uncover [their hair] for many years, in most of the Diaspora that is under the hand of Ishmael, and we are incapable of protesting, how it arose in his heart to forbid it, even if it was forbidden, for even a prohibition from the Torah, we say let Israel be, for it is better for them to be in error than to sin intentionally.[35]

Although Chajes could have used these citations to grant permission, which was the way he leaned, he relied upon the last quoted ruling and decided to prohibit, and this is how he explains it:

> [Alashqar] only ruled leniently because in the land of Ishmael they permitted it, and because it was their way to show their hair and this does not arouse [transgressive] thought, since they always acted that way, and something ordinary does not act on the power of the imagination, and there is not even a distant apprehension, lest there be an impediment from this, but in our country, and also in the country of Germany, where they were accustomed to cover their hair for a long time, and they never permitted hair hanging loose from a braid, like other things that are permitted, but others treat them as forbidden because of modesty, you are not permitted to annul their practice.[36]

Chajes is aware that the eye becomes accustomed to what is accepted, and the imagination that sets the concupiscent heart in motion is not stimulated by what is usual. Therefore, he states that in Sephardic countries, where women are used to show their hair, they are permitted to wear wigs, but in Galicia, Poland, and Germany this is forbidden. He sums up as follows:

> Indeed, wigs, if the entire head is covered, and only some artificial hair are left over on the forehead through their braid, it is truly possible that it is nevertheless permitted. Even though Rabbi Moses Isserles and the *Magen Avraham* agreed with the opinion of *Shiltei Giborim*, to permit wigs, still since the people were used to forbidding any showing of hair of a woman, I do not dare to permit it: ...

---

35 Ibid.
36 Ibid., 786.

> Nevertheless, because in our country they already were scrupulous on this matter, and in the days of my youth I did not hear that they were permissive about this in any Jewish community in the country of Poland, only very recently it came about that many have broken through the barriers, and it is worthy to reprimand them and make them return to the previous custom. However if his excellency [who asked the question] understands that he will not be listened to, then he should avert his eyes and it is better for them to be in error than purposely sinning, and just as it is a commandment to say something that will be heeded, it is also a commandment not to say something that will not be heeded.[37]

Thus we find that Chajes was familiar with all the important Halakhic authorities who permitted wigs, as well as the psychological explanation underlying the permission. His inclination was to permit, but he did not dare. He clung to the matter of local custom to rule stringently in restrictions of modesty, and he added the ills of the times—the permissiveness of the Reform movement to his left, which required him to block any possible opening, and his fear of the zealots to his right—and in fact he decided to adopt the approach of the Ḥatam Sofer here ("the new is forbidden by the Torah"), which was not usually acceptable to him, and to rule stringently. Perhaps we may say that in this instance he believed that the new was forbidden, but not by the Torah, because he left an opening for leniency. He suggested to the questioner that if he knew in advance that his ruling would not be accepted, he could depend on the authorities who permitted wigs and ignore the prohibition.

On the topic of the status of women, Chajes internalized the importance of giving respect and a proper treatment to women, and this led him to approach the subject while discussing other matters. On the one hand, he moderates and sweetens the bitter taste of discrimination, and he splits hairs with the sources in order to attain this sweetness. However, on the other hand, with respect to Halakha, Chajes remains faithful to the classical tradition of excluding women and according them inferior status, both in fact and in the theory meant to explain the

---

37 Ibid., 787.

practice. Fear of the penetration of Reform in his region and fear of criticism from the Hasidim kept him on the narrow path of the tradition.

HIRSCH'S RESPONSE
Background

The status of Jewish women in nineteenth-century Germany was described by Cohen and Feiner as follows: "In Western and Central Europe, there was hardly any second generation of Hebrew Haskala. The intellectual development of the sons and daughters of the second generation of Haskala was channeled in the direction of European culture, and an effort was made to preserve the culture of the Haskala in only a few places."[38]

Thus it may be said that from the beginning of the nineteenth century, the acculturation of the Jews and involvement in modern European culture was taking place in Germany with great intensity in the society and the community. The Jews of Germany lived in relative affluence, and the pace of modernization was rapid. Reform for these Jews was not a theoretical matter. With respect to the status of women, girls and women were able to approach and sample everything that European culture had to offer, and one can speak of the women's struggle for equality from 1848 onward (the process came to fruition in 1918). Women of the middle trend also posed difficult, true, and challenging questions to their husbands, fathers, and rabbis.[39]

Hirsch was aware of all these processes, and unlike Chajes, for whom it was a marginal topic, he had a double fear: Jewish girls were liable to be tempted by the offer of the Reform movement, which took women's religious needs into consideration. Moreover, the charm of European culture seduced girls, who were thirsty for education and for

---

38 Cohen and Feiner, *'Alma*, 42.
39 See Breuer, *'Eda*, 115. Chertok, *Haisha*, did not emphasize the reasons that I have listed—Reform and acculturation—among the main reasons for the importance that Hirsch gave to improving the status of women in Judaism, but he gave more emphasis to the influence of romantics like Schlegel, Schleiermacher, and Humboldt. See Chertok, *Qanqan*, 55-65, 93-99.

whom the door to Hebrew and Jewish studies was blocked. Hirsch had to offer a solution that would deflect the assimilation of the Jewish salon women as well as the alterations in Halakha proposed by the Reform movement, and, finally, would offer a path that would make preservation of the Halakha possible without adopting the theory of natural inferiority, and would encourage as an obligation, from the outset, the organized study of Hebrew and Judaism for girls as well.

Indeed, Hirsch suggested a new and revolutionary interpretation of the immutable Halakha (as was his way), an interpretation that stood the classic Maskilic theory on its head. Today, from a postmodern point of view, this interpretation sounds apologetic, but it seems to me that Hirsch believed in it wholeheartedly and proposed it with utter sincerity, and he did not notice that it drew him into contradictions and raised doubts. Hirsch's views on the status of woman were undoubtedly revolutionary and unprecedented in the Orthodox rabbinate, and without them it would not have been possible to advance on this issue within the realm of Halakha. Hirsch was also one of the few people in Western Europe of his day who put their views into practice, giving the girls in their community formal education that included Hebrew and Judaism, by establishing a school suited for both boys and girls, and he discussed it in essays in the journal *Jeschurun*, in his instructions to young Jewish people in his book, *Horeb*, and in his commentary on the Torah on the verses relevant to the subject.

Revolution: Women are Superior to Men

Because the issue of the status of women in Judaism was burning for him, and in his eyes it was a central goal in his battle to preserve traditional Judaism, Hirsch devoted a special series of essays to discussion of the status of women in Judaism, which he published in *Jeschurun* from October 1863 to December 1864. In the first essay, "Role of the Jewish Woman under the Law of God," Hirsch gives a detailed account of his thesis.

In the beginning of the essay, Hirsch argues that the natural and social sciences as well as the historiography of his day offer mistaken conclusions derived from correct facts, and since these conclusions are popular, they are taken to be true and no one troubles to examine them deeply. This is also true in connection with the status of women in Judaism. Based on the fact that the Jewish people originated in the Orient, scholars conclude based on what is accepted in other religions and in the Ancient Near East that the status of women in Judaism is inferior. Those who hold this opinion are not aware that, in Hirsch's opinion, there is a difference in principle between Judaism and the customs of other religions, owing to the fact that Jewish customs and ways of life were not influenced by human beings but derive directly from the divine law of the Torah. The claims regarding the inferiority of women in Judaism arise from sources that wish to enlist women for the forces of Reform, which ostensibly seeks to rescue them. Ironically, this fact proves how central the status of women is in Judaism:

> Current popular notions about the position of women in the Orient have been exploited to help spread the most baseless fantasies about the degradation and subordination of womanhood in Israel. The modern era is glorified, above all, for its efforts to deliver Jewish womanhood from the yoke of Oriental degradation. Is this not an ingenious bait to dangle before Jewish women in order to win their favor for efforts at Jewish religious reform? In this process only one small consideration has been overlooked: The effort to win Jewish women for the Israel of the future is in itself an eloquent refutation of all the notions about the degradation of women in Judaism: as a matter of fact, it gives most impressive proof of the high position and profound influence enjoyed by the Jewish woman in Israel. The Reformers apparently believe they can win their cause only if they win over the women to their cause.[40]

---

40 Hirsch, *Writings*, VIII, 84. S. Chertok, *Dyoqan Haisha Hayehudit Behaguto Shel Rashar Hirsch* (Jerusalem, 2006), 7; idem, *Qanqan*, 68-69, points out correctly that Hirsch's opponents on this matter were Geiger, the Protestant Bible critics and theologians from the academy, and all the members of the German intelligentsia who wished to deprive the Jews of rights, using the excuse that Judaism was oriental and therefore primitive. See also Hirsch on Gen. 23:18 and 24:67. It should be noted that Hirsch constantly uses the stereotype, "the Jewish woman," and "Jewish womanhood," rather than "the woman in Judaism," as if there were such an archetype and every woman did not have her own personality, like every man. I am grateful to Elisheva Baumgarten for pointing out this Conservative motive in Hirsch and for preventing me from making a similar error.

Now Hirsch turns to an examination of the actual depiction of women and femininity in the Torah and the Sages. From the verses about the Creation in Genesis, he prefers to cite, "And God created man in His own image, in the image of God created He him; male and female created He them. And God blessed them; and God said unto them: 'Be fruitful, and multiply, and replenish the earth, and subdue it'" (Gen. 1:27-28). The change from singular to plural in these verses

> expresses the complete equality, indeed the close union, of man and woman as human beings created in the image of God. The concept of man created in the image of God embraces both sexes; together, male and female comprise the term "human." God has created them both equally close to Him and for the same active purpose according to His Will: זכר ונקבה ברא אתם [He created them male and female].[41]

Hirsch does not ignore the fact that in the Jewish tradition men and women have different functions, but in his opinion this does not indicate the superiority of men. The male functions as the bearer of the message of divine revelation and the intellectual and spiritual achievements of humanity. He was entrusted with the memory and preservation of the tradition of the human race, which is reflected in its processes of development. The male bears historical memory, and in him is knit the connection that binds creation with the end of history. Therefore, in all his actions he must remember the duties and traditions that he received from God and from the past, and in the connection that he makes between them and the phenomena and conditions of his life, he continues the work of creation and shapes the course of history.

In contrast:

> Woman *receives* her purpose in life and accepts it. The male *chooses* a vocation and thus creates a position for himself. The female, on the other hand, receives her vocation and position in life by entering into a union with a man and identifying with the vocation he has chosen and the position he has created for himself. The Jewish maiden becomes a mature human being, a full-fledged adult Jew, only once she has a husband.... Precisely because she is not required

---

41 *Writings*, VIII, 85.

to choose as vocation and attain a position on her own can the woman function as the nurturer of all that is truly human in mankind.⁴²

To explain the woman's vital role in married life, Hirsch uses Jeremiah 31:21, completely reversing the simple meaning of the text: "the Lord has created a new thing in the earth: a woman shall court a man." In his opinion, this is not a prophecy regarding a future when women will change their nature and began to court men, but rather praise for the pure nature of woman since her creation, explaining the role assigned to her to protect and preserve her man, lest he stray from the right path because of his natural tendency to be seduced to commit immoral actions and errors in ethics. Human history is full of errors and warfare because of human mistakes: they regarded acquisition as the greatest good and sensual pleasures of the body as the goal. According to the Jewish outlook, women guide humanity toward spiritual and moral life, and thus the path to redemption. In Hirsch's words:

> As [the man] struggles for success and achievements, he runs the danger of losing himself; he may come to regard his endeavors, which in fact are only means toward an end, as ends in themselves, as the all-absorbing purpose of his life, forgetting his larger purpose, his task as a human being, which all his material achievements are only meant to help him accomplish. Indeed, he may in time come to subordinate and sacrifice the truly human aspects of his life to these endeavors. This error probably accounts for virtually all the errors and delusions that have marked the history of mankind. It is the woman who can lead the man back to true humanity. The enigma of history can be solved when one considers the dominant role of the female. The man is "encircled," i.e., he is kept within the sphere of purely human existence and activity by the female, who has been entrusted with safeguarding the nobler aspects of life. That is how the male can revert from being merely a prestigious public figure to the pristine state of a human being in accordance with the Will of God.⁴³

---

42 Ibid., 86.
43 Ibid., 86-87. See also *Writings*, II, 301-2. Chertok, *Haisha*, 9; idem, *Qanqan*, 71-72, and n. 28 there, argues that Hirsch's words are fuzzy and unclear, and it is not clear which historical errors he is referring to here. He assumes that Hirsch means the error of the builders of the Tower of Babel, which led to an unbalanced system of

Hirsch, basing himself on the Sages, notes that since the verb "כִּבְשֻׁהָ" ("subdue it," Gen. 1:28) is written without the letter "vav," it only obligates the male, who is commanded to support his family—that is to say, to gather the material means needed to sustain a marriage and establish a home—and therefore the commandment to marry a woman and keep a home is also incumbent upon him. However, the fact that this commandment is in fact directed at both sexes shows that performing the task of humanity and building up the world demands harmonious cooperation of male and female on the basis of full equality. The wife is freed from the task of making money and acquiring possessions, from hard labor, and from subduing the earth: "it is only so that she may be free to devote herself to the nobler aspects of human life, the endeavors more closely related to the purposes of true humanity. It is the function of the female to manage and utilize what the male has acquired through his labor for the human and moral purposes of home and family."[44]

---

relations between the status of men and that of women. In my opinion, here Hirsch repeats the essentials of his approach, which is that the mission of the Jewish people is to bring the ethics of the Torah to humanity. These ethics insist that the acquisition of material goods and the consumption of pleasures are only a means to strengthen spiritual and moral purposes, and not an end in themselves. A person must be careful not to separate the body and the spirit, but to sanctify sensuality and thereby achieve moral sanctity. This is the message toward which the woman must constantly direct the man, whose constant preoccupation with attaining a livelihood and moral weakness are easily liable to make him forget the goal. All historical errors and wars between people derived from man's mistaken view that material goods and sensual pleasures were ends in themselves. Women's assurance that men will cling to the moral instructions of the Torah is what will ultimately bring redemption to the world. According to Chertok, *Qanqan*, 75, the correction will come by attaining a balance between the status of women and that of men.

44 *Writings*, VIII, 88. In his commentary on Gen. 1:28 as well, "Be fruitful, and multiply ... and subdue [the earth]" Hirsch explains similarly that "[be fruitful] refers to ... the union of the sexes" and "[multiply] refers to the *family* ... [the parents'] duty is to *form* and *educate* their children.... [Subdue the earth] refers to *property*.... [The commandment, 'be fruitful and multiply'] is given at once to both sexes; they are to collaborate in harmony so as to fulfill the mission of man. Nevertheless, before establishing his home, man must first acquire material assets, and this duty—subduing the earth, so as to further man's aims—is primarily incumbent only upon the male (this is alluded to by the חסר [defective] spelling of the plural וכבשה [vekivshuha, and subdue it]). For this reason, the duty of marriage and of establishing a home is assigned directly only to the man and only to him is it given

As one who subdues the earth and acquires the means that enable him to marry a woman and establish a home, it would be easy for a man to regard himself as the sole factor on earth that cannot be done without, so that, however the spirit moves him, he may act with

---

as an unconditional duty. To the woman it is given as a conditional duty; it applies to her, only when she joins her husband (See *Yevamos* [sic] 65b)." Chertok, *Hirsch*, 145; idem, *Qanqan*, 78-79, concludes from this that Hirsch is deviating from the Sages' Halakhic interpretation of the Bible, which ruled that the commandment to be fruitful and multiply applies only to the man, and that there is a transition here from the standard of the Torah to a human standard. Chertok did not note that Hirsch was very precise in his language, to make it consistent with the Gemara in Yevamot. Both in the two sources presented here and also in the Hebrew appendix to his commentary on Genesis, 473, Hirsch emphasizes his agreement that "the commandment of being fruitful and multiplying is only an obligation for the man, whose way is to subdue, as stated in Yevamot 65b, and this is indicated by the defective spelling of the plural 'כבשוה' as stated there in the Gemara, and I wrote [in my commentary on verse 28] that for the woman the commandment is not from the outset but upon her union with the man who comes to marry her.... It seems that the Bible was very precise, since certainly the commandment like the blessing was said to both of them, but from the defective spelling of 'כבשה' it is hinted that the Halakha is that only the man is commanded to fulfill this commandment, for it is not the way of a woman to subdue, and also it is not her way to seek out the man, but she must wait until a man demands her, who has succeeded in doing well enough to build a home with a wife." (Translation from Hebrew appendix to the commentary mentioned above). That is to say, the deep intention of the Gemara is to say that the active commandment is incumbent on the man, and the commandment for the woman begins after the man has finished subduing. The man acquires enough possessions to establish a home, the woman is chosen by the man and marries him. Up to that time, the woman was dependent on the man's doing his part, but now they are partners in the commandment, both in marriage (be fruitful) and in educating their children (multiply), whereas Chertok writes that "be fruitful" applies only to the man. This is the reason why the verse is written in the plural, and it is the deep, literal meaning of the Gemara. Hirsch supports his approach by reference to Halakhic authorities such as R. Nissim of Gerona, R. Ḥayyim Joseph David Azulai, R. Elijah Mizrachi, and R. Isaiah Horowitz, who are not to be suspected of deviating from the Halakhic interpretation of the Sages. Haran says that although the woman is not commanded, she has a part in the commandment as assisting in its fulfillment. *Birkhei Yosef* explains Haran and says that the woman is regarded as performing the commandment of "be fruitful and multiply" more than an ordinary assistant in fulfilling a commandment, because the commandment cannot be fulfilled without her. In my opinion, Hirsch wrote the entire detailed appendix to preclude discussion of the claim that Chertok makes. However, Hirsch clearly preferred interpretations of the words of the Sages that suited his modern approach to the status of women, but his determination was always on the basis of commentary and not reform.

arrogance and dominance toward his wife. This is why God said to Adam, "It is not good that the man should be alone; I will make him a helpmate for him" (Gen. 2:18)

> to make a man aware of how helpless and joyless he would be without his wife, even in the midst of Paradise, no matter what his own strength and insight, and that only his wife can give him the support he needs to make him whole....
>
> The momentous task that God has set for human beings ... requires the collaboration of two human beings who can share the labor and complete it by complementing one another.... Taking over a portion of the partner's share of the work to be done enables that partner to concentrate his own energies on the work specifically assigned to him.... This is division of labor, pure and simple...
>
> The word נגד [opposite] clearly places the woman on the same level as the man, while at the same time giving each a distinct position of creation and endeavor... Also note that this division of labor between male and female was not a matter of convenience or accident. From the very outset, the female was created כנגדו [*kenegdo*, at his side], in such a manner that she could complement the work of the male. Man and woman were fashioned for each other, and both of them together were created for one and the same purpose. The man regards his wife as part of his very own being but at the same time as a creature distinct from himself.... She belongs to him. It is she that makes him whole; without her, his existence is only half a life....
>
> Here, then, we have the profound significance of marriage as an institution established by God.[45]

That is to say, in Judaism the woman has a status equal to that of the man. At the Creation God determined this equality, and at the same time he implanted different physical and spiritual characteristics in man and woman so that they could, in harmonious cooperation, fulfill the task of maintaining human existence in a moral and humane manner. The husband received the task of leaving the home and acquiring material assets that make physical existence possible, and the woman received the task of building the home and the family on the foundations of faith, morality, and humaneness, according to the

---

45 *Writings*, VIII, 89-90. See also Hirsch on Gen. 2:18, 23-24 and 5:1-2.

words of God in the Torah, and to make certain that the accumulated assets would serve these ends. Thus, if the man feels superiority because of his role as a man of the world, he is making a grave error. He is ignoring the fact that without his wife, he cannot attain his true goal. In certain respects, woman is superior to man. Only she can protect him from the temptations of his instinct, which lie in wait for him outside, because of her pure and moral characteristics, which improve her intellect, and she can continuously direct him always toward the true goal, so that he does not regard the material means as an end in themselves.

> A woman of purity, if she descends from Sarah, does not need an external sign of the covenant [circumcision]; on her own she remembers the covenant with א-ש ל-די [*El Shaday*, a name of God], Who sets limits and allots measure to all things. The warning די! [*dai*, enough] resounds in her heart of its own accord, through the attribute of צניעות [tseni'ut, modesty] which pervades a Jewish woman of purity. She bears within her the tendency to subordinate herself to all pure and godly values.... The father bequeaths spiritual values, whereas the woman of purity bequeaths to her children the emotional sensitivity that is the standard of moral decency.[46]

These words imply that the woman is exempt from many commandments that were imposed upon the man, such as circumcision, because she does not need them. In discussing women's exemption from the commandment of dwelling in the *succah*, Hirsch states that the reason for this is that women are exempt from commandments determined by time. Hirsch emphasizes that this exemption derives both from the pure and elevated character of women and also from the fact that, because of the framework of her tasks within the home, she does not encounter the temptations that stand before a man when he goes out into the public domain. Women are exempt from positive commandments determined by time not because of her inferiority, for otherwise there would not be so many exceptions to this rule, but because of her religious and ethical superiority:

---

46 Hirsch on Gen. 17:15.

> The most likely reason the Torah does not obligate women in these *mitsvos* [sic] is that *women do not need them.* For the whole purpose of מצוות עשה שהזמן גרמא is to represent—through symbolic actions—certain truths, ideas, principles, and resolutions, and to bring these values afresh to our minds, from time to time, so that we take them to heart and put them into practice. The Torah takes it for granted that woman has great fervor and faithful enthusiasm for her calling, and that the temptations awaiting her in the sphere of her calling pose but little danger to her. Hence, it was not necessary to impose on her all the *mitzvos* that are imposed on man. For man requires repeated exhortation to remain true to his calling, and it is necessary to repeatedly caution him against any weakness in the fulfillment of his mission.... Women's exemption from ראייה [*reiya*, seeing] and from חגיגה [*hagiga*, celebrating], however, is apparently to be explained differently: The public national representation of the Torah—which is what summons the nation to the Sanctuary—belonged primarily to the calling of the men.[47]

Hirsch sees the Original Sin in the Garden of Eden and its punishment as a violation of the law of equality in creation, and accordingly he explains the meaning of the punishment, "your desire shall be to your husband, and he shall rule over you" (Gen. 3:16):

> It is in the nature of woman to feel that she can fulfill her life's purpose only when she has joined her husband; yet he will impose upon her a new renunciation: והוא ימשול בך! [and he will rule over you]. When the relationship between man and earth changed, and man could eat bread only by the sweat of his countenance, the woman became dependent on her husband, the primary breadwinner. Thus the original equality between man and woman was shattered. This is the *general* tendency. Only the Torah will bring redemption and spread the canopy of peace. Man and woman will return to their priestly calling and serve God as equals: woman will again become the "crown of her husband" and "pearl" of his life (*Mishlei* 12:4, 31:10).[48]

---

47 Hirsch on Lev. 23:43. In Hirsch's opinion, the entire female sex is naturally more modest than the male sex. The male received a beard from God to hide his lower jaw, which is more active in sensual eating. The woman does not need this. Therefore it is forbidden to the Jewish man to remove his beard. See his commentary on Lev. 19:27.

48 Hirsch on Gen. 3:16. Hirsch's approach appears to be inconsistent. In the article on the Jewish woman cited above, he argues that the burden of earning a livelihood

That is to say, the judgment "and he shall rule over you" does not imply deterministic inferiority, but rather punishment for a sin that can be corrected. Woman's original purpose of self-fulfillment by joining in with the man's purpose on an equal basis was spoiled after the Original Sin. Earning a living became an exhausting matter, and the woman's purpose made her dependent on her husband, and the equality was overthrown. Implementing the moral path of the Torah in the everyday life of the Jewish home is supposed to redeem mankind in this world (as opposed to Christianity), permitting those who walk upon it to correct the situation and restore equality. I found that Hirsch explicitly expresses the view that the characteristics of women, according to Judaism, which are appropriate to her function in the Jewish family, reflect full superiority over men in only one place. Hirsch sums up his position on the status of women in the final essay in the series, which is devoted to the subject, "The Jewish Woman in the Talmud":

> Even though the Sages of Judaism fully appreciate that women, because of their nature, are basically different from men, they regard women as full intellectual equals of the male sex.... Our Sages consider women intellectually superior to men. The Creator has given greater intellectual gifts to the woman than to the man; that is why women attain intellectual maturity earlier than men (נדה מה). This, too, is why the Sages of the Jewish people regard the matriarchs, women such as Sarah and Rebecca, as no less inspired by the spirit of God and no less capable of communicating with Him than the patriarchs.... In general, the view of the Sages of Judaism is that

---

was purposely placed on the man rather than the woman, so that she could guide the man in using the assets he acquired. In his interpretation of the Original Sin and its punishment, he argues that the wife does not support the family because of the punishment and her subjection to her husband. It might be possible to reconcile these positions by saying that the punishment did indeed cause the wife's subjection; however, the division of labor by which the wife fulfills her role properly according to the Torah, rescuing her husband from addiction to acquiring property and guiding him toward the sanctification of sensuality, thereby saves the woman from subjection. Thus they will share a life of equality and partnership, in which the one complements the other, and thus they will return to the Garden of Eden in this world. Cf. Chertok, *Haisha*, 7-12.

every human being, regardless of class, sex, or nationality, is capable of intellectual and moral perfection.[49]

---

49 *Writings*, VIII, 134-35. In the Gemara in Nida, the well-known teaching by Rav Ḥisda appears, explaining Rav's reason for stating in the Mishnah that a woman's vows are valid from the age of twelve, whereas those of a man only from the age of thirteen. "'And God built the rib' teaches that the Holy One, blessed be He, gave more intelligence to the woman than to the man." Cf. Breuer, *'Eda*, 116; Breuer represents the approach of twentieth-century Modern Orthodoxy, and he therefore admires greatly the "reversal" that Hirsch performed, without criticizing it. Ross, *Armon*, 89-91, 101-5, also took note of the reversal in Hirsch's words, but for some reason she does not cite this source, which is the most explicit of all. She is also disturbed by the refusal of Hirsch and those like him to acknowledge the element of women's inferiority in the Jewish tradition, which I explain below. Her further, post-modern criticism is of Hirsch's apologetics, which, even if it is sincere, is no longer persuasive in many circles. She sees a flaw in the modern conservative approaches that rejected the historical conception of religion and preferred a single, eternal meta-program. In my opinion, it is hard to blame Hirsch for not being a post-modern pluralist, so that his approach no longer pleases us. His choice of a meta-narrative of a super-historical Judaism, entirely derived from Sinai, is understandable in its time. He prefers his meta-program to those proposed by others. He explains with great clarity that it is not possible to accept the historicism of the Halakha that was proposed by the Reform movement and the historical positivists. For, in his opinion, if the Oral Law and the written Torah are not from heaven, there is no longer any basis to obligate us to observe them as they are and to prevent us from making corrections in them as our hearts desire, which is what others did, to his regret. My critique is different. I present a wide variety of sources and show that Hirsch's selective apologetics, even if they are sincere, leads to difficulties and contradictions, making it difficult to maintain the meta-narrative that he so cherishes.

Interestingly, Breuer, *'Eda*, 364 n. 111, points out that the Maharal had a similar idea regarding the superiority of women. Examination of the source he quotes and other places in the Maharal produces, in my opinion, a picture of the status of women that is entirely different from the reversal that Hirsch presents. The Maharal discusses there an Aggada in BT Berakhot 17a on Isaiah 32:9, that refers to "women that are at ease" and "confident daughters" in a negative way, warning them of the impending destruction. The Aggada uses this verse in a positive way, promising a larger reward for women than for men, and the Gemara explains that their reward is greater because they are concerned to have their sons and husbands study Torah. According to the Maharal, based on Aristotle and his followers, the woman is matter, and the man is form. The man is active, and the woman is passive. Only the man is the essence of reality, and the woman is defective reality. The woman—even the whole part in her—is not removed from inferiority. True, this inferiority gives her an advantage in one area. Since matter needs form and easily clings to it, it is easy for a woman, who is herself a passive creation, quiet and at ease, "being matter ready for this, then she unites and connects with the Torah [which is form] completely in the most marvelous

This approach constitutes a reversal of the traditional view regarding the inferiority of women, and in Hirsch's opinion it places Judaism in the first place among all the cultures and religions with respect to the status of women. In Deuteronomy, the juxtaposition of the law of divorce and that of taking a new wife "attests to the supreme value the Torah attaches to the wife and to the husband's duty to attend to her happiness and joy. It appears that, to this day, there has never been another society on earth that could boast of such consideration of the wife's welfare."[50]

Why was Hirsch not content with granting equality to women, but insisted on saying they were superior? One may certainly hold it against Hirsch for refusing to acknowledge that the dominant school in the Jewish tradition believed in the inferiority of women and for considering only a minority of teachings in their praise. However, we must understand that this refusal was necessary for Hirsch. Recognizing that there were two legitimate schools among the Sages regarding the status of women was impossible for Hirsch, who believed that just one truth was possible, and it was conveyed at Sinai. Conceding that there was a school that held women inferior would mean that the eternal ethics of

---

eagerness... But men in this respect must work and take pains with the Torah without rest night and day." This advantage enables the woman to receive a greater reward from the study of Torah. However she is not permitted to study Torah, but her activity to assist and encourage her husband and sons to study Torah, which is an act less important than study itself, is enough for that. See Maharal, Juda Loew, *Drush 'Al Hatorah Vehamitsvot* (Pieterkov, 5674 [1914]), 3-31; Maharal, Judah Loew, *Kitvei Hamaharal Miprag, Mivḥar*, ed. A. Kariv (Jerusalem, 1960), vol 2, 340. In Rav Kook as well—the Maharal was one of his spiritual teachers—there is a position that appears to be close to that of Hirsch, but its source is in a Kabbalistic position which also holds woman to be inferior. The man legislates and conquers, and she is legislated and conquered, he is like the spirit, and she is like the soul, and therefore she also has an advantage, in that sanctity is natural to her and does not need to observe a large part of the commandments or to learn the Torah of the men. See Rosenak, *Hanevuit*, 246-51 and nn. 149, 161 there. Chertok, *Haisha; Qanqan* also mentions incidentally that, according to Hirsch's approach, the woman is always intellectually and morally superior to men, and he refers to his apologetics and the selection that he makes in the words of the Sages with considerable forgiveness.

50 Hirsch on Deut. 24:1. Interestingly, Gedalia Ibn Yiḥiye made a similar reversal, according superior status to women, in the sixteenth century. However, his *Ḥibur Bishvaḥ Hanashim* was a voice crying in the wilderness.

God, the source of all the commandments given at Sinai, was inappropriate to nineteenth-century ethics, which Hirsch had internalized. The only way around this difficulty would be to accept that not all the Halakhot derive from God, but this would bring down the structure of Hirsch's ideas about the obligatory source of the Oral Law. Therefore Hirsch chose (intentionally, in my opinion, and he deserves criticism for doing so) to ignore expressions of women's inferiority in the Oral Law, not even trying to interpret them, as he usually did, unless he could not avoid it, and he had an interpretation that suited his approach. Perhaps Hirsch would argue that all the teachings about women's inferiority in the Mishnah and the Talmud were merely Aggadic Midrash expressing the opinion of the Sages who spoke them. As I showed in chapter two, Hirsch believed that Aggada was not from Sinai, and the views expressed in it reflect the views that were current in the scientific and cultural society of its time. However, the multitude of misogynistic teachings that connect women in general with witchcraft, seduction, prostitution, frivolity, and other contemptible traits and the connection between these teachings and the Halakha make it difficult to accept that explanation, since they appear to be a systematic body of opinion.

Hirsch developed the theory of women's superiority, because he had no better explanation of the difference between men and women with respect to the obligation to perform the commandments, which proves that they are not equal. If there is no equality, in his view women's superiority is preferable to their inferiority, which is contrary to his ethical positions. It is also possible to reproach Hirsch, since the apologetics in his writing are so much more conspicuous because of his selection, and this leads him into theoretical difficulties. If women's intellect is preferable, why are women not the bearers of the intellectual and spiritual achievements of mankind over history? If man is morally weak, why is he the one who sets out into a world full of temptation in order to earn a livelihood? Or, on the contrary, why did men, who sally forth into public discourse, not receive the natural immunity that women received? Would it not be more correct to say that if women are left at home, they encounter fewer seductions, but if they are given equality to set out into the public domain like men, we will find that they have powerful urges from which they need to be protected? Most likely Hirsch would reply that this is what Providence regarded as suitable for building perfect and harmonious connubial union, in which one partner complements the other, and whoever wants an answer will get that one. In any event, here we have another expression of Hirsch's Neo-Fundamentalism (as with the subjects of religion and science and Torah with Derekh Erets). When the status of women rises and becomes a solid fact, Hirsch makes this position into the position of the tradition, even though most sources are inconsistent with this argument, but rather point in the opposite direction.

Woman in the Sources

Hirsch devoted four essays to women in Genesis: Eve, Sarah, Rebecca, and Rachel and Leah.[51] In all of these essays he seeks to present them as positive examples and models of women and their attainments, from which we must learn. While Hirsch does not fail to emphasize that the Torah presents the patriarchs and matriarchs as human beings who are liable to err, and we must learn from their mistakes, in general these figures are presented in a favorable light, in which apologetics is evident.

The apologetics peaks in the essay, "The Jewish Woman in the Talmud." As noted, Hirsch systematically ignores all the Aggadot, Midrashim, and sayings of the Sages, which speak disparagingly of women and their inferiority, and he quotes selectively only sayings that praise women and their importance. He begins the essay with this statement: "The manner in which the Sages of the Talmud discuss the position of the Jewish woman mirrors a respect and appreciation, a tender and considerate attitude toward the female sex, which could have originated nowhere else, in theory and in practice, than in the Wellsprings of the Word of God and in the life of the nation drinking from these wellsprings."[52]

---

51 *Writings*, VIII, 90-117. See also Hirsch's encomium of women in his commentary of Proverbs 31 (the Woman of Valor).
52 *Writings*, VIII, 130. See also ibid., VII, 237-38. For the sake of comparison, see J. Elbaum, "Demuyot Nashim Beagadat Ḥazal—Model Leḥiqui," *Hagut 5, Measef*

In this essay, Hirsch cannot ignore the Talmud's prohibition against women learning Torah. He sees no problem in this, and from his point of view, it is enough that they share in their husband's merit for study. This is also because women urge their husbands and sons and inspire them with the desire to study.[53] He does not ask himself why, if women's intellectual level is truly equal to that of men or superior to it, they do not receive an entrance ticket to full Jewish literacy and the spiritual treasures of the nation?[54]

Hirsch was constrained to deal with teachings of the Sages against women only in his commentary on the *Ethics of the Fathers*, which is included in the prayer book, in the framework of his commentary on the prayer book. He did not compose systematic commentaries of the Mishnah and the Talmud, so he was not required to deal with these teachings, some of which explain the reason for Halakhot. The *Ethics of the Fathers* 1:5 reads: "do not converse much with women.... He who converses too much with women brings evil upon himself and neglects the study of the Torah and will in the end inherit Gehenna." Hirsch deals with this with the same apologetics as outlined before. He notes that the Hebrew speaks of "conversing" and not "talking" with women and turns the statement into praise for women. It is not possible, he says, that this teaching could condemn women:

> As a matter of fact, the sayings of the Sages are replete with maxims stressing the high esteem in which womanhood should be held, the respect and honor due one's wife, and particularly the great importance that a husband should attach to the views, opinions and counsel

---

Lemahshava Yehudit: Haisha Bimqorot Hayahadut (Jerusalem, 1983), 13-26, on how to read and understand the attitude of the Sages toward women, without apologetics, grappling with the subject in a sober and courageous manner.

53 *Writings*, VIII, 131. Note that the idea that a wife shares in her husband's merit when he studies Torah, by virtue of fulfilling the roles assigned to her, is found in Hirsch far before the phenomenon in Ultra-Orthodox Judaism of the mid-twentieth century, noted by M. Friedman "Kol Kevuda Bat Melekh Hutsa Haisha Haharedit," in *Barukh She'asani Isha?*, ed. D. J. Ariel et al. (Tel Aviv, 1999), 189-205, which he called modern and feminist. As I showed above in note 49, the idea appears in the Maharal, and it is based on the Midrash in BT Brakhot 17a.

54 See *Writings*, VIII, 131. See below on his distinction between the deep study of Torah and the simple study of Bible, which is permitted to women.

of his wife.... In fact, this very statement may well be founded on genuine appreciation of the vital role played by both husband and wife in the discharge of the task to be fulfilled by the home. *Sichah* does not mean serious conversation but merely idle talk and gossip. Cf. *Sichat yeladim* (3:14) and *mi'ut sichah* (6:6). A man who truly respects his wife will have more to offer her than just trivial talk and idle chatter for her amusement. He will want to discuss with her the serious concerns of life and will derive enjoyment from the resulting exchange of views and counsel. Moreover, engaging in trifling talk with other women and other men's wives may imperil moral purity.[55]

As to 2:8 in the *Ethics of the Fathers*, "the more women the more witchcraft," Hirsch apparently found no way of explaining it according to his approach, so he chose to ignore it. At any rate, Hirsch states here that the Sages could not have differences of opinion in relation to women, and their positive attitude toward women is self-evident. Hirsch does not ask himself why the matter of idle conversation is connected with women. Why is it that only idle conversation with a woman will lead to moral turpitude? Is there not even a hint at deeply rooted disparagement of women in particular? Would it not have been better, to prevent such misunderstanding, to write, "Take counsel with your wife, because she is a partner in building your home," or "Idle conversation with anyone is harmful to study and ultimately leads to hell?" In fact, in *Ethics of the Fathers* 1:17, Shimon Ben Gamliel says exactly that in general terms, using the word "talk" and not "converse": "Whoever multiplies talk causes sin."

In his commentary on problematic passages in the Pentateuch, Hirsch's apologetics led him to inner difficulties. He cannot ignore the Torah law, according to which a woman whose husband suspects her of adultery, is required to drink the bitter water and be tested by it. Hirsch assumes that if the woman is guilty, she will refuse the test and confess. Hirsch is content to state that the Torah is showing us the importance of the institution of marriage, in that when a suspicion that cannot be confirmed blights it, God Himself intervenes and clarifies the situation. It is enough for Hirsch to state that the water

---

55 *The Hirsch Siddur*, 422-23.

is not an effective test (according to the Sages) of the wife, if the husband is not free of sexual sins such as betraying his wife or committing incest, and also that the adulterer is to be punished (according to the Sages) along with the straying wife. Hirsch does not ask himself why the husband should not be tested in the same humiliating way, if a wife suspects him of adultery. Why in general does the Halakha not stipulate an actual punishment if a married man has sexual relations with an unmarried woman, whereas a wife who does that is considered an adulterer and condemned to death? Why is it not possible to examine the suspected woman in a discreet and not humiliating manner?[56]

Absurdly, Hirsch sees the "temporary and local necessity" (which is what he calls Rabbenu Gershom's decree) of denying the permission to a husband, which the Torah gives him, to divorce his wife unilaterally, as a step backward in the development of Jewish culture, rather than as progress. At the outset, Hirsch contends, the Torah of Israel assumed that a wife receives such great admiration and respect from her husband in the framework of marriage, and it relied upon the husband, that he would not exercise the right of divorce except if his wife was truly unworthy.[57]

On the subject of retracting vows, where the law states that a man is independent in his vows, whereas a woman's father or husband retracts hers, Hirsch goes through logical contortions in a similar apologetic mode:

> For a man creates his position in life independently.... Since his is independent, he is able to take this individuality [of his life due to the vow he has made] into account when he shapes the conditions of his life.
>
> Not so for a woman. The moral greatness of the woman's calling requires that she enter a position in life created by another. The woman does not build for herself her own home. She enters the home provided by the man, and she manages it, bringing happiness to the home and nurturing everything inside the home in a spirit of sanctity and orientation toward God. The woman—even more than

---

56 See *Writings*, VIII, 134, and also Hirsch on Num. 5:31.
57 See Hirsch on Deut. 22:18-19, 24:1.

the man—must avoid the constraint of extraordinary guidelines in her life, for they are likely to be an impediment to her in the fulfillment of her calling.

From this standpoint, one can understand the prescriptions instituted here out of concern for the woman.[58]

Woman's purpose and her responsibility for the home and family are so great that she needs that status in life that her husband has built, and any untoward vow is liable to endanger the attainment of that goal. Because of this, and out of concern for her, her husband is permitted to retract her vows. Out of concern for the woman's purpose and her integrity, she was denied independence, public self-expression, and personal responsibility. Here you have "beneficial distinction and not discrimination" (in the words of Menachem Elon).

Hirsch deals with the problematic benedictions that every Jewish man is supposed to say every morning, thanking God for not making him a Gentile, a slave, or a woman, with simple apologetics. His explanation here, and the reversal that he made in the status of woman, were accepted in Modern Orthodoxy until the second third of the twentieth century, and only recently, with a post-modern outlook, have people realized that it is apologetics, and we must face the problem and not avoid seeing it in historical context rather than as given at Sinai. Here are Hirsch's words:

> This is not a prayer of thanks that God did not make us heathens, slaves or women. Rather, it calls upon us to contemplate the task which God has imposed upon us by making us free Jewish men, and to pledge ourselves to do justice to this mission. These three aspects of our own status impose upon us duties much more comprehensive than those required of the rest of mankind. And if our women have a small number of מצות [mitsvot, commandments] to fulfill than men, they know that the tasks which they must discharge as free Jewish women are no less in accordance with the will and desire of God than are those of her brothers.[59]

---

58 Hirsch on Num. 30:4.
59 Hirsch, *Siddur*, 13. Cf. Ross, *Armon*, 91-93.

That is to say, the meaning of the benedictions is not what it sounds like, and the worshiper is not thanking God for creating him as a man, superior to women. Rather, the Jewish man is thankful for the obligation of the commandments, greater than that of a Gentile, slave, or woman, and he promises formally to observe them. Apologetics lead to contradictions. If, according to Hirsch, the Sages believe that the additional commandments incumbent upon men were given to them because of their moral and intellectual inferiority (as I showed above), why should he recite a benediction for that? The Sages should have had men recite the blessing, "who made me according to His will," and women, "who has made me a woman"!

Education of Girls

The Haskala's revolution in education, as proposed by Wessely, was adopted in full by Hirsch (see chapter three above, volume one). However, continued secularization, acculturation, and especially the theories and actions of the Reform movement, required him to pay heed to the education of girls as well, although Wessely does not mention it in his educational platform in *Divrei Shalom Veemet*. Until Hirsch's time, girls were not given formal education in Torah and Judaism, and Haskala and the Reform movement only offered them general education, which distanced them from traditional Judaism. Hirsch dealt with this topic in *Horeb*, which was published in 1838, and there he lays out the school subjects required for Jewish youth:

A. Hebrew language
B. Vernacular [German language]
C. Torah, Prophets, Writings

These were the principal subjects, to which he added the supporting sciences:

A. Nature and man (natural history, physics, physical geography, psychology, and anthropology).
B. History

C. Right Living (teaching of duties from the Written and Oral Law, from Maimonides, *Shulḥan 'Arukh*, and, if possible, if the boy was capable of it, Mishnah and Gemara as well.
D. Writing and arithmetic.[60]

Here Hirsch presents his view on the schooling of girls:

> We have tried to trace the general course for boys; the same, however, holds good for girls. That is to say 1-5 and 7 remain somewhat simplified, but for 6 only systematic instructions in the duties of her future life is required. In the girl's instruction domestic life occupies the central position which in the boy's case is taken by the requirements of a Jew and a citizen. Similarly, the girl finishes up with needlework and house management as the boy with gainful occupation.[61]

That is to say, girls should be taught the subjects that boys study, but at a lower level of difficulty, including Hebrew and Bible. In the study of Halakha, the girls should mainly be taught the laws that apply to them in their expected role as managing the home and the family, and boys are to be taught Halakhot that will help them in the public structures of earning a living, the community, and the state. In addition to teaching the girls school subjects, they are also to learn the skills they will need as housewives, while the boys are to learn a profession so they can make a living.

Hirsch repeats these ideas in a letter to Eliezer Liepman Prins of Amsterdam, who wrote to him in 1867 and asked for details about the school, so that he could establish a similar institution in his city. Here Hirsch emphasizes even more the importance of educating girls in Jewish studies, including grammar and writing in Hebrew and general subjects:

> Our girls study exactly the same subjects, except Talmud and mathematics. Instead of these, they have lessons in handicrafts for women. They study Hebrew grammar and Bible like the boys. Allow me to call your special attention to a matter I mentioned recently, since in our experience this has very positive results, and therefore it appears

---

60 *Horeb*, vol. 2, 411-12.
61 Ibid., 412.

especially important to me, although usually it encounters some resistance at first. People forget that Hannah and Deborah unquestionably understood Hannah's prayer and Deborah's song, and that the future salvation of our men, our homes, and our children depends on our winning the hearts of our future mothers and wives for the holy things of our people. However, we can only inspire the hearts of our daughters for the holy things of Israel if we teach them to drink the spirit from the source and if they prefer, because of their independent evaluation, Isaiah and Amos over Goethe and Shakespeare—and we have succeeded in this, with the help of heaven. If you wish to work for your future, do not forget the daughters![62]

According to these descriptions, Hirsch preferred separate education for boys and girls not only with respect to religion but also practically. However, when he established the *Realschule* in Frankfurt in 1853, in the spirit of Torah with Derekh Erets, he could not effectuate this immediately for budgetary reasons. Hirsch preferred immediate implementation of education for girls to preserving modesty in separate classes, so he opened mixed classes. This innovation was canceled as soon as it was possible, but it does indicate the importance he attributed to the education of girls in a communal framework that included study of Hebrew and the Bible.[63] Hence, Jewish studies and

---

62 Hirsch, *Maamarim*, 33. In this letter, Hirsch tells that the school opened in 1853 with eighty-three pupils, both boys and girls, and in 1867 there were already 300—about 180 boys and 120 girls. There were nine boys' classes and six girls' classes, and the youngest two classes were mixed boys and girls. According to Eliav, *Haḥinukh*, 231-32, in 1871 Hirsch separated the sexes completely, establishing a high school for girls, and in 1885 the two schools had about 500 pupils. In the early twentieth century there were about 600 pupils.

63 See Breuer, *'Eda*, 117, and also 101-2. Ross states that Modern Orthodoxy sought to resolve the tension between the tradition and modernity on the matter of the status of women by dividing Halakha in two: a permanent, eternal foundation, and a less essential foundation subject to change. Hirsch is one of the examples she uses, as Hirsch distinguished between "Torah," as a permanent foundation, and "Derekh Erets," which is a changeable element of positive cultivation, in which the Jewish people is occasionally found, and Judaism adapts itself to it. I seek to show (see chapter 3) that Hirsch regarded Torah and Derekh Erets (which satisfies the necessary prerequisites) as the same, and both derive from the same divine source. That which is scientific truth is also Torah truth, which always was and never will change. In Hirsch's view, this was the Jewish position from time immemorial, and it contains no element of compromise or variability. Judaism does not

Hebrew for girls were not intended only to defend against Reform and acculturation, but they were inseparably connected to the eternal task of women in the family, as Hirsch described it: to sanctify property and the body for ethical and spiritual purposes. The status of woman and education are connected with each other and extremely important to Hirsch.

In his commentary on Deuternonomy 11:19, "and you shall teach your sons to speak of them," Hirsch explains his position on teaching Torah to daughters as well as the meaning of his instructions in *Horeb* to teach girls Hebrew and Judaism, but on a simpler level than the boys. He cites a Halakhic Midrash from BT Kiddushin 29b: "Your sons and not your daughters," and he reads closely, showing that the Midrash did not conclude this from the verse, "and you shall drill your children" (Deut. 6:7), because there is a difference between לימוד [teaching] and שינון [drilling]. The former is more comprehensive than the latter, which means "teaching the content of the mitzvos in short, concise sentences." It is forbidden to teach a daughter, but it is permitted to "drill her":

> The father is exempt only from the duty of imparting to his daughter Torah erudition [למדנות], for the duty to acquire and transmit Torah erudition devolves on the Jewish man. But that understanding of the literature of Judaism, and that knowledge of the mitzvos, that are essential for the fulfillment of ויראו את-ה׳ אלקיכם ושמרו לעשות את-כל דברי התורה הזאת [they may fear God, your God, and conscientiously carry out all the words of this teaching] (below 31:12) must be imparted to our daughters no less than to our sons....
>
> This has always been the [educational] practice, proof of which is a whole literature in Juedisch-Deutsch [German in Hebrew letters] written primarily for the women, to enable them to understand the Bible and the liturgy and to impart to them a general knowledge of the Halachah [sic] and of the moral teachings of the Sages (see also טורי זהב [*Turei zahav*] on יורה דעה [*Yore de'a*] 246:6).

Again, the instruction of girls will have a different character and be on the lower level of "drilling"—and it will have different content, not

---

adapt to any other culture born of time. Rather culture adapts to the Torah. See Ross, "Nashim," 393, and 563 n. 12; idem, *Armon*, 132 n. 18.

Talmud, but the simple meaning of the Bible, the necessary Halakhot, the ethics of the Sages according to the Mishnah. Hirsch's opinion about this is similar to Chajes's. Both of them rely on the same source in Torei Zahav, but Hirsch was the first to establish a religious school for girls, giving them, along with general studies, formal instruction in Hebrew and Judaism from a young age. This gave the girls an opportunity to gain knowledge, to read and understand Judaism from the source.[64]

Personal Status

Hirsch's principal discussion of the personal status of women in Judaism is found in his early book, *Horeb*, in the framework of his treatment of the commandment to be fruitful and multiply, and marriage, which comprise the subject of maintaining a Jewish home. In this discussion, he already distinguishes between the tasks of the husband and of the wife in the framework of the Jewish home and family. Here we find very conservative descriptions of the personal status of women:

> Therefore the man leaves the parental home and attaches himself to his wife in order to found a family, and they become a single human being; and therefore the wife clings to the husband and willingly subordinates herself to him.[65]
>
> The woman belongs exclusively to the man.... The man makes the declaration since he, as the sole representative and rule of the household, consecrates her to himself as a wife.[66]

Later Hirsch explains the meaning of this arrangement, rule, and government in detail:

> The woman should belong wholly to her husband and her household; only for her husband should she adorn herself, she should try to please only him, and her home should be the fairest field of her activity. Her adornment should be modesty and a Jewish way of life. To appear before strangers with her own hair uncovered or, where it is customary to wear a cap and a veil, to appear without veil or cap,

---

64 Cf. Chertok, *Haisha*, 22-27; idem, *Qanqan*, 84-92.
65 *Horeb*, vol. 2, 396.
66 Ibid., 397.

even though covered, to dress gaudily and alluringly, to expose the body immodestly, to seek the company of other men, to be immodest in her manner of speech, to speak contemptuously of her husband's family, etc.—all this is un-Jewish, and the stamp of fashion can never render such conduct permissible. To hide one's own hair under an ornamental covering made from someone else's or even from one's own after being cut is a very old custom which is not forbidden.[67]

Hirsch shuts women up in the house, isolates them from the company of men, and criticizes following fashions, in which modesty is not a major consideration. Interestingly, contrary to Chajes, who was in doubt regarding wigs, Hirsch permits them without hesitation, as an old custom, even if the wig is made from hair that was cut from the woman herself.

A somewhat less conservative position on this subject, which acknowledges the problematic nature of presenting the wife as her husband's property, and the need to explain it, is found at the end of his essay on Sarah, published in August 1864, among the essays on the status of women mentioned above. In this essay, Hirsch formulates the position of the critics and answers them:

> Of course there are those who point with some irony to this legal formula [קיחה קיחה משדה עפרון, "'taking' means 'buying,' from (Abraham's purchase of) the field of Ephron," BT Kiddushin 2a]. "So, you see, Jewish men acquire their wives by purchase," they say. Yes, it is true; the Jew "acquires" his wife. Note, however, that he acquires her not from others but from herself, out of her own free will, and then she remains his most precious possession, his own most sacred treasure, even beyond death.[68]

Permissiveness and Modesty

Modernity posed further challenges to the middle trend. The charm of European culture also contained dangers. Freedom from the yoke of any authority—that of God and that of another person—is liable to lead to general licentiousness, permissiveness, and even wantonness.

---
67 Ibid., 401.
68 *Writings*, VIII, 103. See also Hirsch on Gen. 23:19.

The challenge was to present a modern religion to the youth, which proposed restraint as a model to be imitated. In the chapter of Horeb cited above, which is devoted to the establishment of the Jewish home, Hirsch instructs the Jewish boy in how to find out whether the bride offered to him is worthy, and he lists the desirable and undesirable traits:

> When you choose a wife, remember that she is to be your companion in life, in building up your home, in the performance of your life task, and choose accordingly. It will then not be wealth or physical beauty or brilliance of mind that will decide you, but you will look for richness of heart, beauty of character and good sense and intelligence.[69]

That is to say, the determining criterion must not be wealth, beauty, or verbal facility, but morality, delicacy, and practical skill. What criteria did Eliezer, Abraham's servant, set for himself when he traveled to a foreign country to choose a bride for his master's son? How was he to recognize the worthy woman? "He would recognize her not by her wealth, nor by her physical charms, nor by her intellectual accomplishments, but only by her character, by the humanity and morality of her heart, by her readiness to help others—in short, by her גמילות חסד [gemilut ḥesed, compassionate deed]."[70]

Hirsch is disturbed by the permissiveness that modern men arrogate to themselves while denying the same to their wives and daughters:

> Scripture specially emphasizes: ויהיו שניהם ערומים, האדם ואשתו [and they were both naked, the man and his wife]. Both were naked, and they did not have to feel ashamed. Scripture thus teaches us that man and woman are equal—not only bodily, but also spiritually. Both are equally obligated to be pure, moral, and holy. The whole generation is sick, if a pure and virtuous life is not equally aspired to by both sexes. The human race is sick, if young or adult men grant themselves license on account of their masculinity; if young or adult men allow themselves what is not permitted to young or adult women. The sign of the holy covenant is imprinted on the body of the Jewish

---

69 *Horeb*, vol. 2, 394.
70 *Writings*, VIII, 104.

man, and it bears the warning: התהלך לפני והיה תמים (Gen. 17:1, "Walk before me and be wholehearted"), meaning that God requires of men innocence and purity—just as He requires them of women.[71]

With more than a hint to his generation, Hirsch states that the Jew's uniqueness lies in his sanctifying not only his spirit but also his body by observing the commandments, and this is taught to him by the Jewish woman, for this is the focus of her task in the home:

> It is not sufficient to have ideas about God's unity. To the mitzvah of "שמע" [hear] should be added the mitzvah of "ואהבת" [you shall love], the practical subordination to Him of all faculties and aspirations בכל לב, נפש ומאד [with all heart, soul, and might]. Toward this end it is not sufficient that Avraham is one's father, if Sarah is not one's mother. We are the people with whom the name "Avraham" is associated, and our mission is not limited to disseminating theological and philosophical conceptions of God's unity. Rather, our mission is לשמור דרך ה' לעשות צדקה ומשפט [to keep the way of God and do charity and justice] (cf. Below 18:19), and that requires the subordination of all our faculties, especially physical energies and drives; in other words, it requires sanctification of the body. Only one who sanctifies his body is entitled to be called a Jew.
>
> Ishmael inherited from Avraham the sanctification of the intellect, but he did not inherit from Sarah the sanctification of the body. When a Jewish woman bears, nurses, and brings up her child, the child's body is sanctified from the very beginning. For this reason the story of Sarah and Hagar is placed between ברית בין הבתרים [the covenant between the parts] and ברית מילה [circumcision].[72]

To maintain a high level of modesty, Hirsch made an educational effort to preserve the custom of arranged marriages, which was losing favor among young people. He was unwilling to adopt the modern outlook, which Mendelssohn had already chosen, according to which couples choose one another freely; he regarded this as erroneously basing marriage solely on blind desire. He used the verse describing the marriage of Isaac and Rebecca, in which matrimony preceded love, "And Isaac ... took Rebecca, and she became his wife; and he loved her" (Gen. 24:67), to explain the value of an arranged marriage as

---

71 Hirsch on Gen. 2:25.
72 Ibid., 16:14. See Breuer, *'Eda*, 116.

assuring the length and vitality of marriage among the Jews, in contrast to the Gentiles, where the marriage-broker is passion:

> This, too, is a characteristic that, thank God, has not vanished from among the descendants of Avraham and Sarah, Yitzchak and Rivkah. The more she became his wife, the more he loved her! Like this marriage of the first Jewish son, Jewish marriages, most Jewish marriages, are contracted not on the basis of passion, but on the strength of reason and judgment. Parents and relatives consider whether the two young people are suited to each other; therefore, their love increases as they come to know each other better.
>
> Most non-Jewish marriages are made on the basis of what they call "love." But we need only glance at novelistic depictions taken from life, and we immediately see the vast gulf—in the non-Jewish world—between the "love" of the partners before marriage and what happens afterward; how dull and empty everything seems after marriage, how different from what the two partners had imagined beforehand. This sort of "love" is blind; each step into the future brings new disillusionment.
>
> Not so is Jewish marriage, of which it says: ויקח את רבקה ותהי לו! לאשה ויאהבה [And Isaac ... took Rebecca, and she became his wife; and he loved her]. Here the wedding is not the culmination, but only the beginning of true love.[73]

Another custom adopted by young people, which Hirsch did not like, was the honeymoon following the wedding. This was unacceptable to him both on religious grounds—the prohibition against sexual intercourse when a woman has experienced vaginal bleeding—and also because the custom was not appropriate to the modest Jewish family, which was devoted to building its home as a miniature Temple. In Hirsch's words:

> As for the nuptial journey—please do not be angry with me, young people—this is not a praiseworthy custom, and it derives from

---

[73] Ibid., 24:67. See also Hirsch, *Writings*, II, 264; VIII, 107. Interestingly, Mendelssohn preferred romanticism and the free choice of a spouse over the customs of arranged betrothals and marriages. Jacob Katz regards his falling in love with Frumet Guggenheim and their personal choice of one another as a highly significant turning point in German Jewish society. See Feiner, *Mendelssohn*, 56-57. In the opinion of Chertok, *Haisha*, 37-38, Hirsch was expressing criticism of romantics like Humboldt, who opposed arranged marriages.

thoughtlessness introduced by fashion. It is proper for a young couple aware of its new happiness to reject it out of pride. For the highest joy awaits them, of entering their own home, the dwelling of their future joy and the joy of the happiness of their shared lives and their aspirations together before God, the abode of their creativity and action as man and wife, who according to the conceptions of Judaism partake of the nobility of priests in the Temple of God. And now, instead of devoting themselves to this idea and to ascend on the pathway of life together, in truth and faith, the couple turns their back on the threshold of the temple of their future home, and they take up a life of wandering and hotels that are in direct opposition to their refined and quiet home life, for which they have just become man and wife. Even less acceptable is the making a voyage by a pair of strictly observant young people, especially because of the laws setting down restrictions regarding giving mutual assistance.[74]

Hirsch was apprehensive about the many opportunities for meetings between the sexes offered by modernity and about the influence of fashion on young men and women, and he instructs them:

> Two persons of opposite sex (other than husband and wife or very near relations) should not be alone in a place which is not accessible to others (יחוד). The two sexes should not make merry together! Even if done in merriment, hand-holding and eye-winking, embracing and kissing are sinful. They tempt and provoke sin. Save yourself the battle.
>
> The most beautiful ornament of woman is modesty and moral purity. This should also be apparent in her attire, in her demeanour. The purpose of your clothing should not be to make yourself noticeable, but modest covering; your demeanour and glance should be modest. Married woman should not be seen with her hair uncovered (Even Ha'ezer, 21, 22).
>
> Not everything which fashion decrees is good, O youth and maiden! If your greatest treasure is precious to you, then listen to the call of the Torah, avoid everything which borders upon immorality, even if fashion has consecrated it a thousand times.[75]

Hirsch was very apprehensive about the hazards of modern times: "It is just in the sphere of sexual immorality that the malady of our young generation is to be found.... We have thus paid so dearly, with our most

---

74 Hirsch, *Shemesh Marpe*, 233.
75 *Horeb*, vol. 2, 311.

costly treasure, for the inflow of European culture, which the century has brought into our circle."[76] Later he writes, "Do not be led astray by the large company of those who perhaps share the same sin with you, nor by the voice of a fashionable philosophy which, instead of educating man up to truth, drags truth down to man."[77]

Hirsch was distressed because young people were seduced by modern fashions, and young men were only interested in satisfying their personal needs, and young women "resent the spirit of our fathers, who assigned to them their place in the home. Today, the ideal for which young women are educated is no longer the home, the hearth consecrated to God, but only society and its culture. The rules of fashion and good taste are the laws our daughters are taught to worship."[78]

SUMMARY

On the status of women as on many other subjects, Hirsch is much more modern than Chajes. He is far more aware of the difficulties created by the tension between the tradition and modernity, and therefore he denies the classic and Maskilic thesis of women's inferiority and states, for the first time, that they are superior. The need to preserve the tradition with modernity required him to find new solutions, sometimes revolutionary, which led him to apologetic rationalizations, tendentious selectivity of his sources, and problems in interpretation.

LUZZATTO'S RESPONSE
Background

Cohen and Feiner have the following to say about the particular attitude toward women among the Jews of Italy:

> In all of Western and Central Europe we know of only one woman who wrote in Hebrew, the poet Rachel Morpurgo, in Italy. Morpurgo's uniqueness in Western Europe can be explained to a large degree

---
76 Ibid., 312.
77 Ibid., 387.
78 Hirsch, *Writings*, II, 96-97.

by the uniqueness of Italian Jewish society, which, since the Middle Ages, had managed to combine the Jewish tradition with European culture. A liberal attitude toward woman was integrated into the traditional religious way of life (and this even became the ideal of the Jewish Maskilim outside of Italy), and we know of educated women since medieval times. Thus it is no wonder that in Italy, in the aristocratic, enlightened Luzzatto family, we find a father who gave his daughter Rachel a full, intellectual Jewish education, and this was where the first Hebrew woman poet was active.[79]

The Status of Women

As shown in the previous chapter, in his youth Luzzatto was drawn to Haskala. Like the Maskilim, he took the attitude that women were motivated by emotion and desire, whereas reason guided men, and an enlightened man had to avoid falling into the erotic trap laid by women. In 1817, at the age of seventeen, he wrote a poem entitled "Cures for Love," telling young men how to cure the plague of lust, desire for women. There he writes about women's character:

> Wake up, oh simpleton, wake up, wake up.
> Will you place your trust in woman?
> Know you not that vanity and falsehood dwell with her,
> As if the waters of Jordan flowed beneath her eyelids,
> Yet she has ruses like the heavenly hosts?[80]

In a poem of 1816 entitled, "Lovely Woman with No Sense," he describes woman as a tempting, red fruit, but in fact

> It is a net of entrapment,
> Swords of sharp flints;
> It is the east wind,
> It is the valley of ghosts.[81]

---

79 Cohen and Feiner, *'Alma*, 42.
80 Luzzatto, *Kinor Na'im*, 198.
81 Ibid., 202.

In another long poem from that year, to which he gave the title "Admonition, On Seeking False Honor," he presents, among other things, "the splendor of woman, the net of man," whose only desire is to catch man in her net. For that purpose, every organ in her body receives the appropriate treatment. He briefly describes some of her limbs: the head, the neck, the hands, the hips, and the eyes, and from there he goes on to say: "Now I shall forget them all, I shall sing my song about her br[easts]." He describes how women are aware of men's desire, "thus they wish to show their beauty outside." Women try to make their breasts as prominent as possible and to bare them, "for to catch her escort with her fishing rod, to bring man low, every woman will plot sophisticated plots"; women put the sense of shame behind them and display their wares in public, by sophisticated use of tight clothing, fastened with pressure, which fascinates men's eyes:

> And they brighten their surroundings with the
>   sparkle of their grapes
> Indeed not all the bunch of these grapes is seen outside,
> Only they leave its roots covered by the earth;
> And thus, wonder of wonders,
> Their beauty is increased, and thus they burst out,
> For their root is tightly bound,
> And while their root is pressed, their blood,
> Their grape kernels are pushed up, thus they become red,
> And thus they look plump as well.[82]

However, the tempests of youth pass, and, as a man Luzzatto begins to see more clearly, to free himself from the opinion of the rationalists, and to understand that, as with men, there are good and bad women, and women are not inherently inferior. Indeed, in another poem, "On, the Son of Pelet," which tells the story of On, whose wife saved him from death together with the followers of Korach, he makes that distinction. On's wife plied him with wine, so that he got drunk and

---

82 Ibid., 169-70.

fell asleep at home, and thus did not join the group, and did not perish with it. After his wife's wise deed was known, the tellers of tales sing her praises, singling her out as a valiant woman, intelligent and moral like few others, unlike beautiful and wealthy women:

> Fortunate are you! Man of happiness, husband of
> an intelligent wife,
> She cleaves to the line of honesty, she weighs out charity.
> He who takes a wealthy wife, takes devouring fire;
> He who takes a woman of valor, he will be joyous
> day and night.
> At every moment she will advise him, her advice is sound;
> In his work she will assist him, he will eat the work
> of her hands;
> If he becomes ill, she will nurse him, he will be cured
> by her efforts;
> He who takes a woman of valor, he will be joyous
> day and night.
> Many are the maids of beauty, wisdom was given to few;
> Therefore wear a crown, you have excelled over them all.
> With wisdom, not with wealth, will the fallen
> tabernacle rise;
> Fortunate are you! Man of happiness, husband
> of an intelligent wife.[83]

In contrast to what we saw in Galicia and Germany, the wife does not have a defined function in the house, while the husband supports the family and passes the culture down from generation to generation. A good wife, for Luzzatto, is intelligent. She advises her husband and is a full partner in his work, and thus in supporting the home.

Luzzatto devoted two poems, which he wrote at the age of sixteen or seventeen, to his relative, Rachel Morpurgo. One is called "To a

---

83 Ibid., 316-17.

Wise Woman, the Daughter of my Father's Sister," and in it he describes her as follows:

> Torah, daughter of the Creator of all, daughter
>   of the Creator of spirit,
> My princess among maidens, supporter of the tribe,
> All beauty, all splendor is in her; she will restore spirit,
> She knows every secret, she will wield the pen like a scribe.[84]

As in the second poem, in this poem Luzzatto describes Rachel's prolonged spinsterhood, for she cannot find a man after her own heart, and he wishes for her that God will quickly send her a spouse, her messiah. The second poem is apparently an answer to a letter she sent him, probably in Hebrew, in which she explained that she did not write much poetry because there was no one to read it. She criticized him for writing poetry instead of works in prose that would contain moral instruction and Torah for the foolish and straying people of the generation. He answers her with praise for her good taste, apologizes for writing so much poetry, by means of which he makes an impression on other people, as if he were wise, but he is hesitant to write in prose, meanwhile, for fear of criticism. However, he promises to her that he will yet write so that his wisdom will be revealed. On her poetry and her Hebrew, he praises her and encourages her not to fear critics but to rely on his support:

> No matter what, blessed is your taste,
> All your good sense still stands by you.
> If they draw a line against you,
> Your fragrance has not altered so far,
> Do not speak to just anyone
> For as long as I am the examiner
> Of your writing, I will find favor in it.
> May God hear your words,

---

84 Ibid., 417.

> He who helps Ishmael's mother,
> And raises them from Z to A.[85]

The full equality of men and women in every area and sense is also expressed in Luzzatto's prose. In his commentary on the Torah, *Hamishtadel* (first printed in 1846), he writes about the words in Exodus 21:10, "her food, her raiment, and her conjugal rights, shall he not diminish." Regarding conjugal rights, he adds:

> Behold, the Sages, in their wisdom and righteousness, saw that woman is not a vessel, and was not created only for the benefit and pleasure of man, but that man and woman are partners, and they join together in their desire to help one another in love and brotherhood, and not only did they make certain that the man should not deprive his wife of her rights, but they also made certain of lesser things, that the man should not decrease his wife's pleasure, for example if he says he in his garment and she in her garment (BT Ketubot 48a); and how honorable is what they say about the reward for delaying ejaculation (BT Nida 71a). And the opposite of this on the other hand is the way of scoundrels, who only seek their own pleasure, and they always prowl around and seek lewdness, and their wives are contemptible in their eyes, and they live as abandoned women and living widows. And the opposite of this on the

---

85   Ibid., 420. I am aware that the use of poetry, which is flowery and has rules of its own, to reach theoretical conclusions requires caution. In Luzzatto's case, it is easier to take his words literally. I believe there is no disagreement among scholars of modern Hebrew literature, beginning with Klausner, *Hasifrut* II, 78-79, that Luzzatto's poetry is not intuitive and written with spiritual inspiration, but rather with the intellect. "Luzzatto has a sensitive heart, but that heart is always philosophizing; the expression of this speculation is good for poetry in prose, for prosaic admonitions, but not for rhymed poetry." His poems do not have the mark of true poetry. In my opinion, a true poet writes with his heart's blood all his life, whereas Luzzatto mainly used the poetic method in his youth, like many other thinkers. See also P. Smolenskin, "Vezot Liyhuda," *Hashahar* 10 (Vienna, 1880): 459, who says that, relative to the other poets in Germany, Galicia, and Italy, Luzzatto's language is clearer, but he, too, does not have "purified language, and the spirit of poetry throbs only rarely within him, and usually he merely produced his poems"; cf. R. Bonfil, "'Lashon Sone Kazav,' Bashira, Bamehqar, Uvahazon: Qavim Lidmuto Shel Shmuel David Luzzatto," in *Italia: Shmuel David Luzzatto, Matayim Shana Lehuladeto*, ed. R. Bonfil et al. (Jerusalem, 2004), 13; Y. Friedlander, "Meqomo Shel Shmuel David Luzzatto Behitpathut Hapoetiqa Ha'ivrit," in *Italia: Shmuel David Luzzatto, Matayim Shana Lehuladeto*, 167-76.

other hand are the ways of the sophisticates, whose wives are like servants and handmaidens, and like a drug to preserve their health ("he should not engage in intercourse except when he finds his body is healthy and particularly strong, etc. etc." [Maimonides] Hilkhot De'ot ch. 4, 19). But he whose Torah is the Torah of Moses and of the Mishnah and the Talmud, he will love his wife as he loves his body, and of him it is written and you shall know that peace is in your tent (BT Yevamot 62b).

Like Hirsch, Luzzatto is selective in citing the sources, but since he does not regard the Halakhot of the Sages as Torah from Sinai, he is not reluctant to reject entirely the legends and teachings of the Sages that are not acceptable to him, and his selection is not apologetic, like Hirsch's is. Luzzatto does not conceal divine Halakhot or the stories and teachings of the Sages that do not fit his thesis, as Hirsch did, but he does ignore human rulings and stories and teachings that he finds unacceptable. Moreover, Luzzatto does not distinguish between the separate tasks of husband and wife, and he does not restrict the woman to the inside of the house. He levels severe criticism against licentious people, whose number apparently increased under the influence of modernity, secularization, and acculturation; men who abandon their wives to their sighs; and philosophers and sanctimonious scholars. There are people for whom Maimonides is a culture hero, and, in his wake, they regard women as serving their needs, sex slaves to satisfy a health need, and not human beings who have sexual needs, like their husbands, who must satisfy them in full equality.[86] In his full commentary on the Torah, which was first printed in Padua in 1871-1876, five years after his death, Luzzatto had more to say about the status of women. In his commentary on Exodus 20:10, on the fourth commandment, "Remember the Sabbath day to keep it holy," on the directive, "you shall not do any manner of work, you, nor your son, nor your daughter," Luzzatto noted that the word "your wife" is missing, whereas "your daughter" and "your maidservant," who are also women,

---

86 Mendelssohn's opinion on this matter is similar to that of Maimonides. In Mendelssohn's opinion, natural law destines men and women to a shared life of love, in order to produce progeny, but the satisfaction of desire, sensuality and pleasure from sexual relations were rejected as sinful. See Feiner, *Mendelssohn*, 154.

are explicitly mentioned. He has no doubt that wives are required to observe the Sabbath, so why are they not mentioned? His answer is:

> [the directive] undoubtedly includes the man and his wife, because it mentioned minors, your son and your daughter, and slaves, your male and female slaves. Therefore the wife equals the husband, and she is independent, like her husband, for, if the wife were subordinate to her husband like a slave woman, the husband would have to be admonished not to have her work, just as he was admonished about his children and servants, who are not independent; and this applies to all the commandments in the written Torah given in the masculine, that they include women, and the Sages (BT Berakhot 20b) exempted women from commandments that are determined by time, for it appears that in their day the situation of women changed, and men made the yoke on them heavier.

That is to say, according to the Torah, women are equal to men in every respect, and they are independent in every respect and required to keep all the commandments; although the Torah speaks only in the masculine, it intends to address men and women equally. A wife does not belong to her husband. In time, perhaps because of the influence of the Gentile surroundings, Jewish men "made their yoke heavier" and took control of women, who lost their independence and their ability to keep all the commandments, like men; then the Sages were forced to change the principled divine intention and exempted women from positive commandments subject to time, in order to make things easier for them.

As I showed above, according to Hirsch, the exemption from positive commandments subject to time required apologetics, according to which Judaism held women to be superior morally and intellectually to men, and therefore the Halakha—which was derived from Sinai, and the Sages merely reconstructed these commandments—exempted them. According to Luzzatto, the exemption from these commandments was not a reconstruction of the Halakha that was given at Sinai but a new regulation based on the opinion of the Sages, because of historical changes, for the needs of the time and the nation, and it reflects decline in the status of women in the period of the Sages, and not their ostensible superiority. Therefore, he does not need superfluous apologetics. From his point of view, true equality was sufficient and consistent with what he himself experienced in Italian culture. It appears that Luzzatto would have been pleased, if in his day there were Halakhic authorities on the level of the Sages, who could restore the earlier situation, as should be done.[87]

Luzzatto expressed similar ideas in a letter to Michael Sachs in Berlin on August 2, 1850. He also attacked Maimonides in this letter, and emphasized the full equality that women deserve according to the Torah, which is expressed in the area of sexuality. He tells Sachs that he received a book to read from its author (apparently about Jewish sects during the Second Temple period), which he did not like and did not finish. He explains why:

> The Essenes were always hateful to me, because they hated women (either they did not take wives, or if they took a wife, they only approached her to propagate the species). In my eyes this is a great abomination, because a woman is not a vessel (see Hamisthadel, Ex. 21:10), and I am very angry at Maimonides for writing: "He should not engage in intercourse except when he finds his body healthy and particularly strong, etc." as if the woman's pleasure were not a also a

---

[87] Chertok, *Haisha*, and *Qanqan*, 65-68, also noted this important difference between Luzzatto and Hirsch, but he believes that in principle, they had more in common than what divided them. In my opinion, the similarity between the two is only in the influence of the surroundings on their wish to represent Judaism as an egalitarian religion regarding women. Luzzatto was influenced by Italian culture, and Hirsch was responding to Reform, and, as Chertok shows, influenced by romanticism. However, the result was entirely different: Hirsch represents the woman in Judaism selectively and with apologetics, as having always been superior to men. Luzzatto presents a turning point in history: first there was equality, and then women were subordinated. Luzzatto's apologetics is far more subtle, and his selectivity is anchored in a historical approach. Chertok only mentions Hirsch's apologetics briefly, and his selectivity is mentioned only incidentally or in notes. It appears that Chertok is smitten with Hirsch's position, and therefore he is forgiving and not critical enough of it, regarding it as a combination of traditional conservatism and daring innovation in the spirit of the age. However, in my opinion there is also apologetics in Luzzatto. In several places in his commentary on the Torah, he states, contrary to his words here, that the Bible reflects paternalistic views that were current in its day, and according to which a wife and her children were subordinate to the head of the household. Luzzatto makes these distinctions in order to explain problematic statements of the Bible or statements that alleviated this paternalism already in the Bible or in the Sages. See the statement in Num. 30:2, and the modifications in the Torah or in the Sages in Ex. 31:3, 20.

great duty for her husband. And for several years I wondered about the saying of the Sages, that a woman who emits seed first will give birth to a boy [BT Nida 31a], until now recently God opened my eyes, and I understood that their meaning was only to plant in the hearts of men that their intention should not only be for their own pleasure, but a man whose wife is cold should try to delay ejaculation until her pleasure is full; and so that he would do so, they promised him that thereby he would have male children. And this is stated explicitly in BT Nida 71a: "As a reward for containing oneself during intercourse in the womb, in order that one's wife may emit the semen first, the Holy One, blessed be He, gives one the reward of the fruit of the womb."[88]

Luzzatto explains that, in their wisdom, the Sages knew that they could not change the actual status of woman, which was inferior, because of the influence of the surroundings, and for that reason men will prefer to have male children. To improve the status of women and bring it closer to what the divine Torah desired, the Sages promised men, with hidden irony, "If the woman emits her semen first she bears a male child" (BT Nida 31a). That is, if a man makes sure that his wife has an orgasm before he does, thereby fulfilling his obligation to provide

---

88 *Igrot Shadal*, 1087. Compare this modern interpretation to the classical interpretation of this Midrash on Lev. 12:1: "If a woman gives seed and gives birth to a boy," according to which a natural phenomenon is described (Maimonides, Ibn Ezra, Ḥizquni, Sforno, and even the author of *Torah Tmima*). Luzzatto's criticism of the attitude of philosophers to women is also directed at Spinoza, which is found in a critical essay against the pamphlet, *Teshuva Nitsaḥat*, that Solomon Rubin published against him. In *Otsar Neḥmad*, vol. 2, Luzzatto argued against Spinoza: "From where will come love for one's wife and children and the poor and the sick, who only disturb us from learning," and Rubin answered in his pamphlet: "Love of one's wife? If you have a heart of flesh, raise your eyes and see the rams mount the ewes." Luzzatto responds ironically—comparing both Spinoza and Rubin to billy goats—that Rubin is certainly not so foolish that he does not understand the difference between the love of one's wife and the love of women. "Rams that mount ewes, as well as Spinoza and his disciples, love women, and not their wives (singled out for us by the marriage canopy and the wedding ceremony). They do not take wives, and they do not raise children, because the troubles of raising children and producing them from the woman's womb is too heavy for them to bear and causes them many perturbations and distances them from their (counterfeit) learning" (Luzzatto, *Meḥqerei Hayahadut*, I, pt. 2, 215).

pleasure for her equal to the pleasure he gets from her, the result of the coupling will fulfill his wish for a male child.

Permissiveness and Natural Morality

As I showed in chapter two, Luzzatto regards the ethics of the Torah as strengthening natural morality. This is also true of relations between husband and wife. Luzzatto argues that humans are naturally disposed to social life and long-lasting marriage, and, with the commandments, the Torah and the Sages help and reinforce natural law. In the Hamishtadel commentary on Gen. 2:24, on the words, "He shall cleave unto his wife, and they shall be one flesh," he uses the Bible to present natural law:

> They cleave to each other so much, as if they were a single body.... And behold this was given to show that people are not like the other animals, that when a male encounters a female he mates with her and goes away, so that no family is joined thereby, and they do not form one band, but man is political by nature, and this is because the Creator made it inborn in him that after mating with a woman, his mind does not depart from her after satisfying his desire, so that he leaves her and goes away; rather his soul is bound up with her soul, and he loves to stay with her in society, and thereby families and states came into being. And behold the story of taking Eve from Adam's rib comes to teach that it is proper for a man to cleave to his wife, and not to act like a beast, and this will bring a man to love his wife with his body, and not to enjoy her and leave her afterward, like a donkey and a dog, and like scoundrels who have nothing at heart but enjoying themselves.

That is to say, unlike Chajes, who saw the creation of woman from the man's rib as a sign that she was subordinate to him, but one must take care not to conclude that she is to be disrespected, Luzzatto sees this as a sign that man and woman are a single body, with all that implies.

The second part of the *Lezioni di Teologia Morale Israelitica* [Lessons in Jewish Moral Theology], which Luzzatto wrote for his students in the rabbinical seminary, is devoted to the special obligations incumbent upon a Jew. The first chapter discusses the married couple. Here Luzzatto sets out his ideas about Jewish marital life, how one should choose a spouse, how to assure continuity, and how the laws of the Torah and the regulations of the Sages contribute to this. He begins the discussion by stating:

> Man is born social ... and naturally he tends to bind himself in conjugal society.... Matrimony was therefore desired by nature, which is to say, by God, the Author of nature. Matrimony, desired by nature, was consecrated by the Law of God, which prohibits adultery and punishes it by death.... Stable cohabitation supposes that there is a reciprocal inclination between the spouses, requiring that they must love one another.... Therefore he sins against the nature of matrimony and at the same time betrays the person with whom he is united,
>
> a) anyone who determines his choice by a norm other than mutual inclination;
> b) anyone who unites with a person not well known, or to whom he is not well known;
> c) anyone who unites with a person whom, for physical or moral reasons it is impossible for him to love, or by whom for some reason it will be impossible for him to be loved;
> d) anyone whose heart is occupied by another affection, or is united with a person who is in that condition, without the old passion at least beginning to subside;
> e) anyone who, loving a person, attains her almost by conquest, after having demonstrated [her] repugnance;
> f) anyone who does not know himself to be capable, or who has not firmly decided to remain inviolably faithful to the person with whom he unites in matrimony; and especially where he is infected by the licentious maxims of those who despise matrimonial fidelity, at least in the man, as ancient and primitive; or when he is so vacillating and vile in his virtue, being ashamed in the sight of depraved souls, who boast of their licentiousness.[89]

---

89 Luzzatto, *Lezioni di Teologia Morale Israelitica* (Padua, 1862), 93-96. These lessons recall Hirsch's instructions to the young people of his community on the same subject. Luzzatto condemns adultery severely; see ibid., 58-64. There he cites the words from *The Ethics of the Fathers*, "do not converse much with women" (1:5), and like Hirsch, this is not to claim that women are inferior, but to warn men of weak character, that "chiunque in questa parte alcuna cosa ceda alla concupiscenza, divenuto schiavo dell'occio e dell'immaginazione, due mezzani del peccato (עינא ולבא תרי סרסורי לחטאה), ne viene agevolmente trascinato ove meno ei vorrebbe" [Whoever gives way at all to concupiscence in this matter becomes the slave of the

Luzzatto is more modern than Hirsch. He praises marriage for love, which is more lasting, and requires extensive acquaintance between the prospective spouses before they marry, to be sure of their suitability. Evidently he rejects arranged marriages, at least if they are not preceded by sufficient acquaintance. Like Chajes and Hirsch, Luzzatto also was aware of the permissiveness and licentiousness that was prevalent among some of the young people in his generation, and he was afraid it would spread, so he took care to emphasize the importance of fidelity on every occasion. Later on, Luzzatto explains the ways to ensure successful continuation of happy married and family life—fostering disinterested love, acquiring the respect of one's spouse by ethical behavior, demonstration of respect, and mutual concessions. Later, Luzzatto explains the commandments of the Torah and the rabbinical rulings that promote and support the desired family life, such as: the groom not going to war during the first year of his marriage, the obligation to provide food, clothing, and conjugal pleasure, and the husband's obligation to his wife and hers to him. Since these were lessons for future rabbis, Luzzatto presents the Halakhot of the Talmud as they appear there, but it is evident that he is not content with all of them, and he tries to moderate some of them, such as the woman's obligation to do housework, appear modest, and serve her husband and do his bidding. Here, too, the quotation of ancient rabbinical sources regarding women is extremely selective. Luzzatto lists only the Halakhot that do not explicitly condemn the nature and character of women, and which can be interpreted as contributing to a successful marriage.[90]

On the duty of modesty incumbent upon the wife, Luzzatto says: "any wife who goes out into the street with her head uncovered or her arms bare, and converses or jokes with anyone in the marketplace, is violating the ancient constitutions of the Hebrew nation (דת יהודית; legge giudaica)."[91]

---

eye and of the imagination, two panderers of sin (the eye and the heart are two procurers of sin), is easily led where he would not like to go] (ibid., 60).
90 See ibid., 99-105.
91 Ibid., 102. Interestingly, Luzzatto does not relate to the subject of wigs at all. This is also true of his letter to Salman Stern of Nyitra, Hungary, of April 1837. Stern had sent him two articles that attacked the rabbis, which apparently sought to

It is important to emphasize that Luzzatto did not include Rabbi Eli'ezer's prohibition against women studying Torah. Apparently, Luzzatto thought this was a prohibition in the opinion of Rabbi Eli'ezer and was appropriate to its time as a regulation regarding women when the status of woman had declined under the influence of the surrounding culture, and Luzzatto thought that it no longer applied in his time.

In some of the communities of Italy, especially in the North, which belonged to the Austro-Hungarian Empire, decent schools were established for Jewish boys and girls according to the curriculum set by Wessely in the early Haskala period in Berlin. In addition, boys studied with their fathers and with private tutors to increase their knowledge. This was also true in Trieste, the city where Luzzatto was born and studied as a boy.[92] The question of women's intellectual inferiority was not at all on the agenda. Rachel Morpurgo, who read and wrote in Hebrew on a high level, proves the point.

In the commentary on Deuteronomy 23:2 in *Hamishtadel*, on the words, "No one whose testicles are crushed or whose male organ is cut off shall enter the assembly of the Lord," Luzzatto emphasizes the importance of obeying the commandments of the Torah and the Sages to strengthen natural law on the subject of sexuality. The prohibition against marrying a castrated man was meant to prevent a situation where a woman would be unable to fulfill her obligation to populate the world:

---

rescind the prohibition against married women baring their head as well as the prohibition against shaving on the intermediate days of festivals, and he asked Luzzatto to send them on, with a recommendation, to the editor of *Kerem Ḥemed* for publication. Luzzatto was opposed to permitting married women to bare their heads but agreed with the permission to shave on the intermediate days. However, he decided not to recommend publication of the articles, because of the style: "I am not at all pleased with these articles, and far be it from me to be aroused to help publish slander against the Jewish religion, after everything that I see with my eyes, the leprosy of wantonness and adultery spreading increasingly among the Jews after women began to throw that law behind their back, or, if you will, that custom. While about shaving I have no objection, nevertheless I am not pleased with that article, because you spoke ill of the rabbis of your country, and it was possible and worthy and obligatory to state your opinion without speaking ill of the rabbis" (*Igrot Shadal*, 383).

92 See Klausner, *Hasifrut* II, 48-49.

> You should know that Roman women chose to have intercourse with castrated men, so that they would not become pregnant.... Blessed be God who has sanctified us with His Torah and commandments, and made intercourse to propagate the race and help society succeed, not only for temporary pleasure. The Sages also followed in the footsteps of the blessed Giver of the Torah (as was always their way), and they issued many regulations and warnings to keep all sorts of lewdness at a distance, and to increase suitable unions, and peace in the home, and success of parents and children, and their love for each other; and all of this has been kept by the Jews during the exile, until the generation that was before us.

Luzzatto is therefore well aware of the inroads of modernity, which had recently penetrated the heart of the Jewish community, for good and for evil. He maintains that the laws of abstaining from intercourse during menstruation also contributes to the success of matrimony and preserve the family framework. In a letter to Isaac Blumenfeld, the editor of *Otsar Neḥmad* starting in 1857, he argues against Jacob Reifman's book, *Toldot Rabenu Zeraḥia Halevi*, which was published in 1853. Reifman claimed that Rabenu Zeraḥia Halevi had included nonsense from Greek mythology in his poetry. Luzzatto argued that Reifman had misunderstood the words of the poem: "(ה"הקב) והזהיר אל-אשת נעורים מִגֶּשֶׁת, ותופש הקשת בלי יורה צִדָה" [And God warned (him) not to approach the wife of one's youth, and one who holds the bow not to shoot to her side]. Reifman had explained that "the one who holds the bow" was the god of love, Amor (Eros, Cupid). Luzzatto explained that the poem referred to the Jewish man, gripped by desire—holding the bow—while his wife was menstruating. According to Luzzatto, Rabbi Zeraḥia Halevi was warning the man not to betray his wife on the side while she was ritually impure due to menstruation. Reifman's interpretation, says Luzzatto:

> Is not possible, because it could not be that the Torah said, perish the thought, that a man should not love his wife at all times and hours, and on the contrary the laws of menstruation increase love between the Jew and his wife, because the Jewish woman is always a new bride, and this is a great principle in the success of the home and the nation; and behold desire fires its arrows at all times in the heart of the Jew, and the Torah did not prohibit this, but it did prohibit

closeness in flesh sometimes, not closeness in hearts, and the poet hinted about this with the metaphor used by the Sages of blessed memory of shooting like an arrow [יורה כחץ], and he compared the husband to a hero holding a bow, and he said he must not shoot his arrows to her side.

Moreover, Luzzatto argues, neither Reifman nor Geiger had understood the next lines of the poem: "הפוגה לנוגה בשושנים סוגה תנה מתענוגה בשדות ושדה" [Give repose to נוגה, surrounded by lilies, from giving her pleasure to שדות ושידה]. Reifman interprets נוגה as the star Nogah, Venus, and thus as the goddess Aphrodite, the mother of Eros, who grasps the bow, who arouses the man's lust. Geiger cites the interpretation of Zacharias Frankel, who explained that the poem was referring to the wife, whose light glowed like the planet Venus, and he claims that both interpretations were wrong, and that the poet was referring to the man's soul, which was sad [נוּגָה, *nuga*] during the time of his wife's ritual impurity. Luzzatto is surprised that Geiger had forgotten the Midrash cited by Rashi on the verse in the Song of Songs 7:3, "surrounded by lilies." Luzzatto explains that the poem refers to the sorrowing soul of the man while his wife is ritually impure, and to him Rabbi Zeraḥia Halevi says: "give a rest to your sorrowing soul, which is sorry about (from the expression "בתולותיה נוגות" [her virgins are sad]) the prohibition against menstrual impurity, and it also fences itself off because of the prohibition (as in the words of the aforementioned Midrash) not to seek pleasure with female demons [שֵׁדָה וְשֵׁדוֹת, *sheda veshadot*], that is, with other women, during the days when your wife is impure."[93]

In conclusion, I cite Luzzatto's words, which summarize his opinion and combine the importance of marital union, as expressed in

---

93 *Otsar Neḥmad* 2 (1857): 181. See Geiger's remarks there; he also cites Frankel on page 8. Geiger's words imply that Frankel also interpreted "who holds the bow" the way Luzzatto did. It should be emphasized here that Luzzatto's critique is hermeneutic, not theological. He did not reject Reifman's interpretation because he introduced mythology in Zeraḥia's poem. Luzzatto himself brought mythology into the story of the creation, but he purified it and stated that the mythological figures were human beings, and they are spoken of in the Torah, in order to inform the Jews of this. According to Luzzatto, Jubal is Apollo, Tubal Cain is Vulcan, Na'ama is Venus, and he also mentions Iris, Bacchus, Troy, and Hercules. See his commentary on Gen. 4:20-21, 22; 9:20; 10:4, 9.

the regulations of the Sages, and his view regarding the equal status of women. In a letter to Rapoport from Tishrei 1840, he discusses, among other things, the regulations of the Tannaim presented in the Babylonian Talmud, Mo'ed Qatan 23a, and in the Jerusalem Talmud, Yevamot 4:11: "If a man's wife dies, he is forbidden to marry another woman until three festivals have passed." The Tosafot explain, s.v. "until three festivals": "Until three festivals have passed without joy, and he will not forget his love for his wife. Or else: so that when he marries another woman there will be no memory of the first wife, so there will not be two minds in bed. And also: Lest he mention to her his love for his wife, to spite her."

Luzzatto discusses the first two reasons presented by Tosafot. In his opinion the first reason is also that given by the Rif [Isaac ben Jacob Alfasi ha-Cohen], meaning "that it appears as if he did not care about the death of his wife." In Luzzatto's opinion, Tosafot prefers the second reason, which is also the one offered by the Ran [Nissim of Gerona], meaning, "So that he will forget her and not remember her during intercourse." On these reasons Luzzatto says:

> Both of these reasons are solid for a person of understanding and correct to those with good sense, because the ways of the Torah are pleasant, and all its pathways are peace, and all the laws and judgments that the Torah commanded us and that the Sages commanded, between man and his fellow, all of them are for the benefit of the society and the success of people and their peace with one another. And behold, if it were permissible for a man to take a new wife immediately after the death of his first wife, the importance of matrimony would lose a great deal, and a man's impulse would tell him that woman was created only for his pleasure and utility, and in the eyes of her husband a wife would be like a vessel that one uses for the benefit in it, and nothing else, and if it breaks, one replaces it with another, and one is sorrowful only about the monetary loss. But in fact a spouse was not made for that, and man was not created for this, so that his coupling is the mounting of a beast, only for his pleasure and utility, but the Creator stamped in human nature that a man should cleave to his wife with his soul, and she should be his comrade for the benefit of both of them, and the pleasure of both of them, and one will help the other. And the wife will be an instrument for her husband's success, and the husband an instrument for

> his wife's success, and both of them instruments for the success of their children, and all of them instruments for the success of the society.... And behold the prohibition against taking a new wife immediately after the death of the first one, is also, on the other hand, the reason noted by Rabenu Tam, which is by the cooling off of his love for the first wife, he can love the second one with all his heart, and the joy of three festivals will give relief of his grief and prepare his heart to make a new wife happy.[94]

That is to say, the first reason emphasizes the importance of the wife from the first marriage, and the second, the importance of the wife of the second marriage, and both of them are correct and important. The motive of the rabbis behind both of the reasons is the same: to assure equal status of the woman in the opinion of the man. God, who created nature, did not create women as inferior to men, but as equal to them in pleasure, utility, tasks, and successes, while husband and wife cleave to one another in their souls in mutual love. These are views that post-modern feminism can accept.

SUMMARY

Among the modern Jews who observed the commandments, as early as the nineteenth century we find well-grounded opinions in the direction of improving the status of women. Indeed, as one would expect in the period, when everyone was seeking a meta-narrative to explain man and the world, there is some degree or another of apologetics in these views. The three thinkers of the middle trend were aware that the new era was influencing the issue of the status of women and the relations between the sexes in a significant manner, for good and for evil. For good: in the respect due to every human being, who possesses basic rights, and even full equality. For evil: in the permissive attitude toward sex that they believed was liable to lead to moral degradation. Chajes was the most conservative in this area, as in other areas of modernity. He clung to the classical and Maskilic theory of the natural inferiority of women, which the canonical writings of Judaism support. The moral decline impelled him, on

---

94 *Kerem Ḥemed* 7 (1843): 52-53.

the one hand, to intensify supervision in matters of modesty, such as prohibiting women from wearing wigs and studying Torah. On the other hand, it led him to warn men not to sin and disrespect women because of their inferiority.

Hirsch was under far more pressure than Chajes. The more rapid pace of modernization and acculturation in Germany and the theories of women's equality of the Reform movement made it necessary for him to discover a revolutionary solution to the status of women in Judaism. According to the apologetic and paradoxical theory that he developed, the Sages believed that, according to the Torah, women were superior to men, and therefore they do not need the many commandments that men, weak in character, need for protection against the evil impulse. Therefore, women were exempt according to the divine Halakha from positive commandments dependent on time and from the commandment of Torah study. As a result of the natures of men and women, and despite the equality between them in principle, God determined a division of labor between men and women, so that the woman was responsible for the moral preservation of the home and the family, and the man was responsible for earning a living, involvement in public life, and the transmission of Jewish culture from generation to generation. The state of equality that existed in the Garden of Eden was violated by sin. Woman was made subject to man, who worked for a living, but the way of the Torah saved mankind by maintaining harmonious family life, preserving the family from moral degradation, and ultimately it would restore humanity to the Garden of Eden. Hirsch permitted himself to be selective and ignore the dominant school in rabbinical thought regarding the inferiority of women, quoting only those sayings of the Sages that praise women, and thereby he was able to claim, with egregious apologetics, that the status of women at the time of the Sages was excellent. Ultimately, as a result of his theory, Hirsch ran into interpretative problems regarding several sayings about women in the Torah and several Halakhot. Out of consideration for women's superiority and their important tasks, Hirsch made sure to include girls in his school and to teach them Hebrew and Judaism in a systematic and organized way.

Luzzatto lived in Italy, a more tolerant and egalitarian Jewish society with respect to the status of women, and less tempestuous ideologically. Luzzatto did not believe that the Halakhot of the Sages were from Mount Sinai, and, unlike Chajes, he was not constrained to adopt the thesis of women's inferiority. Nor was he forced to develop an apologetic theory of women's superiority in order to save traditional Judaism from modernity and Reform. Luzzatto was the most progressive and modern of the three. From his point of view, according to the divine Torah and in the ancient period, there was full equality in Judaism between men and women in every respect, including the obligation to keep all the commandments, and it required full cooperation between them in education and Torah study, and in functions in the home and outside it.

If the Halakha exempted women from some of the commandments and from Torah study, this was the result of decline in the status of women during the period of those who instituted these laws, and this exemption was not a reconstruction of Halakhot from Sinai that indicate the natural inferiority or superiority of women. If there are expressions of contempt for women in the Talmud, these can be ignored and dismissed with the argument that they should never have been included in the canon, or to admit with regret that they reflect the unjustified decline in the status of women in the time of the Sages. Like his two predecessors, Luzzatto was also aware of the problem of sexual permissiveness, which modernity brought with it, and it made him very apprehensive. Like them, at every opportunity he emphasizes the importance of matrimony and fidelity, the despicable nature of betrayal and adultery, and the error of obeying the decrees of fashion, showing how the commandments of the Torah and the regulations of the Sages on these matters defend and strengthen matrimony, also promising continued desire and love between the spouses. He speaks of mutual love between spouses who knew each other well before marrying and are willing to provide satisfaction and success to one another in every sense, with lifelong fidelity.

CHAPTER SIX

The Relation to the Other: Religious Tolerance

BACKGROUND

In this chapter I discuss the attitudes of Chajes, Hirsch, and Luzzatto toward the two other monotheistic religions with which they were familiar: Christianity, among whose faithful they lived as a tolerated minority which was beginning to obtain civil rights, and Islam, which they knew mainly from the books available to them, and to a degree from the history and geography they studied in school or by themselves. Only a small fraction of their discussion relates to Islam, and that fraction hardly relates at all to the content of Islam, which was not known to them. Hence, in discussing the background I will only treat Christianity. A reader interested in concentrated information about Islam and its proximity and deep similarity to Judaism may read the writings of Ignác Goldziher and Hava Lazarus-Yafeh.[1]

---

1 I. Goldziher, *Introduction to Islamic Theology and Law*, trans. Andras and Ruth Hamori (Princeton, 1981); H. Lazarus-Yafeh, *Haislam, Qavei Yesod* (Tel Aviv, 1980); idem, *Islam-Yahadut—Yahadut-Islam* (Tel Aviv, 2003). It appears that Chajes, Hirsch, and Luzzatto were unaware of Muslim criticism of Judaism. Had they known about it, most likely they would not have praised Islam without reservation, and they would have related to the criticism, even though that religion did not

Christianity emerged on the stage of history in the first century CE and is based on belief that Jesus was the messiah. In the *Hebrew Encyclopedia*, Christianity is defined as follows: "A monotheistic religion, historical and messianic, one of the largest in the world, according to which the relation between God and man is attained through the intermediary of Jesus, the messiah, the founder of the faith."[2] The article on Jesus in the Hebrew Encyclopedia, written by Gideon Freudenberg and Yeshayahu Leibowitz, states that Jesus was

> the central figure in the Christian faith ... claiming to fulfill and embody the Jewish Torah, Christianity identifies Jesus as the messiah, referred to—or hinted at by the missions of the prophets.... By virtue of the death and atonement of Jesus, every human (who believes in Jesus) is redeemed from the sin that clings to the human race and from the punishment for it. In this respect, Jesus is the redeemer and savor of humanity.... As a continuation of pagan mythology, Christianity presents the messiah as "the son of God"— born of a woman who was made pregnant by the Holy Spirit, the embodiment of the divinity in flesh and blood.... In other words: Jesus is the divinity of Christianity.[3]

In fact, "Jesus was a Jew, lived in the Jewish faith, and died for it. He was born 'beneath the Torah' (Galatians 4:4) and did not want to be an improver or reformer of Judaism."[4]

Thus, according to early Christian sources, it appears that Jesus was a Jew who obeyed the commandments in the manner of the Pharisees, who had a personal ethical teaching. He acted only among the Jews, and it appears that he did not seek to reform Judaism or to establish a new religion, but rather to emphasize the moral aspect of the religion. Since he thought of himself as the messiah, he sought "to plant the idea of the advent of the messiah among his people and to hasten

---

threaten them. No Jewish meta-narrative can ignore the claim that Judaism has falsified its doctrine and concealed information about the prophecy of Muhammad, or that Abraham was the first Muslim monotheist, and that Islam is the original monotheism, which appeared in the religion of Abraham. See Goldziher, *Islamic Theology*, 10; Lazerus-Yafeh, *Haislam*, 27-29; idem, *Yahadut*, 29-31, 75-79.

2 *Entsiqlopedia 'Ivrit*, vol. 25, s.v. נצרות [Christianity].
3 Ibid., vol. 20, 412.
4 D. Flusser, *Yahadut Umeqorot Hanatsrut* (Tel-Aviv, 1979), 448.

the end of days through repentance and good deeds."⁵ However, his disciple, Paul, a Diaspora Jew who had grown up in Hellenistic culture, was essentially the founder of Christianity. Having "decided to cut himself off from the Jews and concentrate on the Gentiles, he began to create the boundary between the two religions."⁶

Both religions were persecuted by pagan Rome until the first quarter of the fourth century, and their relations were complex and intricate,

> sometimes with no distinction between Jew and Christian. Only later was Christianity made the official religion of the Roman Empire.... From that time on, the daughter-sister began to persecute her mother-sister with ferocity. Christianity could not forget the fact that Jesus was Jewish, but it could also not give up the accusation against the Jews of responsibility for the crucifixion and their stubborn refusal to accept his message.⁷
>
> Until the fourth century, the term "Edom" was a synonym for pagan Rome, which had destroyed the Temple and banished the nation, and all the prophecies about future revenge against Edom were applied to Rome. Beginning in the fourth century, when the empire adopted Christianity, the identification of Edom with Rome received double meaning: religious and political, the Christian church and the Roman Empire. The Christians set up the reverse equation, inspired by Paul: Jacob=Christians; Esau=Jews.⁸

Jesus's disciples and followers, beginning with Paul and the Evangelists, laid the theological foundation of Christianity and created the myths around the figure of Jesus. Central to Paul's thinking were the following principles, whose source was Essene:

---

5 Klausner, *Yeshu Hanotsri, Ḥayav Vetorato* (Tel-Aviv, 1969), vol. 2, 203. See 197-203 there on Jesus's Judaism and his goals. See also Flusser, *Hanatsrut*, 448-455; idem, *Haemunot Vehade'ot Shel Haknesia Hanotsrit Harishona*, ed. T. and Y. Katz (based on lectures) (Jerusalem, 1964), 72-76. On the life of Jesus, his place and time, and the messianic idea that motivated him, see O. Limor, *Bein Yehudim Lenotsrim* (Tel-Aviv, 1993), vol. 1, 46-59.
6 S. Simonsohn, *Hakes Haqadosh Vehayehudim* (Tel-Aviv, 1994), 12.
7 A. Shinan, "Petaḥ Davar," in *Oto Haish: Yehudim Mesaprim 'Al Yeshu*, ed. A. Shinan (Tel-Aviv, 1999), 10. See also Flusser, *Hanatsrut*, 449.
8 I. J. Yuval, *Shnei Goyim Bevitnekh* (Tel-Aviv, 2000), 66-67.

1. Justice and divine mercy are attained by faith and not by obeying the laws of the Torah.
2. The dualistic principle of the ancient decree and the compassionate choice of the sons of light; however, whereas for the Essenes the sons of light were the members of their cult, which is to say part of the Jewish people, for Paul, they were the Gentiles who believed in Jesus.
3. The dualistic principle of flesh versus spirit, the sin of the flesh—Original Sin—from which man is powerless to free himself, and only God can choose him and redeem him in an act of grace. According to the Essenes, and certainly for the Pharisees, repentance and performing the commandments of the Torah would lead to their being chosen by God, but according to Paul, the commandments of the Torah lead to increased sin, and only faith in the atonement that Jesus the messiah brought in his death and resurrection leads to choice by God and redemption.[9]

Regarding the Jews and Judaism, Paul and his disciples determined that

> the Jews rejected Jesus and caused his crucifixion, and for these sins God punished them with a double punishment: they lost their special status as the people chosen by God, and they also lost their political independence and the Temple. After Jesus's mission was rejected by the Jews, it was offered to the Gentiles. They accepted it, and the special status of the true Israel (verus Israel) was accorded to them. The destruction of Jerusalem and the dispersion of the Jews throughout the world were thought of both as a punishment to the Jews and as proof of their sins. Several conclusions derive from this structure: the Old Testament belongs to the true Children of Israel; it was taken away from the Jews of the flesh, the ancient Israelites, and transferred to their spiritual heirs, the new Israelites. In their blindness and stubbornness, the Jews refused to admit to these changes and accept them. Most, though not all, of the commandments were also interpreted as having only spiritual meaning, and the events and prophecies of the Old Testament were given

---

9 According to Flusser, *Hanatsrut*, 259-380. On Paul, the background from which he came, and the ideas he developed in Christianity against that background, see Limor, *Lanotsrim*, 59-65. On the doctrine of grace, redemption, and Original Sin, see ibid., 100.

christological meaning. The Jews could not be saved unless they accepted Christianity; but it was to be hoped—indeed it was prophesied—that this would happen one day.[10]

Contrary to the opinions of Joseph Salvador and Joseph Klausner, David Flusser—to whom the Essene library, discovered in the Judean Desert, was accessible—believed there was no significant pagan or Hellenistic influence on early Christianity, and that most of its sources were Jewish. On the first level, in the time of Jesus, there was Pharisaic influence, and, beginning with the second level—the time of Paul—it was also influenced by the Essenes and by Jewish mystics, who possessed mystical traditions. Thus dogmas were accepted and established in Christianity, such as regarding Jesus as a god who returned to life from the dead, the determination that his mother was impregnated by the Holy Spirit, so that she remained a virgin, belief in the redemptive power of eating the god's flesh and drinking his blood, and representation of the divinity as a trinity composed of three essences.[11]

Augustine was the one who determined the status of the Jews among the Christians for many generations.

> The Jews are the enemies of the church, Augustine argued, and therefore Christians must be defended against them. The Jews must be subject to the church and its servants. However, in the end, even they, despite their lowly position, will be saved, when the church and the synagogue unite. Until this takes place, Augustine believed, the presence of Jews within Christian society must be tolerated; for they bear living witness to the origin of Christianity, and therefore they are guarantors of its truth. They preserve the holy scriptures, although they did not understand them and interpreted them incorrectly.[12]

---

10 Simonsohn, *Hakes*, 12.
11 On the holy trinity, see, for example, D. Flusser, *Haemunot Vehadeot Shel Haknesia Hanotsrit Harishona*, ed. Z. Kats and Y. Kats (from lectures, Jerusalem, 1964), 99-114; Limor, *Lanotsrim*, 110-14. On the mass of breads and wine, see Flusser, *Haknesia*, 123; idem, *Hanatsrut*, 115-19. On the virgin birth, see idem, *Haknesia*, 133-35. On the resurrection and ascension of Christ, see ibid., 55-60. On the transubstantiation of the bread and wine, see Limor, *Lanotsrim*, 102-3. On the sacraments, see ibid., 106.
12 Simonsohn, *Hakes*, 14.

Paul's words and those of Augustine, which were ratified time and time again by the popes throughout the Middle Ages, were the background of the hatred of the Jews that developed among the Christians, and the results were the Crusades, the Inquisition in Spain and elsewhere, pogroms, murder and torture, blood libels, and attempts at forced conversion.

Wherever Christianity prevailed, the Jews were relegated to the lowest social class, and they were denied all civil rights. They were not permitted to serve in any governmental or communal position, they were not allowed to purchase land or to receive permanent citizenship, they were forced to support themselves with small businesses and money-lending for interest, and only a small minority of them engaged in international trade and banking, providing financial aid to the rulers, so that they were attached the courts. Despite their low financial state, the Jews were usually exploited by the rulers, who demanded extra taxes from them, and from time to time they were expelled. This trap created the stereotype of the Jew as the enemy of Christianity by nature of his religion, and morally deficient, always suspected of deceit, and culturally backward.

Usually, the Jews showed impressive obstinacy resisting the persecution of the Christians, and there were many instances of martyrdom. The Jews remained faithful to their religion and the Torah of Moses, and they continued to observe meticulously all the religious commandments in the written and Oral Law, as consolidated in the Mishnah and the Talmud. The rabbis—the community leaders—succeeded through their personalities, their leadership, and their mastery of the Torah, in guiding the nation and preventing its assimilation or extinction. The Jews attributed their survival to Providence and persisted in their expectation of the true messiah from the House of David, who would come and redeem them, and they believed that a person's true reward awaited in the world to come. Therefore, their suffering in this world and the success of the Christians were not at all proof that Christianity was right.

Although Christianity was a monotheistic religion and combated paganism, the Jews regarded it as idolatrous, because of the belief in a god that had been embodied in flesh and blood, and belief in the Holy Trinity. Hatred of the persecutor and expectation of God's revenge against him were part of the Jews' messianic hopes.

During the Middle Ages, European rulers held a number of public debates between prominent rabbis and learned Christians or Jewish converts to Christianity. These debates treated the subjects that were always at issue between Jews and Christians, in an effort to determine which was the true religion.[13]

The Jewish response to the figure of Jesus developed over time. In antiquity the subject was ignored (either intentionally or because of censorship) or treated sporadically and partially. During the Middle Ages satirical works were written, as well as works that wrestled with Christian dogmas and arguments, with the aim of refuting them. The following strategies were adopted by those who participated in the inter-religious debates:

1. Denial and contradiction of what was written about Jesus, pointing out the difficulties that arise from the stories of the New Testament.
2. Acknowledgment of what was told about him, while distinguishing him from the Jewish prophets.
3. Positive attitudes toward him, though he still was regarded as a false prophet:
   A. Recognition of his role in spreading the messianic idea.
   B. Distinction between him and the religion that was unjustifiably attached to his figure by his followers.

In the modern period, the latter argument was repeated, and tolerance was shown to Jesus,[14] but there remained a traditional minority who continued the polemic against his figure and actions.[15]

---

13 See Limor, *Lanotsrim*, vol. 3.
14 See, for example, Klausner, *Yeshu*.
15 This account of the historical development of Jewish attitudes toward Jesus is based on Shenan, "Petah," 11-12.

During the Middle Ages, there were vicissitudes in the life of the Jews among the Christians, but even in quiet times they lived as a subjected and tolerated people, mainly because of their economic contribution to the rulers of the state. Where Jews lived under Islam, there was less persecution and forced conversion, and during extended periods the Jews lived in relative peace with their Muslim neighbors, in a golden age.

Judah Halevi and Maimonides—who defined Islam as a monotheistic religion and Christianity as idol worship, and permitted the teaching of Torah to Christians but forbade teaching it to Muslims—developed an approach according to which the other monotheistic religions were part of God's plan for human history and were a preliminary stage preparing for the advent of the true messiah and the true worship of God, through Torah and the commandments, by all of humanity, as Judaism expects.[16]

Despite the Protestant Reformation, inaugurated by Martin Luther (1483-1546) and others, which attacked and sought to abolish the papacy and the corrupt Catholic church, fostered a direct relation between the believer and scripture without the intermediary of a priest or church, and rejected some of the dogmas, Christianity remained steadfast in its hatred of the Jews. Luther himself wrote at first that he understood the Jews in their time, who were repelled, as he was, by corrupt, papal Christianity. However, since they were unwilling to be convinced and convert, even after his reform, he altered his positive attitude toward the Jews at the end of his life. He was furious that

---

16 See the background to chapter four. On Maimonides's complex attitude toward Christians and Muslims, see Ravitzky, *'Iyunim*, 262-75. On page 36, Ravitzky notes that it is not surprising that Judah Halevi addresses religions as a collective phenomenon, whereas Maimonides emphasizes the human figures of Jesus and Muhammad. Each of them follows his general approach: did the leader (like Moses) rise by the power of the nation (Judah Halevi) or did the leader establish the nation (Maimonides)? For a discussion of the attitude toward Christianity of medieval Jewish thinkers, see R. Ben Shalom, *Mul Tarbut Notsrit: Toda'a Historit Vedimui 'Avar Beqerev Yehudei Sefarad Uprovans Biyemei Habeinayim* (Jerusalem, 2007), ch. 3-4. There he discusses the high degree of exposure of the medieval Jews to the history and historiography of the nations among whom they lived, and their conception of the past of Christianity and its culture, which shaped their attitudes toward Jesus, the origin of Christianity, and the history of the Church.

the Jews continued to reject the divine revelation of Jesus, the messiah, and in 1543 he wrote that all the Jews should be sent to the Land of Israel, and if that was not possible, they should be forbidden to lend money for interest, and they should be forced to earn their livings by tilling the soil, their synagogues should be burnt, and their books, including the Bible, should be taken from them.[17]

Luther reviled the Jews vehemently, stated that they poison wells and drink the blood of Christians, and therefore the houses of Jews should be destroyed, their property, accumulated illicitly, should be confiscated, they should not be allowed to enter or pass through the country or to travel on main roads, rabbis should be forbidden to teach, and they should be expelled.[18] The idea of Original Sin was reasserted by the Calvinists, who taught predestination: only divine grace, and not any action by an individual, a priest, or the church, could redeem one from sin.[19]

The Protestants abandoned five of the seven Catholic sacraments, retaining only baptism and the Eucharist. They stated that the church was not the earthly, hierarchical established church, but rather the community of believers, and they rejected monasticism and its institutions.[20]

The situation of the Jews of Europe improved slightly, and became more stable, from the second half of the sixteenth century until the mid-eighteenth century. In many cities, the Jews were restricted to ghettos. They differed from the Gentile population in costume, appearance, and language, and they were considered to be servants of the king. The right of residence always depended on the grace of the ruler, and it was necessary to assure the proper behavior of every individual. Withdrawal and social separation reduced tensions between the two religions and increased indifference. Contact between Jews and

---

17 R. H. Bainton, *Here I Stand: A Life of Martin Luther* (New York, 1950), 379-80.
18 See E. G. Rupp, *Martin Luther and the Jews* (London, 1972), 17.
19 For a readable and still reliable account of the rise of Protestantism, see the classic H. A. L. Fisher, *A History of Europe*, ch. 57, 58, and 60 (originally published in 1935), and the appendix to chapter 3 by R. Kavner in the Hebrew addition, trans Y. Kopelevitsh-Keshet (Jerusalem and Tel Aviv, 1964), 197-208.
20 On the principles of Catholicism and Protestantism, see ibid.

Christians in the areas of the economy, finance, and commerce continued to spread. All of this made possible more moderate thought about Christianity among the Jews. Therefore, there was an increased tendency among Halakhic authorities to state that Christianity and Judaism had much in common, and that contemporary Christians were not the pagans castigated by the Talmud. Thus it was permitted to trade with them and forbidden to cheat them.

This tendency is already present to a degree in the permission granted by Rabenu Tam to accept the oath of a Christian, and in the approach of Meiri, who was the first to remove Christianity from the category of paganism. However, Meiri's writings were not known then, and the one who disseminated this idea was Moses Rivkes, the author of Beer Hagola, in his notes on the Shulḥan 'Arukh from the seventeenth century. His argument was that, like the Jews, Christians believe in the creation of the world, the Exodus from Egypt, the Revelation, and the tradition of the Torah and the prophets, and they observe an organized and reasonable system of laws; this makes relations of trade possible and requires ethical decency toward them.[21]

In the eighteenth century, rationalism and secularism increased in the society surrounding the Jews of Europe, and in its wake came criticism on the part of enlightened Christians of classical, dogmatic Christianity, as well as tolerance toward members of other religions. The centralized state, based on a money economy, ascended onto the stage of history, and the idea of the separation of church and state was spread by thinkers such as John Locke and John Toland, who also advocated granting rights to the Jews.

These developments gave rise on the Jewish side to the need for an outlook that would make easy contact possible between the two societies, when this was necessary. Hence, Jacob Emden determined, "Jesus never intended to revoke the authority of the Torah, and his only purpose was to spread the principles of the Jewish faith, that is, the seven Noahide commandments, among the Gentiles; the conflict

---

21 See Katz, *Masoret*, 19-57; idem, *Bein Yehudim Legoyim* (Tel-Aviv, 1961), 35-56, 116-66; idem, *Hayetsia*, 16-33.

between Judaism and Christianity and the persecution of the Jews by Christians w[ere] therefore the results of tragic misunderstanding."[22]

However, aside from changes in the hostile views on either side, almost nothing changed regarding social separation and ways of life. Emden's unreservedly positive attitude toward Christianity, as expressed in *Resen Mat'e*, provided a source for inter-religious tolerance on the part of the Jews in the nineteenth century. Hence it is appropriate to examine it in greater detail.

Emden thought that there was no difference of opinions between Jesus and Paul. Paul was, in his opinion, a learned man, the assistant of Rabban Gamliel the elder, and expert in the laws of the Torah. Jesus and Paul believed that the Jews must continue to observe the Torah, which is eternal, whereas non-Jewish Christians must only observe the seven Noahide commandments. Christianity is not a new religion but directed at exactly the same things as Judaism.

Emden explained that the Gentiles practiced baptism instead of circumcision, and instead of the Sabbath, they made Sunday the day of rest for the Gentiles. Their slight condemnation of the Jews, as if the Torah were revoked along with the status of the Jews as the nation of the Lord, and that Christians would be in their place, was merely a ruse: on the one hand, to flatter the Gentiles, who hated the Jews, so they would accept the seven Noahide commandments, and on the other hand, to be sure they would not be envious and desire to be like the Jews. This was beneficial to the Jews, enabling them to observe their Torah in peace, because the principles of Judaism would take root and be observed by all the nations.

> But after that the multitude was seduced by the words of ignorant priests, and over time they sank into alien opinions, because they did not understand the advice of their ancestors (who hid their real thought in their heart), and they did not plumb the depths of their thought. They became very distant from the center. For that reason they despise the Jews. And from the stars they brought down those who justify the many. And they reviled the angels of God for being observers of His covenant and His orders to do them. And

---

22 Katz, *Yehudim*, 166; idem, *Hayetsia*, 34-46.

their accusation is idle.... The Nazarene did double good in the world, as it appears clearly and openly as this very day. On the one hand he strengthened and observed the Torah of Moses in all its strength, as mentioned above, very clearly. This cannot be denied, and none of our Sages asserted more than that in assuring the eternal existence of the Torah. And on the other hand, for the nations of the world, he did great good, if they do not overturn his desirable intention for them in the way that several madmen did, who did not fully understand the authors of the Gospels. And they paid evil back for good: ... [The Nazarene] revoked idol worship and removed the statues from the nations, and he required them to observe the seven commandments and also the Ten Commandments. So they would not be like beasts of the field. And he privileged them with ethical principles. And thereby he was far more severe with them than the Torah of Moses, as is known (he commanded them to give everything to the poor. And to one who asks for an outer garment, to give the inner one as well. And who slaps him one cheek, that he will also let him strike the other cheek, and that he will be content with humility, as I said above, and the like. And there are many similar directives with him) and this is also correct in itself. For it is the correct path for acquiring ethical virtues.[23]

That is to say, Jesus, Paul, and the Evangelists only did good for humanity. Jesus spoke about the eternity of the Torah better than all the Jewish Sages before him, and he benefited both Jews and non-Jews. By bringing to the latter some of the laws of Judaism, he planted morality in them. Some madmen (as he put it) who came after them erred and distorted their intention regarding Judaism, thereby causing tragic persecutions throughout the Middle Ages.

Emden added that such an extreme morality as that which Jesus demands from non-Jews suits the education of Christians, but not of Jews, who are subject to the Torah, which weakens the impulse, and they swore from the start at Sinai to moderate their conduct. Emden emphasizes that what he has written in the essay in praise of Christianity is also

---

23 L. Gottlieb, "'Resen Mat'e' Lerabi Ya'aqov 'Emden," in *Bedarkhei Shalom, 'Iyunim Behagut Yehudit*, ed. B. Ish-Shalom (Jerusalem, 2007), 306-8. It is noteworthy that the moral virtues that Emden praises among the Christians are rejected sweepingly by Hirsch, who regards them as characterizing the alienation of Christianity from daily life, because such an extreme morality cannot be observed by them. See the conclusion of the section on Hirsch's response below.

written elsewhere in his works, and he is not hiding them. He claims that Maimonides expressed a similar opinion in *Hilkhot Melakhim*.

After this article was published, Emden found that Rabbi Simon Ben Tsemah Duran (1361-1444) had written a responsum in similar style, as did Rabbi Jacob Sasportas (1610-1698), the author of *Tsitsit Novel Tsevi*, an attack against Sabbateanism.

In this essay, Emden goes on to attack the priests in Poland, who are as bloodthirsty as wolves, accusing the Jews of the blood libel. Their words are nothing but a lying attack, with no basis at all. Although the lie and forgery are revealed time and time again, they continue to make accusations, seizing Jews and torturing them severely. It is clear to every educated man familiar with the religion of Moses that there is no hint of this fiction in them, and ultimately God will take revenge against their persecutors.

Emden compares the horrible situation in Poland to Western Europe, where such libels are unknown and inconceivable, and even the more so in Muslim countries, "Because most of them are smart. And there are well-educated men among them, who are honest and like the Jews."[24]

MENDELSSOHN'S POSITION

Beginning in the mid-eighteenth century, a significant change took place in Jewish-Christian relations, and because of its importance, I give it an extensive place. The Enlightenment movement reached its peak at that time in Germany, and religious tolerance increased. The man who led Jewish Haskala and the call for tolerance with respect to ideas, and unwillingly became the spokesman for European Jewry, was Moses Mendelssohn, and the ones who led the action were Wessely, Friedländer, and especially Eichel.

Katz[25] and Feiner[26] described the events that shaped this turning point, some of which were interwoven in Mendelssohn's life. Feiner devotes his book on Mendelssohn less to his philosophy than to his

---

24 Ibid., 310.
25 Katz, *Yehudim*, 168-79; idem, *Hayetsia*, 47-73.
26 Feiner, *Mendelssohn*.

struggle for religious tolerance, and he shows how these events, which reflected both progress and regression in the struggle, influenced his hopes and disappointments.

Mendelssohn's view of Christianity and the crucial necessity for religious tolerance to ensure the success of humanity and enlightenment is expressed in several of his letters. Against the claim of Johann David Michaelis (see chapter four) that the Jews were hostile to Christianity because of the nature of their religion, and that they are not ethical, because they deal in commerce, which requires them to cheat their customers, Mendelssohn responded in an essay published by Gotthold Ephraim Lessing (see chapter four) in his periodical, *Theatralische Bibliothek*, in 1754.

From the position of an intellectual and making use of the lexicon of the Enlightenment, Mendelssohn demanded of the enlightened European, according to Feiner, "to apply to their Jewish brethren the principle of religious tolerance in the name of the elevated values of humanism and reason."[27] According to Mendelssohn, "the Christian multitude always regarded us as the filth of nature, the sickness of humanity, but from educated men I would expect a more respectable judgment."[28]

Mendelssohn explains that the Jews are willing to be oppressed and deprived of rights, if only they are not deprived as individuals of the possibility of being enlightened, learned, and moral. In 1769, Swiss theologian Johann Kaspar Lavater published a German translation of the book by Charles Bonnet, *Recherches Philosophiques Sur Les Preuves Du Christianisme*. In the dedication to the book, despite the promise he had given to Mendelssohn five years previously, Lavater proclaimed that Mendelssohn had told him that he honored the ethical character of Jesus, and he issued an ultimatum: either refute Bonnet's proofs or convert to Christianity.

Lavater was a zealous, messianic Christian millenarian who expected that Mendelssohn's conversion to Christianity would be the beginning of the process of the conversion of the Jews, which would

---

27 Ibid., 41.
28 Ibid.

lead to the advent of the thousand year kingdom. Mendelssohn answered him in a short letter in the end of that year, "The Open Letter to the Deacon Lavater." Instead of responding to the ultimatum, Mendelssohn explained in his letter:

> Why religious polemics were inherently opposed to the values of enlightened culture, and why, therefore, Lavater's ultimatum was an improper action and a blow to the value of friendship.... Religious polemics are in fact entirely one-sided, and this was because Judaism—in contrast to Christianity—did not claim exclusivity, did not seek to attract converts, and was not missionary.... Judaism did not offer, in Mendelssohn's opinion, the only way to redemption of the soul and the world to come. The Christian church declared that there was no salvation outside of the church, but Judaism believed that whoever obeys the Seven Noahide Commandments (including eschewing idolatry, incest, bloodshed, and robbery)—which correspond to what any reasonable person recognizes on his own as the general human directives of morality—is assured the same heavenly reward that is promised to the Jews: "Those who live according to the laws of this religion of nature and reason are called 'virtuous men of other nations,' the children of eternal blessedness".... This was the first time that Mendelssohn expressed the opinion that the different religions have a common basis in natural religion, which does not require divine revelation or the Scriptures. He also argued that Judaism, which is not fanatical about the principle of exclusivity and superiority, is therefore closer to natural religion and also more tolerant.... These characteristics of Judaism put it in an honorable place in enlightened culture, and in contrast the proselytizing ardor of Christians place their religion in a miserable light, as denying tolerance, freedom of opinion, freedom of religion, and acting against reason.... Mendelssohn explained, "I could scarcely think that he who leads men to virtue in this life can be damned in the next." The universalistic, humanistic view of natural religion, which gave the author of Phaedon eternal fame, is presented here as the basic attitude of Judaism.[29]

---

29 Ibid., 74-76. Quotations from Mendelssohn taken from "Open Letter to Deacon Lavater of Zurich from Moses Mendelssohn," available at http://www.german-historydocs.ghi-dc.org/pdf/eng/15__TheJews__Doc.2__English.pdf. Feiner emphasizes that Mendelssohn bases his words on Maimonides, although he disagrees with his demand of the Gentiles who observe the seven Noahide laws to believe that the source of the obligation is divine revelation to Moses and not reason, as a condition for life in the world to come. Emden wrote to Mendelssohn that there was a source,

Mendelssohn concludes with the argument that the Jews' gratitude toward the ruling nation, which enables them to practice their way of worshiping God, prevents them from disagreeing with the religion of the ruler, and he declares that he will remain faithful to his religion and distant from Christianity.

Mendelssohn expressed his thoughts on the truths of Christianity in a letter to Prince Ferdinand of Braunschweig, in 1770, which he was against publishing and even tried to destroy, in answer to the prince's request to hear his views. In his letter, Mendelssohn stated that

> the Christian conception of God—belief in the trinity and in the incarnation of God in Jesus—was contrary to reason and therefore could not be true... Even reformed Christianity—which lowers Jesus to the level of a man and regards him solely as a messenger of God and a prophet—must pass several tests before a Jew like Mendelssohn could relate positively to it: giving up its claim of exclusivity as the true religion; ... removal of belief in eternal punishment in hell, in Original Sin, in Satan and evil spirits; and finally recognition that Jesus did not want to revoke the Torah of Moses and exempt those who believed in it from the obligation to keep the commandments. Only under these conditions, which practically speaking entailed denial of the principles of Christianity, "would a religion be attained in which Christians and Jews could take part equally".... All the verses [in the New Testament] that serve as proof of the truth of Christianity and herald its appearance even before the time of Jesus are erroneous interpretations or malicious distortions.[30]

In late 1781, Christian Dohm published a work, titled *Concerning the Amelioration of the Civil Status of the Jews*, at Mendelssohn's request following a wave of anti-Jewish incitement that threatened the Jews of

---

though indirect, for Maimonides's argument, which might be correct. Mendelssohn thought differently, that universal, rational justice requires that even someone who did not receive the revelation at Sinai should merit life in the world to come. See Katz, *Yehudim*, 175.

30 Feiner, *Mendelssohn*, 79. Mendelssohn wrote in similar spirit to his friend Elkan Herz in a personal letter. See Feiner, *Hahilun*, 202-3: Feiner himself expresses doubt there—based on Allan Arkush—as to the reliability of these arguments, and he believes that Mendelssohn's effort to reconcile the revelation of the Torah with natural religion was "rather fragile, suspect, and difficult to understand." Some scholars disagree with Arkush and, consequently, with Feiner's doubts.

the community of Alsace, France. To Mendelssohn's disappointment, although Dohm proposed drastic improvement in the situation of the Jews in his work, he made this conditional on a deep change in the education of the Jews and in their occupations.

Dohm refuted most of the accusations leveled against the Jews and argued that an enlightened country could not behave with the barbarity dictated by religious fanaticism, and that the dubious morality of Jewish merchants and the flaws in their education were the unfortunate result of the discrimination against them. The different religious customs of the Jews should not be an excuse for depriving them of their human and civil rights.

Michaelis immediately published a critique of Dohm, in which he described the inherent obstacles preventing the naturalization of the Jews: their consciousness as a nation apart, their messianic hope to return to Zion, and the Halakhic restrictions on contacts with Christians and military service. Michaelis also wondered about the loyalty of the Jews, some of whom had turned their backs on their religion and declared themselves to be deists. In Mendelssohn's opinion, both Dohm and Michaelis expressed prejudices against the Jews, according to which they have a tendency to be cheaters and delinquents. Mendelssohn responded in his introduction to the book by Menasseh Ben Israel, *Vindiciae Judaeorum*, written and published in London in 1656. This book is a defense of the Jews intended to convince Oliver Cromwell and his government to permit their return. In 1782, Mendelssohn decided to publish a German translation of the book and wrote an introduction, of which Feiner says:

> In the Introduction Mendelssohn revealed ... his apprehension regarding the Christian world and his doubts as to the possibility of the desired substantial change at that stage. He asked: Could enlightenment ever erase the traces of fanaticism and barbarity with respect to the attitude toward the Jews?... "They accuse us of having superstitions and being immersed in ignorance, that we lack ethical sensitivity, good taste, and good manners, that we are not fit for crafts, for science, or for the useful arts." However, he continued, the restrictions imposed on us and our relegation to the margins of society do not enable us to develop. Anyone who truly is interested

in the integration of the Jews in society and culture must first liberate them from the restrictions. Otherwise the oppression will continue forever: "they block all the paths to effective reform of our situation, and they make lack of culture an excuse to continue to oppress us. They shackle our arms and reprimand us for not using them."

As to whether religious fanaticism had diminished, Mendelssohn was very skeptical. He claimed that first of all it was necessary to refute all the false stories told about the Jews. In a renewed outburst of pessimism, Mendelssohn told his readers the distressing facts of life: eighteenth-century Enlightenment had not yet succeeded in erasing the "barbaric traces of history." Was there any way of repairing this? asked Mendelssohn. Could one struggle successfully against those "coarse accusations," "barbaric laws," and the entire dark legacy of Christianity, so weighty and oppressive, which was created in the Middle Ages? At this point, Mendelssohn was overcome with despair: "Reason and humanity raise their voice in vain, because prejudice, having grown old, no longer has the sense of hearing."[31]

In this introduction, Mendelssohn also argues with Dohm, who sought in the framework of his plan to leave the Jews with the autonomous authority to punish and excommunicate rebels, those who strayed, and deviants—the same authority given to the Christian church. Mendelssohn believed that such a situation was inconsistent with enlightenment, and this authority, both of the church and of the rabbis, should be abolished. Therefore he wrote: "I do not recognize any right over people and matters that depend on laws governing opinions and based on them.... And less than all do I recognize the right to rule over opinions on the part of religion.... True, divine religion does not usurp control over opinions and views."

Mendelssohn, who was also worried about rumors that certain rabbis intended to ban his Biur, the commentary on the Pentateuch, and on rumors about the persecution of a Jew from Hamburg because he denied the authority of the community, addressed the rabbis, too, at the end of the Introduction, proposing to make "the Jewish community

---

31 Feiner, *Mendelssohn*, 113-15; see also idem, *Hahilun*, 287.

into an open organization, in which membership is not obligatory, and it has no coercive authority." Mendelssohn called upon the Jewish leaders to give up voluntarily and intentionally the use of "the sword of revenge, which only madness believes it can use with safety."[32]

When an effort was made by the zealots to pressure the rabbis to ban Wessely's *Divrei Shalom Veemet* and to banish him from the community, Mendelssohn also worked intensely to prevent this, and in letters he expressed his apprehension that the event would shame Judaism in the eyes of Christian public opinion. This struggle against the rabbis is apparently what nourished the rabbinical tradition from then on regarding the danger that Mendelssohn, "the heretic," and Haskala posed for traditional Judaism.

In 1782, August Cranz published the essay "The Quest for Light and Right," in which he challenged Mendelssohn's fidelity to the Jewish religion because of his call to give up the right to religious coercion, expecting that Mendelssohn would in fact slough off his adhesion to the Jewish religion and stand fully at the side of the enlightened and the deists. In response, Mendelssohn wrote *Jerusalem*, which summarizes his positions in favor of religious toleration and the separation of religion and the state, against any coercive authority of a religious institution, and in favor of assuring human rights to everyone, in favor of the principles of natural, universal rational religion, and in defense of his loyalty to the Torah and commandments which were revealed to the Jews in a particular, historical event, which is the religion most faithful to reason.

Mendelssohn stated that Christianity requires belief in the principles of the faith and punishes those who deny them. Judaism maintains that the essentials of faith are rational and do not require the mediation of clergymen, and at the revelation, the Jews received practical behavioral norms, not beliefs. In answer to Kranz's claim that the foundation stones of Judaism are based on religious coercion, Mendelssohn wrote that in antiquity the law of the Torah was also the law of the state, and the state had the right to impose its laws, as it is today, to assure human

---

32 Feiner, *Mendelssohn*, 120.

happiness and prevent heresy, in order to ensure morality and justice, which are the basis of the state.[33]

Mendelssohn argued that according to Jesus, the separation between what is "to God" and what is "to Caesar" was required in those days of sorrow and grief, when the Jewish state existed under foreign domination, which was very distant from the demands of the religion. Since the unity in affairs has been disrupted, each master must be given his part separately. Until the advent of salvation, this separation will continue, and therefore the Jews in the present must adopt the same approach.[34] Like Emden, Mendelssohn also argues for a distinction between Jesus and the church:

> Jesus of Nazareth himself observed not only the law of Moses but also the ordinances of the rabbis.... Closely examined, everything is in complete agreement not only with Scripture, but also with the tradition ... the rabbinic principle evidently shines forth his entire conduct as well as the conduct of his disciples in the early period. He who is not born into the law need not bind himself to the law; but he who is born into the law must live according to the law and die according to the law. If his followers, in later times, thought differently and believed they could release from the law also those Jews who accepted their teachings, this surely happened without his authority.[35]

The views of Mendelssohn and Lessing and the band of enlightened Jews and non-Jews who gathered around them were in the minority. Many Christians opposed association with Jews and developed an ideology of rejection: stating either that the Christian character of the society could not be changed, or that the Jewish religion and mentality isolated the Jews.

Those who rejected the Jews based themselves on an ancient Christian tradition regarding the classic stereotype of the Jew and of Judaism. This was described, for example, in a book by Johann Andreas Eisenmenger, *Entdecktes Judenthum* [Judaism Revealed],

---

33 See ibid., 127-36. In my opinion, in Jerusalem Mendelssohn prefigured the pluralist, post-modern view of David Hartman, as presented by Sagi, "Hartman," 450-66.
34 See Mendelssohn, *Jerusalem*, 132-33.
35 Ibid., 134.

published in 1711. Eisenmenger, citing Talmudic sources, stated that Judaism was a narrow-minded, intolerant, immoral system, according to which Gentiles were not regarded as human beings.

Another negative approach employed by those who rejected the Jews was that of Voltaire (1694-1778), a deist who wanted to destroy Christianity by demonstrating the immorality of biblical figures and by arguing that Bible stories are merely the legends of a backward tribe with irrational and primitive customs, who separated themselves from anyone who was not one of their own and were contemptuous of them.

However, the days of the Enlightenment were short. Not even a generation passed before it became clear that Mendelssohn's vision of the future was merely an illusion. Under the influence of Kant, Hegel, and Schleiermacher,[36] romanticism conquered the hearts of Western and Central Europe. Nationalism increased, and it was based on historical romanticism and classical Christianity. "German nationalism and Christianity—which was grasped as a world view and as a spiritual heritage more than as a system of belief—were identified with one another, or at least bound tightly together. The Jews found themselves, self-evidently, kept at a remove from every social unit based on identifying signs like these, whether it was the state or another organized body."[37]

In contrast, despite opposition, the political process of granting civil rights to the Jews of Europe continued in country after country: France, 1790; Holland, 1795; Frankfurt, 1811; Prussia, 1812; Austro-Hungary, 1848 (a process completed in 1867); and northern Germany, 1866.

THE REFORM RESPONSE

One of the most important motivations for the creation of the Reform movement in Judaism in the early nineteenth century was the desire to do whatever was possible to persuade the Christians to accept the Jews in social and cultural circles.

---

36 See Meyer, *Reform*, 64-67.
37 Katz, *Hayetsia*, 193-94. The account of Christian opposition is according to Katz, ibid., 82-103.

David Friedländer took the most extreme step. In 1799, he anonymously addressed the head of the church in Berlin, the enlightened Protestant minister Wilhelm Teller, and proposed that he and his friends separate themselves from the Jewish community of Berlin and formally join the church and receive its protection, provided that they should not be forced to accept beliefs that were not natural and rational. Teller rejected the offer categorically, and, having no alternative, the members of Friedländer's group remained Jews and members of the community, though they chose radicalization of Judaism.

The first Reform Jews could not convert to Christianity because of irrational Christian dogmas, or because they did not wish to cut themselves off from their families and Jewish friends, and they also could not sever themselves from any religious community, because of the law that required their adhesion. Therefore they chose to reform the Jewish religion, its laws and customs, with the aim of reducing significantly the difference between Judaism and Christianity; Mendelssohn's vision of a universal, rational, natural religion would be fulfilled, and Judaism would lead all of humanity to it. Therefore, they abolished many of the practical ritual commandments that the Christians thought to be primitive, which had become irrelevant.

The Reform movement abolished many customs, made a selection of the wording of the prayers that eliminated the particularist sting from Judaism, such as the return to Zion, the messiah, sacrifices, medieval hymns, the Kol Nidrei prayer recited on the Day of Atonement, and anything derived from a mystical, kabbalistic source. The most radical of them also wanted to pray in German and to move the weekly day of rest from Saturday to Sunday. The temples were more like churches than synagogues, and organs were placed in them and played on the Sabbaths and holidays. In some communities confirmation ceremonies were held for young people, as in the Christian custom.

The Reform Jews tried to purify Judaism of irrational dogmas and bring out the spiritual element. They emphasized the ethical and humanistic monotheism that Judaism had brought to the world, claiming that it was actually similar to Christianity, and even superior. They embraced the idea of the mission, the claim that Providence had sent the Jews into the Diaspora in order to bring universal salvation to the Gentiles according to Judaism, and this would take place not in Jerusalem but in Christian Europe. In that way they sought to curry favor with the Gentiles, to advance and improve their emancipation, which would enable them more and more to participate in culture, social life, and public functions with Christians. The Reform Jews encountered fierce opposition from the traditional Jews, and both sides even sought the intervention of the authorities, which were inconsistent in their response. Sometimes they authorized the Reform community, in hopes that the Jews would indeed change for the better, and sometimes they forbade their activity, precisely because they were apprehensive about the changes that might bring Jews closer to Christians. In these cases, there was an increase in conversion to Christianity, especially among intellectuals and academics, who wished to assimilate into the culture and the academy.[38]

THE TRADITIONAL RELIGIOUS RESPONSE: THE MEN OF THE MIDDLE ON CHRISTIANITY AND ISLAM

In the first half of the nineteenth century, the men of the middle trend found themselves struggling on three theological fronts. Two of these fronts were within Jewish society: from the left they were attacked by the Reform Jews as men of darkness and fanatics, who were unable to give up the old, primitive ritual in favor of the modern future; from the right they were attacked by the devout Orthodox for their willingness to include European culture within Judaism.

From the outside, the attack of the Christians continued, in the spirit of intolerant romanticism. As usual, they regarded Judaism and the stubborn Jews as the cause of all the evil in the world. The men of the middle trend required a world view that would justify, rationally and morally, attachment to the commandments of the Torah, the importance of the achievements of human reason, which were embodied in European culture, and the existence of the other monotheistic

---

38 According to Meyer, *Reform*, 28-61. On the Friedländer-Teller episode, see Feiner, *Haneurut*, 330-31, 350-55; idem, *Hahilun*, 359-60, 374-76.

religions. Similarly, they needed an explanation that would present the superiority of the Jewish religion, based on observation of the commandments, to Christianity.

In this context it should be pointed out that those who sought to show the superiority of Judaism to Christianity were also assisted by the withdrawal of Christianity from the rational universalism of the Enlightenment period, which advocated a purified Christianity, to a nationalist, romantic Christianity that prized the myths and mysteries of Christianity, with all its classic characteristics. These seekers also were assisted by the research of their contemporaries, which showed that Christianity was a kind of compromise between paganism and spirituality, and this was the root of its success in gaining the acceptance of the pagans and its spread throughout the world. Christianity offered the pagans, who lived in moral corruption and under tainted regimes, a new content for the existing frameworks, and therefore it grew up as half-pagan.[39]

CHAJES'S RESPONSE

The front against Christianity preoccupied Chajes much less than the internal fronts against Reform and the fanatics. In general, Eastern European Jewry did not feel the wave of romantic chauvinism that swept over Western and Central Europe. The Haskala movement continued to be dominant in the East, and the Maskilim of Eastern Europe, especially those in the Austro-Hungarian Empire, continued to await the advent of Mendelssohn's Utopia.

For that reason, the Maskilim emphasized that all the defects that the Gentiles saw in the Jews derive from past persecutions, and the present and egalitarian and tolerant future of enlightenment, demonstrated by the authorities of the merciful Austrian empire, would present Judaism in all its ethical beauty and enable their acceptance in the family of nations and monotheistic religions with full, equal rights. In the margins of this discussion, it should also be pointed out that the

---

39 See, for example, the book by Joseph Salvador, published in Paris in 1818, in French, described by Klausner, *Yeshu*, 152. See also Jacob Fleischman, *Be'ayat Hanatsrut Bamahshava Hayehudit Mimendelssohn 'Ad Rosenzweig* (Jerusalem, 1964).

harsh censorship enforced in the Austro-Hungarian Empire until 1848 did not allow the Jews to speak ill of Christianity, even if they wished to do so.

The Difficult History

Several times in his writings, Chajes described the harsh conditions that prevailed between the Jews and their Christian rulers in the Middle Ages. In the second chapter of his book *Darkhei Hahoraa*, of 1842, he discussed the contradiction that he found between the tendency of Ashkenazic rabbis to be more severe in their prohibitions than the Sephardim, and the leniences permitted by the Ashkenazim in cases of fear of danger, because of "eiva" [hostility] and "Dina Demalkhuta" [the law of the kingdom].

Chajes found that, whereas the Ashkenazim added stringencies to certain prohibitions which were not mentioned in the Talmud or by the Geonim, according to the tradition of Hasidut Ashkenaz, founded by Rabbi Judah the Hasid and El'azar Ba'al Haroqeah of Worms, they were lenient in the aforementioned matters, even regarding prohibitions that were found in the Talmud. He explained these leniencies by the different situation of the Sephardic Jews, in comparison to that of the Ashkenazim:

> The reason for this is known to anyone who examines the history of our brethren the Children of Israel in the countries of Ashkenaz in former days, in contrast to the status of the People of Israel in the countries of Sepharad, behold he sees that in Sepharad under the government of the Arabs our nation, Israel, was very great in number, ornamented in Torah and in wisdom and in great wealth, and they were important and protected in the eyes of the king and the ministers, and filled with all good things, they had property of field and vineyard, and some of them were appointed in office, doing their work in the king's house, and their work was the main thing, and commerce was secondary, and there was not great hostility between the nations and our nation, and they did not suspect them of the aforementioned malice, they were only beloved and important and protected among them, whereas the lot of our brethren in the countries of Ashkenaz was evil and bitter, and they closed the door before them, and they did not give them a holding or remnant in the land, and they did not allow them to join in their settlements,

tortured and open to any misfortune and plague, and they had no portion except commerce and usury, as is known, if so necessity is not to be condemned, and they were forced to conduct themselves in the narrow path accorded to them, even though it also has a prohibited aspect, and the Sages, seeing how bad it was for their brethren, and that their status in those countries was not for the best, permitted them such behavior because of concern that a person is afraid for his money, and he may permit more for himself, see Tur (Yore De'a no. 159, in the name of Tosafot), that in this time it is permitted to lend money for interest to heathens because all our business today is only lending to them, see there, and whoever looks at the history of the Jews in the time of the Tosafists and the Rosh [Asher ben Jehiel] and the Tur [Jacob Ben Asher] will easily understand the reason for the permission, because they left us nothing except usury, and also because of that they were lenient in many matters against Halakha because of fear of hostility and hatred as well, but the Sephardim left all the Halakha of the Gemara in force, because they did not find any necessity to behave other than as the Torah prescribes.[40]

That is to say, in Chajes's opinion, the oppression and discrimination against the Jews in the countries of Ashkenaz, under Christian rule, which also led to a difficult economic situation, required the rabbis to be lenient in certain Halakhot connected to relations with the neighboring Gentiles, and this was to enable the people to cope and survive. In contrast, in countries under Islamic rule, where the Sephardic Jews lived, a golden age prevailed, and there was no need to be lenient regarding Halakhot explicitly stated in the Talmud.

In the first essay in *'Ateret Zvi*, published in 1841, entitled "Drush Nehmad" [Pleasant Homily], Chajes treats three kinds of hatred of the Jews present in his time, and this was based on Maimonides's "Epistle to Yemen." The first type was national and political hatred, and its purpose was physical extermination, as in the time of Pharaoh, Amalek, and Haman. The second kind was religious hatred, and its purpose was nullifying the Torah as in the time of Antiochus and the Expulsion from Spain:

---

40 Chajes, *Darkhei Hahoraa*, 225. Chajes was not aware, like many of his contemporaries, and later as well, of the harsh persecutions that had befallen the Jews under Islam.

> And we have also found in the prophets (Ezekiel 36), "a devourer of men are you," that is, they falsely accused the Jews of mixing human blood in matsot prepared for Passover, see Abarbanel there, and they also claimed that the Jews offered human sacrifices for a pleasant fragrance, and even in our generation and in earlier generations, our opponents held arguments like these against the Jewish people, as I saw in the French satirist Voltaire, that from the thing that happened to the daughter of Jephthah, and from the Bible (Lev. 27), where it says, "anyone who is completely devoted from among human beings is not to be ransomed. He is certainly to be put to death," he hung his craziness that human sacrifice was practiced among us, and against all those lies and similar ones, Josephus [Flavius] the Priest wrote his book [Against Apion], and he demonstrated against the chief persecutor, Apion, that these were lies and false accusations.[41]

The third kind, which Maimonides does not list, belongs more to the modern period, and it is racial hatred. This arises every time there is a discussion among the authorities about granting rights to the Jews, and enlightened people who "are honest in their hearts," speak out in favor of civil rights for the Jews:

> Immediately Satan dances among them, and the opponents come with strange arguments, saying of us, we are a people that must dwell alone, and they have nothing in common with us, the people of that nation regard themselves as strangers, and they hold the opinion that this land is not theirs, and their eyes are raised to another place, and in addition to that they claim about us that this nation is not yet ripe in manners and morals, and they do not walk together with the current of the time like the other residents of the state, and, not only that, they add, look at the flaw that clings to their character, and the root of the Jewish people is defective, they love idleness and deal only in trade, they are peddlers who go among the villages, lend money for interest, sucking out the wealth of many nations, act in cunning, because they look only for money, and they race to get rich, and such and such they say about us, with strange arguments to strike at us with various ruses, to shame and revile us, in order to justify their action against us in sight of the sun.[42]

The Jews are accused of isolating themselves, of treachery, of dual loyalty, of moral corruption, of primitive backwardness, of bad

---

41 Chajes, *'Ateret Zvi*, 354-55.
42 Ibid., 355.

character traits stereotypical of the Jewish race: idleness, avarice, and cunning. Chajes goes on to state that in fact these accusations are not new, and Haman made them:

> Even the new arguments innovated by the persecutor Gasparin in the State of Hungary, that the sons of our nation curse the king and ministers in their prayers every day, were stolen from the father of all persecutors, Eisenmenger, in his book *The Jewish Religion Revealed* [Part 2], however, he stole from a thief, because we have seen here Haman the Agagite speaking in the mouth of Eisenmenger, because he, too, told falsehoods about us like that as testified by the Sages, only the persecutor Gasparin did more, because Haman admitted it, in any event, that at the time of circling the reading platform on Hoshana Rabba, he does not know whether they bless or curse the king, but the foolish and ignorant Gasparin made an absolute declaration, that every day we curse the king and the ministers, and including on Hoshana Rabba.[43]

Naturally Chajes denies all the arguments and shows that the traits of the Jewish character are love, compassion, humility, charity, forgiveness, reconciliation, and cooperation with the kingdom and its ministers. Here Chajes describes ancient Jewish history and shows that their occupation was always keeping sheep, tilling the soil, and crafts, and they distanced themselves from commerce and finance. However, since the persecutions and oppression began, they had no choice, and they became the scapegoat for all the plagues, evils, and disasters of nature.

> Indeed after that, for many years, we were driven from disaster to disaster, persecution without letup, and we found no respite for our wearied souls, and the inhabitants of the land did not allow us to settle in their state, and they prevented us from joining in their estate in any matter of work or public service, and there remained only commerce and money-lending, and what could they do to provide for their souls?... For we are regarded as aliens in the land, and we are prone to every mischance and plague—and they said (Yevamot 63a), "No disaster comes to the world except for Israel," meaning that in every matter of trouble that happens in the world at all, the sons of our nation were the first who were struck by midat

---

43 Ibid.

hadin [strict justice]. If a scourge suddenly kills, the residents of the country said the thing happened because of the Jews, because they threw poison into the water wells, if fire catches from the mouth of God and devours an entire city, behold the Jewish people caused it, and all the time they attributed the fault to the afflicted, to the reviled sect of Jacob, who hear their blame and do not reply, and all the evil natural disasters that happened in the entire world, they did the most harm to the Jewish people, as if all the evils had as a target only the Jewish people.[44]

The Damascus Blood Libel

Chajes devoted an essay titled "Tiferet Yisrael" [The Splendor of Israel] to the Damascus blood libel of 1840. The essay was written in the year of the libel, and was joined to the end of the essay "Darkhei Moshe" [The Ways of Moses] in his book *'Ateret Zvi*.[45] At the beginning of the essay, Chajes is pleased to say that in his time, after six hundred years of blood libels and the killing of many Jews, the enlightened nations and their rulers recognized that there was nothing to merit them. He says that the source of the blood libel was hatred of the religion, and that it was based on confessions extracted with torture, and once the rulers of Europe abolished torture, the libels ceased.

Chajes briefly describes the blood libel of Damascus, which broke out in a less enlightened place, whose leaders were avaricious:

> When our ear heard, our soul fainted, from the torments with which the suspects were stricken, nothing as bad as which has been heard for a long time, because in the city of Damascus men of coarse heart and flesh massed together, to afflict us once more with the old falsehoods, to accuse us falsely and evilly to say of us, you are cannibals, and according to the tenets of the religion the obligation is incumbent upon every Jew, to knead matsot with the mixture of Christian blood, and with revolting things of this kind they slander us, to make our odor foul in the eyes of the residents of the country, and the governors there lend a heedful ear to them, so they can have an excuse to plunder their wealth and property and all they own.[46]

44　Ibid., 357-58. See also ibid., 484, note.
45　Ibid., 483-91. See under the heading "Darkhei Moshe" there, 435.
46　Ibid., 483.

Chajes tells about the efforts of the rabbis of Britain, France, and Germany to help reveal the truth about the Torah of Israel and Jewish customs. The community leadership asked him to contribute "an essay of defense against the blood libel that has been renewed in our time."[47] Indeed, Chajes composed a full Halakhic treatise as a defense brief in which he presented various aspects of the absurdity of the accusations, which were inconceivable in every respect. The proofs that Chajes adduced had been, he said, almost all presented by his predecessors, including Rabbi Menasseh Ben Israel, who had written a special work on the subject and presented it to the rulers of Great Britain two hundred years earlier.

First, Chajes argues, even if, perish the thought, there were such a commandment, it would be forbidden on the grounds of saving lives, because this would be regarded as a revolt against a decree of the king reigning in the state, disobedience of which is punishable by death. Second, the matter has no textual authority, not in the written Torah and not in the Oral Law. At the time of the rise of Christianity, the Sanhedrin had already stopped passing death sentences, and it would be impossible to condemn a Christian child to death; and, moreover, the despotic Roman rulers would not have allowed it. The Sages passed ordinances only for the benefit and safety of the people, and not to place them in situations of grave danger, and if there had been such an ordinance in the past, they would have revoked it. Third, according to the Torah it is forbidden to shed the innocent blood of any person, and this is a severe transgression unparalleled in the entire Torah, and no situation is possible in which this law could be changed or uprooted from the Torah, even if it were possible to commit it at some time without danger. Fourth, the God of Israel hates idol worship, and one of the most abominable practices of idol worship is that in which children are burned as a sacrifice to the god, and therefore it is inconceivable that He Himself could desire such a sacrifice. Fifth, how is it possible to knead matsot with blood, since it would immediately be leavened. Sixth, many of the commandments of the Torah derive from the virtues of compassion and grace, and the Torah is even merciful toward animals

---

47 Ibid.

and prevents them from suffering unnecessarily; moreover, the Jews always have acted with honesty and decency with the Gentiles. Even toward the worst idol worshipers, we segregated ourselves socially so they would not kill us, but were commanded not to be contemptuous of them and not to hate them as long as they did us no harm. According to the Sages, every human being was created in the Image of God and is precious, and we are all children of Adam. The Talmud, and Maimonides in its wake, is full of obligatory Halakhot according to an ethical code of behavior toward the Gentiles with whom they lived, and with instructions of loyalty to the government and to the nation that is host to the Jew in his exile.

The Status of Christianity and Islam in Judaism

Now Chajes explains that if the Jews behaved in that way toward idol worshipers, a fortiori they would behave similarly toward Christians:

> And now if we see the honesty of [the Jews'] behavior with idol worshipers, who burned incense to Baals, and believed neither in the existence of God and His unity nor in Providence and reward and punishment, ever the more so toward the Christians, who believe in religion and Torah from heaven, and in the existence of God, and in reward in the next world, and in other principles and foundations of faith, without doubt their status with us is that of a resident alien [ger toshav], and those who keep the seven Noahide commandments because they were ordered to do so by God according to Moses, they are like the righteous of the nations of the world, and they have a portion in the world to come, according to the established law with us (in Maimonides ch. 3 of Hilkhot Teshuva and ch. 11 of Hilkhot 'Edut and ch. 8 of Hilkhot Melakhim) that the righteous of the nations of the world have a portion in the world to come, and also the Christians who keep the seven commandments and believe in the Torah of Moses, which has come from the mouth of God to Moses, and they believe in the existence of God, and although they associate something else with their worship [of God], as the Ran [Nissim of Gerona] and Yerucham Ben Meshullam wrote in the name of the Tosafot (Bekhorot 2a), as cited in Moses Isserles, Orah Hayim no. 156, that Gentiles were not commanded regarding association [of another component of the divinity].[48]

---

48 Ibid., 489.

Chajes adopts the opinions of the moderate Halakhic authorities throughout history, who regarded Christianity and the Christians in a positive light as followers of a religion very close to Judaism in most of its principles. Here we see a sign of a pattern of behavior adopted by Jews whenever things go slightly better. Even if there are still blood libels in faraway places, the forced conversions and pogroms are forgotten, and apologetics emerge.

Chajes embraces the opinion of Maimonides and Jacob Emden, that a non-Jew who keeps the seven Noahide commandments must do so because God commanded him to, via His prophet Moses in the revelation, and not based on his own reason, which is Mendelssohn's position. Chajes believes that Christians are righteous of the nations and have a part in the world to come, because they do indeed believe in the Torah of Moses and in the revelation of the Old Testament. According to his interpretation of the Gemara (B.T. Hulin 13b; Chajes misquoted the text there), Maimonides (Perush Hamishnayot, Hulin ch.1) and Nachmanides (Lev. 18:25-28), Chajes explains why non-Jews outside the Land of Israel are not prohibited from associating other gods and powers with the divinity. He says that in the Land, non-Jews, like Jews, must know "the conduct of the God of the land," meaning the One God, and if they do not acknowledge Him alone, but worship other gods with Him, they will be punished. On the other hand, outside the Land, where the One God appointed other powers to govern, the non-Jews have "the customs of their fathers in their hands," and therefore the association of other divinities is not forbidden to them. Hence, although they believe in the Holy Trinity and include the Son and the Holy Spirit with God, since "their main intention is only to the God of gods,"[49] they are not idol-worshipers, and it is permitted to have business and social connections with them. Chajes believes that Maimonides thought that the Christians were not idol-worshipers, as Emden stated, and he goes on to lavish praise upon the Christians and Muslims:

> The seven commandments are in general natural commandments, which both the Christians and the Muslims enforce in the places of

---

49 Ibid., 490.

their judgment, and both of them supervise their observance with a vigilant eye, such as incest, shedding blood, civil laws, cursing God, and theft, and they are extremely punctilious in them to punish transgressors, and also about eating from a living animal there is a hint in the words of their emissary Paul, who warned them not to eat from strangled animals, and the Ishmaelites are not idol-worshipers, Yore De'a no. 124, and they also are precise about the seven commandments and are also warned against eating pork and eating blood and carrion, and also that which is not slaughtered to God in the direction of the mosque, see Yore De'a no. 14, par. 7, see the Koran, Sura 2, known as the Cow, and (Sura 5), known as the Table, and everyone who keeps the seven commandments because he was commanded by the Torah according to God by Moses is a ger toshav [resident alien] among us, and see also what our rabbi Maimonides wrote in Ch. 12 of Hilkhot Melakhim (Venice edition), and see the *Kuzari*, section 4, no. 23, who wrote that they, the sons of Hagar "The nations merely serve to introduce and pave the way for the expected Messiah, who is the fruition, and they will all become His fruit. Then, if they acknowledge Him, they will become one tree. Then they will revere the origin which they formerly dispersed, as we have observed concerning the words."[50]

That is to say, in countries where the prevailing religion is and has been monotheistic, they maintain a society according to the minimum prerequisites of Judaism, out of recognition of and faith in the revelation of Moses, who conveyed these minimal requirements to the world. Instructions of this kind prepare and ensure human progress toward one pure faith in a single God, which is Judaism, and the advent of the messiah, the son of David, as Maimonides and Judah Halevi stated. Although the other religions seek to impose their beliefs on others, and even proclaim death to those who deny Jesus as the divine messiah, or the prophecies of Muhammad, in fact modest, non-militant Judaism will win out. It turns out, according to Chajes's own logic, that when things go well for Ashkenazic Jewry, it embraces the doctrine of the great Sephardic Jewish authorities. It should be noted that Chajes read the book about Jesus by Joseph Salvador, *Jesus-Christ et sa doctrine*, of 1838, and he commented: "the French Salvador wrote in our time a

---

50 Ibid.

special book to show the truth of this matter, that these nations are only preparations for the perfection of the world in the kingdom of God and to prepare them to be worthy of receiving the pure religion of the unity of the Creator, and he was not aware that in this principle he was preceded by Maimonides and the Kuzari in this secret."[51]

The Present Situation and Hopes for the Future

The departure of the delegation to Damascus in an effort to free the Jewish prisoners, and the efforts of the authorities, encouraged Chajes. He finished his essay on the Damascus blood libel with the argument that it was forbidden for Jews to murder anyone, even someone of another faith, and especially not young children who never sinned, for

> Who knows whether in the end they will grow into a splendid vine and be among those honest people of the righteous of the nations, who shine today to the House of Israel in their splendor and stand up for us as a shelter and refuge, like the government of our Lord the Emperor Ferdinand, and fortunate are his servants and fortunate are those who represent him the Consul in Damascus and the General Consul in Alexandria.[52]

Chajes also continued the essay "Drush Nehmad" with an optimistic feeling. After developing the argument that anti-Jewish racism is an error, and that the vices of the Jews derive from persecution and pressure over the course of history, he comes to the present and hopes for the future. In the present, where the Jews of France, Holland, and North America are well off, there was an immediate, significant improvement in the behavior of the Jew, proving, in his opinion, that his argument is correct. This is also true in Galicia, in the Austrian Empire:

> And we, too, whose pleasant lot it is to be under the Austrian government, a kingdom of compassion for all the nations that take shelter in its shadow, behold we have seen that we have improved our ways a lot, and if this is the beginning of our path, let us hope that in the fullness of time everyone will acknowledge and know, that we are a

---

51 Ibid., note. See above, Chapter 4 n. 33.
52 Ibid., 490-91.

blessed seed ornamented and splendid in honest virtues and the merciful sons of merciful parents, and we still grasp the virtue of our ancestors, and there is no flaw inherent in our law, perish the thought, only because of the length of exile and the weight of the yoke, things went wrong among us.[53]

In the essay "Darkhei Moshe" [The Ways of Moses], one of the essays that compose the book 'Ateret Zvi, Chajes devotes a long discussion to the sects in Judaism, and of course he also comes to the Reform movement of his day. Comparison of the old sects with the new one brings up two surprising findings. From the religious-theological point of view, the situation today is far graver, because whereas the old sects believed in Torah from heaven, the prophesy of Moses, and keeping the commandments of the Torah, the Reform Jews deny everything. In contrast, whereas in the past it was possible to understand the deviations from the central stream and to see them as the result of the pressure and persecution of the Gentiles, today the situation of the Jews is excellent: "Indeed the Lord has done well for His people in their political status, released us from the hard labor that our enemies subjected us to in the past, and thank God in this age we do not hear about forced conversion and killing and destruction and general expulsion, as we suffered in earlier times with no letup, and on the contrary, in our generation everyone respects us, and in some states we are considered citizens."[54]

In the introduction to his book *Sheelot Uteshuvot Maharats*, in a discussion of the reason for the dispersion of the Jewish people among the nations, Chajes claims that the Jewish people was sent to the nations to teach them the principles of Judaism, and a large part of the task has already been carried out successfully, as proven by the spread of Christianity and Islam, which learned from Judaism.

> [Jesus] taught the nations about the existence of a spiritual essence, that causes all existing things to exist, but is not a body and is not a force in a body, and also they believe in the possibility of prophecy and Torah from heaven, and reward and punishment, and the other

---

53   Ibid., 358.
54   Ibid., 453.

principles in the Torah of Moses, and the Torah of Moses and the stories of the patriarchs are known to the end of the settled world, and all of this was caused by us, and our holy Torah, which we have borne with us in all the lands of our dispersion, was a light before them to prepare the moral path for them, and with respect to perfecting opinions and moral qualities, we have fulfilled our goal, and the obligation that was placed upon us in every respect, and our government, the government of opinions and truths is spread over most parts of the settled world.... And we place our trust in God, that the day will come when they will again believe in the simple unity, and nation shall not lift a vengeful sword against nation, and in matters of faith the whole earth will be filled with knowledge of God like the covering water of the sea, and from now the arguments of our enemies and detractors will pass away entirely.[55]

Chajes goes on to cite the parable of the seed from the *Kuzari* of Judah Halevi, 4:23 (cited above at note 52) and the censored words of Maimonides at the end of chapter 11 of Hilkhot Melakhim. This is the only place where Chajes touches upon the figure of Jesus, but he adds nothing to the quote from Maimonides and states that Jesus imagined he was the messiah and was executed by a Jewish court. Maimonides accepted some of the myths created about Jesus as the founder of Christianity, and Chajes does not deal with this subject on his own. According to Maimonides, Jesus claimed to be the messiah, and the Jews did condemn him to death.

Chajes states that Jesus was a false messiah, because instead of saving the Jewish people, gathering them in their land, and strengthening the observance of the commandments, he caused the killing of Jews, their dispersion and humiliation, the replacement of the Torah, and the theological error according to which one was supposed to worship an entity that was not the God of Israel. Nevertheless, Maimonides states that the teaching of Jesus and of Muhammad are a preparation for the true messiah and the perfection of the world in the future for worship to the true, universal God. According to Chajes, based on the words of Judah Halevi and Maimonides, it is clear "that these nations and religions are means and preparations for the improvement of all the people in the world for the kingdom of God, to prepare

---

55   Chajes, *Shut Moharats*, 607-8.

them so that they will be worthy of receiving the pure religion in the aspect of true unity."⁵⁶

Summary

Chajes does not discuss the figure of Jesus at all (aside from the quotation of Maimonides), and he completely refrains from arguing with Christian dogma (aside from belief in the Trinity, which is permitted to Gentiles outside of the Land of Israel). The belief of the Christians and Muslims, that they are the true Israel, he mentions only incidentally, in answer to the question of whether it was permitted to buy Torah scrolls for use by non-Jewish courts, to swear in Jews who appear before them.

Chajes permits this for various reasons, but, with respect to our topic, in his responsum he denies this belief of the Christians as a

---

56   Ibid., 608. It appears to me that Chajes misreads Maimonides, just as Emden did. It is important to point out that among those who approve in principle of Christianity as a stage in the divine plan before and after Maimonides, the latter is exceptional in that he did not regard the actions of the Christians, who adopted monotheism and Jewish morality and spread them among the pagans, as anything positive with respect to them. M. Goodmann, "Historia Umeta-Historia Behaguto Shel Harambam," in *Darkhei Shalom, 'Iyunim Behagut Yehudit*, ed. B. Ish-Shalom (Jerusalem, 2007), 243-54, showed, according to the Epistle to Yemen, that in Maimonides's opinion, just as the Torah of Moses adopted pagan elements in order to apply them against idol-worship, and it succeeded in turning the Jews away from their habitual paganism to monotheism, so, too, the pagans, who failed in their effort to wipe out Judaism with their ordinary methods, tried to combat it by establishing Christianity and Islam, which adopted parts of Judaism, in order to create confusion and the conversion of the Jews. This effort, motivated by hatred of the Jews, failed so badly that it was paganism that changed, and in fact disappeared, becoming monotheistic itself in a kind of suicide, like an evil version of Samson's "may my soul die with the Philistines." Maimonides's words at the end of Hilkhot Melakhim show that Christianity and Islam continue to spread the ideas of Judaism in paradoxical fashion, through their efforts to deny the views and commandments of Judaism. With their incessant preoccupation with the messiah, with the Torah, and the commandments, though it is negative, humanity comes to know them better and better. Goodmann calls this "the cunning of history" (under the inspiration of Hegel), but in my opinion Maimonides would have preferred to call it "the cunning of Providence." Leibowitz advanced a similar conjecture in *Yahadut, 'Am Yisrael, Umedinat Yisrael* (Jerusalem and Tel-Aviv, 1975), 330, but he does not connect it to Maimonides. Rather, he presents it as his own opinion, against Flusser, who argued that from the eschatological point of view, Maimonides had a favorable judgment of both the other religions.

falsehood. This is according to the testimony of the Oral Law, which directs us as to how to interpret the verses of the Torah and the prophets, which other religions used on the basis of an interpretation different from that of the Sages.[57] No one drew Chajes into polemics against Christianity, and he did not feel threatened by it. His battles were generally directed against antisemites, who tried unsuccessfully to prevent the granting of political rights and citizenship to the Jews. In his discussions of this subject there is quite a bit of apologetics toward the authorities and pronounced optimism that the worst was behind us. Chajes did not need cultural and social equality, because in his surroundings he continued to live in isolation in these areas. He took commercial and business contact with Gentiles as self-evident, according to the existing rulings by Moses Ravkash and Emden, according to which Christianity and Islam accepted many principles of Judaism. Christian and Muslim believers are not idol-worshipers, and we are in the midst of human progress according to the old predictions of Maimonides and Judah Halevi, and the new hopes of Mendelssohn.

HIRSCH'S RESPONSE
Background

The interaction between Jews and Christians in Germany was far stronger than that in the Austrian Empire, and certainly than their relations in Galicia. The Jews of Germany aspired to comprehensive emancipation that would include social, cultural, and academic life, and they wished to take part in every area of life. Acculturation, secularization, and emancipation fragmented the German communities, and rejection of the commandments, Reform Judaism, and conversion to Christianity became common phenomena.

Unlike Chajes, Hirsch could not be content with preserving the situation and with the classical views of Jewish Halakha and the Christian religion, and he had to combat the latter. His task was, on the one hand, to present the ethical superiority of the commandments

---

57 Chajes, *Shut Maharats*, 705-6.

of Judaism, and, on the other, the moral inferiority of Christianity as a religion that was fundamentally pagan. He had to do all this without offending the prevailing opinion in the Jewish tradition based on Judah Halevi and Maimonides (which was also accepted in Europe after Kant, Hegel, and Schleiermacher, from the Christian-romantic point of view), that there was a constant process of progress according to the divine plan in history, toward the salvation of mankind in the spirit of Judaism, and that the appearance of Jesus and Muhammad was part of this plan.

In Hirsch's criticism of Mendelssohn, we find the argument that the latter "treated the Bible only philologically and aesthetically, and did not build up Judaism as a science from itself, but merely defended it against political stupidity and pietistic Christian audacity."[58] In contrast to the defensive, apologetic arguments of Mendelssohn against the Christian world on the outside, Hirsch and the other leaders and thinkers of Judaism in the second third of the nineteenth century were mainly concerned with themselves, inwardly. They focused on the dispute about the essence of Judaism, its place in the world of European culture, and the argument about the centrality of the ritual and the commandments of the Torah in Judaism, and the possibility of reforming them.

Hirsch's outwardly directed struggles were less concerned with issues of emancipation, which was already almost a fait accompli, and more with obtaining the recognition of the authorities of the Orthodox communities' right to organize. In his writings, which were addressed to his Jewish community, Hirsch did not hesitate to attack Christianity theologically and philosophically, to defend the position that classical Judaism and not pure or classical Christianity, which the German idealist philosophers represented, provided the divine ethics that would lead Europe to salvation. Against the ideas of Spinoza, Kant, and Hegel about the superiority of Christianity and its ethics, and the inferiority of ritualized, outdated Judaism, Hirsch argued the opposite—that

---

58 Hirsch, *Nineteen Letters*, 189.

Christianity was outmoded, pagan, and immoral, whereas Judaism was the embodiment of superior, spiritual morality.[59]

The Dreadful Past and the Wonderful Present

Like Chajes, Hirsch also emphasizes the horrors of the past and praises of the present, but less as a defense against arguments from outside and more as an educator explaining the importance of the Jewish commandments to his students. In *Horeb*, he writes about the relations with Gentiles in the context of two commandments. The first is the prohibition of marrying a Gentile and eating with him, and the second is doing what is honest and good, even with a Gentile.

---

59 For the background of Jewish views of Christianity in Germany, a detailed presentation of the opinions and relations between the two religions and their communities, see M. A. Meyer, Chapter 5 of *German-Jewish History in the Modern Times, Vol II: Emancipation and Acculturation, 1780-1871*, ed. M. A. Meyer, M. Brenner, and S. Jersch Wenzel (New, York 1997), 168-98. According to his account of the views of Steinheim, Formstecher, Hirsch, and Geiger, a picture arises that is usually identical to that presented by Hirsch, and for the same reasons. It does, however, appear that their critique was more delicate than Hirsch's vehement criticism. Chertok, *Qanqan*, 25, 108, correctly notes that the polemics in Hirsch's commentary on the Torah were mainly directed inward, within the Jewish community, and at elements in it, and not outwardly against the Christians. Nevertheless, I intend to show that in his commentary there is a major dispute against Christianity, and its purpose is to prevent conversion and to increase the prestige of Judaism within the community, versus Christianity, which was inferior in his opinion. Chertok himself mentions outside targets of the polemics on pages 68-69, and in note 22 there, as well as on page 95. On page 39 as well, Chertok regards Hirsch's words in his commentary about the importance of giving rights to a *ger toshav* [resident alien] in Judaism as a criticism and demand for emancipation leveled against German society, and he asks how he could require behavior of them according to the ethics of the Torah. In my opinion, the criticism of German society here in the commentary is more directed inward, to inform Jewish society and to demonstrate that Judaism is superior to Christianity. Nevertheless, as I show, Hirsch expected the ethics of the Torah increasingly to penetrate the general society, according to the mission of the Jewish people, and in the end it, too, would chose a regime that would grant equal rights, according to Judaism. Rosenbloom, *Hirsch*, states that Hirsch was strongly influenced by Hegel. I do not ignore the fact that, like every cardinal position that influences the spirit of an age, the romantic idealistic theory of Hegel had some influence on Hirsch, and Breuer, too, takes note of this (*'Eda*, 63). Nevertheless, I believe that Hirsch opposed most of the main theses of Hegel, such as, for example, that of the "absolute spirit," and mainly that which regarded the Christian German state as the basis for the salvation of mankind, which Hirsch saw in the Torah and Jewish family ethics.

The first commandment is a barrier against assimilation, and its purpose is to preserve and defend the continuity of the Jewish spirit and life in purity forever. In the situation that has emerged today, the nations show signs of love and friendship to the Jews, and the Jewish people are grateful, thanking and blessing the ruler of their country with faithful love. In this situation, the Jews experience cooperation and closeness of two kinds: closeness in civil business, and closeness in ideas and religion: "Intercourse ... between Jews and non-Jews [becomes closer, and] ... the faith and outlook of other peoples become [allied] in part to those of Israel."[60] In this situation of economic and cultural ties, it is necessary to be more insistent on these prohibitions, because the danger of breaking through the boundaries is great. Hirsch quickly emphasizes that he regards the change as very positive, and he, like Chajes, defines the Christian Gentile as a *ger toshav*:

> Israel can rejoice today in the midst of the peoples among whom it mostly lives. Behold, Israel, how the holy light which God placed among you at Sinai has spread far and wide and has already scared away from a great part of humanity the delusion and abomination of idol-worship. Rejoice that in Europe, in America, and in part of Asia and Africa, non-Jewish peoples also have become illumined by the Revelation of the One God given to you and have adopted a doctrine which teaches them to perform the seven duties which according to your doctrine are binding on all men.... Rejoice in this. According to your law, he who expressly accepts these duties in the presence of three persons as having been enjoined upon all men by God in His Revelation to Moses, such a man is a ger toshav (גר תושב), a "proselyte of the gate" as he is called. Towards such a man you are not only to practise all the obligations of justice—as indeed also towards any idolator—but the Torah also commands you to perform towards him all the duties required by an active love (אתה מצווה להחיותו). You must esteem and love him as a genuine man, since he performs all the duties which God requires from all men.[61]

---

60 Hirsch, *Horeb*, vol. 2, 379.
61 Ibid., 379-80. Here, like Chajes, Hirsch accepts Emden's opinion that, according to Maimonides, the Gentile who observes the Noahide commandments must acknowledge that they were given to Moses, and he rejects Mendelssohn's position.

The second commandment is included in the obligation, "Do not despise an Egyptian, because you resided as foreigners in their country."[62] The meaning of this obligation is to forget all the evil done to the Israelites by the Egyptians and to remember only the good they did for them by allowing them to dwell in their land and subsist there. These words also apply to following generations, and therefore, from this the Jews must learn in our day as well one must forget all the sorrows and pogroms:

> Learn to forget the centuries of oppression and misery, of the inhuman scorn and the inhuman degradation which folly and lack of understanding brought upon you in your wandering in the Galuth, and remember gratefully the good that you found everywhere—and still find.... And now, Jew of today, now, when God has put into the hearts of the princes and the people a spirit of kindness, justice and humanity, and the yoke is lifted, and the chains are unbound and the scorn and degradation disappear and, through tender justice, the sons try to atone for the harsh unkindness with which their forefathers treated your people: with what heartfelt love and gratitude would you advance to meet your non-Jewish brother, if only you pondered carefully the full implication of this Divine commandment.[63]

In Hirsch's opinion, the phenomenon of Christianity is mainly positive:

> The Jew is glad when he sees man increase his acceptance of truth and morality, and foresees for his fellow man the rise of a morning sun which will shed cloudless light upon all mankind. It occurs to him that a single seed from among the multitude of God's saplings was implanted into the lap of mankind some two thousand years ago—although not free of distortion and misrepresentation. Still the seed has blossomed to benefit many.... Then he follows the slow progress the world will have made toward the realization of truth, love and justice for mankind—concepts which, knowingly or not, have been plucked from the Jewish Tree of Knowledge.[64]

---

62 Deut. 23:8.
63 Hirsch, *Horeb*, vol. 2, 443.
64 Hirsch, *Writings*, VIII, 8.

Hirsch develops Salvador's thesis, that the source of Christianity is in Judaism, and therefore it succeeds in influencing only the pagans, but the Jews were not at all convinced because of the pagan dogmas in its message:

> Did not Christianity arise from among the Jews?... The apostles of Christianity sought to bring a ray of true Mosaic monotheism not to the Jews but to the heathens.... The pure Mosaic monotheism was itself diluted and endangered by the Christian doctrine of the Trinity and therefore, from the very outset, had to abandon all hopes of making any great headway among the Jews.... The message of the Christian apostles contains two basic elements—a miracle and a doctrine. The miracle of a god turning into a man was nothing new for the heathens. They knew of a whole list of female mortals—Danae, Semele, Io, etc., on whom Theos or Deus had bestowed his favors and by whom he had fathered sons. The miracle of the "new message" was therefore nothing new to the Greeks, but the doctrine [of "Semitic Mosaism"] was ... [the thing] that gave its newly won adherents freedom and solace, enlightenment and inspiration, which they could never have derived from the wisdom of Theos, Deus, Tyr or Bog.
>
> To the Jews, on the other hand, the doctrine that the Christian apostles had to offer was perfectly familiar. For the wisdom of the "new message" was taken, without exception, even to its very style of expression, from the words of the Sages of Judaism. This is an indisputable fact. The Jews had no need to expect wisdom from the apostles of Christianity. On the other hand, the miracle in which the apostles of Christianity expected the Jews to believe was completely alien and incomprehensible to the "Semitic Jews" and shook the very foundations of the basic Jewish concept of God. One miracle can be substantiated only by another.[65]

The results of the spread of Christianity, many of whose principles are, as noted, derived from Judaism, were beneficial, because they protect both the revelation of the written Torah and the Oral Law:

> The peoples in whose midst the Jews are now living have accepted the Jewish Bible of the Old Testament as a book of Divine revelation. They profess their belief in the God of heaven and earth as proclaimed in the Bible, and they acknowledge the sovereignty of

---

65 Ibid., 314-15, "Nature and the Bible as Seen from the Materialistic Viewpoint," (1864).

Divine Providence in both this life and the next. Their acceptance of the practical duties incumbent upon all men by the Will of God distinguishes these nations from the heathen and idolatrous nations of the Talmudic era.... The peoples in whose midst we live today are regarded by the Talmud as the complete equals of the Jews and therefore entitled to our active charity and compassion in every respect.... Nearer our own day, toward the end of the eighteenth century, such noted Rabbinic authorities as R. Ezekiel Landau, R. Elazar Fleckeles and R. Jacob Emden dealt extensively with this subject in their writings. R. Jacob Emden in particular emphasizes this in his commentary on the Chapters of the Fathers 4:13: "We should consider Christians and Mohammedans as instruments that will help bring about the recognition of God by all men on earth. While the [heathen] nations worshipped their idols and denied the existence of God, and thus recognized neither the power of God nor the principle of reward and punishment, the existence of Christians and Mohammedans helped disseminate among the nations the awareness of God's existence, and introduced into the most distant lands the realization that there is a God Who rules the world, Who rewards and punishes, and Who has revealed Himself to men. Indeed, thinking Christian scholars have not only taught the nations to accept the written revelation but have also acted as defenders of the oral revelation which is equally of Divine origin. For when vicious people from our own midst, sworn enemies of the Law of God, conspired to abrogate the Talmud and to do away with it, there arose from among the non-Jews defenders who fought against these attempts.[66]

Like Chajes, Hirsch, too, explains the low morality of the Jews with the claim that it is the fault of the nations among whom the Jews lived, discriminating against them, by not allowing them to acquire land and engage in agriculture. The Jews did not receive equal rights, and constant fear of expulsion confined them to only certain specific occupations and fostered abilities that enabled them to survive under difficult circumstances.[67] However, unlike Chajes, Hirsch did not hesitate to enter into discussions of the figure of Jesus, on the one hand, and of the preposterous and dangerous dogmas of ecclesiastical Christianity, on the other.

---

66 *Writings*, VII, 226-27, "Talmudic Judaism and Society."
67 See Ibid., 233.

The Figure of Jesus

Hirsch accepted in principle the approach presented during the Middle Ages by Judah Halevi and Maimonides, which Emden adopted in the modern period. This approach was developed by scholars in the Haskala period and after it, headed by Joseph Salvador. According to this approach, a distinction had to be made between Jesus's figure and message, which were mainly Jewish, and Pauline, ecclesiastical Christianity, which was partially pagan and developed after Jesus. Hence, Hirsch regards Christianity in general and the figure of Jesus in particular, as phenomena in the positive direction, as part of the divine plan in history for disseminating monotheism and the unity of humanity, which is derived from it, among the corrupt, benighted pagans—and it had decisive ethical consequences. This is how Hirsch describes the appearance of Jesus on the stage of history:

> On the very eve of the exile, a branch left the parent tree, which was obliged to surrender largely the characteristics of the parent stem, in order to bring to the world, which had relapsed into polytheism, violence, immorality, the tidings of the existence of the All-One and of the brotherhood of man and his superiority to the beast, and to proclaim the deliverance of mankind from the bondage of wealth-and-lust worship, [as opposed to embracing these things as a means to serve the All-One—with its later branch it was a great step toward advancing the goal of history].[68]

The "branch" is Jesus, and from it grew ecclesiastical Christianity. According to Hirsch, Jesus preached the most important ethical principle of Judaism: sanctification of the body and of property for religious and spiritual purposes, which were established in the revelation to the Jews. The source of Christianity is in Judaism, and its basis is the Old Testament:

---

68 *Nineteen Letters*, 81. The English translation by Drachman omits the words in square brackets, see Ben Usiel (Rabbiner Samson Raphael Hirsch), *Neunzehn Briefe über Judentum*, fourth edition (Frankfut am Main, 1911), 46. I am grateful for the assistance of Professor David B. Dollenmayer in translating it—J.G. See also Hirsch, *Writings* II, 369; VIII, 8. Geiger developed this idea later.

> The Jews are said to be a sinful nation, and yet it is the Jewish World of Right and Truth on which nations and sovereigns build their sovereignty and their national life!... Yet it is Jewish history, the stories of Jewish men and women, the stories of Abraham, Isaac, Jacob, Joseph, Sarah, Rachel, Moses, Samuel, Hanna, David, and Daniel which the Christian child is taught in his childhood. And it is the stories of these great people that influence the Christian's moral convictions and humaneness.[69]

Judaism does not proselytize. Therefore it is pleased to accept all spiritual or moral human progress brought by other religions. It regards the other religions as its daughters, proud of their achievements, and regarding them as the accomplishment of their mission.

> It hails every ... triumph of truth and goodness as a triumph of its own mission on earth. The attitude of Judaism toward other religions may be compared to that of a true mother toward her daughters.... Judaism rejoices, and has a right to rejoice, in the harvest of light and goodness produced by its daughter religions in the civilized world for the benefit of universal human happiness and culture, just as if the accomplishment had come directly from Judaism. Judaism regards these advances as triumphs of the concepts that are to be brought to the rest of mankind by the Divinely-selected Jewish people.[70]

Of course, Christianity contains many invalid aspects, and there is much room for improvement. Ecclesiastic Christianity distorted the teachings of Jesus and made him into a god, in absolute contradiction to the principles of Judaism. Hirsch discusses this distortion in his commentary on the beginning of Exodus, which treats the figure of

---

69 *Writings*, I, 369.
70 Ibid., VII, 87. These statements of Hirsch led Breuer, *'Eda*, 89, to write of him: "Most probably there has never been a rabbi who spoke so well, with such positively conditioned admiration of Christianity, with such powers of persuasion." While in comparison to many other observant Jews, this is correct, one cannot ignore the fact that Breuer minimizes, unjustifiably, in my opinion, the severity of Hirsch's critique of dogmatic Christianity, which I present below. In my opinion, his remark applies first of all to Emden, whose position was presented above, then to Chajes and Luzzatto, and only lastly to Hirsch.

Moses in the Bible and describes his genealogy in detail, in order to emphasize his humanity:

> Right from the earliest times it has happened that men who were outstanding benefactors to their people were, after their death, divested of their human image and, because of their "godlike" feats, were invested with a "Divine" origin. We all know of a certain Jew, in later times, whose genealogical record was *not* available,[71] and *because* it was not available, and because he brought people a few sparks of light borrowed from the *man* Moshe, he came to be considered by the nations as begotten of God;[72] to doubt his divinity was a capital crime.
>
> *Our* Moshe was human, remained human, and will never be anything but human…. This "certificate of origin" is meant to negate in advance and forevermore any erroneous deification, any illusion of an incarnation of Deity in human form. It is meant to uphold this truth: Moshe, the greatest man of all time, was just a man, and the position he attained before God was not beyond the reach of mortal human beings.[73]

In contrast to the position of Judaism, which presents a transcendent deity outside of the material world, which He made, the Christian church took a pagan position, according to which Jesus is God, the son of God, who was incarnated in a material person for a certain time.

Hirsch also makes a comparison between the miracles attributed with great pride to Jesus in the Gospels, and the miracles attributed to Moses in the Torah, emphasizing the unexpected outcome of this comparison on their respective images:

> People of other faiths tell of miracle workers who provided the multitude with loaves and performed all sorts of wonders—but what is all that compared to providing for the nutritional needs of two and a half million human souls for forty years on their journey through

---

71 This remark of Hirsch is based on an argument of Salvador, who believed that the whole matter of the virgin birth by the Holy Spirit was meant to deflect arguments that Jesus was born of an incestuous union or illegitimate. Flusser argued that the source of this belief is also found in Judaism.
72 The original German here is "gotteserzeugten." In Breuer's Hebrew translation of the commentary, he wrote "created by God," which is a term that would apply to everyone.
73 Hirsch on Ex. 6:14-30. See also Hirsch on Gen. 12:10-13.

the heart of the wilderness! Another person—even if of only slightly lesser stature than Moshe—would certainly have been unable to resist the temptation of basking in the glow of such Divine glory!

Yet here we see that "the man Moshe" shrinks from assuming such glory.... His whole desire was to diminish his own personality in the eyes of the people, to dispel the notion that he stood between the people and God. Moshe wished to be a man—and no more. This was his supreme greatness.[74]

Of course, Hirsch denied that Jesus was the messiah. He made use of Zechariah 9:9, which the Christians applied to Jesus, in particular to show the difference between Christian and Jewish messianism. According to classical Christianity, the messiah has come once, in the figure of Jesus. He is God, who was incarnated in man, and he will save everyone who believes in his messianic essence. In Judaism, by contrast, the messiah has not yet come, and the world still awaits his advent. In Judaism, the messiah is a redeemed righteous man who comes to teach that if the Jews are righteous as he is, and they take the path he shows them, they will be saved by God together with him.

The messiah himself is poor and rides on a simple donkey. "צדיק [*tsadiq*, righteous] and נושע [*nosha'*, saved] is he. *He is not a [moshia', savior]* מושיע, he is saved. *He is not a God who saves,* but a *man,* whose whole power is in his righteousness, *and for the sake of his righteousness God will save him and help him to victory.*"[75]

The whole idea of suffering and pain on behalf of others and the ethic of turning the other cheek and humbling oneself as an ideal is unacceptable in Judaism. "The Jewish 'lamb' is not a meek, sad creature that bears the troubles of the world upon its shoulders, allowing itself to be led to the slaughter without offering resistance: שה תמים זכר בן-שנה יהיה לכם [Your lamb shall be an unblemished male a year old] (Exodus 12:5): Whole in body, with manly vigor and the freshness of eternal youth—thus shall it symbolize our character."[76]

According to Hirsch, Jesus was therefore a Jew who wished to benefit his people and who preached the unity of God and the moral

---

74 Hirsch on Ex. 16:8.
75 Hirsch on Gen. 49:11. Hebrew and italics in source.
76 Hirsch on Ex. 12:3-6.

message of human brotherhood, and thereby he became an outstanding figure, who brought the idol-worshipers out of corrupt paganism according to the divine plan. His followers erred and were dazzled by the small light that he brought them, and they accepted him as a messiah and even made him into a god, and thereby they stamped Christianity with the seal of paganism. Unlike Emden, Chajes, and Luzzatto, or their predecessors Meiri and Rivkes, and following Maimonides, Hirsch regards Christianity as marked by paganism.

Original Sin: A Pagan Dogma

Paul introduced the doctrine of Original Sin in Christianity. Whereas the Pharisees believed in a doctrine whose components were sin, repentance, and atonement, Paul stated that the components were sin, crucifixion, belief, and redemption. The saved would attain paradise, and the rest would be condemned to eternal damnation. Martin Luther developed Paul's deterministic thesis of Original Sin and stated that physical and spiritual life must be entirely separated. Man did not have free will. He was not master of his deeds, and therefore positive commandments could not be imposed on him. The believer must be free of the need to do good deeds, in order to ascend to the spiritual level, because outward human deeds have no influence on inner spiritual life. The believer is therefore not judged by his outward actions, of which he is not the master, and the inner, spiritual foundation must be liberated from the outer bonds of actions.[77]

Hirsch sees this Christian doctrine as extremely dangerous, and he discusses it in many places in comparison to Judaism. In his opinion, the idea that man is essentially evil and subject to his appetites in this world, with no possibility of escape by means of repentance, out of free will, and only the believer in Jesus receives divine grace in the next world, without any obligation on his part to act morally, is deterministic, pagan, abominable, and corrupt.

---

77 On Luther's separation of corporeal and spiritual life, see R. Schechter, *Luter Berei Haleumanut Vehaantishemiut Hagermanit Hamodernit* (PhD Dissertation, Hebrew University, Jerusalem, 1973), 10-13.

Judaism is preferable to Christianity ethically speaking because it teaches that man is created in purity, and he has the full potential, with no intermediary, to repent of his own free will, and return to God, and to paradise, at any time, and to gain the world to come in this world by fulfilling the will of God, which is embodied in the morality and commandments of the Torah. In place of Christian love and faith, Judaism offers fidelity to duty and law. In discussing Adam's sin and his punishment, Hirsch states unequivocally that the dogma of Original Sin is erroneous and false:

> *The Divine judgment directs a curse at the earth and at the serpent, but this judgment contains not a hint of a curse against man. Man is not cursed in any way. Nothing was changed in man's lofty calling or in his ability to fulfill it.* Only the external conditions, only the stage on which he is to fulfill his mission have changed—and even this happened only for his own good. The mission itself, his Divine calling and his ability to fulfill it, have not changed one iota. To this day, every newborn infant emerges from God's hand in purity, as did Adam in his time; every child comes into the world as pure as an angel, to live and become a man. This is one of the cardinal points in the Torah of Israel and in Jewish life.
>
> But what a miserable and hopeless picture of man is drawn by those who err and deny his purity. On the basis of the story of גן עדן [*gan 'eden*, the Garden of Eden], they have concocted a lie that undermines the moral future of mankind. We are referring to the dogma of "Original Sin," on the basis of which they have build a spiritual structure against which the Jew must protest with every fiber of his being.
>
> It is true that, on account of the sin in the Garden of Eden, all of Adam's descendants inherited the task of living in a world that no longer smiles at them as it once did, but this is so only because this same sin is still being committed over and over again. However, the express purpose of the present conflict between man and earth and of man's resultant "training by renunciation" is to guide man toward moral perfection, which will pave the way for his return to Paradise.
>
> But to say that because of "Original Sin" *sinfulness is innate* in man, that man has *lost the ability to be good* and is now *compelled* to sin—these are notions *against which Judaism raises its most vigorous protest.*
>
> Man as an individual and mankind as a whole can, at any time, return to God and to Paradise on earth. Toward this end, man needs

no medium other than devotion to duty, which is within the capacity of *every human being*. Toward this end, there is no need for an intermediary who has died and then been resurrected. This is attested to by all of Jewish history, from which we learn that, in subsequent generations, God drew as near to men of purity as He did to אדם הראשון [*adam harishon*, the first man] before the sin. Avraham, Moshe, Yeshayahu, Yirmeyahu, and others like them attained God's nearness simply by their faithfulness to duty. The first principle of Judaism—the one, free God—goes hand in hand with the second principle, namely that of the pure and free man.

The dogma of Original Sin is a most regrettable error of an alien faith. They think that, in consequence of this sin, sinfulness is innate in man, and that man can be saved from the curse of sin, only by virtue of the belief in a certain fact. In the story of גן עדן, however, there is no mention of a curse against man. To this day, every Jew avows before God: נשמה שנתת בי טהורה היא, "The soul that you have given me is pure," and it is up to me alone to keep it pure and to return it to You in its original state of purity. As our Sages teach us: ... there is no age in which people like Avraham, Ya'akov, Moshe, and Shemuel do not live" (*Bereshit Rabbah* 56:7). *In every age, in every generation, man is capable of ascending to the highest levels of morality and spirituality.*[78]

The thesis of Original Sin undermines the ethical future of humanity by denying it the hope of returning to paradise in this world of its own free will. This thesis is not mentioned in the Hebrew Bible. The principles of Judaism are a single God who rules over the forces of nature, and a pure, free man to whom God grants free choice to obey His instructions in the Torah faithfully, and thus to overcome the sensual forces of nature that are in flesh. Hirsch repeats his opposition to the Christian idea that man is evil by nature several times. For example, on the verse, "every *yetser* [יצר] of the thoughts of his heart was only evil

---

78 Hirsch on Gen. 3:19. Italics, insertion of Hebrew words, and spelling of biblical names as in the published translation. See also Hirsch, *Writings*, I, 178-80, 216; II, 10. Interestingly, on the one hand Kant accepts the Christian dogma that man is evil by nature, while, on the other hand, he does not accept the idea that grace depends solely on faith in Jesus, and he requires moral action as a condition for receiving divine grace. See Bergman, *Kant*, 150-57, based on E. Kant, *Religion Within the Limits of Reason Alone*, trans. T. M. Greene and H. H. Hudsor (New York and Evanston, 1960).

continually"⁷⁹ Hirsch writes, "It is unfortunate that יצר is so often translated as 'drive' or 'impulse,' as though there were a force in man that urges and impels him to do evil. This is the source of that bleak view which is one of the basic concepts of a large 'religion': the dogma of the *power of evil* which holds man in its power and from which he can be saved only by virtue of a certain belief. Thus the word יצר is twisted into a cord of falsehood by which mankind is bound and gagged."⁸⁰

Elsewhere Hirsch emphasizes that this idea is immoral, since it teaches people that there is no reason or need for moral action, and it is not effective or necessary to remove people from the state of sin:

> To offer such a חטאת [*ḥatat*, sin offering] would mean one of two things: either it would represent the condition of חטא [*ḥet*, sin], sinfulness, as the normal condition of the human being, or it would express the very opposite extreme, that man is sinless. Such spiritual arrogance, no less than the idea of unrectifiable sinfulness, means the demise of all moral perfection. The one—because one believes there is no *need* for ascent; the other—because one believes there is no *possibility* of ascent.⁸¹

Hirsch states that the theory of Original Sin, according to which man comes to this world condemned to a life of sin and defers reward only to the world to come, cannot be proven. Therefore its truth cannot be guaranteed. Only in Judaism are promises kept in this world, to someone who sanctifies his life according to the morality of the Torah, and thereby its truth is manifest. Judaism (and not Christianity) is thus the only hope of humanity for the fulfillment of the ideas of romantic idealism about the general progress of mankind toward an epoch of justice and peace in this world:

> Other religions teach what man must do in order to attain closeness to God in the *next* world; Judaism teaches what we must do so that God will draw near *to us* in *this* world. Judaism teaches that עיקר שכינה בתחתונים [*'iqar shekhina bataḥtonim*, the essence of the divine

---

79 Gen. 6:5.
80 Hirsch on Gen. 6:5. See also his commentary on Lev. 4:11-12.
81 Hirsch on Lev. 4:24.

presence is in the lower worlds] (*Bereshit Rabbah* 19:7); God seeks, first of all, to dwell on earth together with man; He says ועשו לי מקדש ושכנתי בתוכם (*Shemot* 25:8), "Let them make of their lives on earth a sanctuary to Me, and then I will dwell in their midst." To perfect the world through the reign of the Almighty—not only in the heavens above, but also on the earth below—is the mission of Israel and the purpose of its Torah.

That is why all the Torah's promises relate to *this* world. Any charlatan can sign checks that are payable in the next world; it is easy to promise reward or punishment—in heaven or hell. But only ה׳ אלקים אמת ומלך עולם [the Lord God is truth and eternal king] can make promises that are fulfilled on earth before our very eyes.

The Torah's ideal is שכינה [*shekhina*]. Wherever man sanctifies his home and makes his camp holy, ה׳ מתהלך בקרב מחנהו [God walks about in His camp]; God fills him with rapture on earth and allows him to experience in this world מעין עולם הבא [something like the world to come]. This is the Torah's aim and goal for the Jewish people, and this is destined to be the lot of all mankind, when they return to "the way that leads to the tree of life."[82]

The same idea, expressed in different words, is found elsewhere: "Other religions teach man how to merit the next world by renouncing this world. Judaism teaches man to perform his duty in his lifetime, so that he may attain bliss already in this world, and so that the life of the world to come should begin even during his life on earth."[83]

Some Criticism

While the thesis of Christianity is not very reasonable, Hirsch's demagogic writings are not convincing either. Is it true that the righteous never suffer, and that the wicked sometimes prosper? This is what the prophets protested against, without receiving an answer. Did he forget the words of Rabbi Jacob, who taught, "there is no reward for [observing] a commandment in this world"[84]? Historical

---

82 Hirsch on Gen. 9:27.
83 Hirsch on Lev. 29:13. Other critics of Christianity commented on its rejection of this world, including Joseph Salvador, Elijah Ben-Amozegh, and Joseph Klausner (*Yeshu*, vol. 2, 250-52). It could be that Salvador aroused Hirsch to take up this burden.
84 BT Kidushin 39b, Hulin 142a. And also the Ethics of the Fathers 2:17, citing Rabbi Tarfon: "And you must know: the giving of the reward of a righteous man is to come in the future."

evidence shows that in periods of forced conversion and persecutions, such as when the Roman pagans persecuted Jews and Christians without mercy, it was reasonable to think that the righteous would receive their reward only in the world to come. In contrast, in a time of tranquility, tolerance, and emancipation, Hirsch could advance his claim. In any event his treatment of the problem of reward and punishment is superficial and fundamentalist. Hirsch argues that in Judaism it is possible to sever the connection between past sin and future life, so that the sin will not adversely affect the possibility that a pure future will bloom after a faulty past. The severance and atonement are effectuated by an omnipotent God, who also creates the causal connection between sin and its consequences. The past is buried for someone who repents and takes it upon himself with all his soul to devote himself to the duty that has been commanded to him. However, silent acceptance is insufficient, and confession is also necessary.

> When God's grace, by its absolute power, comes to "bury" the blemished past, it is a person's duty not to bury it and conceal it from his own consciousness; rather, his sin should remain ever before him, vivid and unobscured by illusions.
> This is the Jewish conception of וידוי [*vidui*, confession]. It does not entail confession to another person, or even to God. Rather, it is an admission to oneself ... that one has sinned.... By recognizing the freedom of the moral will, he rejects any excusing of present or future sin.[85]

That is to say: Hirsch adopts the Pharisaic position, as it took shape in Jewish law and tradition, regarding the process of atonement, which includes remorse, confession from the depths of the heart, and acceptance for the future, which makes the sinner into a new, pure person, whose past is erased by God. Simple outward confession by a person who believes that he is incapable of removing himself from the state of sin, and which does not oblige him to accept ethical norms in the future, is ineffective and immoral.

---

85 Hirsch on Lev. 16:6.

Hirsch puts forward the comprehensive theory that according to Judaism, God, who created the laws of nature, is of necessity free and not bound by them, and He may change them and subject them to His will. That God created man in His image, the meaning of which is the granting of the characteristics of freedom to man, who was created as a being with moral freedom, and his spirit is free to liberate itself from subjection to the laws of nature and to sanctify his body. According to the view of Judaism, man must sacrifice the forces of nature within him to the free God, to subjugate them with the powers of the spirit within him, which are assisted by the commandments of the Torah, and thereby to attain true freedom and salvation in his lifetime. In contrast, Christianity is deterministic, and Hirsch includes it among the materialist theories, which he calls "modern heathenism." The position of Christianity is that man is subject in a deterministic and arbitrary manner to the laws of nature and the desires of the flesh, which his body imposes upon him because of Original Sin, and he must sacrifice himself to the forces and laws of nature and hope that, upon his death, he will attain grace and salvation. Judaism is therefore freedom, and Christianity is subjugation.[86] This is how Hirsch describes Judaism versus "modern heathenism":

> In any case, this expression [abhorrence] is characteristic of Judaism's attitude toward ancient and modern heathenism [materialism]. That to which other peoples sacrifice themselves, the Jew offers to his God. The gods of the other nations are the mighty forces of nature, to which man must submit, and the powerful forces of nature within man, to which he is subject. The heathen idolizes the forces of nature that are around him and within him, and he submits to them helplessly. The Jew, however, in his offerings, kills the representatives of these forces, and thereby makes himself aware of his ability to master the forces of nature within himself. By mastering these forces through the exercise of his freedom, and by submitting them to the one free almighty God, he also frees himself from the dominion of all the blind external forces of nature. By offering up the idol that is within himself, he breaks the chains of the external bondage posed by nature.[87]

---

86 See Hirsch on Gen. 1:27; Lev. 16:10.
87 Hirsch on Ex. 8:22. See also on Lev. 9:2 and 10:1.

There is, in effect, no difference between paganism, which submits to the external forces of nature, and "modern heathenism"—which also includes Christianity, according to which, because of Original Sin, man is subject to the forces of nature within him, the sensual appetites of the flesh—and he does not have the moral freedom to subjugate them. Luther's development of this thesis was also criticized vehemently by Hirsch. Judaism is opposed to all dualism of body and soul. The body, too, is divine, and combined with the soul, and sanctification of the body in this world, in order to raise man up to the spiritual level, is the task of man, endowed with free will, and not ruled by the forces of nature:

> Nothing undermines morality more than that erroneous conception that splits the human נפש [*nefesh*, soul]. This view recognizes the Divine dignity of the spirit, and instructs the spirit to elevate itself to higher worlds, but allows the body unbridled license, to indulge animal-like in the smut of sensuality. And to great men of intellect, this view even grants special immunity in the moral degeneration of the body. Not so is the destiny of man as depicted in God's Torah. Sanctification of the body and preservation of man's Divine form are the cornerstone of all moral refinement and the condition for all spiritual ennoblement; and the higher the spirit seeks to ascend, the greater the demand for bodily sanctity.... Many *mitzvos* written in the Torah are intended solely for the benefit and rectification of the body.... so that the body should continue to be צלם אלקים [the image of God], and not שקץ, טמא [*tame*, *sheqets*], and תועבה [*toeva*, impure abhorrent, and an abomination].[88]

Christianity as a Religion of Death: The Ultimate Source of Ritual Impurity, and the Place of Religious Leaders

Along with the theory that Christianity is a combination of Judaism and paganism, Joseph Salvador also developed the theory that Jesus regarded himself as the messiah. At the same time, he believed that his doctrine of the messiah was essentially different from the one taught by

---

88 Hirsch on Gen. 1:27. I wonder whether Hirsch saw any of Nietzsche's writings about the Dionysian spirit.

the Pharisees. The latter sought to offer earthly happiness to people as much as was possible, without damaging their spiritual lives. Hence Pharisaic Judaism dealt with settling in the world and improving it, a doctrine of life for a nation living on its land. Jesus, in contrast, was not at all concerned with social life, but with the morality and religion of the individual believer. Jesus, according to Salvador, was contemptuous of life in this world and sought life in the world to come—the future kingdom of heaven—and he denied life in the present, on earth. Jesus was concerned only with the life of souls after death and not with human society in the world. Seeing the sharp opposition of his Jewish brethren to his life's work, he despaired of human society and preached asceticism and radical morality. Jesus believed that this world would soon become a new creation—the kingdom of heaven, and thus there was no need for material possessions or family life. Jesus developed a gloomy and pessimistic system of ethics of the end of days.[89]

Hirsch appropriated these two theories and used them for his own purposes, to show his fellow Jews that Christianity was pagan, that it sanctified death and the world to come, and that it could not bring salvation to humanity—contrary to the arguments of Kant and Hegel. Humanity requires moral correction in this world, and only Judaism frees man from the consciousness of subjugation to the sensual forces of nature, sanctifies life on earth, and teaches ethics that also sanctify the body in this world.

Hirsch develops a model according to which he explains the meaning of [טומאה] "contamination," [חטאת] "purification" or "sin," and [טהרה] "purity," as they appear in the Bible. According to Judaism, man must free himself from subjection to the forces of nature, which restricts the divine powers of the spirit that are within him. When a person is stuck in certain situations, where his mind and consciousness are filled with the feeling of inability to free himself from the coercion of the forces of nature and bodily necessity, and his free ethical will is paralyzed, he is in a state of "contamination." This situation occurs when contact is made with a human corpse or an animal carcass, with a

---

89 See J. Salvador, *Jésus Christ et sa doctrine* (Paris 1818), vol. 1, 356-414. Klausner accepted this theory in full. See Klausner, *Yeshu*, vol. 1, 151-52, 233-36, 250-51.

woman who is menstruating or has given birth, a person with genital discharge, or a leper. A person frees himself from this situation by ritual immersion and by sprinkling the purifying water [מי חטאת], or sacrificing a sin-offering [קרבן חטאת] and he restores to his consciousness the perpetuity of the free morality and spirit in man, by which he is able to overcome the sensual, ephemeral forces of nature, and then he returns to the state of "purity."

> The human corpse demonstrates the power of death for all to see, and the superficial observer perceives in the corpse the power of nature dominating everything, including man. If the *whole* man has succumbed to death; if the corpse lying before us, overwhelmed by the compelling forces of nature, represents all that there is to man, then man, even during his lifetime, is no different from any other living thing. He is under the spell of a universally compelling necessity. If all this were indeed so, then this physical "must" would not leave room for any moral "thou shalt." Then moral freedom would be an illusion, God's moral law would be inconceivable, and its demands to freely dedicate one's existence and will to the purifying and vivifying fire of the Sanctuary would rest on baseless suppositions....
>
> The whole purpose of the laws of [*tuma*, impurity] טומאה and טהרה [*tahara*, purity] ... is to negate this idea. These laws confront the demoralizing illusion of physical nonfreedom with the Divine guarantee that man does indeed have moral freedom. Throughout our lives, whenever the energy of moral awareness is threatened by reminders of bondage to physical forces, the Law reminds us of the טהרה-elements of moral freedom.... Man *can be free of sin, can clear himself of sin, and can remain free of sin....*
>
> Man is indeed capable of controlling himself in the face of any physical temptation. This חטאת *proclaims the general fact that man is endowed with moral willpower.*
>
> However, in proclaiming man's freedom, it recognizes that he is subject to physical forces; it demonstrates moral freedom in connection with physical subjection. It does not teach man to close his eyes and ignore the physical subjection which is a part of his nature. Rather, it shows man in the whole contrast of his nature. For he is mortal, and at the same time he is eternal; he is fettered, and at the same time he is free; he is endowed with physical powers along with moral powers. By placing him, in the totality of his dual nature, before the Sanctuary of the one sole God, Who is the only One with absolute freedom, this חטאת [*ḥatat*, purifying water] elevates man

> with his whole nature, with his transient physical powers and with his eternal moral powers, into the free, eternal sphere of the one, sole God, and says to him: Do not be misled by the sight of corpses and of death; become free, become immortal, not *despite*, but *along with* all those aspects of your existence that are mortal and physically fettered. Be the immortal master of your mortal body; in the midst of טומאה, preserve your טהרה!⁹⁰

Denial of the freedom of God and of man is idol-worship, which has not yet left the world, and, in contrast, freedom from the coercion of the powers of nature is sanctity:

> טומאה [impurity] is a state in which every living thing—including man who is called to moral freedom—submits to the ruling force of the body. The essence of this force is embodied in death; hence טומאת מת [dead corpse impurity] is אבי אבות הטומאה [the ultimate source of impurity]. טומאה signifies the compulsion of natural forces, the power that basically has been considered a deity by pagans throughout the ages, people who deny the freedom of God as they deny the freedom of man, and who think that everything is subject to the physical compulsion of blind governing necessity.... The proclamation "קדש לה'" [sanctified to God] ... plac[es] all the sacred things of the altar under the sovereignty of the Only One, the God of freedom, life and truth, Whose creations and servants are all the physical forces and laws of nature, before whom the pagans bow in trembling fear.
>
> Just as He, in His almighty power and freedom, reigns supreme over all the compelling forces of nature, He also summons man, whom He created in the image of His Divine freedom, to rise above all the compelling forces of blind nature and lead a life of continually expanding moral freedom, a life of serving God *and God alone*, a life of holiness—and holiness means liberation from domination by the forces of blind nature.⁹¹

Pagan doctrines, which submit to the forces of nature and to death are identical to the materialist doctrines prevalent in Europe: "Whereas death brings to mind man's frailty and his submission to the forces of nature, man must stand tall in the midst of the physical world, proud of

---

90 Hirsch on Num. 19:22. See also his commentary on Gen. 2:7, Lev. 11:43, and Num. 5:2-3.
91 Hirsch on Lev. 28:38. See also his commentary on Num. 6:6.

his vital freedom; he must immunize himself against the doctrine of materialism, which undermines all morality and draws its wisdom from post-mortem examinations."[92]

As I have shown above, in the discussion of Hirsch's ethical doctrine, he uses the terms "modern heathenism" or "the heathenism of all times" in reference to all the immanent philosophical theories that do not accept the dogma of a transcendent God. Among these is Spinoza's pantheistic-deterministic philosophy, according to which God is identical to nature, to an object. He also uses those terms in reference to Hegel's philosophy, which made a dialectical move between Spinoza's object and Kant's rational subject, and according to it God is embodied and actualized in human history. History for Hegel is a kind of divine spirit, which transcends nature and sublates it, according to the Christian dogma of the incarnation of God in the flesh of Jesus. These terms also are applied to the Marxist materialistic theory, and even, perhaps, to Nietzsche's philosophy (if Hirsch was acquainted with it), and, in contrast, panentheistic Kabbala, according to which natural reality is part of the divinity.[93] In his discussion of the three prohibitions, "They shall not make baldness upon their head, neither shall they shave off the corners of their beard, nor make any cuttings in their flesh" (Lev. 21:5), Hirsch develops the argument even further and points out new facts from the Christian world that strengthen his claim that Christianity is the religion of death:

> Heathenism, both ancient and modern, tends to associate religion with death. The kingdom of God begins only where man dies. Death and dying are the main manifestations of divinity. For, in the heathen view, the deity is a god of death, not of life; a god who kills and never revives, who sends death and its harbingers—sickness and poverty—so that men, mindful of his power and their own helplessness, should fear him. For this reason, heathen temples stand beside graves, and the foremost place of heathen priests is beside a corpse. There, where the eyes are dimmed and the heart is broken, they find fertile soil for the dissemination of their religion. He who bears on

---

92 Hirsch on Lev. 11:46-47.
93 On the theories regarding God's immanence of Spinoza, Kant, Hegel, Marx, and Nietzsche, and their connection with Christianity, see Yovel, *Spinoza*, 275-305.

> his flesh a mark of death [viz. baldness, shaving, cutting]—a symbol of death's power to conquer all—and thus remains ever mindful of death, performs the religious act *par excellence*, and this especially befits a priest and his office.
>
> Nor so are the priests in Judaism, because not so is the Jewish concept of God and not so is the Jewish religion. God, Who instructs the כהן [*kohen*, priest] regarding his position in Israel, is a God of life. The most exalted manifestation of God is not in the power of death, which crushes strength and life. Rather, God reveals Himself in the liberating and vitalizing power of life, which elevates man to free will and eternal life. Judaism teaches us not how to die but how to live, so that even in life we may overcome death, an unfree existence, enslavement to physical things, and moral weakness. Judaism teaches us how to live every moment of earthly life as a moment of eternal life in the service of God; how thus to live every moment of a life marked by moral freedom, a life of thought and will, creativity and achievement, and also pleasure...
>
> When death summons the other members of the people to perform acts of loving kindness for the physical shell of a נפש [*nefesh*, soul] that has been called home to God, 'כהני ה [the priests of God] must stand back and keep away. By standing back, they raise the banner of life beside the corpse. They awaken in people's consciousness the idea of life and remind them of moral freedom, of man's godly existence, which is not subjugated to the bodily forces that suppress all moral freedom. They reinforce in people's consciousness the idea of life, so that it is not overshadowed by the idea of death.[94]

Hirsch argues that the location of graves around the church and the place of the priest, crossing himself at the bedside of a dying person, like the tattoos and scarification that pagans apply to their bodies, excellently symbolize the connection of Christianity to death, whereas Judaism sanctifies life, removes graves to the outskirts of towns and priests from contact with the dead. The comparison between the Christian priesthood and that of Judaism, in Hirsch's opinion, is clearly disadvantageous to Christianity, whose priests exploit conditions of suffering and poverty and employ emotion in an extreme manner, sorrow and weeping, and, in a manipulative way they make cheap use

---

94 See also Hirsch on Ex. 16:25 and *Writings*, II, 43, 68.

of them to promote religious fanaticism, and they are called priests [כמרים (*kemarim*, Gentile priests)] because of the expression "נכמרו רחמיו"—["his mercy was stirred"; play of words on the root כמר]. In contrast, the Jewish priests employ pure reason to improve man's power of judgment.

> The Jewish כהן [priest] is not dependent on devotion, emotion. Jewish Divine service is not designed to excite dark mysterious feelings. The Jewish Sanctuary appeals *primarily to the intellect*: התפלל [*hitpalel*, prayed] means to rectify one's *judgment* and to make clear to oneself one's relationship to things in general, one's duties. Feelings are very cheap. One can weep copiously before God in prayer, and then get up and be no better than one was before! The כומר [*komer*, Gentile priest] counts on exciting the emotions. The כהן [*kohen*, Jewish priest], however, has to be כן [*ken*, sincere] with himself and מכין [*mekhin*, prepares], provide others with firm direction and a firm basis. Heathenism works on the emotions and thereby shackles the intellect. The emotions, however, are like a clock mechanism without hands, restless movement that knows not whence or whither, which can be exploited for any purpose. The כומר fans the flames of hell and arouses fanaticism; he celebrates his triumph when נכמרו רחמיו, when the innards of the believers reach a point of total ferment.[95]

In Christianity there is an ecclesiastical hierarchy, while there is no priestly hierarchy in Judaism, and authority always rests in the hands of the Halakhic authorities. "Nowhere do we find even the slightest hint of such an idea that the כהן גדול [high priest] was a prototype for the authority of a 'pope.'"[96] The distinction between a Christian priest and a Cohen is epitomized in the question of what satisfaction he is supposed to provide: that of man with the actions of God or that of

---

95 Hirsch on Gen. 43:30. Hirsch's explanation of prayer as directed toward the person praying and not to God with the expectation of influencing Him, penetrated deeply into Jewish thought after him. One prominent proponent of this view was Leibowitz, who also emphasized that prayer was a person's duty as part of service of God, and a human could not influence God. Leibowitz went on to develop this position with the argument that prayer did not open a dialogue, and the worshiper should not expect to satisfy his needs by means of it. See Y. Leibowitz, *Yahadut, 'Am Yisrael Umedinat Yisrael* (Jerusalem, 1975), 385-90.

96 Hirsch on Lev. 4:3.

God with the actions of man? "*It is not the task of the* כהן *to suit God to man's needs;* the כהן's task does not square with the modern conception of 'meeting the religious needs of man.' Rather, *the task of the* כהן *is to prepare man for, and suit him to, God's Will;* his duty is to act so that God finds satisfaction in man and in man's deeds."⁹⁷ The same distinction is made between the Jewish temple and the Christian church.

> The Jewish Temple is not a place of "wonder-working grace," to which primarily the infirm and the aged, the blind and the lame, the weak, women, and those stricken with misfortune and grief go on pilgrimages from the "vale of troubles," to seek salvation, consolation, and miraculous healing for the maladies of body and soul. The Temple of the living God is the Sanctuary of His Torah, not a hospital for the infirm and the incurable, not a shelter for the crippled and the wretched. It is the elite of the nation—the vigorous and virile, the very backbone of the people, on whom all action of the present depends, and with whom all hope for the future rests—that the living God summons to the Sanctuary of His Torah.⁹⁸

Hirsch's position may be summed up with a final quotation from his discussion of the three prohibitions, cited above, where Hirsch links the sanctification of death with the Christian doctrine of Original Sin, seeing them as a single, invalid unit: "Heathenism—both ancient and modern—not only deifies the power of death, but also embraces the deification of the sensual powers. Heathen priests build their edifices not only on man's fear of death, but also on the power of sin, which exerts control over man."⁹⁹ That is to say: Christianity, which made death and sensual appetites into divine forces that cannot be

---

97 Hirsch on Gen. 14:17-18. In my opinion, this anticipates Leibowitz's central thesis regarding the Torah for its own sake and not to satisfy human needs, which would be idol-worship, but Hirsch limits himself to the intermediary, the Cohen, who should not be expected to satisfy needs, whereas Leibowitz completely denies the possibility of supplying the needs of the believer as a result of his service of God, an argument from which Hirsch is distant. See Leibowitz, *Yahadut*, 22-29.

98 Hirsch on Ex. 23:17. See also his commentary on Lev. 21:17. At the same time, Elijah Ben-Amozegh in Italy expressed similar criticism of Christianity. It should be noted that women are listed here among the inferior people. Although, according to Hirsch, women are not supposed to act in public, is this the figure of women superior to men, that Hirsch proudly presents, as seen in the previous chapter?

99 Hirsch on Lev. 21:5.

resisted, is merely a new form of paganism. In Judaism, by contrast, the free individual stands before God, a person made in the image of God, who received a partially free essence from Him, and free choice to accept God's commandments in moral liberty and thereby to defend himself against sensuality, or to oppose Him, and to act against His will, and to sin:

> Implicit in the concept of freedom, however, is the possibility of opposing God's will. It is absurd to say that the ability to sin and the temptations of the senses are only consequences of man's degeneration. For without the ability to sin and the alluring temptation of sensuality, man ceases to be man. For man's whole virtue is contingent upon his ability to sin; and man's whole dignity lies in his ability to disobey God's will.[100]

Therefore this is man's excellence and not a flaw that cannot be repaired. God calls upon man constantly to exploit his freedom, to control his sensuality, and thus to gain the sanctity that is in closeness to God during his life: "You are to use that freedom and the power to master, with a strong hand, your own world of inner drives and impulses, subordinating them all to the laws of My will. Thus ... you will be close to Me."[101]

Monasticism and Asceticism

The dogma of Original Sin and the messianic ideas that were developed in Christianity after Jesus's death as well, which included sanctification of death, the centrality of the world to come, and dismissal of the importance of life in this world, led Christianity to sanctify monasticism and asceticism as well. Central to all the various theories about monasticism is the determination that the higher a person rises in the hierarchy of religious leadership, ascends in spirituality, and sanctifies himself, the more he must reject the pleasures of this world, sexual and family life, the acquisition of worldly goods, and also must afflict his body in order to purify the soul in preparation for the world to come. Thus in Christianity and in Eastern religions, monasticism emerged,

---

100 Hirsch on Lev. 21:5.
101 Ibid.

stating that men and women who have devoted their lives to God and to spiritual life must deprive themselves as much as possible of ordinary social life, of public and political involvement, and from the pleasures of this world, including family life. Hirsch states that the idea of *nezirut* in Judaism is entirely different, and that Judaism opposes asceticism and mortification of the flesh and it favors the acquisition of goods for the purpose of doing good. It also requires the religious leadership to be involved in the public life of the community. Of the religious leaders in Judaism, Hirsch says: "Secluding oneself from others is not the Jewish way. Our צדיקים [*tsadiqim*, righteous men] and חסידים [*ḥasidim*, pious men] lived among the masses, with the masses, and for the masses.... The Torah opposes ascetic seclusion, which is based on the erroneous notion that godliness lies outside the sphere of ordinary life."[102]

Hirsch expresses the importance of acquiring possessions, which is a sacred duty according to Judaism, in the following way:

> The Law ... firmly and unyieldingly opposes ... the deification of wealth and lust as the sole aim and controlling impulse of our lives; but it not only permits their pursuit within the limits set by Divine wisdom, but declares the effort to gain them a duty as sacred and binding as any other human obligation, and condemns the purposeless and unreasonable abstinence from permitted indulgences as sin.[103]

A similar statement of the duty to acquire property as a means and not as an end is found in his commentary on the word "וכבשה" [and subdue it] in Gen. 1:28:

> Man is commanded to master the earth and subdue it. His task is to acquire the products of the earth and to transform them, so that they become fit for his purposes. Acquisition of property is prerequisite for the tasks of home and society. Property serves as an instrument with which home and society achieve their aims. Thus, the acquisition of property becomes a moral duty.
>
> The mitzvah of וכבשוה, however, is written here last, which implies a limitation: There is no moral value to property, unless it is

---

102 Hirsch on Gen. 5:4-27. See also his commentary on Num. 6:2.
103 *Nineteen Letters*, 139. In a footnote he relates this position to BT Ta'anit 11b and 20a. See also his commentary on Ex. 16:25. See above, Volume 1, Chapter 3, in the discussion of Hirsch's ethical doctrine.

devoted to home and society. It is a person's duty to acquire material assets, in order to build a home, and to further the society. He should not build a home and support the society in order to increase his assets and his wealth.

In his commentary on the passage about the *nazir* (Num. 6:1-21), Hirsch discusses the laws governing the Jewish *nazir* and the restrictions imposed on his vows, and in his commentary on verse 6, "all the days that he consecrates himself unto the Lord he shall not come near to a dead body," he warns against being drawn toward Christian monasticism:

> Now, just as טומאת מת [*tumat met*, corpse impurity] must be kept out of מחנה שכינה [*maḥane shekhina*, the camp of the divine presence], so must it be kept out of the Naziritic circle. The meaning of these two exclusions is identical, only that the exclusion of טומאה [ritual impurity] from מחנה שכינה [camp of the divine presence] is for the sake of the national Sanctuary, as the Sanctuary is meant to educate the nation to moral perfection, whereas the exclusion of טומאה [impurity] from the נזיר's [nazirite's] circle is for the sake of his limited individual sphere, within which he seeks to attain his moral perfection.
>
> Human society—from which the נזיר [nazirite] temporarily withdraws in order to live more in himself and his relationship to God—fulfills itself through the synthesis of two elements: moral freedom and physical compulsion. For the synthesis of these two elements—the physical and the moral—is what makes a human being. Partial withdrawal from human society can help a person devote himself more fully to his moral freedom. However, it can just as easily lead him to concern himself primarily with his physical needs; and the God to whom the נזיר [nazirite] in his self-isolation devotes his thoughts and meditations can easily become the all-powerful force of nature, which celebrates its triumphs in the sensual grave of morality's absence, and which bears its flag in the wasteland of graves and tombstones.
>
> But that should not be the case. Rather, the God to Whom the נזיר dedicates the isolating circle of his נזירות [period as a nazirite] is the free and personal God, Who enables man to become a free and moral personality. The God of the נזיר is 'ה [the Lord], and it is to His Torah that the נזיר should devote his thoughts and aspirations. In limiting himself, he should increase his personal holiness, so as to live in God's presence in moral freedom. His withdrawal into himself should be dedicated to life at its fullest, not to death and dying. His

מחנה [camp] is to be a מחנה שכינה [camp of the divine presence] of אלקים חיים [the living God].

So that he should bear all of this in mind, he must, like a כהן גדול [high priest], keep away from death and dead bodies.

That is to say, Jewish *nezirut* is temporary and intended to strengthen the component of moral liberty in man, so that the corporeal component will not prevail. However, if *nezirut* is permanent, and the *nazir* is educated according to Christian principles of Original Sin, according to which man is subject to the corporeal element within him, without the ability to struggle against it, and of the sanctification of death, he is liable to attain the opposite goal of despair of life, prolonged sorrow, and devotion to the corporeal and sensual element of all-powerful nature. Hirsch emphasizes that there is a basic flaw in the vow of *nezirut*, and therefore it must be temporary and have a defined goal: "The נזירות [naziritic] vow in itself appears like antisocial arrogance, like the presumption of one who separates himself from the community in order to stand out, and it is the only goal to which the נזיר [nazirite] aspires—spiritual and moral ennoblement—that purges the vow of this reprehensible semblance."[104] With the fulfillment of his time of *nezirut*, the *nazir* must offer, among other things, a קורבן שלמים [peace offering], which, in Judaism, symbolizes joy and the sanctified pleasure of life in this world, which are the opposite of *nezirut*, which in essence is negative asceticism. Thereby hope is expressed that the positive goal of temporary *nezirut* will be achieved:

> The focal point of the נזיר's offering is the איל לשלמים [the ram peace offering], which constitutes the antithesis of the נזירות [naziritic status]. For the נזיר withdraws from social contact and abstains from wine, which gladdens the heart. He thereby seeks to attain closeness to God through the inwardness of spiritual and moral refinement. But this effort, directed primarily inward, does not reflect a permanent state; its whole purpose is to educate. True נזירות leads only to a temporary withdrawal from communal life; one temporarily withdraws from society, so that afterward one can dedicate himself with redoubled force to fulfilling the tasks set for him by God. Just as formerly he distinguished himself by his withdrawal and

---

104 Hirsch on Num. 6:12.

renunciation, now he is to lead the people…. In the midst of the aspirations and enjoyments of social communal life, upheld by the עולה [*ola*, burnt offering], and חטאת [*hatat*, sin-offering], sanctification of a life rich in deeds and morally pure, one attains the blissful harmony of a life lived in the presence of God.[105]

Withdrawal from society and the pleasures of life is negative in Judaism, and someone who withdraws temporarily must offer a sacrifice for his withdrawal and return to society and positions of public leadership, and to a life full of joy. Hirsch concludes the discussion of the passage about the *nazir* by repeating that Judaism requires enjoying this world and not withdrawal and asceticism: "The נזיר now re-enters the social community. Re-entering the social life of the community is not only permissible, it is a mitzvah, a duty. It is a mitzvah to rejoice and enjoy life in God's presence, and to live a life imbued with the spirit of שלמים [*shelamim*, feast offering]. Such a life is greater than נזירות, which demonstrates its moral strength merely through self-isolation and separation; only if it leads to such a life does נזירות have value."[106]

Elsewhere Hirsch also emphasizes the importance of joy in Judaism, in contrast to Christianity which emphasizes sorrow and suffering:

> As a result of man's feeling of purposelessness, there is a preoccupation with death which from time immemorial has found its place in the anguish of man … "whose jubilation begins, when people wrap themselves in mourning" (Hosea 10:5).
>
> Man is told: not only is a smile foolish, not only is joy useless, but a smile is sinful, and joy is a crime. The destiny of earthly life is pain, misery, sorrow, and distress. Man should yearn for the next world, he should thirst for salvation. He should find happiness in a doctrine which claims that bliss and joy can ultimately be found only in death.[107]

To summarize the discussion of Original Sin and Christian monasticism according to Hirsch, who binds both of them up with depression and death, I will cite his explanation that in Judaism, which calls for

---

105 Hirsch on Num. 6:14.
106 Ibid, 6:18.
107 *Writings*, II, 84.

elevation and life, it is the קרבן עולה [burnt offering] and not the קרבן חטאת [sin offering] that expresses the basic idea of the sacrifices. He states:

> Not by a permanent חטאת-consciousness of sin and guilt, not by a permanent state of penitent contrition, will the heart be moved to yearn for God, or the spirit be uplifted with inspiration to serve God and work for the rectification of His world. עולה, עולה, עולה—up! upward! aloft! Up to the light of God's closeness, and higher, for ever and ever! That is the call that comes continually from God's Sanctuary to the sons and daughters of Israel, a call that awakens and revives and dispels depression and death. This call of the living God of the Jewish Sanctuary is the loudest, most forceful protest against all the heathen theories of mortification and against the doctrine of the self-deprecation of unrectifiable sinfulness, which the blasphemers impute to the Sanctuary of offerings of the eternally living God.[108]

Original sin and permanent monasticism are therefore anti-moral and anti-human.

The Importance of the Practical Commandments and their Place in the Religion

As noted above, Paul and his followers freed the believer in the New Testament from the yoke of the practical commandments, which underwent a process of spiritualization. In the deterministic world where sin is immanent, the commandments have no value or purpose, and only belief in Jesus, who suffered for man's salvation, offers a chance for grace and salvation of the soul in the next world. As an Orthodox Jew, Hirsch regarded this idea as unacceptable and dangerous.

However, unlike earlier Jewish thinkers, Hirsch had a far more bitter enemy within the Jewish community, which posed a similar threat. In the previous chapter I showed that the Reform Jews who wanted to draw closer to Gentile society and cooperate with it, argued that the time of the practical commandments had passed. Unlike classical Christianity, Reform Judaism was based on a rational, scientific,

---

108 Hirsch on Lev. 4:24.

and modern position, according to which the Torah was written by man, and therefore it was possible to dismiss the importance and need for most of the practical commandments, those which no longer were consistent with reason and the values of the generation. Thereby they cooperated with the progressive and modern Christians, who wished, in the name of reason, to refine Christianity from its dross and from some of its dogmas, and to present a pure, rational, more spiritual Christianity, which advocated ethical love and the importance of good intention, spontaneity, and a religious experience of spiritual elevation. The Reform Jews wanted to adopt this direction, which rejects dry law and ritual without spiritual and ethical content.

Hirsch attacked this trend of the Reform movement with all the means at his disposal. I presented this polemic in detail in chapter two, mainly in the discussion of Hirsch's ethical teaching, emphasizing his argument that the revealed commandments, in fact, embodied divine ethics, free of the bonds of natural sensuality, and they brought correct morality to mankind, and the path to salvation. It is impossible to obligate whole communities to act ethically by means of abstract theories and ideas. Education for morality requires written, detailed divine law, which demands obedience in all the areas of life, out of acknowledgement of the duty. Good intentions and humaneness, which are taught by human rationalism, which is bound up with the flesh, are insufficient, because people are liable to be drawn after their impulses. There is a need for a concrete deed, which is done intentionally, and the yardstick for the quality of the action is God's will, as embodied in His Torah.

Here I will only add that the polemics that Hirsch waged against Reform necessarily included, as well polemics against everyone who denied the practical commandments: against Christianity as established by Paul and his followers; against modern, purified Christianity; and also against the deistic views that distanced God from the world and of course rejected the possibility of revelation. The argument against Christianity is formulated as follows: "Faith can transform spirits and minds, but only deeds can accomplish the transformation of the world.... [The] Law ... is not content to say to man: be holy and clean;

and to say to society: practice love and righteousness. The Law tells man how to be holy in the eyes of God. And it tells society how a profound Divine Wisdom weighs out what is right, and comprehends and determines what is love."[109]

Another one of Hirsch's central arguments for the commandments was that Judaism did not believe in the principle stated by Jesus, "Then render to Caesar the things that are Caesar's, and to God the things that are God's,"[110] according to which a distinction must be made between God's areas of responsibility and those of the emperor, between the church and the state. The judiciary, the government, and public order are the responsibility of the state, whereas religion and charity are the responsibility of the church. Hirsch claims that Judaism is total, and it penetrates and fills all areas of life—both active life and spiritual life, and it guides them:

> Don't our Gentile fellow citizens also have a religion? But their religion is reasonable, because to them religion isn't everything. They have a legitimate place for religion, just as they have for their concerns as human beings and as citizens. They have people for whom religion is a full-time profession, people who devote all their working hours to the promotion and cultivation of religion, who attend to ecclesiastic and doctrinal matters, people who are ready at any time to bestow the blessings of religion upon anyone feeling a need to flee from everyday life to the altars of religion. By offering spiritual uplift to men, they attempt to satisfy men's higher celestial yearnings so as to win them for the heavenly bliss of the world to come. For them, religion is allowed free rein, but it never exceeds the limits set for it, and permits human and social affairs full autonomy to develop as they will. Practiced in this manner, religion is entirely compatible with personal and civic life. When will we learn from our fellow men, who are wiser than we, to "render unto God what is God's and to give our fellow men what is theirs?"

---

109 *Writings*, I, 216. See also ibid., 355, and Hirsch on Gen. 17:1, Num. 18:6-7, and Deut. 11:28.
110 Luke 20:25, Mark 12:17, Matt. 22:21. Note that Hirsch, like the Church commentators, interprets this saying of Jesus's as representing a desirable situation from Jesus's point of view, unlike Mendelssohn, who interprets it as an imposed situation. See note 33 above.

> When will we learn to do that? Never! Not as long as we are Jews.... [God's chosen] people are to counteract the compartmentalization of life into Divine and mundane, clerical and civil. They are to prevent the banishment of the Divine from the home, the temple from the State, and the inevitable result of such developments: the desecration and degradation of every aspect of true life—work, accomplishments, creativity and pleasure—depriving God of His world and mankind of its God.... [In the Jewish kingdom] every citizen would be a priest ... every home would be a temple, every table an altar and every act of domestic or public life an act of Divine worship, glorifying God.[111]

The Ten Commandments on the tablets of the covenant represent the opposite of the separation of church and state, and religious and civil law are inscribed without distinction on both sides of it.[112] On the verse, "you shall take him from my altar, that he may die,"[113] Hirsch explains:

> The Jewish altar does not grant protection to the criminal. We do not have here two principles mutually controlling and modifying each other, such as church and state, justice and mercy, and the like. The chamber of the highest court of justice was located right next to the altar, over which the sword must not be swung.... The principle cultivated by the altar is the same principle actualized by the Sanhedrin.
>
> The whole idea of the right of pardon is absent in the code of law of the Jewish state. Justice and judgment are God's, not man's. When the precisely defined Law of God—which leaves no room for human arbitrariness—ordains death for a criminal, the execution of the sentence ... is itself a most considerate atonement.[114]

---

111 *Writings*, VII, 405-6. This also shows that Hirsch opposed the separation of religion and the state in a Jewish state.

112 On the tablets of the covenant, see *Writings*, I, 268.

113 Ex. 21:14.

114 Hirsch on Ex. 21:14. Mendelssohn, who advocated separation of religion and state in the Jewish community as well, wrote in Jerusalem that the authority of the Jewish court in matters of religion was only in the distant past, when God was sovereign in the Jewish state, but today this authority must be rescinded. Hirsch disagrees. Hirsch's distinction between Christianity and Judaism was later developed by Hermann Cohen, who argued that Christianity, in contrast to Judaism, distinguishes between salvation and sanctity in the realm of religion and history, which is in the area of the state.

The Hebrew language has no special word for all the virtues together, and there is no term parallel to the European concept of religion. Hebrew relates to every virtue separately, and the word דת [*dat*, religion] includes all aspects of life:

> In Hebrew ... there is no one word that encompasses all virtues. For us the supreme value is מצוה [*mitsva*], and the virtues are counted separately: משפט, חסד [*mishpat*, kindness; *hesed*, justice] and so forth.
>
> The same applies to "religion." Every European language speaks of "religion." We, the people of religion *par excellence*, have no term for "religion." If religion is just one aspect of life, it can be assigned a name; its name defines and delimits it, isolating it from other things. The other aspects of life are not included in religion, which has its own separate realm. If, however, all of life is connected with religion, from birth until after death, then no one can fathom the character of religion or assign it a name, inasmuch as it informs everything, and everything is included in it.[115]

The Status of Islam

The Muslim world was distant from Hirsch, and he had only a vague understanding of it. Nevertheless, he did not refrain from discussing Islam briefly when it suited his needs. Hirsch regarded Islam in principle, like Christianity, in a favorable light, and his remarks about Islam are even more sympathetic than those about Christianity, of which he also had severe criticisms. Unlike Christianity, Muslim monotheism is clear and strong, and it does not have unacceptable pagan dogmas. However, like Christianity, it lacks the commandments, which alone enable the subjection of all powers, including the sensual, to the path of God and attaining the goal of sanctification of the body.

Hirsch's central discussion of Islam is found in his commentary on the story of Hagar and Ishmael, in Hagar's flight from Sarah, as recounted in Genesis 16:1-16. On the words, "therefore the well is called Well of the Living One Who Sees me," in verse 14, Hirsch explains:

> These two ideas, חי and ראי —God is the absolute Master of space and time, He watches over and guides all—were gifts given to the

---

115 Hirsch on Gen. 11:7.

Arabian people by their matriarch and patriarch. All the Arabian thinkers and philosophers worked at developing these ideas for mankind. This work constitutes the essence of the Arabian people's treasury of ideas.

The story of the genesis of the Ishmaelite nation contains all the elements of the Ishmaelite character, which later emerged from potentiality into actuality. Cham's sensuality, Hagar's thirst for freedom, Avraham's spirit—these are the basic threads from which the Arab national character was woven.

The Arab nation, descended from Avraham and Hagar, is *one-sidedly* Jewish.

We, the Jewish people, have been assigned by God a dual mission: (a) אמונה, intellectual truths, which we are to absorb in our hearts and through which our minds are to develop; (b) מצוה, shaping—in harmony with these truths—all of life according to the dictates of God's will.

In one respect—viz., the intellectual—the Arab nation occupies a position of prominence. It developed with keen insight the idea of God, an idea bequeathed to it by Avraham. Consider the magnitude of the Arab influence: the ideas on the unity of God in the writings of the Jewish philosophers—to the extent that these ideas are developed philosophically—are based largely on the intellectual work of Arab thinkers. They attained אמונה —but they did not attain the מצוות.... It is not sufficient that Avraham is one's father, if Sarah is not one's mother. We are the people with whom the name "Avraham" is associated, and our mission is not limited to disseminating theological and philosophical conceptions of God's unity. Rather our mission is לשמור דרך ה' לעשות צדקה ומשפט ... and *that* requires the subordination of all our faculties, especially physical energies and drives; in other words, it requires sanctification of the body. *Only one who sanctifies his body is entitled to be called a Jew.*

Ishmael inherited from Abraham the sanctification of the intellect, but he did not inherit from Sarah the sanctification of the body.

That is to say: the faith aspect is so well developed and deep among the Muslims, that the medieval Jewish philosophers depended upon it to develop their thought. This dependency is positive in Hirsch's view, in his attitude toward Islam, but it is well known that he was unsparing in his criticism of Maimonides for depending on foreign sources rather than on the source common to all: the Torah of Israel. According to Hirsch, Islam has a love of freedom derived from Hagar, but also great sensuality, derived from Ham. Ishmael did not inherit sanctification of the body from Sarah—the archetype of the Jewish woman, who maneuvers and protects the Jewish man from falling in the trap of instinct—and therefore his desire for freedom is exploited by sensuality without the guidance and direction of the commandments. Instead of Sarah's influence, there is Hagar's. Ishmael's descendants inherited "Hagar's strong tribal urge for freedom, which led them to adopt a nomadic way of life, free of all restraints."[116] Hirsch states that the combination of these qualities, between Abraham's monotheism, Ham's sensuality, Hagar's thirst for freedom, and zealous belief in Divine Providence "shaped the traits for which the Arabs are known to this day and with which they have made their own contribution, in the form of poetry and scholarship, to the spiritual symposium of humanity."[117]

Summary

According to Hirsch, both Christianity and Islam are positive phenomena in themselves, since they are a stage in the divine plan for the victory of Judaism and the advent of salvation to mankind. Following Maimonides, he states that Islam is preferable, because it is free of idolatry, though it lacks the commandments. However, the theological and philosophical part of Christianity is defective because it includes pagan elements. As a religion that claims to be bringing salvation to humanity, Christianity is a total failure both because of its unacceptable dogmas and because it rejected the commandments of the Old Testament and does not include the commandments and the path of practical guidance. This denial of the commandments cut the religion off from life, separated it from the state, and set it apart for the church and aspirations for the world to come, doing away with the possibility of redemption through return to the Garden of Eden in this world. Hirsch's conclusion is therefore sharp and clear: Christianity did not succeed in its mission of bringing salvation to mankind. The doctrine of Original Sin, death, and monastic asceticism as a system gave rise to a policy of evil and fanaticism, leaving humanity exposed, without hope:

---

116 *Writings*, VII, 321.
117 *Writings*, VIII, 98.

Christianity did not succeed in coming ... close to solving the task it set for itself: the redemption of the world from physical and moral evil. On the contrary, the specifically Christian elements in its philosophy are [neither] designed nor intended to bring about a radical change in the state of human relationships.... [Christianity] ideologically excluded "this world" from its "religious kingdom," a teaching that considered death to be the "ideal exit" and the "instruments of torture" to be confession-inducing tools to "educate the sinner." As a religion Christianity taught its adherents to despise those who do not conform to its precepts and prescribed as a duty of the highest order the elimination of non-believers who were seduced by a mysterious "evil." It proclaimed that immersion in the nebulous fog of the supernatural and yearning for an otherworldly paradise were the only salvation from the fleshy cesspool of earthly pleasures. All its specific teachings were rooted in the total rejection of temporal earthly pleasures. "if somebody takes away your coat, give him also your shirt," or "if someone strikes you on the right cheek, offer him your left." While this may sound like a lesson of appeasement and reconciliation, it is actually a doctrine celebrating the contempt for a man's honor and his concern for material possessions.

This religion was committed to the idea that human society could not be freed from the shackles of evil, and that the redemption of the individual and of mankind as a whole could not be effected by the vision of a paradisiacal kingdom of justice and morality. Thus it became a comforter for the beaten rather than a guide for those who are active, a lighthouse for the shipwrecked rather than a compass for a joyful journey through life. Yes, hospitals for the sick, altars for the oppressed, graves for the dead—but no market places and public centers anywhere for the freshly pulsing life... Human interrelationships were thus left to themselves, to be influenced by Hellenistic sensuality and Roman power.... [Christianity] failed to inspire a spring-like awakening in the human society.... The redemption has still not arrived and the redeemer is still supposed to come.[118]

---

118 *Writings*, VIII, 242-43. Breuer, '*Eda*, 89, briefly describes Hirsch's attitude toward Christianity. In his opinion, Hirsch regarded Christianity favorably as a bearer of the message of Judaism. However, it seems to me that my analysis here, according to which Hirsch was harshly critical of Christian dogmas as a modern heathenism, is inconsistent with Breuer's statements, according to which Hirsch expressed his criticism of Christian dogma pleasantly and in disguise, and he was not interested in a dogmatic argument. True, the argument was internal and not directed toward Christians, but internal needs were also important and led Hirsch to express this sharp criticism. M. A. Meyer, *German-Jewish History in the Modern Times*, 190, also

LUZZATTO'S RESPONSE
Background

Unlike Hirsch, Luzzatto was not upset by Christianity as a religion competing for the hearts of his fellow Jews, and Reform was not active in his region. His principle task was to teach the students in the rabbinical seminary in Padua what they needed in order to be successful modern rabbis. That is to say, they should know and master Jewish studies with an academic approach, which would enable them to cope with the challenges of leading a Jewish community within a non-Jewish majority, a society that was discussing whether Jews could enjoy the full rights of citizenship. These discussions do not evince outright hatred of the Jews, as existed in Central and Southern Italy, whose Catholic leaders were highly influenced by the pope at that time. Tolerance in northern Italy was also greater than that in the more conservative culture of Galicia.

Having internalized the Enlightenment, which advocated equal rights, and being a romantic who sought to preserve the national heritage—but who also recognized the right of every nation to retain its values—Luzzatto followed Mendelssohn in favoring pluralistic universalism among nations. Nations should live alongside one another in ethical brotherhood common to them all, while every nation retained its religion and customs, and the Jews would dwell among them as guests, preserving their particularity. Individuals and groups should be judged only according to their good or bad actions, and not according to their beliefs. In the light of these ideas, Luzzatto developed a positive attitude toward the monotheistic religions, without criticizing them.

I will now focus on his few discussions of Christianity and Islam.

---

failed to notice Hirsch's harsh criticism of Christianity. In his Christianity was a greater threat to the Reform than to the Orthodox. My analysis shows that the Orthodox were also wary of Christianity, and from their point of view Reform Jews and Christians posed an identical threat, in that they rejected the commandments of Judaism as outmoded, not suited for the modern world.

The Status of Christianity

As a youthful rationalist, Luzzatto believed in the doctrine of the mission of the Jewish people to bring the true religion to the Gentiles, following Judah Halevi and Maimonides. The publishers of *Beit Haotsar, Lishka B*, included Luzzatto's essays on synonyms, research that he undertook as a youth and then abandoned. In these essays he frequently tends to digress from the main topic and discuss beliefs and opinions. In sections 7-14 he discusses, among other things, the word ברך (to bless), going on to discuss the choice of Abraham, who is blessed by God, and by whom all the nations will be blessed. Luzzatto quotes Sforno about the verse that appears just before the giving of the Torah, which speaks of the choosing of Israel: "You will be a kingdom of priests for me" (Ex. 19:6). Sforno writes that the Jewish people will serve as a priest to the nations, who, in the future, will also be called by the name of God. Luzzatto corrects Sforno, saying that this does not apply only to the future, because we are already in the midst of the process:

> Truly the light of our Torah, the Torah of grace, has already appeared in half of the world, since all the masses of Christians and Turks [i.e. Muslims] believe in it, and they worship a single God, and they observe the path of the Lord in doing charity and justice: and what more is to be wished of them? Should they observe the 613 commandments? Why? For even in the future, they will not observe more than the commandment of Sukkot, because the commandments were only given to the Jews, so they would be a kingdom of priests and a holy nation: hence, that which is still to happen is merely the total extirpation of idols and images.[119]

Here Luzzatto asks Mendelssohn's well-known question: Why, as claimed by Judaism, did God discriminate among His children and grant revelation only to the Jews, since the other religions also claim sole revelation, and they all cannot be right? Here is his answer:

---

119 Luzzatto, *Beit Haotsar, Lishka B*, 42-43.

> If there is a truly divine Torah in the world, it must be the same Torah, whose light went out to the entire world, not only to a single nation: and what is it? It is undoubtedly the Torah of Moses; because from it were born, and upon it were established all the other doctrines that proclaim the unity of God, which have grown strong on the earth and sown the seed of truth, justice, and charity. In giving His Torah to the Jews, God did not intend to benefit only us, but rather to benefit the entire human race; and as for His giving it specifically to the Jewish people, it is because those generations were so deeply immersed in falsehoods, that their dull eyes could not receive the light of truth, and only the Jews were worthy of receiving it. Therefore He sowed His seed in them, which later blossomed and sprouted and filled the world with knowledge of God: therefore the Jews are called "my eldest son," because the Gentiles were also to be the sons of God, but Israel came first; and behold everyone who believes in a single God and walks in His ways to do justice and love of grace, is called a son of God, and he is our brother, of our flesh.[120]

That is to say, the Jews did not receive the Torah because they have some essential, immanent quality preferable to other nations (as Judah Halevi and Nachmanides thought), but because they were the first and only ones at the time of the revelation who were worthy of it and capable of receiving it. The Torah of Israel is the true revelation, since all the other monotheistic religions were established according to it and learned from it. Luzzatto, like Hirsch, believed that all human beings were children of God, and the status of the Jews was that of the eldest son. Christianity and Islam accepted the principles of Judaism regarding belief in a single God, and they adopted Torah's ethical norms of justice and law. Everyone who maintains these is our brother, flesh of our flesh. Our task, together with Christianity and Islam—which helped spread the principles of Judaism over half the world—is to complete this dissemination to those who have not yet received it.

Did Luzzatto ignore the painful past of hatred and persecution, and the arguments of Christianity against Judaism? No. Later in the essay, at the end of the discussion of the word "העיד" (he testified) in sections 18-23, he presents a commentary on the entire Haazinu

---

120 Ibid., 43.

poem (the Song of Moses) from Deuteronomy, interpreting verses 32:37 and 39.

> It would appear that it is the enemy who says against us, "'Where are their gods, The rock in which they sought refuge?" Just as they say against us *now* that God has rejected us, *because we did not accept the new faith*. God says, "See now that I, I am He, and I, God have not changed," I am the one who loved Israel in ancient times, and I am the one *who loves them now* in the end of days: and why is this? Because "there is no god with me," *who is joined to me* as you [Christians] say, and therefore, why should I reject the seed of Israel *because they did not accept the new faith?* On the contrary: I must love them for that, because they are faithful to my covenant.[121]

In discussing the word רפא (to heal) in sections 39-42, Luzzatto once again explains only those two verses in the Song of Moses, saying similar things, but with more detail and force:

> And thus what is written in the Torah will be well understood: "See now that I, I am He, and there is no god besides Me; It is I who put to death and give life. I have wounded and it is I who heal, and there is no one who can deliver from My hand" [Deut. 32:39] What does it say before this? The disparaging remarks made by our enemies about us and about our God: "And he [the enemy] will say, 'Where are their gods, the rock in which they sought refuge?'" (In the opinion of Rabbi Nehemia cited by Rashi). And after it, what does it say? Vengeance against the wicked: "Indeed, I lift up My hand to heaven, etc.," and "If I sharpen My flashing sword, etc.," "I will render vengeance on My adversaries." This is the meaning of the verse. You nations who deny my Providence over the Children of Israel, as if I had violated my covenant with them and exchanged them for another nation (*as they say in this place of exile*), see now that I, the Lord, have not changed, and the sons of Jacob will not die out; see now that I, I am He, I am the God of Israel from ancient times, and I am their God in recent generations: And why is it that I am He, and I have not violated my covenant with them? Because there are no gods with me: not the way [Christians] *say that there are others with me, emanated from me, and therefore I rejected Israel, because they did not accept that opinion: this is not so, and there is no god with me, close to me, standing together (the exact opposite of their*

---

121 Ibid., 77.

error, and therefore we find the term "with me" used only here in connection with the blessed Creator, since He is speaking about [the views of] the recent gentiles).[122]

Luzzatto is willing to accept the other religions as equals, but he is not willing to accept Paul's claim—used by the Christians in modern Europe to disqualify the Jews and remove them from the family of nations, with no rights—according to which the Jewish people were abandoned by God after they did not agree to accept Jesus as the messiah, and they were replaced by the Christians, the true Israel. For this purpose he employs the verse in which God declares that He does not change His mind, as befits a single God: "I, the Lord, have not changed." He bases his argument that the verses of the prophetic song refer to the Christians who would exist in the future—that is, in the present Diaspora—on the fact that they believe they have replaced Israel and adopted the Holy Trinity. The meaning of the Trinity is that there is another god alongside God. The Bible only uses the word "עמדי" (with Me) in relation to God here, and thereby it prophesies to those who claim that other divinities emanated from God, and it says to them, "There is no god with Me." Therefore your whole argument against the Jews, that they supposedly were abandoned for not accepting Jesus as a messiah and god, is incorrect. I, God, did not abandon My people, and I will yet cure them, despite your opinion. Luzzatto, like

---

[122] Ibid., 100-1. The italics in this quotation and the previous one appear in handwritten square letters in the photocopied edition that I consulted. It appears that they were erased by the censor because they attacked the principles and dogmas of Christianity, and because they refer to contemporary Christianity. R. Nehemia's approach is mentioned by Luzzatto in his commentary on the Torah there, and he writes that it is presented in Midrash Sifri, Haazinu, no. 327. There, too, he writes that Rashi also follows R. Nehemia's approach, as do Rashbam [Samuel Ben Meir] and Abraham Ibn Ezra. In the Rashi in our possession, the opposite opinion is stated: that the word "and he said" refers to God, who speaks to Israel in anger (and not to the nations who mock the Jews). One of two things must be explained: either Luzzatto had a different version of Rashi, where the opinion of R. Nehemia is also presented, or he wrote from memory and meant to say Nachmanides. Support for the latter explanation, which is also presented as a note by the editor, is found in the fact that both Nachmanides and Luzzatto cite the verse, "Why did the nations say, where is your God?" On the other hand, in *Beit Haotsar* Luzzatto says, "Rashi cited it," a quotation that the editor might not have seen, which supports the first explanation. See also Luzzatto, *Igrot Shadal*, 46.

Hirsch, also denies Paul's principle, that the advent of Jesus heralded the revoking of the commandments, and that the only way for people to gain salvation is faith in Jesus, or even just a declaration of faith without understanding it:

> The great Judah Halevi speaks thus of faith, which others [the Christians] see as a theological virtue, sufficient to ensure eternal joy for the soul: "[This] applies to the statement made by believers in other faiths—that man, by the pronunciation of one word alone, may inherit paradise, even if, during the whole of his life, he knew no other word than this, and even if he did not understand its meaning. How great must be the significance of this word, which raises him from the ranks of a brute to that of an angel. He who did not utter this word would remain an animal, though he might be a learned and pious philosopher, who yearned for God all his life" (*Kuzari* I: 110). "Now we do not allow any one who embraces our religion theoretically by means of a word alone to take equal rank with ourselves, but demand actual self-sacrifice, purity, knowledge, circumcision, and numerous religious ceremonies" (ibid., 115).[123]

Luzzatto goes on to explain that the meaning of the word אמונה, generally translated as "faith," in biblical Hebrew, is to cleave to the truth, fidelity, and integrity, sincerity, and justice. He rejects Paul's interpretation, based on the Septuagint, of the Prophet Habakkuk, saying: "we have no right to attribute a different meaning to the noun אמונה in the verse, 'the righteous shall live by his אמונה' (Hab. 2:4), as if it meant that the righteous will live by virtue of his faith (the later meaning of the word: faith in the existence of God), but rather it means: 'the righteous will live by virtue of his just deeds.' And this is how the Targum understood it: 'וצדיקיא על קושטיהון יתקיימון' [the righteous will be sustained by their truths], as did Rashi: 'צדקו לו יעמוד' [his righteousness will sustain him]."[124]

Unlike Hirsch, who regarded Christianity as a competitor and considered it idolatrous, Luzzatto is not disturbed by the irrational dogmas of Christianity. His critique is focused only on the Christian principles that depreciate the Jewish people and their Torah. According

---

123 Luzzatto, *Ketavim*, vol. 1, 74.
124 Ibid., 75. See Flusser, *Hanatsrut*, 370-78.

to Luzzatto, the attitudes of Christianity regarding the end of the Jewish people's task and their replacement by Gentile believers in Jesus, and the substitution of faith or mere declaration of faith for the moral actions embodied in the commandments of the Torah strike at the soul of Judaism, and one cannot be tolerant of them.

Interestingly, Luzzatto does not hesitate to mock the memory of Jesus when, as a romantic, nationalist religious Jew, he angrily attacks conversion to Christianity. In a letter of 1838 to Meir Halevi Letteris, he writes about the philo-Semitic scholar of the Bible and of Jewish studies, the German Christian Franz Delitzsch, who apparently changed his position in order to retain his academic appointment: "And I saw him bear the name of the hanged man upon his lips for glory and splendor, and I saw that he was flattering the members of his religion, and I said to myself: that poor man needs bread, and the members of his nation will not support him and will not place him in the chair of a professor if he does not wear a Christian cloak for the sake of denial."[125]

Jewish Tolerance for Other Religions

In the lessons he prepared for his students in the rabbinical seminary in the early 1830s, in his *Lezioni di teologica morale israelita*, Luzzatto devotes extensive discussion to the idea of tolerance for other religions in Judaism. In this discussion he explains the problematic opinions about the Gentiles found in the Mishnah and Talmud, arguing that they do not apply to Christians, and he launches a frontal attack against Maimonides for adopting them as practical Halakha for all time in his *Mishneh Torah*. In the introduction to the first part, which is devoted to the Jew's general obligations, Luzzatto states that

> the general duties of justice and of humanity that the religion imposes on us obligates us [to act] in favor of all humans, without any distinction.... The Torah of Moses ... makes no express distinction between the Israelite and the non-Israelite (*nokhri*) in any of the laws that justice and humanity have suggested to all civilized people.... The term רע (neighbor, companion) that is frequent in the Pentateuch does not exclude non-Israelites at all.... Moreover, any statement,

---

[125] *Igrot Shadal*, 420.

and any story, which might be found in the Talmud or in other Talmudic writings, which might be in opposition to these sentiments of universal humanity and justice, instilled equally by nature and by the Holy Scriptures, must be regarded not as dictates of the religion and not even of the tradition, but as uncouth suggestions of calamitous circumstances, and of the public and private vexations and cruelty, to which the Hebrews were exposed during the centuries of barbarism.

The injustice and inhumanity that the Romans allowed themselves toward the Israelites, and the almost universal corruption of morals among the Romans during the first three centuries of the Common Era, inspired the Sages of the Mishnah [to adopt] various measures of prudence and self-preservation and defense against the oppression of the gentiles.... I say, that same injustice, inhumanity, and depravity of the Romans of their time, the lords of the world at that time, rather naturally inspired some of the Talmudists [i.e. Amoraim] with the idea that people so corrupt and so inhuman should not be regarded as brothers and friends; and thus every time the sacred text uses the term "your neighbor," it could only refer to an Israelite. This interpretation, contrary both to the spirit of Holy Scripture and to the nature of the Hebrew language, is not traditional; and it is only the invention of some Talmudists, who tended to endow with the authority of the sacred text this doctrine and these measures, which circumstances made them judge necessary for the conservation of their co-religionists. These should not be regarded otherwise than certain Talmudic laws and decisions, of which the Talmud itself says they are rabbinical institutions, and that the text from which they are deduced is a mere *asmakhta*, that is to say a support [*appogio*], a pretext [*appicco*], but not a true authority [*autorità*].[126]

The later barbarism, which covered Europe during the Middle Ages, and the calumnies and the persecutions of which the Israelites were then constantly the target, sustained the same sentiments in the Rabbis of those later generations.

Any Talmudic or rabbinical statement marked with an antisocial imprint is evidently the daughter of circumstances, never the

---

126 Luzzatto, *Lezioni di Teologia Morale Israelitica* (Padova, 1862), 25-35. This accords with Luzzatto's approach, which I presented in Ch. 3 above, according to which the Halakhot of the Oral Law are not from Sinai, and they are preventive legislation by the Sages. Naturally the fundamentalists, Chajes and Hirsch, could not accept such an opinion, because in their opinion, the Sages' interpretation of the Bible is its primary meaning. Therefore, they would justify the position of those who usually interpret the term רֵעַ as referring solely to Jews.

doctrine of the religion, which breathes sweetness, and of whom all the paths are paths of peace (Prov. 3:17). And it is so true that the antisocial Talmudic statements were never spoke by the religion, but only because of the conditions of the time, that the celebrated and authoritative Rabbi Moses of Couci (Smag, Negative Precept no. 152) stated: And even according to the view that it is not forbidden to steal from a Gentile, this refers only to one who has done harm to an Israelite, and also in that case his ruling was not adopted; aside from this case every Talmudist recognizes that it is forbidden to steal from a Gentile.... The question of whether the Sages of the Mishnah and the Talmud, in speaking of the Gentile, were referring to our Christians, can be answered in the negative. Indeed, among the festivals of the Gentiles the Mishnah names the Calends and the Saturnalia; certainly not holidays of the Christians.... Diversity of religion and of opinions of any person does not authorize us to hate him or harm him, nor does it dispense us in any manner from adopting the general duties of humanity and justice toward him.... The religion does not command proselytism and, even less so, coercion.... Maimonides's assertion (Hilkhot Melakhim, ch. 8) that Moses has commanded to force, with sword in hand, all people to observe the seven Noahide commandments, which is to say to observe natural religion, is entirely gratuitous and devoid of any scriptural or Talmudic authority[127]....

This great author, instead of removing from his halakhic work certain intolerant statements contained in the Talmud, or at least to moderate them, added new ones, both in relation to non-Israelites and also regarding heretical Israelites, or misbelievers, and the latter (in his commentary on the Mishnah, Sanhedrin, ch. Ḥeleq), claims they must be hated and destroyed.... This judgment is quite surprising for the great philosopher that Maimonides was. But the surprise will cease if one considers that Maimonides, while a philosopher, was one according to the Aristotelian-Arab philosophy that prevailed in his time[128].... Now that upside down [*stravolta*] philosophy taught that the human soul was not a substance, but a potential, an attitude, by

---

127 Ibid., 36-40. Here Luzzatto accepts Mendelssohn's opinion in the controversy on this subject with Emden. As noted above, Hirsch, the fundamentalist, agreed with Maimonides.

128 Ibid., 41. Luzzatto's approach rejects Maimonides's philosophy, because it includes and is based on foreign elements that are opposed to the spirit of Judaism. Luzzatto also prefers his culture hero here, Judah Halevi. Interestingly, Luzzatto is not willing to include Maimonides among those who wrote against the Gentiles in the Middle Ages because of persecutions and forced conversions which he experienced or knew about, but rather he attributes it to his philosophical opinions.

which man is capable of becoming intelligent, and to know God and spiritual beings; and that only by passing from potential to action, the soul, perfecting itself and identifying itself with these conceived spiritual substances, becomes a substance, a spiritual and therefore immortal being. This doctrine, which before Maimonides was already exposed and combated by Judah Halevi in his *Kuzari* (Dialogue V:12, 14), was adopted by Maimonides; and it was what suggested to him all the intolerant statements, which darken his great halakhic work, inspiring him with the philosophical dogma, that a man who had no correct idea about God, but who professed polytheism or some other erroneous doctrine, had no immortal soul, and he was almost not even human. There is good reason to deplore the miserable condition of the centuries of barbarism and ignorance that produced such aberrations; but it would be a grave sin to attribute them as doctrines of the religion, which has the universal aim of charity and justice. Any Jew would be committing the worst nefarious impiety if today, living in the midst of a humane and just people, whose governors benevolently foster his life and goods, to nourish toward it the lightest trace of such antisocial and equally anti-religious sentiments. He would be violating the Law of God, natural and revealed which in the duties of humanity and justice makes no distinction of people or beliefs; and he would be adding to that sin another even more atrocious one, which is ingratitude. He must repeat to himself the words of Joseph: How could I commit such a great evil deed and sin against God?[129]

This is a clear and unequivocal praise for religious tolerance, in favor of solidarity and brotherhood among all people, as long as they maintain the ethical norms of justice and law. Judaism, as embodied in the Torah, in the words of the Sages—after we have purified them of temporary, unfortunate teachings—and in the words of the medieval rabbis, is identical to natural religion and relates to all men with equality, as long

---

129 Ibid., 43. See also *Meḥqerei Hayahadut*, I, pt. 2, 165-69, "Ktivat Hamishnah Veharambam." There he argues against Maimonides and repeats the accusation that he introduced hatred of other religions and of heretics, and he embraced the temporary things said against non-Jews in the Talmud because of the exigencies of the time. Thereby "he gave us to the horror of all the nations of the land," and he also corrupted our morals. This was all because of his erroneous theory of the soul, based on Aristotle, and according to which only the wise would gain eternal life by making their soul merge with the intelligible and by the loss of its independence. In order to gain such a world to come, he taught us the thirteen principles, "and we did not see the snake that was entwined in the heel of your words."

as they are cultivated and ethical, independent of their beliefs and opinions. In any event, the Talmud does not refer to Christians at all, and all the harsh statements in it are directed against idol-worshipers, who were cruel and corrupt, and this is what impelled the Sages to utter them. It is difficult not to see an apologetic selection in Luzzatto's words, because many of the statements against Rome in the Talmud have the double meaning of the Roman Empire and of the Christian church, beginning in the fourth century CE, under the appellations of Edom or Esau. Luzzatto could easily have said that these, too, were merely applicable in their time, because of the cruel persecutions by the Christians, whose religion became the official religion of the Roman Empire, against the Jews who refused to believe in Jesus, and who constantly reminded the Christians that Jesus was a Jew. However, Luzzatto insists on arguing that only Rome was called Edom in the Talmud, and not the Christians:

> All the time that the First and Second Temples stood, only the actual sons of Esau were called Edom, but after the destruction of the Temple the Jews began calling the Roman Empire Edom, and this was because the Edomites were mostly persecutors of the Jews, and for that reason the name of Edom was an abomination for us, especially since King Herod, who was an Edomite, caused great harm to the Jews, and when the Temple was destroyed by the Romans, the hatred of the Jews was transferred to Roman Edom. Therefore (and also because of fear) they called Rome "Edom." This does not refer at all to the believers in the new religion, but to the Roman Empire, which destroyed our Temple, and to the places where their dominion and language spread. And do not believe the words of Ibn Ezra, who said that the members of the new religion [Christianity] were called Edom because the first ones to believe in Jesus were from Edom; because this is a complete lie, since the first to believe in Jesus were Jews and Greeks and Romans, not Edomites, and the name of Edom is an epithet for the Romans and other nations because at that time they were under Roman dominion, and not because of their faith.[130]

---

130 Luzzatto on Gen. 27:40.

Luzzatto briefly repeats his position on the subject of the mission and status of the Christians once more in his *Yesodei Hatorah*, written in 1839-1840. In the beginning of the essay he discusses the Patriarch Abraham, who, according to Luzzatto, chose monotheism in his wisdom, and therefore God chose him to retain his faith, pass it on to his progeny, and, through them, to all mankind. The foundations and principles of the Jewish religion were already known to Abraham's family, and the Torah of Moses was only conveyed to them when they became a great nation and required general, obligatory norms. Here are his words on the mission and on Christianity:

> The intention of Divine Providence in choosing this nation was not beneficial solely to the nation, but to all the nations ... and R. Judah Halevi (*Kuzari* 4:23) believed that the dispersion of the Jews in exile is one of the secrets of Providence, and that is beneficial to all the nations—this divine intention is implemented gradually over all the generations. And if a person should say that the Christians are idol-worshipers (as in the words of Maimonides in Hilkhot Maakhalot Asurot 11:7, in old printings, and here are his words: but the Christians are idol-worshipers, and their wine is forbidden for enjoyment) we will reply that this is not the truth, and that was also Rashi's belief, that they are not idol-worshipers (*Tur Yore De'a*, no. 148).[131]

---

131 Luzzatto, *Meḥqerei Hayahadut*, I, pt. 1, 10 n. 2. I discussed the development of Luzzatto's position regarding the mission of the Jews in detail in Chapter 4 above. For the reader's benefit I cite here the words of Jacob ben Asher in *Arba'a Turim*, ibid., 12: "In this time Rashbam wrote in the name of Rashi (*Rashi's Responsa*, 327), that everything [which was forbidden in the eleven previous sections] is permitted because they are not idol-worshipers and do not go and acknowledge [idol-worship]. Also because most of our livelihood is earned from them, and we trade with them every day of the year, and if we withdrew from them on the day of their holiday, we would be liable to hostility, therefore it is permitted." And Beit Yosef— Rabbi Joseph Karo (1488-1575)—on this passage (and the *Prisha*, R. Joshua Falk Katz, agrees with him) writes of these words: "That is to say, everything that was mentioned in this section [148] as forbidden, is permitted today. And the reason is that they are not idol-worshipers, meaning that they are not so aware of idol-worship, and as we say in Ch. 1 of Ḥulin (13b), Gentiles outside of the Land are not idol-worshipers, but they practice the customs of their ancestors, and they do not go and confess." That is to say, Rashi, Rashbam, and the Tur ruled that Christians are not idol-worshipers. In addition, the Tur says that there is another reason, because of hostility, which is liable to cause monetary loss. The commentators on the Tur restrict this categorical ruling. Christianity is in fact idol-worship, but the

In his commentary on the Torah, *Hamishtadel*, Luzzatto also adds regarding the second commandment, "You shall have no other gods before Me," that paganism favors the existence of evil gods and causes divisions among nations, and only Jewish monotheism, which has already been spread among all the believers in a single God, is the moral hope of mankind: "Only believers in the single God who know that there is one father of everyone, and one God created us, and that all human beings are beloved before Him, may He be praised; and in truth only after the Torah of Moses was spread in the world did the nations begin to acknowledge that we are all brothers."[132]

Luzzatto retained this opinion of Christianity all his life. In his important letter to Eliezer Silverman of 1858, in which Luzzatto as an old man shows himself as a radical who does not believe in the Jewish mission or in progress, he repeats that Christianity is not idol worship, but expresses implicit criticism of Christian proselytism. In addition, Luzzatto speaks negatively of Jews who regard the Christian religion and its believers with paternalism: "The believing Jew should not slander the faith of the people among whom he lives, and he should not try to weaken their faith, because he was never commanded to spread his faith in the world; and he should not flaunt his belief in a single God before his neighbors, since they truly intend to worship a single God; and such a man is beloved above and precious below and finds favor in the eyes of God and man."[133]

In his polemics against Reform Jews and Bible scholars who deny prophecy and state that the Torah is not from heaven but the work of human hands, he states that they are worse than believing Christians:

> There is no doubt that anyone who says there is only a single God but errs in understanding the unity, and imagines it as his father and

---

    believers in their time do not actually know how to worship its idols, and they only possess the custom of their ancestors—who once lived in the Land of Israel and founded Christianity—and it is possible to relate to them, by extension, as "captured children."

132 Luzzatto, *Hamishtadel* (Vienna, 1847), on Ex. 20:3. Luzzatto also discusses the choice of Abraham in detail here, the reason for the revelation to the Jewish people, and their mission.

133 *Igrot Shadal*, 1336.

mother taught him, and he admits the truth of the prophecy of Moses and the wonders of his Torah, and he observes the seven Noahide commandments, is better for heaven and for humanity than a Jewish man who acknowledges the pure Unity, clear of any addition and error, but does not admit that the Torah is from heaven.[134]

SUMMARY

A positive view of Christianity as monotheism apparently began in the Talmud and was continued by Rashi, the Tosafists, the Meiri, the Tur, Judah Halevi, Rabbi Shimon Ben Tsemaḥ Duran, Sasportas, Rivkes, Emden, Mendelssohn, and others—to varying degrees, and with larger and smaller doses of apologetics.

Maimonides was among those who saw pagan elements in Christianity, and in his opinion it was created by pagans who included monotheistic elements in order to attract the Jews, but they failed and brought about the defeat of paganism. Islam was universally regarded as monotheistic. In the modern period, beginning with Emden, a distinction began to be made between the origins of Christianity and the church. Recognition spread that Jesus was himself an observant Jew who did not seek at all to establish a new religion, but rather to bring the advent of the messiah. In the early nineteenth century, the opinion expressed by Salvador and others spread that after Jesus, who was a normative Pharisaic Jew, Paul actually established the Christian religion and attracted the pagans to it, by including pagan dogmas. Only today, with the discovery of the Dead

---

[134] Luzzatto, *Meḥqerei Hayahadut*, I, pt. 2, 20, "Haemuna Betorat Moshe," first published in *Hamagid* 1, no. 3 (5218 [1858]). It is noteworthy that Luzzatto voiced similar criticism of the teachers of purified Christianity, the Protestants of our day. In a letter to Rapoport of 1832, he repeats the question that had been addressed to Rapoport by a student of Luzzatto's, the answer to which displeased him. "My friend, the wise rabbi Hillel Hacohen [de la Torre], who sends you greetings, is somewhat upset by your answer to his question regarding the Protestants... Our question and request is about the men of our generation, how can they call themselves Christians, since most of the sages of their faith (Doctores Theologiae) publicly deny Torah from heaven and the marvelous prophecies? This is something that the mind cannot tolerate." See *Igrot Shadal*, 227.

Sea Scrolls, could Flusser determine, on their basis, that Christianity mainly drew upon Pharisaic, Essene, and mystical Jewish sources.

I have analyzed the positions of Chajes, Hirsch, and Luzzatto on the subject of religious tolerance, showing that they were influenced by all that was said about Christianity before them and in their time. I showed that Chajes was the most tolerant and optimistic of the three, and his critique of Christianity was minor, relating mainly to past persecutions and the blood libels that took place far away. In his opinion, this favorable view of Christianity and Islam was shared by all his predecessors, including Maimonides: they were not idolatrous, and they were part of the divine plan for the correct service of God by all of humanity, and the future would be good for the Jews among the Christians.

Luzzatto is more critical than Chajes. However, he only rejects the principles of Christianity that detract from the status of the Jews and their Torah. He developed a doctrine of universalistic tolerance, and he also believes that the two other monotheistic religions help spread monotheism among mankind, and the goal of all three religions is to do so. He does not agree with Maimonides, that Christianity is pagan, and he attacks him strongly because of his intolerant attitudes. Nor does Luzzatto count Maimonides among those who agree with his opinion and regard Christianity as a stage in human progress.

Hirsch, who sees Christianity as a competitor and threat, is the most critical of all. He agrees with the others that Jesus was a positive figure who observed the commandments and did not intend to found a new religion, and that early Christianity, which adopted some of Judaism, was a chapter in human progress, according to the divine plan. However, in his opinion, apparently based on Salvador's suggestions, Jesus's followers adopted pagan dogmas and included them in Christianity.

Hirsch attacks these dogmas vehemently, because in his opinion they bring about the separation of the divine realm from the human, civil realm, causing moral corruption and hopeless impotence among human beings, enslaved to Original Sin and unable to free themselves from the bonds of the sensual forces of nature. Only the Torah of Israel can save mankind from this materialistic determinism and restore it to the Garden of Eden in this world, because only it teaches man to sanctify his body by overcoming the sensuality of the flesh by ethical choice, making possible the existence of an ethical society. In contrast to Christianity, Islamic monotheism is perfect, but it lacks the practical guidance of the commandments of the Torah so as to take part in the period of redemption in which everyone will serve God shoulder to shoulder.

Summary

In this book I have presented and analyzed the responses of three religious thinkers to six phenomena of modernity. These thinkers are Rabbi Zvi Hirsch Chajes, Rabbi Samson Raphael Hirsch, and Samuel David Luzzatto, who lived and were active in Europe between 1820 and 1870. This period in Jewish history was characterized by emancipation in stages, and by decline in the power of the community in favor of the central regime. The three thinkers absorbed some of the ideology of the Haskala period, and they experienced the transition in the thought and in spiritual atmosphere of Europe from egalitarian, universal rationalism to romanticism, which limited reason and elevated nostalgia for the past, concern with personal and national experience, and emotional life. Despite their romantic leanings, all three of them, having internalized Haskala, distinguished between these characteristics of romanticism and mysticism and Kabbalah, which they rejected, and they were able to limit their emotion and set it within boundaries, according to clear, healthy reason.

All three experienced the strong emphasis placed on historical studies, but they did not all understand the meaning of this and the difference between the old unified view of history and the awareness of historical development that took its place. They had to cope with signs of the new age, in which the view that God intervenes in history gave way to the view that human reason rules the world and conquers the forces of nature with the tool of modern science, which it developed for the benefit of humanity. Religion was shunted to the side, and secularization, throwing off the yoke of the commandments, and pursuit of luxuries and material goods increasingly characterized the entire society. The Jews were drawn inexorably to European culture and to scientific research, which opened their gates to them, and the fate of Judaism as an independent factor was in jeopardy. These three thinkers were not philosophers. Chajes and Hirsch were community rabbis, and Luzzatto was the head of a rabbinical seminary. However, these developments forced them to formulate a religious ideological response. As I showed in the Introduction, they viewed themselves as "men of the middle" between those who rejected religion and the deists, on the one hand, and the extremely devout, who closed themselves off from anything new and avoided rational inquiry.

I include in the Middle Way those who were active up to mid-century and sought to combine the tradition with modernity without changing or modifying the Halakha, at least in practice. These men tried to preserve the religion and its commandments, which they regarded as a gift from God and as the correct way of life, and to combine with it everything that was true, ethical, and aesthetic in European culture, in order to produce a more perfect Jew. The middle position is complex, because it is vulnerable to attacks from two sides, and to dialectical tensions that derive from the desire to live in two worlds at the same time. These tensions—between the tradition and modernity, between reason and revelation, between religion and science, between faith in Torah from heaven and philological research, and between sensuality and sanctity—present difficult tests to those who stand in the center and wish to espouse both poles. The Middle Way grappled with them in full confidence that theirs was not a position of compromise but rather the true Jewish way.

The phenomena of modernism that I examined are:

A. Bible Criticism;
B. The Reform movement and the historical-positivist school;
C. Haskala and Wissenschaft des Judentums;
D. The attitude to the Land of Israel and a real return to Zion;
E. The status of women and religious tolerance.

Despite the shared political and social background in Germany and Austria, and despite the common cultural and philosophical environment, and despite the shared position that sought to combine the tradition with modernity, the responses to these phenomena were varied. Differences in biographical and social circumstances gave rise to a variety of opinions within the middle trend.

CHAJES: THE TALMUDIST AND RATIONALIST, AND THE RESTRICTIVE IDENTICALITY APPROACH

Chajes was relatively isolated from European culture compared to the other two. The northern end of the Austrian Empire was far from the centers of culture in Europe, so every change reached there after it was already consolidated in Western Europe. Judaism in Chajes's area largely remained devout, and Hasidism was very powerful. Therefore, Chajes remained more faithful to the old rationalism than the other two, anchored in the Talmud and loyal to Maimonides, though also influenced by romanticism.

Chajes's home city, Brody, where he studied and where his personality was formed, was exposed to moderate Haskala, but not to Reform Judaism, and it was a center of systematic study of the Talmud and of Maimonides. This determined the axis around which his opinions revolved. As a rationalist Talmudist, who had absorbed Haskala, Chajes focused on studies whose aim was to prove the truth of the chain of reception from Mount Sinai, according to the Talmud. As a classical fundamentalist, his reading of Maimonides was very moderate; the Biblical revolution did not reach Chajes. He categorically rejected both the higher and lower criticism of the Bible, but not because modern scholarship was necessarily illegitimate. Unlike his friend Krochmal, he did not internalize developmental historical consciousness, and therefore he ruled that biblical scholarship was not new: the Sages had engaged in it on the strength of their authority to interpret scripture, and that was sufficient. The tools of modern scholarship were to be applied to the Oral Law, and this he did. Because of the influence of his romanticism and fundamentalism, Chajes was troubled by issues such as:

A. What does the Torah intend to teach?
B. What is man's purpose?
C. Is ethics superior to philosophical inquiry or not?

He did not fully accept Maimonides's position regarding the philosophy implicit in the Bible and contemplation as man's purpose because of the romantic attacks on rationalism, and the emphasis in European culture on ethics as a goal and anti-elitism as a method. Therefore, Chajes proved to be only partially consistent.

He related to Reform with fury. At first he thought it was a moderate and transitory phenomenon, over which Judaism would triumph, and he believed the struggle against it should be waged politely, to restore those in error to the right way. Later, as Reform spread, the number of its supporters increased, and its rabbinical conventions were held, Chajes understood that the danger was increasing, and he attacked Reform with detailed polemics. He argued that the approach stating that the written Torah and the Oral Law were created by humans was dangerous to Judaism, and its motivations were not honorable, but rather were intended to support the aspiration to find favor in the eyes of the Gentiles and to throw off the yoke of Halakha. This conviction also led Chajes, the fundamentalist, to a very moderate reading of Maimonides. He claimed to have analyzed Maimonides's view of the components of the Oral Law, but Maimonides's claim, that most of the Oral Law was a creation of the Sages, might have helped those who rejected Halakha and sought to reform the religion. Therefore Chajes distorted Maimonides's approach, and adopted Krochmal's Aristotelian tactic for his own purposes. He believed that, by their wisdom, the Sages actualized what already was actual with God, the Lawgiver at Sinai and only in potential with the recipient, and they revealed it. Contrary to Maimonides, who stated that these Halakhot stood on a lower level, which was not from Sinai, and contrary to Krochmal, who stated this principle in order to retain some obligatory authority for the Halakha, which was created in a developmental process, Chajes raised these Halakhot to the level of the written Torah from Sinai. In a dialectical process he combined the poles of the contradiction between the cumulative codex of the Halakha, according to Maimonides, and the Oral Law from Sinai. Chajes also regarded Aggadic Midrash as part of the Oral Law from Sinai, and he stated that it was possible to issue Halakhic rulings from it. Things in Aggada appeared to contradict reality because of faulty understanding of the Aggada, or because "nature changed." According to Chajes, the ethics of the Torah embodied in the two Torahs from Sinai was the correct one, and he did not accept Luzzatto's criticism of Maimonides, according to which the latter regarded contemplation as superior to morality. At the same time, on this topic as well, one finds contradictory messages in Chajes.

Since he did not dismiss research completely, Chajes accepted the Wissenschaft des Judentums gladly, as well as Haskala literature, for he regarded them as preserving the honor of the nation and assuring its continued existence. He even regarded those whose opinions differed from his with respect. Scholars of Jewish literature and history, from the time of Tannaim to the present, were none other than a single unified continuum, and they were all positive in his view. The combination of tradition and modernity must be subject to constant control. Chajes did not accept Luzzatto's critical opinion that Maimonides regarded autonomous reason and Aristotelian rationalism as a standard for understanding revelation. He preferred a moderate reading of Maimonides, according to which philosophy and revelation were identical, and in instances of difficulties and contradictions, the restrictive approach should be taken, and revelation should be the sole yardstick for the examination and purification of philosophical and scientific propositions. It is also possible to find a Mendelssohnian position in Chajes: that the Torah does not teach eternal [philosophical] truths. To resolve the contradiction between this principle and the fundamentalist view that the entire Torah is from Sinai, Chajes made a dialectical move, claiming that the entire nation received not only a constitution at Sinai but also intellectual perfection. Chajes did not internalize the principles of Haskala on the matter of secular studies. In his opinion, they were permitted only to adults in their leisure time. On this, he followed Emden's path.

Regarding the Land of Israel and the return to Zion, Chajes was faithful to Mendelssohn's neutralizing approach, just as he was faithful to his universalistic positions. The Jew's prayer for the return to Zion was a prayer for the end of days, beyond history, when all the nations would gain salvation, and it was not a sign of the Jews' dual loyalty. The Jewish people were subject to the three oaths, and the more rights countries granted them, the more faithful and useful they would be as citizens. Here Chajes based his opinion on his reading of the prophet Jeremiah (29:7). In contrast to Reform, Chajes was faithful to the tradition regarding the future salvation and the ingathering of the Jewish people in Zion, where they would rebuild the Temple and the kingdom, but he postponed this to the end of days, placing it beyond real history.

Chajes remained faithful to the central tradition in Judaism regarding women's inferiority, though he warned his listeners that this inferiority did not justify the humiliation of women in any way. He was deeply disturbed by the sexual permissiveness and corruption of modern times. The distance of Galicia from the centers of culture and from Western Europe prevented the issue of the status of women from being raised there in public discussion. Even when he felt and thought that there was room for leniency, Chajes was reluctant to grant it, for fear of the reactions of the Hasidim and of the possibility that this would open the way to Reform.

Chajes was tolerant toward Christianity, and his tolerance was not free of apologetics. He accepted the opinion of Judah Halevi and what he thought was also Maimonides's opinion. That Jesus and Christianity as well as Islam were part of the divine plan to bring humanity to accept the ethical monotheism of Judaism. He believed that the difficulties and errors of the past, which gave rise to persecution and forced conversion, were no longer possible.

HIRSCH: THE ROMANTIC EDUCATOR AND THE POSITION OF NEO-FUNDAMENTALIST IDENTICALITY

Hirsch lived and was active in the center of polemical battles, in the eye of the storm. He experienced closely the decline of the prestige of reason and metaphysics, and the transition to romanticism, as well as the prolonged struggle with Reform and then with the historical-positivist school, and also the collapse of the communities. In his youth in Hamburg, where he experienced the unsuccessful struggle of Orthodoxy against the Reform Temple, his decision took shape: to devote himself to saving the tradition and the Torah in a new way.

His studies in the spirit of Wessely, which combined religious and secular subjects, Jewish philosophy from Hakham Bernays based on Judah Halevi, and Talmud study from Rabbi Ettlinger, formed a middle way for Hirsch, by which he hoped to bring the Torah back into Jewish life. He called this path, "Torah with Derekh Erets," which was the path of Modern Orthodoxy, or Neo-Orthodoxy. Hirsch devoted himself to the communal rabbinate, while emphasizing the campaign and the educational system. He also had a brief acquaintance with the academic world and studied the speculative philosophy of the time on his own.

He completely rejected Bible criticism. In contrast to Chajes, he perceived the danger latent in the new developmental historical approach, and therefore he objected in principle to the application of philological and historical tools of research to scripture. Hirsch declared categorically that the Torah was unified, divine, inerrant, and authentic, and that it could be studied only from within itself, as it presents itself, as the word of God. The Torah is perfect and free of any error, and it contains truths that the generation of those who received it did not know. Man's mission was to raise itself toward the Torah and not to lower it to his level, as demanded by the religious reformers. Therefore neither higher nor lower criticism was permissible.

Hirsch did not accept the position expressed by Chajes regarding the Sages' Bible criticism, and in his opinion they did not engage in criticism, but merely transmitted or reconstructed information. Regarding man's purpose and the question of what the Torah teaches Hirsch was determined in his romantic, post-Haskala position, that the Torah contained no philosophy or mysticism, but that it was a book of divine ethical norms, whose acceptance by humanity would bring about their salvation. Man's purpose was the attainment of ethical sanctity in every area of life—spiritual and physical—not an elitist goal, and the ethics of the Torah is the sole means for attaining it. It is a divine morality, free of all sensuality that prevents reason from maintaining pure morality. Hirsch was greatly influenced by the Biblical Revolution: he devoted himself more to interpreting the Bible than to the Talmud, although for him the Talmud remained the guiding book of Judaism.

Hirsch devoted his whole life and educational activity to the struggle against Reform. When the historical-positivist school appeared on the stage, he immediately perceived the danger to his views that followed from that approach. He regarded the idea that the Oral Law was the independent creation of the Sages as a challenge to all the foundations of Judaism, because it implied that anyone, in fact, could continue to change the Halakha according to his own understanding and the requirements of the age.

Hirsch took the fundamentalist position of the Geonim and Nachmanides, according to which the entire Torah—the written Torah as well as Halakhic Midrash—was from Sinai, and its source was divine. The public event at Sinai was proof of that. In order to dispense with the position of the reformers as much as possible, Hirsch made a revolution beyond the position of the Geonim and Nachmanides: he explained that the Halakhot in the Oral Law were all given to Moses from the mouth of God. Only afterward, during the wanderings in the desert, was the written legal code given to him, in which the Oral Law was stated in brief, in the best possible way, and the thirteen hermeneutic principles were also given to be used as a key to decipher the code and reconstruct forgotten Halakhot. All of this was intended to ensure that the Halakha would not be forgotten and that the connection between the Oral and written Law would be retained.

Thereby, like Chajes, Hirsch elevates the level of Midrash, but he goes even farther, by making it—with his characteristic fundamentalism—into the primary level, and the written Torah into the secondary level. Clearly, according to Hirsch as well, the ethics of the Torah, embodied in the two divine Torahs, is supreme, and the only ethics that can bring salvation to humanity. Only this ethical system can raise man up to the sanctity whose meaning was man's control over his sensual appetites and devotion to the spiritual God.

Like Chajes, Hirsch imbibed important principles of Haskala. The equality of rational men, universalism, and the combination of the sciences of man with that of the divine teaching were basic to his thought. However, unlike Chajes, he rejected the Wissenschaft des Judentums, because in his view it expressed the aspiration for reform in religion according to the spirit of the age, and especially the invalid principle of applying the modern tools of scholarship to the Torah, and the developmental, historical position regarding the Halakha. Hirsch regarded the Torahs from Sinai as ahistorical, beyond time and place, and therefore he engaged in prolonged polemics against Graetz and Frankel of the historical school, who regarded the Sages as the creators of the Halakha and not only as restoring and transmitting what was received at Sinai.

The view that the Sages were great men who created the Halakha according to their human tendencies and their deep understanding of the needs of the nation and the age appeared to be a diminution of the status of the Sages for Hirsch, and legitimizing reform in Halakha. As for Aggada, Hirsch was more daring than Chajes and stated decisively that it was not from Sinai but reflected scientific opinions that were accepted by all men of science at that time, and in this matter the Sages might err, and one should not issue Halakhic rulings according to it.

Hirsch did not agree with Mendelssohn's position regarding the relation between revelation and reason. Mendelssohn saw them as two important but separate realms in Judaism, while—as Maimonides also stated—autonomous universal reason served as the yardstick. Relying on Kant, Hirsch stated that reason, which was subject to the senses, could not serve as a standard. Philosophy and revelation were principally and theoretically identical, and anyone who did not accept the position of identicality was a heretic, because nature, reason, and the Torah all had their source in God, but the yardstick for resolving difficulties and contradictions was, as Judah Halevi stated, revelation.

Being a neo-fundamentalist, who believed that both the Torahs were from heaven and could not err, and that they reflected an absolute, supreme truth, Hirsch moved inconsistently within the position of identicality between the restrictive and interpretative approaches. When it was a question of matters that had not yet been proven, and which seemed to him as speculative science or philosophy, he took the restrictive view. But when it was a question of experimental knowledge, which in his opinion had been proven beyond any reasonable doubt, he was prepared to make use of the interpretative approach and to make the Torah harmonize with science, but only to avoid admitting that there were errors either in the Torah or in the Halakhic Midrash of the Sages.

Unlike Chajes, Hirsch had entirely absorbed the educational revolution of Haskala and believed that secular subjects should be taught from an early age, but that they should be taught in an integrative manner from the viewpoint of the Torah, by the method of Torah with Derekh Erets. Hirsch believed that the inclusion of secular studies was not a compromise with the needs of the age, and that Judaism always believed that truths from outside of Judaism must be accepted, and that they had intrinsic value. Hirsch daringly stated that the correct combination of Torah and general studies would give rise dialectically to a result that would be greater than a simple sum of the parts.

On the subject of the Land of Israel and the return to Zion, Hirsch, like Chajes, adopted Mendelssohn's neutralizing position. Careful reading of the texts shows that there is no possibility of regarding Hirsch as a precursor of Zionism. Bound by the three oaths, Jews were faithful to their present homeland, and the return to Zion was a Utopian dream. In his view, the Diaspora became an ideal that enabled the Jewish people to fulfill its mission to the nations and to teach them the ethics of the Torah for their salvation. Hirsch adopted Maimonides's opinion, which denied the inherent sanctity of the Land of Israel and the Jewish people. As a universalist who desired emancipation, Hirsch, contrary to Judah Halevi, stated that the Jewish people was only the first among equals, and that the Land of Israel was only an instrument for fulfilling the Torah, an instrument that had disappointed. It was a dangerous instrument that had corrupted the nation with its bounty.

Faithful to the tradition, like Chajes, he stated that the ingathering of the Jews in their land and state would take place in the Utopian future at the end of days, though he showed little enthusiasm for that as well. Integration as a Jewish religious community in a cultured, flourishing Germany, which had been redeemed and acted according to the norms of the Torah of Israel, charmed him far more. Nor did Hirsch point out the advantage of the separate national existence of the Jewish people in their land at the end of days.

On the subject of the status of women, Hirsch created a revolution, according to which women were superior to men in Judaism. Pressure for women's equality for moral reasons on the part of the general society and of the Reform Jews forced him to ignore the central stream of the Jewish tradition and to create an apologetics, stating that according to Judaism, women had always been superior to men intellectually and morally. Men, easily seduced, need far more commandments than women in order to avoid moral corruption. Women do not need a large part of the commandments, and they are given a special role in the home, in the framework of which she must watch over her husband and ward off the moral dangers that lie in wait for him in his tasks outside the home. Like Chajes, Hirsch was also very fearful of the spreads of permissiveness in the modern age, and he devoted efforts to educate and direct youth on the subjects of sexual and ethical sanctification.

As for Christianity, Hirsch had one opinion about Jesus and a different one about his followers. He saw Jesus as mainly a positive figure, who brought some of the light of the ethics of the Torah to pagan nations. However, the Christianity established by his followers never shook off its pagan elements: the incarnation of God in human flesh and Original Sin, which left a curse upon man, making him unable to escape the moral corruption in the bonds of flesh, are pagan ideas. Therefore, Christianity cannot lead mankind to true morality or salvation, and only Judaism can do so.

LUZZATTO: THE ROMANTIC SCHOLAR AND THE POSITION OF DUAL TRUTH

Although he lived in geographical isolation and in a relatively small community in Italy, Luzzatto kept up close connections both with the men of Wissenschaft des Judentums in the West and also with his friends, men of Haskala literature throughout the Austrian Empire, and he quickly became informed of what was taking place around him.

Luzzatto was faithful to rationalism and Maimonides only in his youth, but he rapidly fell under the influence of romantic ideas, which rejected intellectual elitism and developed fondness for the past and the national, religious experience, cultivating morality and sentiment. The emancipation brought the Jews of Italy to abandon Halakha and made them indifferent to the commandments, but Luzzatto had no close contact with either Reform or Hasidism. The threat he faced was ignorance. Like Hirsch, Luzzatto was a post-Haskala romantic who rejected mysticism and Kabbala. He imbibed the Haskala principles of equality and universalism, and he embraced free scholarship, which strove impartially to reach the pure truth, as the motto of his life. Being faithful to the idea of Torah from heaven and to observance of the commandments out of belief in their supreme ethical value, Luzzatto found himself as a man of the middle way, standing in the breach between the religious reformers and Bible critics who denied Torah from heaven, prophecy, and divine reward and punishment, and the Orthodox who rejected all rational research as endangering the tradition. As was common in Italy, Luzzatto studied both secular and religious subjects, and later, on his own, he studied general and Jewish philosophy. His appointment at the rabbinical seminary in Padua determined that his life work would be writing commentary and research on the Bible, the Hebrew language, and Jewish thought and history.

As a romantic, Luzzatto was decisively influenced by the Bible revolution, and the Bible became the formative book of Judaism for him. After conducting impartial research, Luzzatto reached the conclusion that the Torah was authentic, and the information it offers about its divine origin is trustworthy. Among other things, he based his conclusion on the repeated miracle of the manna, and on the full preservation of the text throughout history. In the light of this conclusion, he devoted great effort to disputing those who claimed that the source of the Torah was human and later than the time of Moses.

Like Hirsch, Luzzatto stated that the Torah contains neither philosophical nor mystical information, but rather divine ethical guidance, and that its purpose is not to offer truth to mankind, but rather to make people better. Luzzatto was interested in the literal meaning of the text and, contrary to Hirsch, he believed that the Torah was given in a form that was appropriate to the level of those who received it, and that it refined the prevalent beliefs of the time it was given. In general, Luzzatto accepted the positions of the tradition regarding the dates that the books of the Bible and the prophets were composed, and he agreed to adopt a different opinion only if there was irrefutable proof. Therefore, he rejected the position of Krochmal and Rapoport regarding two Isaiahs and the late date of certain psalms.

Like his comrades in the middle trend, Luzzatto saw Reform as a danger to the existence of Judaism, and he viewed the reformers as insincere, whose purpose was not to search for truth, but rather to throw off the yoke of the Halakha, to pursue wealth and honor, and to flatter the Gentiles. In contrast, he saw no danger in the idea of the historical development of the Halakha. In fact, his position was close to that of the historical-positivist school, and he should be viewed as one of its precursors.

Luzzatto eventually took a developmental position regarding the Halakha as he progressed in his study of the Bible and the Mishnah, and he reached the conclusion that the Halakhot in the Oral Law were largely the splendid creation of the Sages, who legislated them with lofty inspiration, sincerity, and deep insight into the needs of the nation, and who also invented the thirteen hermeneutic principles to connect their regulations to the Bible and to give them more authority. Luzzatto concluded from this that it was not permissible to institute even moderate reforms in his day, because he believed that people were not on the exalted level of the Sages, who could effect a true, impartial reform, out of deep understanding of the needs of the nation.

Conversely, Luzzatto concluded that the primary meaning of the Bible could not in any way be the interpretation of the Sages, contrary to the opinion of Chajes and Hirsch. The Bible stood on its own, and it must be interpreted according to what was commonly thought at the time of those who received it. Luzzatto stated that the Sages had an esoteric doctrine of their own, which was lost in the interim, and they issued rulings according to it. Thus he endowed the Oral Law with obligatory authority. He abandoned that explanation later and stated that the obligation to obey the Halakha lay in the directive of the Torah: "and you must do everything you are instructed." This view was similar to Maimonides's opinion, based on Deuteronomy 17:10.

Luzzatto explained that the Jewish ethical doctrine, as reflected in Jewish literature, was, therefore, the only ethical doctrine that could successfully educate the masses. This Torah was divine and not subject to the sensuality to which human reason was subject, and it was based on a natural human characteristic: the feeling of compassion. It also provided a deterrent: divine reward and punishment.

Luzzatto was a product of the Haskala in every fiber of his being. He was a member of the Haskala literary movement of Eastern Europe and maintained wide-ranging contacts with all the Jewish scholars of his day. Use of philological and historical tools of research was his forte. At first he took the identicality approach with the interpretative position, but he soon reached the conclusion that it was difficult to find a compromise between philosophical truth and the purpose of revelation, which was to educate mankind to be better but not necessarily learned in philosophical truths. Hence he adopted the compartmental position, changing his opinion when certain scholars in Germany and Galicia adopted rationalist philosophical opinions, based on Aristotle, Maimonides, and Spinoza, which were foreign to Judaism in his view. That phenomenon, in his opinion, led to throwing off the yoke of Halakha and rejection of the idea of Torah from heaven.

Luzzatto called this philosophical trend "Atticism," which he distinguished from "Judaism." He regarded it as turning away from Jewish scientific scholarship, which did not dismiss prophecy and divine reward and punishment a priori. It led to moral corruption and preference for settling accounts rather than compassion. However, the compartmental approach also failed to satisfy him, because he realized that philosophy contradicted revelation and any compromise between them was illusory.

In Luzzatto's opinion, there was no flaw in such a view, nor was it heretical, as Hirsch thought. The human mind is unable to heal the rift, and therefore God cannot formulate a unifying Torah in human language, and He preferred moral goodness—the religious truth—over philosophical truth. Consequently, Luzzatto adopted the doctrine of dual truth, which he learned from an earlier Italian thinker, Elijah Delmedigo. This position holds that there is a pure, correct philosophical truth, which has yet to be formulated as a single, independent position, and it contradicts the other correct truth—free of all speculative rationalism and mysticism—of revelation. The educated believer must know both truths and learn to live with them and to love both of them. He must understand that a dialectical synthesis between philosophy and revelation is impossible for human beings, and that the contradiction between them reflects a cosmic rift that can be bridged only in infinity, in God. Thus it appears that those who called Luzzatto a fundamentalist were wrong. On the contrary, according to one way of understanding, he accepted the possibility that the Bible, though it is divine, does not provide philosophical truth. Moreover, essentially, as a divine book of moral guidance, the Bible forgoes truth to educate for goodness. Another way of putting this is to say that Luzzatto accepted the conception that the Torah presents one truth, and science presents another truth, which contradicts it—a view that anticipates post-modernism. The contradictions between science and religion did not disturb Luzzatto in the slightest, because they were merely a possible consequence of the doctrine of dual truth.

Secular studies at a young age were common in Italy, and thus Luzzatto gave no attention to the topic in his writings.

On the subject of the Land of Israel, Luzzatto's position was very similar to his comrades in the middle trend. Like Mendelssohn, he believed that return to Zion was a vision for the end of days, for a time beyond history, when all the nations would be redeemed. Thus he was no precursor of Zionism. The early Luzzatto was a universalist who believed in the mission of the Jewish people to educate humanity in Jewish ethics. Luzzatto came to change this view. He understood that such a position, adopted by the Reform Jews and the Atticist rationalists, endangered the independent existence of Judaism, nor did it suit the compartmental approach and the doctrine of dual truth that he developed. Therefore he rejected the value of emancipation, the idea of educating mankind, and the mission of the Jewish people as illusions and fruitless dreams.

Luzzatto believed that the Jewish people must preserve its uniqueness as a family among the nations, leave the completion of God's plans to Him, and await the end of days, the time when they would be gathered in Zion and establish their kingdom.

In general it may be said that Luzzatto lived before his time. He acknowledged the development of the Halakha, determined that the text of the Bible was dependent on the culture, place, and time of its recipients, like any human text, although its source was in God. He perceived that the realm of religion was entirely separate from that of science, and they had different languages of discourse, which could only be bridged in God, outside of the world and of history. In this world, one must live with contradiction. The planning of history, salvation, and the return to Zion must be left to God, without trying to interpret historical events such as the dispersion of the Jewish people among the nations, emancipation, and progress as events of religious significance and without seeking to take part in them.

With regard to the status of women, Luzzatto was a faithful son of the Italian Renaissance and of his view of the historical development of the Halakha. In his opinion, according to the Torah, women were equal to men in duties and rights both in the home and in public, and they are obligated by all the commandments. When the Jews were influenced by the surrounding society and adopted the idea of the inferiority of women, the Sages, in their wisdom, were forced to exempt them from some of the commandments, to alleviate their suffering. Luzzatto was contemptuous of sexual corruption and permissiveness, which he regarded as pathology of the modern age.

Luzzatto's critique of Christianity was less severe than that of Hirsch. He did not agree with Maimonides, that Christianity was a pagan religion, and he did not attack its dogmas. He only attacked the views that denied the status of the Jews and that of the Hebrew Bible. In his view, as well, Christianity and Islam took part in disseminating monotheism in the world.

As religious thinkers, the men of the Middle Way, Chajes, Hirsch, and Luzzatto, struggled against opinions to their right and left, and they formed positions that combined revelation with human wisdom and science. Usually the three men developed common general positions in their responses to modern phenomena. However, close reading of all their writings reveals important and critical differences among these positions. In some critical areas, each of them developed a different position, according to the social surroundings and cultural and ideological background in which he was active, his education, and his life experience.

These positions place Luzzatto to the left of Chajes and Hirsch. While the other two adopted fundamentalist attitudes, Luzzatto presented a more daring and modern approach. This approach was expressed in his attitude toward the use of modern research tools both in relation to the source of the Oral Law and also to the place of reason versus revelation. The present study can be developed in two directions: in latitude, to examine the responses to other phenomena of modernity such as the attitude toward government and the state, permissiveness, the judiciary, Halakha and medicine, and more; or in longitude, to examine the influence of these three thinkers on those who followed them, such as Hermann Cohen, Franz Rosenzweig, M. D. Cassutto, Yeshayahu Leibowitz, and others. The present study could serve as the foundation for such research.

Epilogue

In this book I have surveyed the changes that took place during the nineteenth century in the world views of important aspects of traditional Judaism, observant of the Torah and the commandments. According to my definition, the Jews about whom I wrote belonged to the middle trend, which was influenced by the abundant work in philosophy, scholarship, science, and technology that came to Europe on the wings of modernity. This influence motivated them to make an intellectual effort intended to find the correct combination of the marvelous Jewish tradition and the wonderful achievements of modern European culture, in which they wished to take part.

These efforts did indeed give rise to important changes within this trend, in comparison to earlier generations.

TORAH FROM SINAI AND HALAKHA FROM HEAVEN

This area is the one least susceptible to change. Challenge to this principle appears to undermine all of Judaism, which is build on the axiom that the Torah and the Oral Law were received from God by Moses in the Sinai Desert, and therefore they are valid and authoritative forever.

However, changes took place in this principle among those faithful to the tradition even before the appearance of the historical-positivist school. Although Rabbi Samson Raphael Hirsch was unwilling to budge from this principle, following his culture-hero Judah Halevi, with the others there was movement. With regard to Rabbi Zvi Hirsch Chajes, I showed that, following Maimonides and Krochmal, he acknowledged that not all the Halakhot were actually instituted by Moses, and that large parts of the Halakha existed only in potential among those who received the Torah, and only over the course of history did they emerge from potentiality to actuality, through the wisdom of the Sages. His argument that such moves left the Oral Law on the same level as the written Torah, which actually existed at the time of Sinai, is debatable. Not everyone would agree that what was attained by one Sage or another, even by application of the thirteen hermeneutic principles, truly reveals what already existed in potential at Sinai.

In contrast to the former two, Luzzatto took a daring step forward. His scholarship led him to the conclusion that, indeed, a large part of the Halakhot in the Oral Law was invented by the Sages, including the hermeneutic principles. Their authority derives from:

A. Their genius and spiritual elevation, to legislate according to the needs of the nation, impartially.
B. The instruction of the Torah to the people: "be careful to do everything they will teach you."

Isaac Samuel Reggio of Gorizia, Zacharias Frankel, and Heinrich Graetz were also inspired by Maimonides and Krochmal, and then the middle way divided into two: the Neo-Orthodoxy, on the one hand, and Conservatism, on the other. From here to actual changes in Halakha, the way was long, and none of the thinkers mentioned above was willing to make an actual change. Only the Reform movement did so, and that is a subject in its own right.

RELIGIOUS FANATICISM

The three thinkers I have presented were repelled by religious fanaticism and also suffered from it. They insisted that the middle way they chose was not a compromise between tradition and modernity, but a difficult and complex path that sought to combine, in dialectical fashion, two poles that could not dwell together in peace. The truth is not in the ease and simplicity of either extreme, but complex and challenging. They regarded fanaticism, which rejected rational inquiry completely, did not agree to accept truth where it was found, and adopted the mystical ideas of the Kabbala, as contemptible. The embodiment of fanaticism was, in their opinion, Hasidism, and Chajes, who lived among Hasidim, suffered mistreatment at their hand.

UNIVERSALISM AND SECULAR STUDIES

This was the area in which our three thinkers went the farthest in the direction of modernity and European culture. Someone who thinks that human reason is capable of inquiring and finding philosophical, theological, and ethical truths in addition to scientific discoveries, necessarily advocates universalism to one degree or another, and he must include the wisdom of the Gentiles in his children's school curriculum. Chajes was not yet prepared to take that daring step, and self-directed study by adults was sufficient for him. Luzzatto lived in a culture where non-Jewish studies were already an integral part of the education that every Jew received. The one who was most daring in the traditional world was Hirsch, who established a school based on the theories of Wessely, combining secular and religious studies for the boys and girls of his community for ideological reasons. Hirsch believed that this had been that path of Judaism in splendid periods of the past, and that this combination produced a more complete educated and cultivated person than the sum of the individual components of the curriculum.

THE COMBINATION AND CONTRADICTION OF REVELATION AND REASON

Each of the three thinkers arrived at a different combination. Chajes and Hirsch stated that revelation and reason were, in principle, identical. However, when contradictions emerged, Chajes believed that revelation took precedence, and that it was the determining standard. Hirsch agreed with him in general. However, he thought that whenever the claims of rational science had been proven, and there was a contradiction, the propositions of revelation must be interpreted so as to accord with the achievements of reason, which, in essence, gave precedence to reason. Luzzatto went farther, believing that there were two contradictory truths that could not be bridged by human reason. We must not fear contradiction, because there is not always as clear and unequivocal answer to every question. It was preferable to live in a complex world, where there were unresolved contradictions, than to live in a simplistic world that clung to one extreme or another of the spectrum.

THE STATUS OF WOMEN

The campaign for women's equality began in the nineteenth century. Judaism could not stand on the sidelines and stick to the classical chauvinistic position of women's inferiority. The Reform Jews began by outwardly improving the status of women in the synagogue service, but they did not truly change the classical views of women. For Chajes, the required change was difficult. He was not willing to change the principle, but he demanded of men not to err because of it and think that they were permitted to insult women's honor. Hirsch, as was his wont, made an apologetic revolution. He chose to ignore all the negative statements about women in Jewish sources and argued that women had always been regarded as superior to men in intellect and morals, and this was the source of their exemption from certain commandments. Luzzatto thought that in the biblical period women were equal to men, and only during the period of the Mishnah and the Talmud, when their status was lowered because of Gentile influence, were the Sages lenient with them and exempted them from some of the commandments. All three men were worried about the increase in sexual permissiveness and corruption, and they instructed their students to grant as much equality as possible and full honor to women. Hirsch even opened a school in which girls studied religious and secular subjects from an early age, with some restrictions.

THE LITERAL MEANING OF THE BIBLE

Both Hirsch and Luzzatto rejected the approaches according to which the Torah is to be interpreted by speculative philosophical codes or by mystical, kabbalistic codes. Hirsch regarded the Sages' interpretation of Halakhic verses as their primary meaning, whereas Luzzatto sought the primary meaning by linguistic, grammatical, and literary means, and according to current research on the Ancient Near East, which was the world of those who had received the Torah. They both viewed the Torah as a book of moral instruction, which the Jewish people had to preserve for the benefit of all humanity, so that people could sanctify their bodies and their lives and attain the next world in this one.

THE ATTITUDE TOWARD THE WEAK IN SOCIETY

Since the Torah is a book of moral guidance, Hirsch and Luzzatto make it clear that the purpose of the commandments of the Torah is to strengthen and fortify the moral virtues that are natural to man. Hirsch called this "conscience," and Luzzatto emphasized "the virtue of compassion," which underlies many of the commandments of the Torah. This does not refer to paternalistic pity derived from a feeling of superiority, which is unacceptable to the modern way of thinking, but compassion that comes from full and authentic identification with the suffering of one's weaker fellow. This natural morality is not sufficient to oppose the weakness of the impulses, which are driven by sensuality, and God gave mankind a system of ethical norms in revelation in order to wage war against the instincts and strengthen the quality of compassion, and to assure its implementation by establishing a system of reward and punishment. This assured a proper attitude toward the stranger, the orphan, the widow, the minority of strangers within our midst, the poor, and the slaves.

INFLUENCE IN THE TWENTIETH CENTURY

During the twentieth century, the middle trend spread in depth and breadth. Prominent thinkers among Modern Orthodox Jews were Hermann Cohen and Franz Rosenzweig, on the one hand, and Rav Kook and Rabbi Joseph Soloveitchik, on the other, and—so to speak—on a third hand, Professor Yeshayahu Leibowitz. The former two came from the assimilated world that lived with German philosophy after Kant, Hegel, and Fichte. With a huge intellectual effort they paved the middle way and built a world of thought that combined Post-Kantianism with Jewish religiosity. Rav Kook and Rabbi Soloveitchik strongly experienced the difficulty of living in a dialectical world. They struggled to heal the cosmic rift between their religious world and their cultural and civil world. Their success is a matter of debate among scholars, but neither of them was willing to sacrifice one of these worlds to the other, despite the pain they felt because of the rift. Rabbi Kook moved from the world of Kabbala and the Talmud into the secular Zionist world in the Land of Israel, and Rabbi Soloveitchik came from the world of the Brisk Yeshiva into the academic world of the United States, and both of these men lived very well in both worlds. Yeshayahu Leibowitz was a European religious rationalist who moved to Israel and struggled against both the extremism of the haredim and the settlers and also the secular world, which had no God, in his opinion. He definitely clung to a compartmentalized view, arguing that religion reflects the service of God, which is man's duty in his world, whereas humaneness and morality are human areas that belong to man's reason. He developed an approach in which human history and nature reflect the way of the world, without either sanctity or miracles, whereas God is transcendent and should not be regarded as supplying human needs. The commandments, products of the wisdom of the Sages of Israel, are the only way of serving God that does not answer human needs, but rather is intended to bear one beyond instinctive sensuality and help one combat it.

Professor Umberto Cassutto should also be mentioned, a Bible scholar who also observed the commandments. All his life he opposed scholars who espoused the Documentary Theory and wished to blur the unity of the Bible and rip it to pieces. He tried to combine the world of religious faith with Bible scholarship and argued for the unity of the Bible under a single editor, a genius who combined various oral traditions into a unified text with consistent meaning.

TODAY

Should modern religious Jews, followers of Hirsch, Chajes, and Luzzatto, stop where they stopped, or should they continue to seek and try other ways, like their predecessors? The answer is clear: in the twenty-first century, we know far more about the universe around us and about our history and that of other nations. Research tools have improved, libraries have been opened, and genizas have been discovered. In various excavations, findings have been made that change attitudes toward the ancient past, the parallel ancient cultures and religions, and ancient texts.

I believe that progress cannot be halted, and we must ask what it means. Is it really so relevant whether the Revelation at Mount Sinai actually took place? Can we not be content with spiritual reality and with consciousness of the great patriarchs? Does what Judaism has bequeathed to mankind and what is implicit in Jewish views and norms depend on one miracle or another, without which it must be erased? Or can we be proud of the world of our ancestors and cling to it for life today? I believe that we must make the Bible speak as it stands before those living today, and we must understand its message for the present. The Halakha should be active, life should be breathed into it, and it should be brought into our lives. It must be recognized that the Halakha is a developing, living organism. Ways must be found to improve more and more the lot of the Other among us. Women should not be the Other at all. Every person's sexual orientation must be left in the private realm, and it should be acknowledged that these orientations are largely inborn and not acquired. In postmodern age, we cannot be satisfied with tolerance, but we must advocate pluralism. The meaning of pluralism is that you keep to your path, even though you no longer can have assurance that it is the sole truth. The pluralist recognizes that there are other legitimate opinions, perhaps more correct than ours, but we cannot know that, and if we ask about it, we will receive no answer. So we should cling to what is ours because it is our heritage, the world and consciousness of our ancestors, and our anchor and that of our community in the world.

We must restore conscience, feeling, and compassion, which in our era have lost their place to acquisitive accounting, swinish capitalism, and globalization, where the individual gets lost, and to New Age, which immerses people in metaphysical worlds disconnected from reality. We must go back to reading the simple meaning of the Bible, the literal meaning that teaches ethical ways and correct behavior toward the Other and the disadvantaged. Temporary workers, minorities, foreign workers, many people in Israel who seek to convert, abandoned women, and women whose husbands refuse to divorce them—these are the weak people of today. The Torah requires that we feel their suffering on our flesh, and that we act on their behalf, since they are part of the nation, or dependent on it, and we must not relate to them from a sectoral religious point of view. Just as the Sages instituted laws for the people's needs, we, too, should act in that direction, and remove contemptible racism from our midst.

We must refrain from all religious extremism and fanaticism. We cannot give either intellect or emotion a supreme position. We must learn from Luzzatto and Hirsch, and even from Chajes, that when we rely solely on the intellect, we miss spiritual religious experience and community life, and we restrict humanity to a narrow area, from which one cannot see the beauty of God's world or the beauty of spiritual and ethical life. On the other hand, relying solely on emotion is also dangerous. It ignores the world of knowledge and research, and proper guidance for correct living in the world. It is liable to make one sink into a world of delusion, illusion, religious ecstasy, and efforts to cleave to God, and thus lose connection with the real world and its demands. In this era of the New Age, that danger is even greater, and we must avoid falling into the trap of emotional charlatanism. We must combine our worlds, recognizing that such a combined world is complex, dialectical, and sometimes contradictory, but we must take up that challenge: on the one hand, to rely on the basic academic achievements of the intellect, and, on the other hand, to obey the commandments, to live in a prayer community, and to deepen our knowledge of Judaism and its literature—everyone according to his or her ability and propensity. People are composed of material bodies and a divine spirit, and both of them together are essential to them, and they must live fully in both worlds, even if sometimes there are contradictions between them. All extremism is invalid, and the middle way is difficult and sometimes paradoxical, but it is correct. For the past two centuries, Jews have tried all three of the possible extremes, and all their efforts failed. These extremes are: religion; nation and state; culture and education. The haredim proposed religion without culture and without the state. The Reform Jews and the extreme Maskilim offered a lukewarm religion and culture without nation and state. The secular left offered culture and state, without religion; and the extreme Orthodox nationalists offer religion and nation, without culture and education. Along with extremism, today we also experience a return to the center from the extremes in all the streams of Judaism, and this movement must be strengthened. I share in the world of Avi Sagi and Yedidia Stern, and the dialogical Judaism they propose, in that projected by Moshe Meir and his secular religiosity, which lives in contradiction; in that of Dov Berkovitz, and the combination of opposites that he proposes; in that of Micah Goodmann, and the challenging life of a skeptical Judaism, without certainty, that he offers; and in that of Elḥanan Shilo, and the variegated Judaism he offers. It appears that the era of dichotomies has passed, and once again the time of the center has come, which combines and contains opposites without rejecting them. Those who seek to take the middle way can prevent division and loss of direction and succeed, finding grace and good will in the eyes of God and man.

Appendices

APPENDIX TO CHAPTER ONE: WHO IS A *GER*?

To emphasize the essential difference between Hirsch's commentary on the Torah and that of Luzzatto, I chose to present their treatment of the meaning of the concept *ger* in the Torah. Both of them use the considerate attitude of the Bible toward the *ger* to shed light on the universal character of the Torah. I discuss the universalism in their doctrines in more detail in chapter four. Here I will demonstrate the difference between their understandings of the primary meaning of the term *ger* in the Bible. Hirsch chooses to base his interpretation on that of the Sages, which is that in general, when the term *ger* appears in the Torah, this refers to a *ger tsedeq*, a person who has undergone a process of conversion in order to join the Jewish people. However, according to the Sages, there are exceptions, in which the term simply means a person who lives with you, not someone who has converted. Hirsch tries to make coherent sense out of the matter, but with only slight success, with inner contradictions. In his interpretation of the commandment about the Sabbath in the Ten Commandments, Exodus 20:10, he tries to put matters in order, stating that the term "your *ger* who is in your gates," usually refers to a *ger-toshav*, a resident alien who observes the seven Noahide commandments. However, here, your *ger*, disregarding the phrase, "who is within your gates," is a convert, as stated in the Midrash, and he is included in the prohibition against working on the Sabbath. In contrast, Exodus 23:12, regarding the commandments of the Sabbath, says, "and the *ger*," and there it means, according to the Midrash, a resident alien, because it refers to rest on the Sabbath, to which the stranger is also entitled. Hirsch states: "Apparently, a distinction is to be drawn between גר [*ger*] and גרך [*gerkha*], in that גרך always denotes a גר צדק [*ger tsedeq*, a convert], who has attached himself to you completely" (on Ex. 20:10). In his commentary on Exodus 22:20, "And a stranger [גר, *ger*] shall you not wrong, neither shall you oppress him; for you were strangers [גרים, *gerim*] in the land of Egypt," he ignores the simple analogy between the two situations that are described, as well as the principle that he himself had stated two chapters earlier, and he insists, following the Sages, that this refers to a convert.

> One who was born a heathen is entitled to complete equality and full rights among Jews under Jewish law from the moment he joins the Jewish fold by accepting the basic principles of Judaism and Jewish worship.... Personal and civil rights, and personal worth, do not depend on descent, place of birth, or property ownership; nor do they depend on any external, incidental factor that bears no relationship to the individual's true character.... Your whole misfortune in Egypt was that you were גרים there, and that as such, in the view of the other nations, you were not entitled to land, homeland, or existence there, and they could do with you as they pleased. As גרים you were without any rights in Egypt; *this* led to your עבדות (*avdut*, enslavement) and to your עינוי (*inuy*, affliction). Therefore we are warned: When you have a state of your own, do not make human rights dependent on anything other than the pure humanity inherent in every person. Any deprivation of human rights will open the door to all the abominations of tyranny and abuse that were practiced in Egypt.

All this is well and good, as a declaration that Judaism is not racist and that it opposes racism, but why should the granting of human rights require conversion? After all, the Israelites in Egypt did not have the status of converts, but that of resident aliens. Hirsch himself says elsewhere that "the Jewish state is ready to grant rights of domicile, with all the attendant civil rights, to any *man*, even if he does *not* become a Jew, as long as he becomes a גר תושב [*ger toshav*, a resident alien] and accepts upon himself the obligations emanating from his vocation as a human being."[1] Why then should the prohibition against wronging and oppressing be contingent upon conversion?

On Lev. 25:35, "Now in case a countryman of yours (אחיך) becomes poor and his means with regard to you falter, then you are to sustain him, like a stranger (גר) or a sojourner, (תושב) that he may live with you (וחי עמך)," Hirsch explains, according to the Sages in the Talmud, Baba Metsia 71a (ignoring the Midrash in *Torat Kohanim*), that "stranger" and "sojourner" do not refer to different statuses, but to a single status of the resident alien, who dwells with you. The conclusion is reached as follows:

> Since a גר צדק [convert] is included in גר ותושב אחיך, גר ותושב should be understood in the same sense of Abraham's statement: "גר ותושב אנכי עמכם" (Gen. 23:4); I come from a strange land, but live here among you. I am neither native born, nor have I acquired citizenship—yet I live among you. This is precisely the concept of a גר תושב. He has not become a member of the Jewish national community; but by renouncing עבודה זרה [*avoda zara*, idolatry] and accepting the Noachide [*sic*] laws, he has acquired the right to live in the Land of Israel.... You must also help the stranger who lives in your midst and who is not אחיך; you must support him, so that he can make his living among you.

This is a new status, with specific definitions that have no written source. However, the following verse poses a serious difficulty for Hirsch: "Do not take usurious interest from him, but revere your God, that your countryman may live with you." According to the Halakha, it is permissible to charge interest to someone who is not Jewish, but here it appears that the גר-תושב is included in the prohibition against charging interest, so Hirsch performs an impressive but unconvincing maneuver, based on the teaching of Rav Naḥman Bar Yitsḥaq in the

---

1 Hirsch on Ex. 12:48. Chertok, *Qanqan*, 36, explains Hirsch's deviation from his own rule by the proximity to the preceding verse, which Hirsch points out.

Gemara there: "Is it then written, 'Take thou no usury of them'? [No,] 'of him' is written, [meaning] of an Israelite." Hirsch places the words "גר ותושב וחי עמך" in parenthesis, so that the verses require Jews to help the resident alien, but permit them to charge him interest.

In contrast to this interpretation of a verse where the words "brother" and "*ger*" both appear, Hirsch offers an entirely different interpretation of other verses where "brother" or "*ezraḥ*" [citizen] and "*ger*" appear close to one another, in order to be consistent with the interpretation of the Sages. Deut. 1:16 reads, "judge righteously between a man and his brother and his *ger*." Here Hirsch's conclusion is different: "It makes no difference to you whether the case on which you are to render your decision is between two of your native-born countrymen or between one native-born citizen and a stranger who has come from outside to live among you. Upon his entry into the community of Israel, the גר became גרו [*his* convert]; he is equal in status to every native-born citizen." Instead of saying, as he had earlier, that since the word "brother" had been used, *ger* must refer to a foreigner, he states that equality under the law must be accorded to the native-born brother and to the stranger *who has converted*. This contradiction between two conclusions drawn regarding the same matter and the maneuvering within the verse derive from the need to cling to the Halakhic Midrash of the Sages, which, according to Hirsch, is the only correct interpretation of scripture.

A similar contradiction is found in his commentary on Numbers 15:13-14, regarding the sacrifice of libations: "All who are native [אזרח] shall do these things in this manner.... If a *ger* sojourns with you ... just as you do so he shall do." The native-born Israelite is required to offer libations, and, according to Hirsch, the verse excludes the foreigner, but includes the *ger*, who is regarded as a convert here, a person who has been made equal to the native-born with respect to the duty and permission to offer libations. Here, too, Hirsch avoids drawing the first conclusion: since a convert is regarded as equal to native, the *ger* in this verse must be a foreigner.[2]

---

2 In his doctoral dissertation, page 24, as well as in *Qanqan*, 36-38, Chertok, contrary to my analysis here, argues that in his interpretation of the term "*ger*" in the Bible,

Now let us consider Luzzatto's commentary. Exodus 12:48 reads: "But if a stranger [*ger*] dwells with you, and celebrates the Passover to the Lord, let all his males be circumcised, and then let him come near to celebrate it; and he shall be like a native of the land. But no uncircumcised person may eat of it." In his commentary on this verse, Luzzatto presents the rules regarding the meaning of *ger, ger toshav,* and *ger tsedeq*:

> The opinion of the Sages of blessed memory (BT Pesaḥim 93a) is that this refers to a *ger tsedeq* who has accepted the entire Torah, but this verse shows clearly that even before being circumcised, he is called a *ger*. Hence, the *ger* has not taken all the commandments upon himself, and he is not circumcised like the Israelite males. And behold, according to the meaning of the words, it appears that a *ger* is of lower status than a *toshav*, because a *toshav* has settled in the land, and a *ger* comes to sojourn there and return to his own country after some time. Accordingly, how could it be that the verse simply says of a *toshav*, that he will not eat of it, and of a *ger*, that he must be circumcised, and then he can approach? Johann David Michaelis wrote that a *ger* does not own land, and a *toshav* has no house, and I say that a *toshav* is someone who comes alone, without wife and children, and he settles in the house of an Israelite (and that is the meaning of "תושב כהן" [tenant of a priest] in Lev. 22:10), and he is a slave and servant ("As a hired servant [שכיר], and as a settler [תושב], he shall be with you; he shall serve with you until the year of jubilee," Lev. 25:40); but the *ger* comes with his whole household,

---

Hirsch deviates from the interpretation of the Sages and from the traditional view. He bases this argument on Hirsch's commentary on Ex. 23:9 and Deut. 10:19. According to him, in the commentary on these verses, where the *ger* is presented as a resident alien and not as a convert, Hirsch moves from a Torah standard to a human standard. I disagree with Chertok. It should be noted that Hirsch was aware that his readers might err in reading his commentary on these verses without reference to his general approach, which follows that of the sages, which is presented here. Therefore, he takes pains to refer the reader of these two verses to his commentary on Exodus 23:20, which is meant to serve as a necessary introduction for the reader. In that commentary, quoted above, he states axiomatically that the stranger must convert as a condition for receiving full rights and quality, and not only the private rights of residence, which are due to all resident aliens. See also Ex. 12:43, 45, and 48. In general I agree with Chertok, *Qanqan*, 38-41, that Hirsch leverages these verses and preaches a humane attitude toward the resident alien in the framework of his efforts to achieve improvement in social emancipation for the Jews of Germany.

his wife and children, and he dwells alone with his family, and not with an Israelite like a *toshav*. Therefore it says, "let all his males be circumcised," meaning the men of his household; and there is no doubt that the *toshav*, too, if he wants to be circumcised, ate of the paschal lamb, but the verse states this regarding the *ger*, because it is a new ruling, that he can offer the sacrifice by himself, as I interpreted in the previous verse. And as for what is written in Lev. 25:45, and also the sons of the *toshavim* and their family who are with you, it already states explicitly there, "who were born in your land," that is to say, that the *toshav* married a resident woman or a Canaanite maidservant, and not that he came married. And accordingly, there is no doubt that the *toshav* was not an idol-worshiper, and that he was in the home of an Israelite, and we find that the Torah regards him as fit to eat the produce of the sabbatical year like Israelites and slaves (Lev. 25:6), and he was punished if he killed someone, and the cities of refuge would also receive him (Num. 35:15). And the *ger* appears from this verse itself (if a stranger [*ger*] dwells with you ... let all his males be circumcised) as if he did not take upon himself all of the commandments, and we do not find that there must be one Torah for you and for the *ger* regarding all the commandments in general, but rather on the matter of Pesaḥ, that if he wants to make it, he should do it according to the commandment and not eat it if he was not circumcised; and similarly in offerings, if he wants to bring a burnt offering "as you do so shall he do" (Num. 15:14-16); and he received ritual impurity like any Israelite, and if he wanted to be purified, he needed the ashes of the heifer like any Israelite (ibid., 19:10), and we also find (ibid., 15:26), "And all the congregation of the children of Israel shall be forgiven, and the *ger* that dwells among them," and also, "You shall have one law for him who does anything unintentionally, for him who is native among the sons of Israel and for the *ger* who dwells among them" (ibid., 15:29), and "But the person who does anything high handedly, whether he is native or a *ger*" (ibid., 15:30). All of this appears to refer to a *ger* who wishes to be circumcised and to enter the community of Israel, and he is called a *ger tsedeq*, but not every *ger* is a *ger tsedeq*, as I have shown regarding this verse ("and if a *ger* dwells with you"), and therefore, as to being commanded to love the *ger* and not to oppress him (Lev. 19:33-34), this applies to any *ger*, even if he is not a *ger tsedeq*.[3]

---

3   Luzzatto, commentary on Ex. 12:48. See Y. Levi, "Ger-Toshav," in *Leqsiqon Hatarbut Hayehudit Bizmanenu*, ed. A. A. Cohen and P. Mendes-Flohr (Tel-Aviv, 1993), 77-85 on the interpretations of this concept from the biblical period to modern times. He places Luzzatto and Hirsch together on page 81.

This shows that Luzzatto also believed that the term *ger* could be interpreted in several ways; but unlike Hirsch, who generally followed the Sages and took it to mean "convert," for Luzzatto the term *ger*, unmodified, usually meant a stranger who had settled in the land with his family, and had not accepted the commandments. Only with regard to a small number of commandments, in which his status was equal to that of a native Israelite, was he regarded as a *ger tsedeq*, a man who was circumcised and had accepted Judaism willingly. There was no decisive criterion for distinguishing between them, so one must apply logic according to the context. A *toshav* was someone who had come alone and lived in the home of an Israelite, who did not worship idols, and also did not keep the commandments (ibid., 19:45). The conclusions that derive from this literal reading were that there was no concept of *ger-toshav* in the Bible, and it was created by the Sages. According to a literal reading, the commandment to love the *ger* and not to harm or cheat him does not apply only to a convert, as the Sages stated, but to any foreigner. Regarding Leviticus 25:35, which Hirsch manipulated, Luzzatto says that in his book, *Ohev Ger*, he had interpreted it as "he will dwell and settle," but this interpretation seemed wrong to him now, so he reverted to his approach: "and perhaps the intention is that whether he is a *ger* (who has a wife and children) or a *toshav* (who is unmarried), he will live with you." This explanation obviates the difficulties and contradictions into which Hirsch had fallen, because he clung to the Midrash of the Sages. In any event, the prohibition against taking interest also applies to either a foreign *ger* or a *toshav* if he is poor. Indeed, in Deuteronomy 23:21, with respect to the prohibition against charging interest, he distinguishes between reference to a foreigner, who does not dwell among us, and who has come to do business with us, from whom it is permissible to take interest, and reference to one who lives with us, whom we are commanded to sustain, and therefore, if he is poor, it is forbidden to take interest from him, as from a poor Jew. It is permissible to charge interest to a foreign merchant, but if he is a poor foreigner, it is forbidden. "If the Torah spares a foreigner who lives among us, a fortiori it spares the Gentiles among whom we live."

Hence, one must not charge interest to the citizens of the countries that host the Jews in their exile, if they are poor and not engaged in commerce. Evidently this is contrary to the Halakha of the Sages, which rules that it is permissible to charge interest to any Gentile, and forbidden to take interest from any Jew.

APPENDIX TO CHAPTER TWO:

Illustration and Comparative Table for Clarification

THE MIDDLE TREND

Three religious thinkers: religious — traditional — modern
The Written Torah is from Heaven, no Halakha can be changed
The superiority of the ethics of the Torah: Because of its divine origin and its independence of reason, which is limited by the flesh
The return of the Jewish People to their land will take place only in the Utopian future
The status of women is inferior and must be improved
Christianity and Islam also have positive content

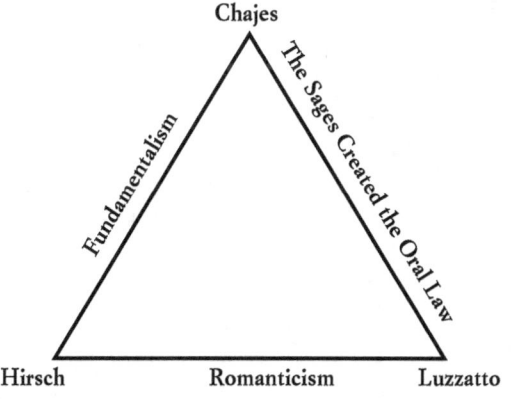

		Chajes	Hirsch	Luzzatto
Motive	Ideology	Rationalist (follower of Maimonides)	Romantic, follower of Judah Halevi	Romantic, follower of Judah Halevi
Motive	Fundamentalism	Classic Fundamentalist	Neo-Fundamentalist	Not Fundamentalist
Motive	Formative Book	The Talmud	The Talmud	The Bible
Outcome	Relation between Religion and Science	"Limiting identical" approach. In the dispute between religion and science, the criterion for determining the truth is revelation and not reason	The "limiting identical" or "interpretative" approach. In the dispute between religion and science, the criterion for determining the truth alternates between revelation and reason	The "dual truth" approach. Religion and science are truths that contradict each other, and neither is the criterion for the other
Outcome	Inerrancy	The Torah, Midrash Halakha, and Midrash Aggada are all inerrant	The Torah and Halakhic Midrash are inerrant, but Aggada is the creation of the Sages and need not be inerrant	The Torah does not have to be inerrant, and even less so Midrash, which is the creation of the Sages
Outcome	Research Tools	Use of philological and historical research tools on the Bible is permitted only to the Sages	Use of philological and historical research tools on the Bible is forbidden to everyone, including the Sages	Use of philological and historical research tools on the Bible is vital

Illustration and Comparative Table for Clarification

Conclusion	Strata of Halakha and the role played by the Sages	Only some of the Halakha was actually given at Sinai. The rest was only in potential. By means of the 13 hermeneutic principles, the Sages revealed parts of the Oral Law, bringing the potential into actuality, and they attached them to the upper stratum with the Written Torah	The entire Halakha was actually given at Sinai. The Oral Law preceded the written Torah, and is above it. The action of the Sages was the reconstruction of portions of the Oral Law, which had been forgotten, by means of the 13 principles, which are from Sinai.	Only the written Torah was actually given at Sinai. The Sages, by their acts of legislation, created the Oral Law and the 13 principles, which they employed. The Written Torah is above the Oral Law.
Conclusion	Interpretation	The interpretation of the Sages is the primary meaning of the Bible.	The interpretation of the Sages is the primary meaning of the Bible, which was formulated on the highest stratum, and which has not yet been fully understood	The simple, rational meaning is the primary meaning of the Bible, which was formulated on the level of those who received it at Sinai

In order to bring out the innovations in the present study, the three thinkers are presented here in a triangular table. One of the three is placed at each vertex of the triangle. Each side of the triangle represents what is common to the two thinkers at the vertices, and the distance between each side and the vertex opposite it represents the distance and contrast between them and the thinker at the opposite vertex. The result is the visual representation of a model that has not previously been proposed, while the table represents in schematic fashion the basic characteristics of each thinker, which were not discussed in earlier scholarship.

APPENDIX TO CHAPTER THREE:

The Importance of the Study of History

INTRODUCTION

Chajes, Hirsch, and Luzzatto all accorded great importance to the study of history, both Jewish and general, like everyone in the nineteenth century who had imbibed Haskala. Nevertheless, there was a significant difference among them. For Chajes and Hirsch, the Haskala approach was an innovation introduced by Mendelssohn and Wessely. Hirsch accepted this innovation in full and placed the study of Jewish and general history, along with other subjects, in the curriculum of his school for all the pupils from an early age. Chajes believed that study of history by adults was sufficient, and claimed that the Sages had already dealt with history. He distinguished between Jewish and general history, and he regarded its study as a peripheral matter. In contrast, Luzzatto did not regard the inclusion of secular studies as an innovation, stating that this had been the method of the rabbis and sages of Italy from time immemorial. Nevertheless, it should be emphasized that all three of them believed in full Divine Providence, personal and general, so that in their opinion history should be taught and studied according to the principle that God intervenes in history and acts according to a general master plan, which the student of history must try to find and understand from events. Hence, in their opinion the miraculous existence of the Jewish people during history results from special Divine Providence and testifies to the centrality of the Jews in the divine plan. Yosef Hayim Yerushalmi has shown that Spinoza, who came before his time and removed God from history, argued that the hatred of the Jews, who kept themselves apart (with their customs and with circumcision), and not Divine Providence was what maintained their existence throughout history, but this view was not accepted until the late nineteenth century by historians who had ceased to believe in Providence.[1]

CHAJES

It should be remembered that Chajes was a close friend of Krochmal, a philosopher of history, and he certainly was familiar with the latter's approach to the uniqueness of Jewish history, which had rises, falls, and rises once again, in continued cycles. The Jewish people bears with it the absolute spirit that it received with revelation, and it will bring humanity to its peak, whereas the history of other nations has only rises and falls. This approach is based on Hegel's theory, but it does not agree that Christianity is what will ultimately bring salvation in a dialectical process that will do away with all the other religions and ideas and sublate them. Acquaintance with Krochmal's theory doubtless reinforced the importance of the study of history for Chajes, and an allusion to it can be found in the following passage:

> Behold no sensible person will deny that knowledge of the history of our nation in general and in detail is very necessary for any educated man, for whom the Torah of his God is his portion, so that he should know what God did for this nation, and how the people of our nation from of old have risen and declined, and they conduct themselves with His special Providence, blessed be He. And that in every generation they rise up against us to destroy us, and the Holy One, blessed be He, raises up a faithful redeemer, who risks his life to save this great multitude, and great is the shepherd who saves them, and see the book *Mor Uqtsi'a* by the great rabbi Jacob Emden, Hilkhot Shabbat 307; on the matter of studying books of wisdom on the Sabbath, he wrote, and these are his words: "And therefore I say

---

1   See Spinoza, *Treatise*, 55; Yerushalmi, *Zakhor*.

that it is a commandment for every Jewish person to be familiar with the pleasant book *Shevet Yehuda*, and with other books about the history of the Jews, to remember God's mercy for us in every generation, for we have not ceased to be despite all the many decrees [against us], and incidentally he will learn sweet and precious things from it, a wise heart will acquire knowledge in the ways of polemics, see there.... And it appears that Maimonides went too far specifically about those who deal with the history of the kings of Arabia, because their main interest was in erotic stories and non-existent [imaginary] things, like the Arab stories that have been translated among us today, but the history and sources of nations and the history of states and ruling families is very necessary wisdom to know the wisdom of Providence and the supreme leadership.[2]

In a responsum to question number 12 in *Shut Maharats*, on the study of books of secular knowledge on the Sabbath, Chajes quotes Emden again and adds that on the Sabbath it is permissible to study books of Jewish history that do not contain sorrowful matters, but the others may be studied only on weekdays. However, regarding books of general history, even if they were written in Hebrew by a Jewish author, they may only be read in free time on weekdays and days when yeshivot are not in session, so as not to make scholars cease their studies, because there is no vital need to know these facts. The benefit of this study is marginal:

> To learn pure and clean language from them, and also so that a Torah scholar will not be naked of this knowledge of the history of bygone days and changes in times, so that he will know how to respond to his reviler, and that he will not be thought of as foolish and ignorant of matters of the world, and they will not say, only an ignorant nation poor in knowledge is this one, and sometimes one must peruse these stories that belong to the nations, and to learn from them about them, or good advice and wisdom might come out of it, in matters of the world that are also needed for us, and especially in matters of intervention with the king and ministers.[3]

---

2 Chajes, *'Ateret Zvi*, 406, and note.
3 Chajes, *Shut Maharats*, 648-49. A detailed discussion of God's ways in leading His nation in history can be found in his *Mavo Hatalmud*, 328-29, and *Shut Maharats*, 607.

Chajes chose to quote Emden rather than Wessely, from the previous generation, because in traditional Galicia of his day, quotations from Maskilim were not welcome. Chajes found it difficult to present history, even Jewish history, as having inherent value as a subject of study in a school or *cheder*, and he clung to the views that were current prior to the educational revolution. In the introduction to his commentary on the Talmud, he claims that the Sages always sought to learn natural sciences and humanities, as they existed at the time of the Sages, for use in the study of Torah. He refers to a number of scientific subjects and states that "above all, [the Sages] dealt with matters of the history of the world, especially the history of our nation from the time of the building of the Second Temple until the sealing of the Talmud.... And they plumbed the depths of human knowledge and by that means attained many matters touching upon laws and Halakhot."

That is to say, just as the Sages dealt with Bible criticism, they also dealt with the study of history, and this was no innovation. Chajes also criticized the devout rabbis in Galicia, who refused to acknowledge the importance of the study of the history of their nation and ignored everything that was happening to the Jewish people in Germany in their day: "And as for the rabbis of our country, who do not endeavor to provide themselves with knowledge of the history of our people, I will not preach a sermon [to them] here, since from the start I know that they would be surprised at the object that I bring in my hand, saying, look, this man has brought us matters of much talk and weariness of flesh, which are a loss of time in their opinion, and what is known to everyone will be like a sealed book to them, which they do not know how to read, and because of that they will raise their voice against me."[4]

Another allusion to Krochmal's approach can be found in the following passage:

> You have no more mighty proof of particular Providence than the existence of the Jewish nation, which stood fast against the times that raged to wipe them from the face of the earth, and the names

---

4   Chajes, "Minhat Qenaot," 1016.

of several ancient nations have been erased, and their memory has been forgotten from the world: Babylonia, Assyria, Persia, Media, Greece, and Rome, who once ruled with force and pride and high heart, but as for us, who were always the smallest of nations, persecuted without cease, were thrown from the land of our fathers and we went into exile after exile, and we ceased being an individual nation, behold: nevertheless the staff of the persecutor only wounded and destroyed the body and external things of the nation, but the spiritual life, that is, the achievement of the intellect and true opinions, they are still with us, thank the Lord, in purity and glory and splendor. We have borne them with us in all the places of our dispersion.... And at the time when the Greeks increased and succeeded, we had already gone into exile, and then the Romans exiled us completely, and no remnant was left in the land of our dwelling. We were mocked and reviled, a despised and persecuted nation among the neighbors, and nevertheless, they died out and faded from the face of the earth, and we, an ancient nation, an old and antique people, the smallest of nations, have remained in spiritual life, the father of all the dwellers on the earth in the study and knowledge of the presence of God and other pure beliefs. Who does not know that only the hand of God did that, and His Providence protected us at every time and moment.... By virtue of the Torah we are distinguished" [Note to Efi: As in "melamed she-hayu Yisrael metzuyanim sham."] among the nations and just as the intelligibles are eternal, so, too we will always stand against time, and all the natural causes of the destruction of the nation do not act at all upon us.[5]

The following passage contains similar ideas:

> For 1800 years that we have ceased being an independent nation, and a spoken language, and nevertheless we have still remained splendid and superior in the countries of our dispersion, and the staff of the tyrant only wounded us in matters external to the life of the nation, but their spiritual and moral life did not ever submit under the rule of despots, and just as intelligibles do not fall under natural causes, so, too, the people that bears these truths will stand forever.[6]

The presence of the Maskilim of Brody and closeness to Krochmal influenced Chajes's attitude toward general studies and especially

---

5   Chajes, *'Ateret Zvi*, 464-65.
6   Chajes, *Shut Maharats*, 607.

history. As I have shown, he was knowledgeable about history and quite familiar with the books by Jost. In the introduction to *Imrei Bina*, among other things, he sings the praises of Jewish historians, including the Tanna Rabbi Yose, who wrote *Seder 'Olam*, Rav Sherira Gaon, Joseph Ben Samuel Bonfils, Maimonides, *Sefer Yuḥasin* by Zacuto, Azariah Dei Rossi, and others.[7]

Chajes himself wrote historical studies when he needed to do so to strengthen his arguments. Thus, for example, he investigated the history of the Aramaic translations of the Bible in *Imrei Bina* (section 4) as well as the history of the various versions of the prayers in "Minḥat Qenaot" (978-80).

Ḥaim Gertner states that Chajes planned to publish a new and corrected version of *Seder Hadorot* by Jehiel Heilprin, first published in 1769, and there is evidence of this in the introduction to *Imrei Bina*. However, Chajes died before he was able to carry out the plan upon which he had been working.

Chajes was one of the first supporters of an initiative to publish an orthodox yearbook to be called *Pleitat Sofrim*, as we see from his letter to Joshua Heschel Levin. Here Gertner identifies a general phenomenon, according to which the rabbis of Eastern Europe responded to the biographies written by the scholars of the Wissenschaft des Judentums. Because of the diminution of their power and that of the rabbinate, these rabbis sought to oppose the pantheon of personalities presented by modern Jewish scholarship by presenting an alternative pantheon of orthodox rabbis. The goal was that those who were loyal to the tradition no longer had to feel isolated, because they were continuing a splendid rabbinic tradition.[8]

However, it must be pointed out that Chajes restricted use of modern historical-philological research tools. Only the Sages were permitted to perform research on the written Torah with their special analytical power, and the Oral Law could be investigated so long as one did not undermine the Halakhot, which have come down to us in a

---

7   See Chajes, *Imrei Bina*, 872.
8   See Ḥ. Gertner, "Reshita Shel Ketiva Historit Ortodoksit Bemizraḥ Eiropa: Ha'arakha Meḥudeshet," *Zion* 67, 3 (2002): 305-7, 323, 329, and nn. 73, 181.

special process of the actualization of what was delivered in potential at Sinai. That is, the Torah and the Halakha are above history, the former in fact, and the latter in potential.

HIRSCH

Hirsch completely accepted the innovations of the Maskilim in the area of secular studies, and in any event the study of Jewish and general history was an integral part of the curriculum in his school. The influence of the philosophy of history that traversed Western Europe did not pass over him. In all of his writings the historical outlook and consciousness are reflected, as well as the importance of the study of history for understanding the tasks of the present generation. While the Pentateuch and the prophets did not intend to teach philosophical knowledge but rather ethical conduct, they are definitely trustworthy books of the history of the Jewish people and the divine plan in history.

In his commentary on the Torah, Hirsch takes every opportunity to point out this plan, as he sees it, in contrast to the idealist philosophy of history of the nineteenth century. The stories of the Torah prove that when the trials of the Garden of Eden, the Tower of Babel, and the Flood fail to educate humanity in ethical monotheism, God decided to choose a special man, from whom he would build a nation in a special way, and to remove it miraculously from the situation of a nation of slaves on the lowest possible social and political level, to the situation of a free nation. God entrusted to that nation, whose claim that it owed its existence solely to God, was undeniable, the task of educating humanity by observing the moral code of the Torah in its land, and for it to be an example that all the nations would wish to imitate.

When that nation failed to fulfill its mission and was corrupted by excessive bounty, the divine plan failed once again, and the Jews were exiled and dispersed among the nations as emissaries of God, to dwell among them. Since then, their mission was to observe the ethical code of the Torah among themselves, and thus to bring the nations, in a long process, to acknowledge God and His morality as embodied in the

Torah, to overcome sensuality, to understand that the spirit was preferable to physical power, and to sanctify themselves in the daily routine of life and to bring about human salvation. In parallel to this task of the Jewish people, empires that idolized power and the material arose, and for that reason corruption and decay were inevitable, but they fell, never to rise again, proving that only the Jewish spirit would abide forever.

The Jewish people alone continued to exist so as to fulfill its destiny according to the divine plan. Christianity, Islam, Emancipation, and Enlightenment were signs of the success of this plan, which was now approaching its advanced stages. To understand this and the task of the Jew in our generation, one must study history. In his article on the relevance of secular studies to Jewish studies, Hirsch wrote, among other things, about the importance of the study of history for Jewish pupils: "Here, then, we have a people that emerged from the course of world history, that was placed into the midst of the nations to advance the goals of world history, and that was endowed with historical vision. Should not the sons of such a people understand that historical studies of the development of nations are truly not superfluous, but that they are, in fact, virtually indispensable?"[9]

Here are several quotations of his statements about Jewish history:

1. Israel's whole development was a miracle. Its very first entry into the circle of politically independent peoples, without power, without land of its own, with no prospect of friendship or alliance with other nations, was miraculous.[10]
2. שמנת-עבית-כשׂית ["You grew fat, you grew stout, you kicked," Deut. 32:15] was the outcome whenever God granted us a period of good fortune, and so it has always been.... Israel was expected to remain always master of its abundance. Abundance was supposed to be a tool in Israel's hands, a mere tool for accomplishing the Task set by God's Law … .שמנת, when Israel became fat, when a great abundance of material goods flowed upon him, עבית, he did not become

---

9 Hirsch, *Writings*, VII, 97.
10 Ibid., I, 299.

stronger, more filled with life, more determined to unfold his true nature. Instead he became corpulent and sluggish. His better self—the spiritual, Godly life-principle within him—went to sleep. Instead of gaining dominion and mastery over the abundance, כשיח, he was covered by it. His true nature was buried by it.[11]

3. The Purpose of the Destruction and the Exile: (a) *The immediate purpose:* Destruction of the worship of property and self ... the raising of Israel to the adoration of God alone. Their possessions which became the very gods of their life disappeared, their independence was destroyed.... To one blessed possession they clung throughout their wanderings, the Torah, and to one source of strength, God.... (b) *A further purpose:* ... When the knowledge of God and righteousness and morality are lost everywhere, then must Israel become by its own example the beacon for the avowal of God, the testimony to the Providence of God, the witness to the dignity of man and the exalted task of man... To be a holy people and a kingdom of priests, bearer of the Divine scheme, and God's instrument.[12]

4. [The] prophets were torn with grief when they were bidden to foretell the imminent ruin of the enemies of their people. They were the ones that stood at the cradle, and subsequently at the grave of the earliest civilized nations—Egypt, Babylonia, Nineveh, Tyre, etc.—declaring that the history and the downfall of these nations were not due to the fortunes of battle but resulted from the internal corruption, the voluptuousness, the tyranny and the utter disregard for human dignity that were rife in these lands.[13]

5. As Judea's state and temple collapsed under the tread of the Roman legions, the Roman world itself—its own states and temples included—was already putrid internally and decomposing rapidly. There then came a long succession of centuries, in which aging, dying, decomposition, disintegration, separating into atoms, and fitting together into new forms in raw and barbaric beginnings

---

11 Ibid., 302.
12 Hirsch, *Horeb*, vol. 1, 144.
13 *Writings*, VII, 268.

constituted the history of the nations of mankind on earth. There was only *one* nation that had already surmounted death, that had already *become* and did not have to become any further. This nation was not affected by this decomposition process, by this journey through death to a belated new life. It remained the only living nation amid the corpses of all the other nations. This nation was Israel, our nation.¹⁴

6. The whole secret of the drama that we call world history is based on the factual truth that any power which has developed its maximum potential by force will be blinded by its illusion of might and, believing itself invincible, will look down on the skills of cunning as attributes of weakness. It thus deprives itself of the only means that would assure its survival. Force spurns union with intelligence, and that is why, emasculated and without a future, it will perish. No conqueror has ever succeeded in creating a world empire that managed to survive beyond a limited span of time.¹⁵

7. Look at Jewish history! From the very beginning, this nation was shown its mission in world history, in all its glory but also in all its solemn import, and the heights to which it would have to ascend over centuries and millennia of error and sorrow. Israel's inspired "Yes!" at the foot of Mount Sinai was not demanded for the acceptance of some illusion but for the acceptance of real Jewish life and Jewish destiny with all its vicissitudes. The Jewish nation knew from the very onset that its mission would lead it though a rocky path, winding upward over cliffs and sudden, sharp drops. It knew that it would arrive at the summit of perfection implied by its unqualified "Yes!" only באחרית הימים [at the end of days] in the far distant future, at the end of days…. Israel was not to start out, like the ancient Hellenes, as a nation filled with enthusiasm for "beauty and goodness," only to end pitifully and glorified only by the feeble halo of past splendor. Nor was it to ascend the stage of history like Rome, as a world-conquering nation nurtured by wolves' milk, living by the sword and devious politics, only to end in misery as a

---

14 Ibid., I, 261.
15 Ibid., II, 118.

conglomerate of peoples enslaved by priestlings and foreigners. Israel's shame came at the beginning of its history; its everlasting glory still beckons to it from the high places of its future.[16]

8. The Jews were destined to be the eternal people of history, to wander the earth as the "eternal Jew"; to stand at the cradle and grave of all nations; to undergo the evolutions and revolutions of history; to suffer in the catastrophes of nations. From the shipwreck of the past we were assigned the task of successfully salvaging the eternal spiritual heritage of all mankind. From the onset of history we were given stern notice: do not be dazzled by material might, no matter how brilliantly and meteorically it beckons on the historical firmament of nations. Do not tremble when sword-carrying nations subdue and brutalize the defenseless. Always be aware that the days of any power are numbered which fails to accept the certainty of the ultimate victory of man's spiritual and moral destiny.[17]

9. Such is the faith which, after centuries of dark, trial-filled nights, has now been called to step forth into the bright new daylight of European national entities and to prove its immortal, ever-youthful vigor in the free arena of human, moral and spiritual endeavors.[18]

10. The entire course of world history will culminate in the worldwide celebration of the Festival of Sukkoth. At that time סוכה, "the hut," will no longer be the hut of Israel but סוכתו של לויתן, the "hut" of mankind united. This is the ultimate objective of the education given to the nations בעולם הזה [in this world], and the attainment of this goal will mark the beginning of the earthly עולם הבא [the world to come], the new future era on earth.[19]

In these passages, Hirsch demonstrated fully and in detail how history should be taught, in his opinion. Just as nature and the Torah are both divine creations, so, too, the course of history reflects the divine plan,

---

16 Ibid., 265.
17 Ibid., 380.
18 Ibid., VI, 163.
19 Ibid., II, 120.

and it should be studied from that point of view. This plan began with the patriarch Abraham, continued through the Exodus from Egypt, the establishment of the kingdom in the Land of Israel, corruption, and exile. In exile, the Jewish people lives a life of exemplary morality according to the Torah of Israel, as an educational example for the Gentiles. The culmination of this plan is the salvation of mankind under the influence of this Torah. Judaism will not be assimilated in a dialectical process that will raise up Christianity as the savior of mankind, as Hegel thought. Judaism bears that destiny. The Jewish people has left behind the corpses of physically powerful empires that collapsed.

It must be emphasized that Hirsch's historical consciousness was very limited. The Jews are a people above history, and with its super-historical Torah—which sanctifies ethics and the spirit—in its possession, it will bring humanity to salvation. This kind of historical study, in which revelation is the yardstick, is one-sided and lacks developmental motives. Hirsch limited the use of modern research tools of historians and set preconditions for it. Since the written Torah is a divine text, it is forbidden to investigate it with the tools appropriate for human texts. The Halakhot in the Oral Law were also given at Sinai, and therefore the tools of research are restricted in advance and cannot challenge this axiom. The Torah and the Halakha are actually above and beyond history.

LUZZATTO

Luzzatto was not impressed by Wessely's and Mendelssohn's educational revolution. According to him, secular studies for everyone had been accepted in Italy for ages. From his point of view, the study of history, like any other subject, was self-evident. His scholarship is imbued with historical consciousness and based on examination of the text according to its author and the historical background of its writing. One of Luzzatto's central claims was that the scholar must place himself in the time and environment of the author and know the theories, beliefs, and world views of the period in order to understand his words. He also bases his ideas on this understanding of Jewish history, according to which the Torah reflects the world view of those who received it, and the Halakha is a human development. Mature historical and critical consciousness led him to the conclusion that the Kabbala was a forgery, with good intentions, written by Jews who wished to keep the people away from speculative philosophy, so they erected a parallel structure, which was also baseless. However, speculative philosophy has also adopted an invalid critical attitude, which continues to endanger Judaism and it is the main reason for heresy and Reform in our day. Luzzatto also believed that Abraham and his descendants were chosen by God to preserve healthy, anti-pagan opinions and promote exalted morality as a mission for the benefit of mankind, which will acknowledge God as king in the end of days, when human progress and improvement have reached the desired elevation.[20]

Luzzatto bases the credibility of Judaism and its divine source on the public miracles, which were never denied and regarded as true in past generations, even by non-Jews. Therefore, in his view, they are historical. He bases it on the tradition as well, which transmitted the customs and holidays that were established in memory of events from generation to generation. Luzzatto also points out that the existence of the Jewish people throughout history is miraculous. Accordingly, in addition to the dogma of reward and punishment, God's covenant with the Jewish people is the second dogma taught by Judaism. This covenant, which includes the promise of the Land, and the punishment of exile and persecution, also includes the promise "that even if exile and persecution are very widespread, God will not destroy the people.... This, too, has been fulfilled until now, and there is no similar phenomenon with any other nation";[21] and the last part of this dogma—which in fact comprehends all of Jewish history—is the ingathering of the exiles and the eternity of the Torah.

---

20 Luzzatto, *Ketavim*, vol. 1, 51, 99.
21 Ibid., 103.

Luzzatto praises the way in which the Jewish people preserved Judaism throughout history, and he fears that things will change in his time.

> And who cannot wonder at the sanctity of this nation, which, in its wanderings and displacements, its poverty and tribulations, the delightful songs that make the human heart glad were lost to them; but the books of laws and judgments, and the responsa, and the commentaries on the Bible and the Talmud, and all these matters, which weigh upon it and which are the cause of all the hatred that has pursued it from generation to generation—they were not lost; but in all its displacements the nation bore them in its bosom and preserved them, the way a person saves his infants and children from a fire, and his silver and gold. See how the generations have changed! But I will block my mouth, lest I open it and speak and no longer keep silence."[22]

As someone believing that the written Torah was from heaven, and the Oral Law was developed by human beings, Luzzatto did not hesitate either to express the historical consciousness that he had imbibed or to adopt the use of historical and philological research tools without preconditions, or to emphasize that everything that research showed to be true with these tools had to be accepted, even if it went against the tradition. This research led him to accept the Jewish tradition regarding the divine source of the written Torah, but in the wording and world view of the generation that received it, and it led him to the conclusion, contrary to the accepted tradition, regarding the human source of the Oral Law as a developing codex created by the Sages according to the needs of changing times and the spirit of the nation. After a historical and philological examination he concluded that the message of the written Torah is above history, but the textual framework that Moses placed in writing and the entire content of the Oral Law are within history. This is in contrast to Hirsch and Chajes, who stated, as I have shown, that the written Torah and the Oral Law were from Sinai, and therefore the use of historical research tools was, in

---

22 Luzzatto, *Kerem Ḥemed* 4, 96.

their opinion, forbidden or restricted, and in any event it was subject to preconditions.

Luzzatto was a very active man, and he was involved in every area of research on Judaism. He also set his hand to historical research and wrote two books taken from the lectures he gave to his students, which dealt with Jewish history from the time of the Second Temple until the sealing of the Mishnah. One of these books was intended for the students in the rabbinical seminary, and the second for Jewish students at the University of Padua. In the second book, there are no innovations, because it contained only general concepts. However, in the first, which preceded Graetz and appeared after Jost, once again the true, sharp-witted scholar is revealed.[23]

---

23 See also Klausner, *Hasifrut* II, 83-84. On historical consciousness in the nineteenth century in comparison to earlier times, and the controversy between Yerushalmi and Funkenstein on this matter, see Funkenstein, *Tadmit*, 13-30.

Bibliography

PRIMARY SOURCES

Albo, J. *Sefer Ha'iqarim*.
Ben-Amozegh, E. *Mavo Latorah Shebe'al Pe*. Sde Eliahu, 2002.
Bikurei Ha'etim. Edited by Sh. Hacohen and M. Landa. Prague, 1821-33.
Bodek, J. *Haroe B'*. Affen, 5598 [1838].
———. "Keter Torah." *Kokhvei Yitshaq*, 17-20 (1852-5).
———. "Qorot Nosafot." *Le-qorot Ha'itim Shel A. Tribitsh*. Lvov, 1851. Sign 41 for the year 5589 [1829].
Chajes, Z. H. "Maamar Minḥat Qenaot." *Shut Hoharats* pt. 3 (5609 [1849]). In *Kol Sifrei Maharats Ḥayut*, 973-1036. Jerusalem, 1958.
———. "Sefer 'Ateret Zvi" (5601 [1841]). In *Kol Sifrei Maharats Ḥayut*, 351-503. Jerusalem, 1958.
———. "Sefer Darkhei Hahoraa" (5602-5603 [1842-3]). In *Kol Sifrei Maharats Ḥayut*, 205-80. Jerusalem, 1958.
———. "Sefer Mavo Hatalmud" (5605 [1845]). In *Kol Sifrei Maharats Ḥayut*, 281-350. Jerusalem, 1958.

———. "Sefer Sheelot Uteshuvot Moharats, pt. 1" (5410 [1850]). In *Kol Sifrei Maharats Ḥayut*, 505-867. Jerusalem, 1958.

———. "Sefer Sheelot Uteshuvot Moharats, pt. 2" (5409 [1849]). In *Kol Sifrei Maharats Ḥayut*, 870-972. Jerusalem, 1958.

———. "Sefer Torat Haneviim Hamekhune Ele Hamitsvot" (5596 [1836]). In *Kol Sifrei Maharats Ḥayut*, 1-206. Jerusalem, 1958.

———. *Hagahot Lashas* (5603-5604 [1843-4]). Printed at the end of every tractate of the Vilna Talmud.

Chajes, Z. P. *Tsevi Perets Ḥayut Neumim Vehartsaot*. Boston, 1953.

Dei Rossi ('Azariah Min Haadumim). *Meor 'Einayim*. Vilna, 1862.

Delmedigo, Elia of Candia. *Sefer Beḥinat Hadat* (Vienna, 1833). Edited by J. J. Ross. Tel Aviv, 1984.

Ettlinger, J. *Sheelot Uteshuvot Binyan Tsion Hashalem, Binyan Tsion Hahadashot*. Jerusalem, 2002.

Frankel, Z. *Darkhei Hamishnah*. Edited by I. Nissenbaum. Tel Aviv, 1959.

Geiger, A. *Hamiqra Vetirgumav*. Translated by Y. L. Baruch. Jerusalem, 1940.

Girondi, N. (Haran). *Sefer Hadrashot*. Edited by Feldman. Jerusalem, 1976.

Gottlieb, M., ed. *Moses Mendelssohn: Writings on Judaism, Christianity, and the Bible*. Waltham, MA, 2011.

Graetz, H. *History of the Jews*, vol. II. Translated by B. Lowy. Philadelphia, 1893.

———. *The Structure of Jewish History and Other Essays: Studies in Jewish History, Literature, and Thought*. Translated by I. Schorsch. New York, 1975.

Halevi, J. *Kuzari*. Translated by H. Hirschfeld. New York, 1905.

Hamagid, Mikhtav Qorot Hayamim. Edited by A. L. Silverman. 1856-1903.

Hegel, G. F. "Introduction." In *Phenomenology of the Spirit*. Translated by A. V. Miller. Oxford, 1977.

Hildesheimer, E. *Igrot*. Jerusalem, 1966.

Hirsch, S. R. *Horeb: A Philosophy of Jewish Laws and Observances.* Translated from the German original by Dayan Dr. I. Grunfeld. London, 1962.

———. *The Hirsch Chumash*, 5 vols. Translated by Daniel Haberman. New York, 2002.

———. *The Psalms.* Translated by Gertrude Hirschler. New York, 1997.

———. *The Nineteen Letters of Ben Uziel.* Translated by Bernard Drachman. New York and London, 1899. Printed in Germany: Ben Usiel (Rabbiner Samson Raphael Hirsch). *Neunzehn Briefe über Judentum,* fourth edition. Frankfurt am Main, 1911.

———. *Maamarim, Teshuvot, Igrot Vekhitvei Yad She nesfu Leyom Hapetira Hameah, Tadpis Me"hama'ayan." Tishrei-Tevet 5749.* Jerusalem, 1989.

———. *Shemesh Marpe, Shut, Ḥidushim Veigrot.* Edited by A. M. Klugman. New York, 1992.

———. *The Collected Writings*, vol. I-VIII. Translated by I. Grunfeld et al. New York, 1997.

———. *The Hirsch Siddur.* Translated by the Hirsch Publication Society. Jerusalem and New York, 1969.

Horowitz, I. *Shnei Luḥot Habrit.* Warsaw 1863; photocopied edition, Jerusalem, 1963.

Ibn-Daud, Abraham (Rabad). *Sefer Haqabala.*

Kant, Immanuel. *Religion Within the Limits of Reason Alone.* Translated by T. M. Greene and H. H. Hudson. New York and Evanston, 1960.

———. *Critique of Practical Reason.* Translated by L. W. Beck. Indianapolis and New York, 1956.

Kerem Ḥemed, vols. 1-9. Edited by S. L. Goldenberg (vols. 1-7) and S. Sachs (vols. 8-9). Prague, 1833-56.

Krochmal, N. *Moreh Nevuchey Hazman (MONH"Z).* Ravidovics Edition. Berlin, 1924.

———. "To Samuel Leib Goldenberg." Letter No. 27 of Ḥeshvan 1839. *Kerem Ḥemed* 4 (1839): 260-74.

Landau, E. "Drasha Leshabbat Hagadol 5542." *Drushei Hatslaḥ.* Warsaw, 1886. Drush no. 39, fol. 53.

Levinsohn, I. B. *Te'uda Beyisrael,* photo offset edition. Jerusalem, 1977.
Luzzatto, S. D. "Mavo Leviqoret Ulefarshanut Hatora." In *Ketavim,* vol. 2, 97-134. Translated into Hebrew by M. E. Artom. Jerusalem, 1976. Written in Italian in 1829 and first published in Padua, 5631 [1871] as the introduction to his commentary on the Torah, entitled "Introduzione Critica ed Ermeneutica."
———. "Torah Nidreshet." *Mehqerei Hayahadut,* vol. I, pt. 1, 49-109. First printed in *Kokhvei Yitshaq* 16-26 (5612-5621) [1852-1861].
———. "Vikuah 'Al Hokhmat Haqabala Ve'al Qadmut Sefer Hazohar Veqadmut Hanequdot Vehate'amim." In *Mehqerei Hayahadut,* vol. I, pt. 1, 111-240. First printed Gorizia, 5612 (1852).
———. *Yesodei Hatorah.* In *Mehqerei Hayahadut,* vol. I, pt. 1., 1-48; Lemberg, 1880; *Al Hahemla Vehahashgaha,* 31-83. Tel Aviv, 2008.
———. *Beit Haotsar, Lishka A.* Lemberg, 5607 [1847].
———. *Beit Haotsar, Lishka B.* Przemyśl, 5648 [1848].
———. *Beit Haotsar, Lishka C.* Cracow, 5649 [1849].
———. *Betulat Bat Yehuda.* Edited by J. Hauben (Nevo), 135-226. Tel Aviv, 1996. First printed in Prague, 5600 [1840].
———. *Divan Yehuda Halevi.* Edited by J. Hauben (Nevo), 135-226. Tel Aviv, 1996. First printed in Lyck, 1864.
———. *Epistolario italiano, francese, latino di S. D. Luzzatto,* publicato da suoi figle. Padova, 1890.
———. *Hamishtadel.* Vienna, 1847.
———. *Heleq Meigrotav Haitalqiot Shel Shadal.* Translated by A. Cahana; *Pardes* 3 Odessa (5657 [1897]): 93-127.
———. *Igrot el M. H. Letteris.* Edited by Y. Zemora. Tel Aviv, 1943.
———. *Igrot Shadal,* vols. 1-9. Przemyśl-Cracow, 5642-5658 [1882-98].
———. *Ketavim,* vol. 1-2. Edited by M. E. Artom. Jerusalem, 1976.
———. *Kinor Na'im.* Warsaw, 5673 [1913]. First printing: pt. 1, *Bikurei Ha'etim* 5586 [1826] and pt. 2, Padua, 5639 [1879].
———. *Lezioni di Teologia Morale Israelitica.* Padua 1862.
———. *Lezioni di Teologica Dogmatica Israelitica.* Trieste, 1863-4.
———. *Magish mishirei Rihal.* Edited by J. Hauben. Tel Aviv, 1996.
———. *Mehqerei Hayahadut,* vol. I, pts. 1-2. Warsaw, 5673 [1913].
———. *Peninei Shadal.* Przemyśl, 5648 [1888].

———. *Peraqim Bemishnato Shel Shadal.* Selected and translated by M. E. Artom. Jerusalem, 1968.

———. *Perush 'Al Ḥamisha Ḥumshei Torah.* Padua, 5631-5636 [1871-6]; Tel Aviv, 1965.

———. *Perush 'Al Yesh'ayahu.* Padua, 1855-67. Photo offset edition, Jerusalem, 1966.

———. *Perush 'Al Yirmiahu, Yeḥezqeel, Mishlei, Veiyov.* Lemberg, 1876. Photo offset edition, Jerusalem, 1969.

———. *Pirqei Ḥayim.* Edited by M. A. Schulwas. New York, 1951.

Maharal, Judah Loew. *Drush 'Al Hatorah Vehamitsvot.* Pieterkov, 5674 [1914].

———. *Kitvei Hamaharal Miprag, Mivḥar.* Edited by A. Kariv. Jerusalem, 1960.

Maimonides, Moses. *Haqdama Leferush Hamishnah.* Mosad Harav Kook Edition. Jerusalem, 1966.

———. *Haqdma Lefereq Ḥeleq.* Mosad Harav Kook Edition. Jerusalem, 1966.

———. *Mishneh Torah Hayad Haḥazaqa.* Mosad Harav Kook Edition. Jerusalem, 1958.

———. *Sefer Hamitsvot.* Edited by C. B. Chavel. Jerusalem, 1981.

———. *The Guide of the Perplexed.* 2 vols. Translated with an introduction by S. Pines. Chicago and London, 1963.

Mendelssohn, Moses. "Open Letter to Deacon Lavater of Zurich." Available at http://www.germanhistorydocs.ghi-dc.org/pdf/eng/15__TheJews__Doc.2__English.pdf.

———. *Jerusalem.* Translated by A. Arkush. Hanover and London, 1983.

Modena, Leon (J. A.). *Sheagat Arieh Veqol Sachal.* Edited by I. S. Reggio. Gorizia, 5615 (1855).

Nachmanides, Moses. *Hasagot Lesefer Hamitsvot Larambam.* Edited by C. B. Chavel. Jerusalem, 1981.

———. *Perushei Hatorah,* A-B. Edited by C. B. Chavel. Jerusalem, 1959.

Otser Neḥmad. Edited by Y. Blumenfeld. Vien, 1863-56; reprint Jerusalem, 1967.

Rapoport, S. J. *Divrei Shalom Veemet*. Prague, 1861.

———. *Igrot Shir*. Przemyśl, 5645 [1845].

Reggio, I. S. *Behinat Haqabala*. Introduction to *Sheagat Aryeh Veqol Sachal*. Attributed to Leon (J. A.) Modena. Gorizia, 1852.

———. *Hatora Vehapilosofia*. Vienna, 1827.

Rosenzweig, F. *The Star of Redemption*. Translated by W. W. Hallo. New York, 1970.

Sa'adia Gaon. *Sefer Hanivḥar Beemunut Vede'ot*. Translated by Y. Qapaḥ. New York, 1970.

Salvador, J. *Jésus Christ et Sa Doctrine*. Paris, 1818.

Schelling, F. W. J. *System of Transcendental Idealism*. Translated by P. Heath. Charlottesville, VA, 1978.

Sefer Haḥinukh. Edited by C. B. Chavel. Jerusalem, 1984.

Sofer, M. *Sefer Ḥatam Sofer Al Hatorah*. Edited by Y. N. Stern. Jerusalem, 2003.

———. *Sheelot Uteshuvot Ḥatam Sofer*. Bratislava, 1841.

Spinoza, B. *Theological-Political Treatise*. Translated by M. Silverthorne and J. Israel. Cambridge, 2007.

Tevele, D. "Derasha Leshabat Hagadol 5542." *Jahrbuch der juedische-literarischen Gesellschaft* 12 (1918): 182-94.

Wessely, N. H. *Divrei Shalom Veemet*. Berlin, 1882.

Zunz, Yomtov Lipman (Leopold). *Gottesdienstliche Vorträge der Juden* (1832). Hebrew translation: *Hadrashot Beyisrael* (from II ed., 1892), including additions by Ḥ. Albeck, translated by M. A. Zhak. Jerusalem, 1974.

SECONDARY SOURCES

Amir, Y. *Qol Demama Daqa*. Jerusalem, 2009.

Artom, M. E. "Mavo." In *Laketavim Shel Shadal*. Jerusalem, 1976.

Assaf, S. *Meqorot Letoledot Haḥinukh Beyisrael*. Tel Aviv, 1985.

Bainton, R. H. *Here I Stand: A Life of Martin Luther*. New York and Nashville, 1950.

Balaban, M. "Igeret Ratzhach LeShir." In *Maamarim Lezikhron R. Zvi Perets Ḥayut Z"l*, edited by A. Aftovitzer and Z. Schwartz, 174-80. Vienna, 1933.

Baron, S. "Shadal Vehamahapekha Bishnot 5608-5609." In *Sefer Asaf: Qovets Maamarei Meḥqar*, edited by M. D. Cassutto et al., 40-63. Jerusalem, 1953.

Barr, J. *Fundamentalism*. Philadelphia, 1978.

Bartal, I. "Teguvot Lamoderna Bemizraḥ Eiropa: Haskala, Ortodoqsia, Leumiut." In *Tsionut Vedat*, edited by S. Almog, Y. Reinhartz, and A. Shapira, 21-32. Jerusalem, 1994.

———. "The Heavenly City of Germany and Absolutism à la Mode d'Autriche: The Rise of Haskalah in Galicia." In *Toward Modernity*, edited by J. Katz, 33-42. New Brunswick and Oxford, 1987.

Barzilay, I. *Shlomo Yehuda Rappaport and his Contemporaries*. Ramat Gan, 1969.

Baumgarten, E. *Imahot Veyeladim: Ḥayei Mishpaḥa Beashkenaz Biyemei Habeinayim*. Jerusalem, 2005.

Beit Halevi, I. D. *Rabbi Zvi Hirsh Ḥayut Parshat Ḥayav Ufo'alo*. Tel Aviv, 1957.

Ben Shalom, R. *Mul Tarbut Notsrit: Toda'a Historit Vedimui 'Avar Beqerev Yehudei Sefarad Uprovans Biyemei Habeinayim*. Jerusalem, 2007.

Ben Shalom, I. *Beit Shammai Umaavaq Haqanaim Neged Romi*. Jerusalem, 1994.

Benayahu, M. "Ḥalifat Igrot 'Al Hareforma Bein R. Mordekhai Shmuel Girondi LeR. Zvi Hirsch Ḥayut." In *Gevurot Haromaḥ*, edited by Z. Falk, 271-92. Jerusalem, 1987.

Bergman, S. H. *Hafilosofia Shel Immanuel Kant*. Jerusalem, 1984.

Berlin, I. "The Counter-Enlightenment." In *Against the Current*, edited by H. Hardy, 1-24. London, 1979.

Bonfil, R. *Bemaraa Kesufa Ḥayei Hayehudim Beitalia Biyemei Harenesans*. Jerusalem, 1994.

———. *'Azaria Min Haadumim*. Jerusalem, 1991.

———. "'Lashon Sone Kazav,' Bashira, Bameḥqar, Uvaḥazon: Qavim Lidmuto Shel Shmuel David Luzzatto." In *Italia: Shmuel David Luzzatto, Matayim Shana Lehuladeto*, edited by R. Bonfil et al., 11-24. Jerusalem, 2004.

Breuer, E. *The Limits of Enlightenment*. London, 1996.

———. "Hatarbut Harabanit Veyaḥasa Lahaskala Hagermanit 1800-1840." In *Hahaskala Ligvaneiha*, edited by S. Feiner et al., 137-48. Jerusalem, 2005.

Breuer, I. "Rashar Hirsch Kemore Derekh Ledoro Veladorot Habaim." In *Bema'agalei Shana, Kitvei Rabbi Shimshon Refael Hirsch*, vol. 2, 9-21. Bnei Brak, n.d.

Breuer, M. *'Eda Udyokna*. Jerusalem, 1991.

———. "'Tradition in the Age of Reform' by Rosenbloom, Noah H." *Tradition* 16, 4 (1977): 140-49.

———. "Maamar R. Shimshon Refael Hirsch Zt"l Al Agadot Hazal." *Hama'ayan* 16, 2 (1987): 1-16.

———. "Harav Sh. R. Hirsch Vehaortodoqsia Hamodernit." *Hama'ayan* 34, 3 (1994): 1-11.

———. "Ḥokhmat Yisrael—Shalosh Gishot Ortodoksiot." In *Sefer Yovel Lichvod Morenu Hagaon Rabi Yosef Dov Soloveitchik*, edited by S. Yisraeli et al., 856-65. Jerusalem, 1984.

———. "Peraqim Mitokh Biografia." In *Harav Shimshon Refael Hirsch Mishnato Veshitato*, edited by Yona 'Imanuel, 11-41. Jerusalem and New York, 1980.

———. "Rabbi Shimshon Refael Hirsch Beyeshivat Rabbi Ya'aqov Ettlinger Bemannheim." In *Harav Ya'aqov Ettlinger Z"l—Qovets Maamarim*, edited by Y. Emanuel, 37-50. Jerusalem, 1972. (Originally published in *Hama'ayan* 12, 2 [1972]: 55-62.)

———. "Shitat Tora 'Im Derekh Erets Bemishnato Shel Harav S. R. Hirsch." *Hamaya'an* (Tevet 1969): 10-29.

———. "Galut Veerets Yisrael 'Al Pi S.R Hirsch Uvnei Doro." In *Sefer Zikaron Lemordekhai Viser Pirqei Ma'as Vehagut*, edited by S. Schmidt, 160-68. Qevutsat Yavna, 1981.

Cassirer, S., and S. Glicksberg. *Misinai Lelishkat Hagazit*. Jerusalem, 2008.

Cassutto, M. D. *Torat Hate'udot Vesiduram Shel Sifrei Hatorah*. Jerusalem, 1959.

Chertok, S. *Dyoqan Haisha Hayehudit Behaguto Shel Rashar Hirsch*. Jerusalem, 2006.

———. *Qanqan Yashan Male Ḥadash*. Bnei Brak, 2000.

———. *Hayaḥas Lamoderna Befarshanuto Shel Rashar Hirsch Latorah*. PhD Dissertation, Ben Gurion University, Beersheba, 2005.

Cohen, T., and S. Feiner. *Qol 'Alma 'Ivriya: Kitvei Nashim Maskilot Bameah Hatsha' 'Esre*. Tel Aviv, 2006.

Dinur, B. *Bemifne Hadorot*. Jerusalem, 1972.

Dubin, L. C. "The Rise and Fall of the Italian Jewish Model in Germany: From Haskalah to Reform, 1780-1820." In *Jewish History and Jewish Memory*, edited by E Carlebach et al., 271-95. Waltham, 1998.

Elbaum, J. "Demuyot Nashim Beagadat Ḥazal—Model Leḥiqui." *Hagut 5, Measef Lemaḥshava Yehudit: Haisha Bimqorot Hayahadut*, 13-26. Jerusalem, 1983.

Eliav, M. *Haḥinukh Hayehudi Begermania Biyemei Hahaskala Vehaemantsipatsia*. Jerusalem, 1951.

Elior, R. "'Nokheḥot Nifqadot,' 'Teva' Domem,' Ve'alma Yafa Shein La 'Einayim': Lesheelat Nokheḥutan Vehadaratan Shel Nashim Beleshon Haqodesh, Badat Hayehudit, Uvametsiut Hayisraelit." *Alpayim* 20 (2000): 214-70.

Ellenson, D. "Traditional Reactions to Modern Jewish Reform." In *Emancipation*, 154-83. Cincinnati, 2004.

———. "The Orthodox Rabbinate and Apostasy in Ninteenth-Century Germany and Hungary." In *Jewish Apostasy in the Modern World*, edited by T. M. Endelman, 165-88. New York and London, 1987.

———. "German Jewish Orthodoxy: Tradition in the Context of Culture." In *The Uses of Tradition*, edited by J. Wertheimer, 5-22. New York and Jerusalem, 1992.

Elon, M. *Ma'amad Haisha Mishpat Veshiput, Masoret Utmura, 'Arakheiha Shel Medina Yehudit Vedemokratit*. Tel Aviv, 2005.

Endelman, T. "The Englishness of Jewish Modernity in England." In *Toward Modernity*, edited by J. Katz, 225-46. New Brunswick and Oxford, 1987.

———. *The Jews of Georgian England 1714-1830: Traditional Change in a Liberal Society*. Michigan, 1999.

Etkes, I. "Hahaskala Bemizraḥ Eiropa—Divrei Mavo." In *Hadat Vehaḥayim: Tenu'at Hahaskala Hayehudit Bemizraḥ Eiropa*, 9-25. Jerusalem, 1963.

———. "Lesheelat Mevasrei Hahaskala Bemizraḥ Eiropa." In *Hadat Vehaḥayim: Tenu'at Hahaskala Hayehudit Bemizraḥ Eiropa*, 25-44. Jerusalem, 1963.

———. *R. Yisrael Salanter Vereshita Shel Tenu'at Hamusar*. Jerusalem, 1984.

Ettinger, S. "Hayehudim Bitsvat Hahaskala." *Zmanim* 3 (1980): 48-61.

Feiner, S., and I. Bartal. "Petaḥ Davar: Liqrat Siaḥ Ḥadash Beḥeqer Hahaskala." In *Hahaskala Ligvaneiha 'Iyunim Ḥadashim Betoledot Hahaskala Vesifruta*, 7-12. Jerusalem, 2005.

Feiner, S. "Shadal Vehahaskala Shekeneged." In *Italia: Shmuel David Luzzatto Matayim Shana Lehuladeto*, edited by R. Bonfil et al., 145-65. Jerusalem, 2004.

———. *Haskala Vehistoria*. Jerusalem, 1995.

———. "Hamifne Beha'arakhat Haḥasidut—Eli'ezer Zweifel Vehahaskala Hametuna Berussia." In *Hadat Vehaḥayim Tenu'at Hahaskala Bemizraḥ Eiropa*, edited by I. Etkes, 336-79. Jerusalem, 1993.

———. *Shorshei Haḥilun: Metiranut Vesafqanut Beyahadut Hameah Ha-18*. Jerusalem, 2000.

———. *Mahapekhat Haneorut, Tenu'at Hahaskala Hayehudit Bamea Ha-18*. Jerusalem, 2002.

———. *Mendelssohn*. Jerusalem, 2006.

Fish, M. *Lada'at Ḥokhma: Mada', Ratsionaliut Vetalmud Torah*. Tel Aviv, 1994.

Fisher, H. A. L. *A History of Europe*. Originally published in London, 1935.

Fleischman, J. *Be'ayat Hanatsrut Bamaḥshava Hayehudit Mimendelssohn 'Ad Rosenzweig*. Jerusalem, 1964.

Flusser, D. *Yahadut Umeqorot Hanatsrut*. Tel-Aviv, 1979.

———. *Haemunot Vehadeot Shel Haknesia Hanotsrit Harishona*. Edited by Z. Kats and Y. Kats (from lectures). Jerusalem, 1964.

Frankel, M. "Ketivat Hahistoria Shel Yehudei Artsot Haislam Biyemei Habeinayim—Tsiyunei Derekh Vesikuyim." *Pe'amim* 92 (2002): 24-30.

Freudenthal, G. "Ein Symbolischer Anfang der Berliner Haskala: Vitel Ephraim, David Franckel, Aron Gumperz und die Patriotische Feier in der Synagoge am 28 Dezember 1745." *Judaica* 61, 3 (2005): 193-251.

Friedlander, Y. "Meqomo Shel Shmuel David Luzzatto Behitpathut Hapoetiqa Ha'ivrit." in *Italia: Shmuel David Luzzatto, Matayim Shana Lehuladeto,* edited by R. Bonfil et al., 167-76. Jerusalem, 2004

Friedman M. "Kol Kevuda Bat Melekh Hutsa Haisha Haharedit." In *Barukh She'asani Isha?,* edited by D. J. Ariel et al., 189-205. Tel Aviv, 1999.

Friezel, E. *Atlas Karta Letoledot 'Am Yisrael Bazman Hehadash.* Jerusalem, 1983.

Funkenstein, A. *Tadmit Vetoda'a Historit Bayahadut Uvisvivata Hatarbutit.* Tel Aviv, 1991.

Gelber, N. M. "'Arim Veimahot Beyisrael." In *Toledot Yehudei Brody,* edited by Y. L. Maimon, 173-219. Jerusalem, 1955.

Gelber, Y. *Hahistoria Zikaron Veta'amula.* Tel Aviv, 1997.

Gertner, H. "Reshita Shel Ketiva Historit Ortodoksit Bemizrah Eiropa: Ha'arakha Mehudeshet." *Zion* 67, 3 (2002): 293-336.

———. *Rabanut Vedayanut Begalitsia Bemahatsit Harishona Shel Hameah Hatesha'-Esre.* PhD Dissertation, Hebrew University, Jerusalem, 2004.

Gilat, I. D. *Mishnato Shel R. Eli'ezer Ben Horqanos.* Tel Aviv, 1968.

———. *Peraqim Behishtalshelut Hahalakha.* Ramat Gan, 1992.

Goldberg, R. "Vikuah Bein Shadal Leeichenbaum." *Tarbitz* 38, 2 (1969): 175-81.

Goldziher, I. *Introduction to Islamic Theology and Law.* Translated by A. and R. Hamori. Princeton, 1981.

Golinkin, D. *Ma'amad Haisha Bahalakha, Sheelot Utshuvot.* Jerusalem, 2007.

Goodmann, M. "Historia Umeta-Historia Behaguto Shel Harambam." In *Darkhei Shalom, 'Iyunim Behagut Yehudit*, edited by B. Ish-Shalom, 243-54. Jerusalem, 2007.

———. *Sodotav Shel Moreh Hanevukhim*. Or Yehuda, 2010.

Gottlieb, L. "'Resen Mat'e' Lerabi Ya'aqov 'Emden." In *Bedarkhei Shalom, 'Iyunim Behagut Yehudit*, edited by B. Ish-Shalom, 295-322. Jerusalem, 2007.

Graetz, H. *History of the Jews*, vol. II. Translated by B. Lowy. Philadelphia, 1893.

———. *The Structure of Jewish History and Other Essays: Studies in Jewish History, Literature, and Thought*. Translated by I. Schorsch. New York, 1975.

Graupe, M. H. *Hayahadut Hamodernit Behithavuta*. Translated by D. Singer. Jerusalem and Tel Aviv, 1990.

Grossman, A. *Hasidot Umordot: Nashim Yehudiot Beiropa Biyemei-Habeinayim*. Jerusalem, 2003.

———. *Rashi*. Jerusalem, 2006.

Guttmann, J. *Dat Umada'*. Jerusalem, 1979.

———. *Hafilosofia Shel Hayahadut*. Jerusalem, 1989.

HaCohen, R. *Mehadshei Habrit Hayeshana*. Bnei Brak, 1997.

Halbertal, M. *'Al Derekh Haemet. Haramban Veyetsirata Shel Masoret*. Jerusalem, 2007.

———. "Sefer Hamitsvot Larambam, Haarkhitektura Shel Hahalakha Vehateoria Haparshanit Shela." *Tarbiz* 59, 3-4 (1990): 457-80.

———. *Mahapekhot Parshaniot Behithavutan: 'Arakhim Keshiqulim Parshaniyim Bemidreshei Halakha*. Jerusalem, 1997.

———. *Harambam*. Jerusalem, 2009

Harris, J. M. *How Do We Know This?* Albany, 1995.

———. *Nachman Krochmal, Guiding the Perplexed of the Modern Age*. New York and London, 1991.

Hartman, D. *Maimonides: Torah and Philosophic Quest*. Philadelphia, 1976.

Harvey, W. Z. "Moshe Mendelssohn 'Al Erets-Yisrael." In *Erets Yisrael Bahagut Hayehudit Ba'et Hehadasha*, edited by A. Ravitzky, 301-13. Jerusalem, 1998.

———. *R. Ḥasdai Crescas.* Jerusalem, 2010.

Heinemann, I. "Hayaḥas Shebein Sh. R. Hirsch Leyitsḥaq Bernays Rabo." *Zion* 16 (1951): 44-99.

———. *Ta'amei Hamitsvot Besifrut Yisrael*, pt. 2. Jerusalem, 1955.

Heller, J. E. "'Iqarei Torato Shel Shmuel David Luzzatto." *Melila, Qovets Meḥqarim* 3-4 (1950): 276-88.

Heller-Vilenski, S. "Hayaḥas Bein Haemuna Vehatevuna Etsel Rihal." In *Mishnato Hahagutit Shel Rabi Yehuda Halevi*, edited by H. Schwartz, 41-53. Jerusalem, 1978.

Hershkovitz, M. *Maharatz ḥayut, Toledot Rabbi Zvi Hirsh Ḥayut Umishnato.* Jerusalem, 1972.

Heschel, A. J. *Torah Min Hashamayim Beaspaqklaria Shel Hayahadut*, vol. I. Jerusalem, 1962.

Hoffmann, D. Z. *Mesilot Letorat Hatanaim.* Tel Aviv, 1988.

Horvitz, R. "'Al Haqedusha Bamaḥshava Hayehudit Haḥadasha." In *Minḥa Lesara O. Heller Vilenski*, edited by M. Idel, D. Dimant, and S. Rosenberg, 135-54. Jerusalem, 1994.

———. *Zecharia Frankel Vereshit Hayahadut Hapositivit-Historit.* Jerusalem, 1984.

———. "Mavo." In *Sefer Devar Azhara Leyisrael Meet Hila Wechsler*, 11-47. Jerusalem, 1991.

———. "Yaḥaso Shel Shimshon Refael Hirsch Leerets-Yisrael." In *Erets Yisrael Bahagut Hayehudit Haḥadasha*, edited by A. Ravitzky, 447-66. Jerusalem, 1998.

———. "Mendelssohn Veshadal Vehamodelim Shel Dat Bnei Noaḥ Vedat Avraham Behagutam." In *Avraham Avi Hamaaminim*, edited by M. Ḥalamish et al., 265-80. Ramat-Gan, 2002.

———. "Motivim Haskalatiyim Veanti Haskalatiyim Bemishnato Shel Shadal." *Eshel Beer-Sheva'* 2 (1980): 287-310.

———. "Shadal Uspinoza." In *Barukh Spinoza 300 Shana Lemoto*, edited by S. Fuchs, 167-86. Haifa, 1978.

———. "Hachacham Yitshaq Bernays Kemaqor Lehaguto Shel Shimshon Refael Hirsch Beigrot Tsafun." In *Haqongres Haolami Lemaḥshevet Yisrael*, vol. 11, 3, 2 (1994): 109-16.

Hutner David, B. *The Dual Role of Rabbi Zvi Hirsch Chajes, Traditionalist and Maskil*. PhD Dissertation, Columbia University, New York, 1971.

Idel, M. "'Al Erets-Yisrael Bamaḥashava Hamistit Shel Yemei-Habeinayim." In *Erets Yisrael Bahagut Hayehudit Biyemei Habeinayim*, edited by A. Ravitzky et al., 193-215. Jerusalem, 1991.

Ish-Shalom, B. "'Al Mada' Ushlemut Haruaḥ—Biqoret Hamoderniut Vehapostmoderniut, R. Y. D. Soloveitchik Vehehagut Haneo-Ortodoksit." In *Emuna Bezemanim Mishtanim*, edited by A. Sagi, 347-81. Jerusalem, 1996.

Ish-Shalom, B. *Harav Kook Bein Ratsionalizm Lemistika*. Tel Aviv, 1990.

Kahana, M. *Yatsivut Utmura Beshut Haḥatam Sofer*. MA Dissertation, Hebrew University, Jerusalem, 2004

Kaplan, L. "Tora Umadda in the Thought of Rabbi Samson Raphael Hirsch." *B.D.D.* 5 (1997): 5-31.

———. "Scholarly, Non-Traditional Fundamentalism: On Samuel David Luzzatto's Approach to the Bible." *Conservative Judaism* (Winter 1982): 15-25.

Katz, J. *Hahalakha Bameitsar*. Jerusalem, 1992.

———. "Hamaavaq 'Al Qiyum Brit Mila Bamaḥatsit Harishona Shel Hameah Ha19." In *Hahalakha Bameitsar*, 123-49. Jerusalem, 1992.

———. *Haqera' Shelo Nitaha*. Jerusalem, 1995.

———. *Hayetsia Min Haghetto*. Tel Aviv, 1986.

———. "Rabbi Shimshon Refael Hirsch, Hamaymin Vehamasmil." In *Torah 'Im Derekh Erets*, edited by M. Breuer, 13-31. Ramat-Gan, 1987.

———. *Halakha Veqabala*. Jerusalem, 1984.

———. *Bein Yehudim Legoyim*. Tel Aviv, 1961.

———. *Masoret Umashber*. Jerusalem, 1958.

———. "Haortodoqsia Keteguva Layetsia Min Haghetto Uletnu'at Hareforma." In *Hahalakha Bameitsar*, 9-20. Jerusalem, 1992.

Kavner, R. Appendix to the Hebrew edition of H. A. L. Fisher, *A History of Europe*, translated by Y. Kopelevitsh-Keshet, 197-208. Jerusalem and Tel Aviv, 1964.

Kellner, M. "Sinat Nashim Pilosofit Biyemei Habeinayim: Haralbag Le'umat Harambam." In *Meromi Leyerushalayim. Sefer Zikaron Leyosef- Barukh Sermoneta*, edited by A. Ravitzky, 113-28. Jerusalem, 1998.

Klausner, J. *Hahistoria Shel Hasifrut Ha'ivrit Haḥadasha*, vol. II. Jerusalem, 1937; 2nd Amended Edition, 1952; vol IV, Jerusalem, 1941; 2nd Amended Edition, Jerusalem, 1954.

———. *Darki Liqrat Hateḥiya Vehageula*, vol. 1. Tel Aviv, 1955.

———. *Haemunot Vehade'ot Shel Haknesia Hanotsrit Harishona*. Edited by T. and Y. Katz, based on lectures. Jerusalem, 1964.

———. *Yeshu Hanotsri, Ḥayav Vetorato*. Tel-Aviv, 1969.

———. *Hashpaato Shel Hegel Al R. Nachman Krochmal*. Jerusalem, 1936.

Klugman, A. M. "Quntres Vayehi Biyeshurun Melekh." In *Sefer Shemesh Marpe*, 271-377. New York, 1992.

Kurzweil, B. *Bemaavaq 'Al 'Erkhei Hayahadut*. Jerusalem and Tel Aviv, 1971.

Laḥover, P. *Toledot Hasifrut Ha'ivrit Haḥadasha*, book 2. Tel Aviv, 1939.

Lau, B. *Hakhamim*, vol. I. Jerusalem, 2006; vol. II. Jerusalem, 2007.

Lazarus-Yafeh, Ḥ. *Haislam, Qavei Yesod*. Tel Aviv, 1980.

———. *Islam-Yahadut—Yahadut-Islam*. Tel Aviv, 2003.

Leibowitz, Y. *Yahadut, 'Am Yisrael Umedinat Yisrael*. Jerusalem and Tel-Aviv, 1975.

Levi, J. "Ger-Toshav." In *Leqsiqon Hatarbut Hayehudit Bizmanenu*, edited by A. A. Cohen and P. Mendes-Flohr, 77-85. Tel-Aviv, 1993.

Levi, Z. *Hermanoitika*. Tel Aviv, 1987.

———. "Erets-Yisrael Bamaḥshava Hayehudit Begermania Mehirsch V'ad Rosenzweig." *Kivunim* 4 (1979): 54-67.

———. *Hermenoitika Bamaḥshavah Hayehudit Ba'et Haḥadasha*. Haifa-Jerusalem, 2006.

Levinger, J. S. *Harambam Kefilosof Ukheposeq*. Jerusalem, 1990.

Liberles, R. *Religious Conflict in Social Context: The Resurgence of Orthodox Judaism in Frankfurt am Main*. Westport, 1985.

Limor, O. *Bein Yehudim Lenotsrim*. Tel-Aviv, 1993.

Mahler, R. "Milḥamato Shel Yosef Perl Baḥasidut." In *Hadat Vehaḥayim, Tenu'at Hahaskala Hayehudit Bemizraḥ Eiropa*, edited by I. Etkes, 64-89. Jerusalem, 1993.

Luz, E. "Naḥman Krochmal Uve'ayat Hahistorizatsia Shel Hayahadut." In *Minḥa Lesara*, edited by M. Idel et al., 238-58. Jerusalem 1994.

Mahler, R. "Milḥamato Shel Yosef Perl BaHasidut." *Hadat Vehaḥayim, Tenu'at Hahaskala Hayehudit Bemizraḥ Eiropa*, edited by I. Etkes, 64-89. Jerusalem, 1993.

———. "Sovlanut Veḥofesh Dei'ot Beyisrael Pulmus Shir VeShadal." *Orlogin* 1 (1950): 83-94.

Malach, D. "Hishtanut Hatva'im Kepitron Lestirot Bein Dat Lemada' Da'at Harambam." *Teḥumin* 18 (1998): 371-83.

Margolin, R. "Tafqido Umeqomo Shel Regesh Haḥemla Behaguto Shel Shmuel David Luzzatto." In *Italia: Shmuel David Luzzatto Matayim Shana Lehuladeto*, edited by R. Bonfil et al., 115-143. Jerusalem, 2004.

Margolis, M. B. *Samuel David Luzzatto, Traditionalist Scholar*. New York, 1979.

Mendes-Flohr, P., and J. Reinharz, eds. *The Jew in the Modern World: A Documentary History*. Oxford, 1995.

Mendes-Flohr, P. "Mavo." In *Ḥokhmat Yisrael*, 9-31. Jerusalem, 1980.

Meyer, M. A. *Response to Modernity a History of the Reform Movement in Judaism*. New York and Oxford, 1988.

———. "'Elohei Avraham Vesara,' Ma'amad Haisha Bayahadut Halo Ortodoksit." In *Barukh She'asani Isha?*, edited by D. J. Ariel et al., 179-88. Tel Aviv, 1999.

Meyer, M. A. Chapter 5 in *German-Jewish History in the Modern Times, Vol II: Emancipation and Acculturation, 1780-1871*, edited by idem and S. Jersch-Wenzel Brenner, 168-98. New York, 1997.

Michael, R. *J. M. Jost*. Jerusalem, 1983.

Nehorai, M. Z. "Erets-Yisrael Betoratam Shel Harambam Veharamban." In *Erets Yisrael Bahagut Hayehudit Biyemei Habeinayim*, edited by A. Ravitzky et al, 123-38, Jerusalem, 1991.

Niehoff, M. R. "Targumo Shel Moshe Mendelssohn Le'Tsion Halo Tishali' Shel R. Yehuda Halevi." In *Erets Yisrael Bahagut Hayehudit Ba'et Hehadasha*, edited by A. Ravitzky, 313-25. Jerusalem, 1998.

Orlian, J. L. "Zemana Umeqoma Shel Shitat Rashar Hirsch." *Ma'agalei Shana Kitvei Rabbi Shimshon Refael Hirsch*, vol. 4. (Bnei Brak, 1966): 11-29.

Pedaya, H. "Erets-Shel-Ruah Veerets Mamash: R. 'Ezra, R. 'Azriel Veharamban." In *Erets Yisrael Bahagut Hayehudit Biyemei Habeinayim*, edited by A Ravitzky et al., 233-90. Jerusalem, 1991.

———. "Erets-Shel-Ruah Veerets-Mamash: R. 'Ezra, R. 'Azriel Veharamban." In *Erets Yisrael Bahagut Hayehudit Biyemei Habeinayim*, 260-62. Jerusalem, 1998.

Perziger, A. "Zehut Ortodoksit Uma'amadam Shel Yehudim Sheeinam Shomrei Halakha: 'Iyun Mehudash Begishato Shel Harav Ya'aqov Ettlinger." In *Ortodoqsia Yehudit Hebetim Hadashim*, edited by Y. Shalmon et al., 179-210. Jerusalem, 2006.

Ravitzky, A. *Haketz Hamegule Umedinat Hayehudim*. Tel Aviv, 1967.

———. *'Iyunim Maimoniyim*. Jerusalem and Tel Aviv, 2006.

———. "'Hatsivi Lakh Tsiunim' Letsion: Gilgulo Shel Ra'ayon." In *Al Da'at Hamaqom*, 34-74. Jerusalem, 1991.

———. "'Kefi Koah Haadam': Yemot Hamashiah Bemishnat Harambam." In *Al Da'at Hamaqom*, 74-105. Jerusalem, 1991.

———. "'Shelo Ya'alu Bahoma': 'Al Rishuman Shel Shalosh Hashevu'ot Betoledot Yisrael." Appendix to *Haqets Hamegule Umedinat Yisrael*, 277-305. Tel Aviv, 1993.

———. "Erets Hemda Veharada: Hayahas Hadu-Erki Leerets-Yisrael Bimqorot Yisrael." In *Erets Yisrael Bahagut Hayehudit Hahadasha*, 1-41. Jerusalem, 1998.

———. "Sitrei Torato Shel Moreh Hanevukhim: Haparshanut Bedorotav Uvedoroteinu." In *'Al Da'at Hamaqom*, 142-82. Jerusalem, 1991.

———. *'al Haluhot*. Tel Aviv, 1999.

Rawidovicz, S. "Mavo Lekitvei Nahman Krochmal." In *Biqoret ufharshanut*, Rawidovicz edition, 17-225. Berlin, 1924.

Rofe, A. *Mavo Lehibur Hatorah*. Jerusalem, 1994.

———. *Mavo Lesifrut Hamiqra*. Jerusalem, 2006.
Rosen, T. "Haobyekt Hamedaber: Vikuaḥ Bein Ish Veisha Bamaqama Shel Alḥarizi." *Biqoret Ufarshanut* 39 (Jerusalem 2007): 97-124.
Rosenak, A. *Hahalakha Hanevuit, Hapilosofia Shel Hahalakha Bemishnat Haraiah kook*. Jerusalem, 2007.
———. *Harav Kook*. Jerusalem, 2007.
Rosenak, M. *Tsarikh 'Iyyun*. Jerusalem, 2003.
Rosenberg, S. *Lo Bashamayim Hi*. Alon Shvut, 1997.
———. "Galut Veerets-Yisrael Bahagut Hayehudit Bameah Ha16." In *Galut Veerets-Yisrael Bahagut Hayehudit Biyemei-Habeinayim*, edited by A. Ravitzky and M. Ḥalamish, 166-93. Jerusalem, 1991.
———. "Ḥeqer Hamiqra Bemaḥashava Hayehudit Hadatit Haḥadasha." In *Hamiqra Veanaḥnu*, 86-119. Tel Aviv, 1979.
———. "Hitgalut Vetorah Min Hashamayim." In *Hagut Vemiqra*, edited by H. Schwartz, 13-25. Jerusalem, 2005.
———. "Lev Usgula Ra'ayon Habeḥira Bemishnato Shel Rihal Uvapilosofia Hayehudit Haḥadasha." In *Mishnato Hahagutit Shel Rabi Yehuda Halevi*, edited by Ḥ. Schwartz, 109-19. Jerusalem, 1978.
———. "Musag Haemuna Behagut Harambam Umamshikhav." In *'Al Haeumuna: 'Iyunim Bemusag Haemuna Uvetoledotav Bamasoret Hayehudit*, edited by M. Halbertal et al., 245-79. Jerusalem, 2005.
———. *Be'iqvot Hakuzari*. Jerusalem, 1991.
———. *Torah Umada' Bahagut Hayehudit Hahadasha*. Jerusalem, 1988.
———. "Masoret veortodoqsia: 'Al Hagdarot Umusagei Yesod." In *Ortodoqsia Yehudit Hebetim Hadashim*. Edited by Y. Shalmon, A. Ravitzky, and A. Perziger, 55-78. Jerusalem, 2006.
———. "Bein Peshat Lidrash Peraqim Al Parshanut Veideologia." *Deot* 37 (1969): 91-99.
Rosenblit, P. "Galut Veerets Yisrael 'Al Pi S.R Hirsch Uvnei Doro." In *Sefer Zikaron Lemordekhai Viser Pirqei Ma'as Vehagut*, edited by S. Schmidt, 160-69. Kvutzat Yavne, 1981.
———. "Bein Shnei 'Olamot." In *Torah 'Im Derekh Erets Hatenu'a Isheiha Ra'ayonteiha*, edited by M. Breuer, 33-43. Ramat-Gan, 1987.
Rosenbloom, N. H. *Tradition in an Age of Reform*. Philadelphia, 1976.

———. *'Iyunei Sifrut Vehagut Mishilhei Hameah Ha Shmone-'Esre 'Ad Yameinu*. Jerusalem, 1989.

Rosenheim, J. "Rashar Hirsch—Mevaser Umagshim Ḥazon Hayahadut Hanitshit." Introduction to *Ma'agalei Shana Kitvei Rabbi Shimshon Refael Hirsch*, vol. 1, 9-41. Bnei Brak, 1965.

Ross, T. "Ortodoqsia, Nashim, Veshinui Hahalakha." In *Masa' El Hahalakha*, edited by E. Berholtz, 387-437. Tel Aviv, 2003.

———. *Armon Hatora Mim'al La: 'Al Ortodoqsia Ufeminism*. Tel Aviv, 2007.

Ross, J. J. *Mavo Lesefer Beḥinat Hadat Ler. Elia Delmedigo*. Tel Aviv, 1987.

Rostovsky-Halprin, S. *Shadal Vehitnagduto Larambam*. Tel Aviv, 1954.

Rotenberg, M. *Rabbi Zvi Hirsh Ḥayut: His Personality and Books*. PhD. Dissertation, Yeshiva University, New York, 1963.

Rotenstreich, N. *Hamaḥshava Hayehudit Ba'et Haḥadasha*. Tel Aviv, 1987.

Roth, C. *The History of the Jews of Italy*. Philadelphia, 1946.

Rubinstein, B. *Hama'arechet Letiqun Hadat Vesidrei Haḥayim Beyisrael Bemaḥashevet Sifrut Hahaskala Ha'ivrit Mipulmus Haheichal Ve'ad Shnot Hashishim Shel Hameah Ha19*. PhD Dissertation, Hebrew University, Jerusalem, 1958.

Rupp, E. G. *Martin Luther and the Jews*. London, 1972.

Sagi, A. "David Hartman: Hagut Yehudit Modernistit—Pirqei Mavo." In *Meḥuyavut Yehudit Mitḥadeshet*, edited by idem and Z. Zohar, 445-91. Tel Aviv, 2002.

———. "Haemuna Kepitui." In *'Al Haemuna, 'Iyunim Bemusag Haemuna Uvetoledotav Bamasoret Hayehudit*, edited by idem et al., 39-118. Jerusalem, 2005.

———. "Leibowitz: Hagut Yehudit Lenokhaḥ Hamoderna." In *Yesaaya'hu Leibowitz 'Olamo Vehaguto*, 162-75. Jerusalem, 1995.

———. *Elu vaelu*. Tel Aviv, 1996.

———. *Hamasa' Hayehudi-Yisraeli*. Jerusalem, 2006.

———. *Yahadut: Bein Dat Lemusar*. Tel Aviv, 1998.

Salvador, J. *Jesus Christ et sa Doctrine*. Paris, 1818.

Samet, M. *Heḥadash Asur Min Hatorah*. Jerusalem, 2005.
Sandler, P. *Habiur Latorah Shel Moshe Mendelssohn Vesi'ato Hithavtuto Vehaspa'ato*. Jerusalem, 1984.
Schechter, R. *Luter Berei Haleumanut Vehaantishemiut Hagermanit Hamodernit*, PhD Dissertation, Hebrew University, Jerusalem, 1973.
Scholem, G. *Devarim Bego*. Tel Aviv, 1975.
———. *Meḥqarim Umeqorot Letoledot Hashabtaut Vegilguleiha*. Jerusalem, 1982.
Schorsch, I. *From Text to Context the Turn to History in Modern Judaism*. Hanover and London, 1994.
Schwartz, D. *Haguto Hapilosofit Shel Harav Soloveitchik*. Alon Shvut, 2004.
———. *Hara'ayon Hameshiḥi Behagut Yehudit Biyemei Habeinayim*. Ramat Gan, 1997.
Schwartz, M. *Hagut Yehudit Nokhaḥ Hatarbut Hakelalit*. Jerusalem and Tel Aviv, 1976.
Schweid, E. "Two Neo-Orthodox Responses to Secularization—Samson Raphael Hirsch." *Immanuel* 19 (1984-85): 107-17.
———. *Bein Ortodoqsia Lehumanism Dati*. Jerusalem, 1977.
———. *Moledet Veerets Ye'uda*. Tel Aviv, 1979.
———. *Toledot Hehagut Hayehudit Bameah Ha-20*. Tel Aviv, 1990.
———. *Toledot Hehagut Hayehudit ba'et Haḥadasha*. Jerusalem, 1978.
Seidler, M. "Le'fitron Haba'ayot Hamerkaziot Beyoter Shel Hatoda'a Hayehudit,' Hasimboliqa Shel Harav Shimshon Refael Hirsch 'Al Reqa' Tequfato." In *Bedarkhei Shalom*, edited by B. Ish-Shalom, 323-51. Jerusalem, 2007.
Shahar, S. *Haisha Betarbut Yemei Habeinayim—Hama'amad Harevi'i*. Second revised edition. Tel Aviv, 1990.
Shapiro, M. B. "Rabbi Samson Raphael Hirsch and Friedrich von Schiller." *Torah u-Madda Journal* 15 (2008-09): 172-87. Also available online at: http://www.yutorah.org/lectures/lecture.cfm/745805/Professor_Marc_B_Shapiro/07_Rabbi_Samson_Raphael_Hirsch_and_Friedrich_von_Schiller.
Shavit, Y., and M. Eran. *Milḥemet Haluḥot*. Tel Aviv, 2003.

Shavit, Y. *Hayahadut Biree Hayavnut Vehofa'at Hayehudi Hahelenisti Hamoderni*. Tel Aviv, 2003.
Sheli, Ḥ. *Meḥqar Hamiqra Besifrut Hahaskala*. Jerusalem, 1942.
Shinan, A. "Qodem Kol Sifrut." Introduction to B. Lau, *Ḥakhamim*, vol. III, *Yemei Hagalil*, 19-29. Jerusalem, 2008.
———. "Petaḥ Davar." In *Oto Haish: Yehudim Mesaprim 'Al Yeshu*, edited by A. Shinan, 9-14. Tel-Aviv, 1999.
Shoham, H. *Betsel Haskalat Berlin*. Tel Aviv, 1996.
Shohat, A. *'Im Ḥilufei Tequfot: Reshit Hahaskala Beyahadut Germania*. Jerusalem, 1961.
Silber, M. K. "The Emergence of Ultra-Orthodoxy: The Invention of Tradtition." In *The Uses of Tradition*, edited by J. Wertheimer, 23-84. New York, 1992.
Silman, Y. "Haguto Shel Shadal Min Hahebet Hashitati." In *'Iyunim Besugiot Pilosofiot*, 32-68. Jerusalem, 1992.
———. *Qol Gadol Velo Yasaf*. Jerusalem, 1999.
———. "Artsiuta Shel Erets-Yisrael Besefer Hakuzari." In *Erets Yisrael Bahagut Hayehudit Biyemei Habeinayim*, edited by A. Ravitzky et al., 77-90. Jerusalem, 1991.
Simon, A. E. "Az Eitam 'Al Hatemimut Hasheniya." In *Haim 'Od Yehudim Anaḥnu?*, 135-69. Tel Aviv, 1982.
Simonsohn, S. *Hakes Haqadosh Vehayehudim*. Tel-Aviv, 1994.
Sinkoff, N. B. *Tradition and Transition: Mendel Lefin of Satanow and the Beginning of Jewish Enlightenment in Eastern Europe 1749-1826*. PhD Dissertation, Columbia University, New York, 1996.
Slymovics, P. "Romantic and Jewish Orthodox Influence in the Political Philosophy of S. D. Luzzatto." *Italia* 4 (1985): 94-126.
———. "Spinoza Uviqoret Hamiqra." *Meḥqerei Yerushalayim Bemaḥshevet Yisrael*, vol. 2(B), 232-55. Jerusalem, 1983.
Smolenskin, P. "Vezot Liyhuda." *Hashaḥar* 10 (Vienna, 1880).
Soloveitchik, M., and Z. Rubashov. *Biqoret Hamiqra*, vol. I. Berlin, 1925.
Sorkin, D. "Hahaskala Beverlin: Perspektiva Hashvaatit." In *Hahaskala Ligvaneiha, 'Iyunim Hadashim Betoledot Hahaskala Uvesifruta*, edited by S. Feiner and I. Bartal, 3-13. Jerusalem, 2005.

———. *Moses Mendelssohn and the Religious Enlightenment*. Los Angeles, 1996.

Spicehandler, E. "Mavo Leyehoshu'a Heshel Schorr." In *Maamarim*, 7-37. Jerusalem, 1972.

Stern, E. *Ishim Vekivunim*. Ramat-Gan, 1987.

Tas, L. *Yehudei Italia*. Tel Aviv, 1978.

Tebli, D. "Drasha Leshabbat Hagadol 5542." *Jahrbuch der juedische-literarischen Gesellschaft* 12 (1918): 182-94.

Tishby, I. *Mishnat Hazohar*, vol 1. Jerusalem, 1949.

Tov, S. *Torat Hegel Bemishnat Naḥman Krochmal*. Tel Aviv, 1954.

Twersky, I. "Erets-Yisrael Vegalut Bemishnato Shel Harambam." In *Erets Yisrael Bahagut Hayehudit Biyemei Habeinayim*, edited by A. Ravitzky et al., 90-123. Jerusalem, 1991.

Urbach, E. *Ḥazal Pirqei Emunot Vede'ot*. Jerusalem, 1969.

Vargon, S. "'Derekh Hapeshat,' Beferusho Shel Shadal Latorah." *Talpiot* 11 (1999-2000): 59-73.

———. "'Emdato Shel Shadal Besheelat Aḥduto Shel Sefer Yesaa'yahu." *Meḥqerei Morashtenu* 1 (1999): 7-25.

———. "Shadal Keḥaluts Ḥoqrei Hamiqra Hayehudim: 'Al Gishato Leva'ayot Benusaḥ Hamiqra." *'Iyunei Miqra Ufarshanut* 6 (2003): 71-148.

———. "Zehuto Shel Meḥaber Yesaa'yahu 56:9-57:13 Uzmana Shel Hanevua 'Al Pi Shadal." *Beit Miqra* 45, 2 (2000): 97-109.

———. "Yaḥaso Habiqorti Shel Shadal Klapei Parshanut Hahalakha Shel Ḥazal Hanogedet Et Peshuto Shel Miqra." *JSIJ* 2 (2003): 97-122.

———. "Yaḥaso Habiqorti Shel Shadal Klapei Peirushey Hazal Shelo Bithum Hahalakha." *Mehqarim Betalmud Uvemidrash* 5 (2005): 135-58.

———. "Havikuaḥ bein Shmuel David Luzzatto Le'amitav 'Al Hayaḥas Le R. Avraham Ibn Ezra Keḥeleq Meolama Shel Tenu'at Hahaskala." In *Italia: Shmuel David Luzzatto Matayim Shana Lehuladeto*, edited by R. Bonfil et al., 25-63. Jerusalem, 2004.

Verses, S. "Baaspaqlaria Hakefula: Be'iqvot Ḥalifat Hamikhtavim Bein Shmuel David Luzzatto Lishlomo Yehuda Rapoport." In *Italia:*

Shmuel David Luzzatto Matayim Shana Lehuladeto, edited by R. Bonfil et al., 79-99. Jerusalem, 2004.

Verses, S. "Shadal Be'einei 'Atsmo, 'Iyun Beigrotav Ha'ivriot." *Measef* 5, 6 (1955-56): 703-15.

———. "Haḥasidut Beeinei Sifrut Hahaskala—Min Hapulmus Shel Maskiley Galizia." In *Hadat Vehaḥayim Tenuat Hahaskala Hayehudit Bemizrah Eiropa*, edited by I. Etkes, 45-64. Jerusalem, 1993.

———. *Megamot Vetsurot Besifrut Hahaskala*. Jerusalem, 1990.

Weinberg, Y. Y. "Torat Haḥayim." Introduction, *Ma'agalei Shana Kitvei Rabbi Shimshon Refael Hirsch*, vol. 3, 11-24. Bnei Brak, 1966.

Weiner, M. *Hadat Hayehudit Bitqufat Haemantsipatsia*. Translated by L. Zagagi. Jerusalem, 1974.

Westreich, E. *Temurot Bema'amad Haisha Bamishpat Ha'ivri: Masa' Bein Masorot*. Jerusalem, 2002.

Wolfson, H. A. "The Double Faith Theory in Clement, Saadia, Averoes, and its Origin in Aristotle and the Stoics." *The Jewish Quarterly Review,* New Series, 33, 2 (1942): 230-42.

Yerushalmi, Y. H. *Zakhor*. Washington, 1982.

Yuval, I. J. *Shnei Goyim Bevitnekh*. Tel Aviv, 2000.

Yovel, Y. *Spinoza Vekofrim Aḥerim*. Tel Aviv, 1988.

Zinberg, I. *Toledot Sifrut Yisrael*, vols. 3-7. Tel Aviv, 1958-71.

Zivan, G. *Dat Lelo Ashlaya*. Jerusalem, 2006.

Zweifel, E. Z. *Shalom 'Al Yisrael*, vol. IV. Zhytomyr, 1873.

Index

INDEX OF SUBJECTS

A

Absolute, the, **1**:30, 197, 198–99, 410; **2**:332
acculturation, **1**:7, 65, 278n102, 344n, 363; **2**:1, 135, 187; in Germany, **2**:152, 171, 174, 199, 238
agnosticism, **1**:483n
antisemitism. *See* hatred and persecution of Jews
archaeology: and biblical criticism, **1**:25, 63, 67, 83, 90
atheism, **1**:104, 125n96, 332, 402, 471n180, 476

B

behavior: ethical, **1**:209, 215, 377, 392, 509; **2**:164–65, 175, 193; rules of, **1**:213, 231, 270, 353; **2**:8, 17
Bible, **1**:42, 232, 346, 359, 392, 428; **2**:202, 215, 284; and Chajes, **1**:75; **2**:21; and Christianity, **2**:208; and biblical criticism, **1**:4, 19, 24, 59–60, 86n, 88–89, 102, 104, 105, 124–28, 141n125, 146, 151–52, 154, 155, 250n138, 375, 393, 473, 505; **2**:295, 299–300, 316; as divine text, **1**:8, 23, 66, 68, 74, 116–18, 149n, 150, 232, 346, 360, 388, 392, 428, 433, 496, 504; **2**:10, 119, 206, 208, 215, 284, 296; fragmentary hypothesis, **1**:62; and Haskala education, **1**:359; and Luzzatto, **1**:53, 56, 121–31, 133–44; and Maimonides, **2**:145; Source Criticism, **1**:61–62, 63; source history, **1**:61n6; Spinoza's attitude to, **1**:60–61; study of, **2**:135, 145, 172; traditional Jewish approach, **1**:62. *See also* biblical criticism; Biblical Revolution, influence of; revelation; *Torah*

min hashamayim; translations, ancient Bible; Written Torah

biblical criticism, **1**:4, 7-18, 9-68, 96-99, 108, 146, 150, 151, 155, 156, 176n138, 232, 248, 303, 339, 364, 454; **2**:221; and archaeology, **1**:25, 63, 67, 83, 90-91; attitude of Hildesheimer and Hoffmann to, 91n; and Chajes, **1**:67-82, 155, 180, 367n27; **2**:295-96, 297, 334, 344; and the Church, **1**:59; Hirsch's attitude to, **1**:25, 64, 82-106, 154-55, 253, 263n157, 301, 393; **2**:154n, 299, 300, 342; and Hirsch's Bible commentary, **1**:103, 405, 418-22; and historical-philological tools, **1**:7, 19, 25, 46, 63, 67, 79, 83, 105, 143, 145, 146-47, 151, 155, 156, 173, 174, 243; 346, 361, 393, 404, 405, 474, 502; **2**:239, 294, 299, 301, 306, 309, 314, 328, 336, 342, 344; and historical research, **1**:63; and Jost, **1**:70, 130; and literal meaning, **1**:152; and Luzzatto, **1**:104-16, 141-54, 257, 475, 505; **2**:344; and Luzzatto's commentary principles, **1**:25, 26, 110-41, 482-97; **2**:306; and Mendelssohn, **1**:64, 65n; and Reform, **1**:7, 173, 174; and Spinoza, **1**:59-61, 62, 70, 134, 136, 473; and tradition, **1**:24-26. *See also* Bible: biblical criticism; Bible, as divine text; historical positivism and movement; Wissenschaft des Judentums

Biblical Revolution, influence of, **1**:65-66, 74, 154, 155, 499, 508; **2**:295; on Chajes, **1**:155; on Hirsch, **1**:104, 155, 300; on; Luzzatto, **1**:104-5, 156; **2**:304

C

Catholic Church, **1**:45, 59, 419; **2**:208, 277. *See also* Christians
change: as goal, **1**:2, 3
choirs, mixed, **2**:136, 136n17
chosenness of the Jewish people, **1**:31, 375; **2**:111; and Hirsch, **2**:81, 81n, 86, 111, 246; and Judah Halevi, **2**:81n, 100, 101, 121n; Luzzatto, **1**:340; **2**:81n, 100, 111, 112, 121n, 343; and Maimonides, **2**:100; and Mendelssohn, **2**:101. *See also* Jewish people; mission, Jewish
Christianity, Christians, **1**:4, 28, 32, 40, 45, 50n45, 174, 361; **2**:8, 12, 35, 128, 201-14, 222, 237n, 238, 332; and Bible criticism, **1**:63, 70, 75, 126, 127; in Bismarck's Germany, **1**:45; and Chajes, **1**:68, 186; **2**:23, 25, 147, 224-25, 244, 246n70, 249, 291, 298; erosion of status of, **1**:4; and free will, **2**:249; fundamentalism, **1**:149-50, 149n131; and Hegel, **1**:9, 296; and Hirsch, **1**:104, 273, 275, 283, 287, 289, 290n200, 293, 296, 299, 413, 443; **2**:55, 75, 76, 77, 154n, 162, 212n23, 238-276, 291, 272n114, 327, 338, 342; and Jesus as messiah, **2**:202, 204, 209, 236; and Judah Halevi, **2**:233, 236, 238, 239, 290, 298; liberal, **1**:23; and Luzzatto, **1**:121, 125n96, 329, 333; **2**:100, 108, 109, 115, 119, 246n70, 277-90, 291, 309; Maimonides on, **2**:100, 213, 236, 237n56, 238, 239, 245, 249, 288, 290, 291, 298, 309; and

Mendelssohn, 2:8–9, 213–21, 271n110, 290; and the Middle Way, 2:224; and national redemption, 2:1; Rashi on, 2:100, 281n122, 288, 288n131, 290; and Reform, 2:222–23; Reformation, 2:208; and romanticism, 2:223, 239; and status of women, 2:128, 134. *See also* determinism; hatred and persecution of Jews original sin

civil rights, 2:40, 133, 136, 271–72, 320; Hirsch on, 1:287n193; Jews', 1:34, 40; 2:16, 17, 115n; 2:1, 2, 39, 46–47, 50, 66, 68, 83, 206, 210, 214, 217, 221, 224, 227, 235, 277, 298; and women, 1:136. *See also* equal rights; humanism

commandments, 1:15n, 26, 298; 2:8, 206, 310–11, 314, 315, 318; and Chajes, 1:39, 71, 78–79, 80, 81, 189, 211–15, 220, 367, 379; 2:151; and Chajes, and ethical training, 1:220; and Chajes, and observance of, 1:211–15; 2:26; connected to the Land of Israel, 1:305; 2:2, 71–73, 74, 97, 232; and Hirsch, 1:19, 85, 94, 98, 275, 279, 284, 290–93, 298, 299, 392, 395, 400–401, 402, 405; 2:42, 43, 70, 167–70, 240–41, 250, 255, 256, 260–61, 266, 282, 294; and Hirsch, on "be fruitful and multiply," 155, 157n44; and Hirsch, and importance of practical, 269–76; and Hirsch, on interpretation of, 1:102–4; and Hirsch, on observance of, 1:98, 188, 284, 290–92, 294, 300–1, 402, 445–47; 2:51n, 56, 60, 61, 62, 68, 85, 89, 91, 93, 97, 98, 174–76, 240, 291; and Hirsch, and settlement of the Land of Israel, 2:73, 74; and Hirsch, on Sages interpreting, 1:102; and Hirsch, on women's exemption of observing many, 2:160–1, 165, 199, 303, 313; Judah Halevi, 1:355; and Krochmal, 1:234, 248; and Luzzatto, 1:51, 106, 108, 118, 126, 131, 133, 135–36, 146, 302, 305, 337, 339, 340, 463, 503; 2:101, 109, 111, 113, 115, 121, 278, 282, 283, 294, 304; and Luzzatto, and acceptance of, 1:148; and Luzzatto, and rejection of, 1:450; and Luzzatto, and commandments' exempted for women, 2:309, 313–14; and Maimonides, 1:182; 2:56, 208, 237n; and Maskilim, 1:11; and Mendelssohn, 1:508; 2:8, 13, 216, 219, 220; and the Middle Trend, 1:33; 2:223; Noahide, 1:217, 219, 377–78, 386; 2:23, 25, 32–35, 39, 77, 79, 97, 210, 211, 215, 231, 232–33, 241, 241n61, 285, 290, 320; observance of, 1:4, 10, 14, 51, 57; and Reform Jews, 1:63, 173, 209, 470; 2:270; Spinoza's attitude to, 1:60; and status of women, 2:129, 131, 134, 136–38, 139, 144–47, 157n, 161, 163n, 165, 167–71, 172, 174, 186, 187, 193–97, 313–14. *See also* Halakha; Oral Law; philosophy: inference

community, 1:23, 176, 409; 2:5, 14, 39, 41–42, 85n115, 130–31, 146, 152, 265

community, Jewish: crisis of, 1:3–6, 14n, 191, 274, 363; 2:14, 238, 293; disintegration of frameworks, 1:5–6; loss of autonomy of, **1:**4, 18n, 40; loss of political power of, **1:**3. See also state: and Jews and Jewish community

Conservative movement, **1:**12, 177n, 278; **2:**311

conversion and converts to Christianity, **1:**104, 126, 312–13, 362; **2:**14, 135, 207, 214, 223, 237n, 238, 240n, 283; **2:**135, 207, 214, 222, 223, 235, 237n, 238, 240n, 283; proposed collective, **1:**18n15

culture, general, 434–37, 434n134

D

Damascus Blood Libel, **1:**230n118; **2:**22, 24–25, 229–31, 234,

Decree of Tolerance, **1:**3, 5, 34; **2:**1

deism, **1:**4, 59, 89, 145, 171, 333, 349, 361, 461; **2:**101, 270, 294; and Jews, **1:**325; **2:**217, 219; and Maskilim, **1:**5, 173; rationalist, **1:**394, 403, 456, 458; and secularization, **1:**346; and Voltaire, **2:**221

determinism, **1:**284, 496; **2:**78; and Christianity, **2:**255; with Crescas's philosophical, 490n197; and Maimonides, 490n197; materialistic, **2:**292; pantheistic, **1:**296, 297, 335, 473; **2:**260. See also Free Will; original sin

dialectical tension, **1:**12, 23–28, 494n; **2:**294

dialectics in Middle Way thought, **1:**9, 12, 23–34, 354, 354n, 356, 493; **2:**315, 318; and Chajes, **1:**18, 77n33, 380; **2:**297, 298, 312; and Hirsch, **1:**94n, 399, 406n92, 416–17, 434n134, 435, 511; **2:**81n113, 166, 301, 302, 312; and Krochmal, **1:**77n33, 199, 320, 325n; and Luzzatto, **1:**148–49, 152, 320, 325n, 357, 457, 459, 482–97; **2:**104; and Luzzatto's commentary principles, **1:** 116–41

Divine Providence, **1:**347; **2:**206; and Chajes, **1:**212, 213, 379, 382, 388; **2:**19, 23, 231, 321, 332, 333, 334, 335; and Hirsch, **1:**276, 402; **2:**54, 60, 76, 77, 84, 87, 96, 166, 244, 275, 331, 321; and Krochmal, **2:**334–35; and Luzzatto, **1:**106, 117, 143, 145, 148, 154, 304, 306, 334, 338, 339, 451, 457, 464, 475, 492; **2:**99, 100, 102, 108, 113, 115, 280, 288; and Maimonides, **1:**347, 491n; **2:**6; and Mendelssohn, **1:**358; **2:**9, 12, 13, 102; and Nachmanides, **1:**164; and Reform, **1:**394; **2:**222. See also God

dual loyalty, **2:**2, 9–12, 14, 25, 217; and Chajes, **2:**25–32, 227, 228, 298; and Hirsch, **2:**46, 49, 276, 302; and Luzzatto, **2:**105–7; Mendelssohn on, **2:**10. See also hatred and persecution of Jews

E

Edict of Tolerance, **1:**3, 5; **2:**1

education, **1:**19, 28, 49, 50–51, 187n, 210, 220, 224, 279, 312, 392, 404; **2:**47, 21, 214, 217; of boys, **1:**51, 304, 348, 349, 350, 387, 430, 499; **2:**139, 153, 172, 173, 173n72, 194, 312; and Chajes, **1:** 387–92; **2:**175, 298, 312, 331, 333, 334; of Christians, **2:**212; and Enlightenment, **1:**346; of girls, **2:**134–35, 136, 139, 153, 172–73, 173n62, 174, 312; Haskala revolution in, **1:**357–61, 387, 393, 425,

428, 508; **2:**298, 302, 334, 342; Hirsch and, **1:**11, 19, 20, 23n, 44, 45, 90, 187n, 257, 262, 266n, 269, 291–92, 328, 393, 399–400, 403, 406, 407, 416, 425–42, 511; **2:**60, 69, 80, 84, 85, 86, 97, 98, 173–75, 178, 266, 267, 270, 300, 302, 337, 341; and Hirsch, and educational value of Judaism, **1:**417–18; and Hirsch's educational system, **1:**393, 416n103, 427–28; **2:**299, 312, 331, 337; and human progress, **1:**28, 33; **2:**12, 84, 85–86; and Jewish tradition, **1:**26, 33, 95–96, 179, 220, 349–51; and Luzzatto, **1:**23n, 50, 51, 52–53, 323–24, 331, 337; **2:**194, 497–500; **2:**109, 123, 194, 308, 312, 331, 342; Limud Torah school (Hamburg), **1:**42; modernization of Jewish, **1:**5, 29, 34, 40, 42, 47n, 52, 65, 404; in Reform, **2:**136, 226, 227; revolution in, **2:**171, 194; and Wessely, **1:**393; **2:**294, 312. *See also* Hebrew: study of
elite, elitism, **1:**4, 5, 30, 331, 345, 350, 359, 364, 385, 386 508, 509; **2:**304
emancipation, Jewish, **1:** 3, 15n 57, 191, 209, 310, 346, 363, 506; **2:**1–2, 14, 21n23, 25, 133, 293, 338; Chaje's view, **2:**16; in Germany, **2:**238; Hirsch's view, **2:**43–46, 79, 85, 87; **2:**239, 240n, 303, 323n; in Italy, **1:**48–49, 50; **2:**304; Luzzato's view, **2:**103–4, 105 n. 149, 117, 121n, 126, 127, 308; and the Middle Trend, **1:**32; and Reform, **1:**7; **2:**223; and status of women, **2:** 130, 133. *See also* civil rights; Edict of Tolerance; human rights; humanism

end of days, **1:**7, 56, 91, 211, 298, 487n; **2:**90, 95, 96n, 113, 280, 343; and Christianity, **2:**203, 257; and Messiah, **2:**113, 340; and mission of the Jews, **2:**97, 114; and Return to Zion, **2:**11, 38, 120, 122, 124, 125, 173n, 298, 303, 308

Enlightenment. *See* Haskala, Maskilim

equal rights, **1:**40, 209, 210, 226; **2:**40, 46, 85, 116, 137, 139, 224, 240, 244, 277. *See also* civil rights; humanism

equality, **1:**27, 29, 31, 32, 40, 104, 345, 405; **2:**39, 40, 44, 142, 244

ethical behavior. *See* behavior: ethical

ethical choice, free. *See* free will

ethical monotheism. *See* monotheism: ethical

ethics, **1:** 26, 179, 258, 263n, 331–32; **2:**81, 160, 164–65, 174, 312; and Chajes, **1:**208–11, 215, 216–217, 367, 376, 385, 386, 464; **2:**32, 36, 37, 198, 296, 297; and character, **2:** 128, 160, 177, 182; Christian, **1:**333; and free choice, **1:**425; and Hirsch, **1:**23n, 100–2, 270, 271, 274–97, 393, 405, 425, 430, 435, 437; **2:**39, 40n36, 42, 44, 51n, 54, 55, 60, 64, 67, 72, 84, 98, 156, 160, 164, 165, 174, 175, 238, 292, 301, 303, 337, 342; and Hirsch, on woman's role, **2:**174, 177, 199; and Jesus, **2:**202, 257; and Luzzatto, **1:**23n, 52, 53, 108, 305, 329–42, 458, 462, 464, 466, 477, 488, 489, 497, 498, 499, 503, 508; **2:**99, 103, 110, 115, 116, 117, 121n, 122, 306, 308;

and Luzzatto, on permissiveness and natural, 2:191–98; and Maimonidean polemic, 1:216–20, 321, 464; and Maimonides, 1:377, 464; 2:296; and Mendelssohn, 1:209, 274, 283, 423, 462; and prophets, 1:174, 209; and reason, 1:27, 213n, 283, 306, 336, 365; and Reform on Torah, 1:176, 222; and revelation, 403; and Spinoza, 1:60; Torah, 1:176, 179, 209, 210, 275, 279–80, 283–90, 306, 333–34, 337, 386; 2:40n, 51n, 84, 99, 116, 122, 156n43, 191, 240, 297, 300–303, 327. *See also* morality

Exile, the, 1:118, 144, 278, 300; 2:2, 5, 46, 49, 50, 52, 62, 68, 86, 89, 91, 108, 335, 339, 342, 343; Chajes' attitude to, 2:15, 20, 25, 27, 35–36, 37, 234, 335; Hirsch's attitude to, 2:15, 44, 45, 52, 57, 62, 63–69, 68n90, 71, 78, 80, 82–83, 84, 86, 87–93, 106, 108, 245, 302, 303, 337, 339; as Jewish mission to the nations, 2:5–13, 35–36, 37, 38, 67, 69, 78, 82, 83, 84, 90, 337; Judah Halevi's attitude to, 2:68n90, 93, 100, 288; Luzzatto's attitude to, 1:304, 310; 2:15, 100, 104, 105–7, 118, 120, 124, 280, 281, 343; Maimonides' attitude to, 2:93; Mendelssohn's attitude to, 2:94; and Middle Trend, 2:32; Nachmanides' attitude to, 2:94; and Reform, 1:82. *See also* mission, Jewish; Three Oaths, the

F

faith religious experience, 1:293, 352; and Chajes, 1:17–18, 85, 205, 210, 213, 216, 218, 367, 378, 379; 2:29, 31, 36, 37, 231, 237; and Christianity, 2:249; and enlightened education, 1:360; and Hirsch, 1:98, 225, 292, 293, 299, 394, 397, 400, 401, 402, 403, 410, 423–24; 2:159, 204–5, 250, 251–52, 270, 274, 341; and Kalam, 1:355; and Luzzatto, 1:54, 105–6, 107–8, 111–12, 114, 116, 142, 144, 148, 156, 305–6, 323, 324, 333, 335, 336n, 338, 340; 454, 455, 463, 477n186, 481, 483, 483n, 492, 503, 504, 508; 2:99, 105, 105n149, 109, 110, 113, 121, 277, 282, 287, 288; and Maimonides, 1:348; and Mendelssohn, 2:216, 219; and Reform, 1:173; 2:14, 222; thirteen principles of, 1:218–19, 463; 2:286n. *See also* religion

Free Will, 1:205, 426, 496; and Chajes's view, 1:205, 379; Hirsch's view, 1:101, 275n166, 282, 284, 291, 292, 293n204, 393, 403; 2:39, 249–50, 254–56, 292; and Kalam, 1:355n15; Luzzatto's view, 1:113, 490, 490n197; and Maimonides, 1:490n197; and Middle Trend, 1:29; and morality, 1:415, 417

freedom, moral, 1:280, 295, 296, 404; 2:255, 256, 258, 259, 261, 266

French Revolution, 1: 4, 5; 2:1, 5, 13, 133

fundamentalism, fundamentalists, 1:244, 249, 253, 371n30; and Chajes, 1:71, 72, 103, 215–16, 220, 365, 368, 375, 392, 512; 2:15, 140, 284n126, 295, 296, 297–98, 309; definitions, 1:149–51; and Geonim, 1:163,

300; and Hirsch, 1:46n, 103, 238, 249, 263n157, 411, 419; 2:38, 58, 89, 96, 254, 284n126, 285n127, 309; and Jewish Bible commentary, 1:25; and Luzzatto, 1:106, 115, 145, 149-54, 474n, 496; 2:307; and Mendelssohn, 1:405; and the middle trend, 1:25-26; and Nachmanides, 1:25, 300; Neo-Fundamentalism, 1:25, 104, 149n, 405, 420, 421, 439, 511; 2:166, 302. *See also* Orthodoxy, Ultra-Orthodoxy

G

Geonim, 1:72, 76, 158, 159, 163, 166, 172, 194-95, 258, 264, 342, 367, 466; 2:5n2, 300; and place of women, 2:129, 129n, 130

ger, concept of, 2:319-25

German (language): and girls' education, 2:7, 135; prayers and sermons in, 1:42; 2:136

girls, 2:152; confirmation ceremonies for, 2:136; education, 1:351, 429, 429n126; 2:7, 134-35, 145, 194; and Hirsch's educational approach, 2:153, 171-75, 172n63, 199, 312, 314; in Maskilic school, 2:139

God, 1:23, 26, 27, 28, 31, 363; 2:138, 176, 260, 314, 315; basic Jewish concept of, 2:243; and Chajes, 1:214, 373, 375-76, 379, 383; 2:140, 142, 143, 232, 294, 332; and Haskala, 1:345; and Hirsch, 1:284, 285-86, 287-88, 296, 393, 413, 418, 420, 422, 424; 2:56, 76, 85, 86, 92, 260-61, 269, 273, 301, 337, 339; and Hirsch, on act of creation by God in history, 63; and Hirsch, and denial of existence of God, 1:89; 2:244; and Hirsch, and the divine plan, 60-61, 66; and Hirsch, on attaining closeness to, 2:252-53; and Hirsch, on atonement and, 2:254; and Hirsch, on belief in, 1:398-99; and Hirsch, on Christianity and, 2:77; and Hirsch, on fear of, 1:404; and Hirsch, on history and, 1:411, 2:81, 331; and Hirsch, on human beings reflecting image of, 2:39, 43-44; and Hirsch, on innocence and purity required by, 2:178; and Hirsch, on Israel as instrument of, 88-92; and Hirsch, on Israel's relationship with, 2:51, 59-60; and Hirsch, on Jewish people's mission and, 1:275; 2:274; and Hirsch, on the modern Jew and, 1:44; and Hirsch, on nature and, 1:394, 405, 411; 2:255, 259; and Hirsch, on the nazirite and, 2:266-67; and Hirsch, on neutralization of the Temple of, 2:68-70; and Hirsch, and path to, 1:286; and Hirsch, on a personal, 1:101; and Hirsch, on purpose of revelation and, 1:392; and Hirsch, on unity of, 1:102, 415, 416, 421; and Hirsch, on will of, 1:100, 280, 287, 293, 410; 2:90, 244; and Kant, 1:27; and Krochmal, 1:198; and Luzzatto, 1:117, 135, 143, 144, 338, 339; 2:99-101, 102-3, 107, 110, 111-12, 113, 115, 116, 122, 126, 192, 278-79, 289, 294, 307, 308, 331-32; and Luzzatto, and the Creator, 1:493; and Luzzatto, and imagining God positively, 1:470; and

Luzzatto, and love of, 1:482–86; and Luzzatto, and Revelation, 1:480; and Luzzatto, and Torah, 1:481, 493; and Maimonides, 1:356, 375, 376, 377, 381, 491n; 2:3, 208, 291; materialization of, 1:403; and Mendelssohn, 1:358; 2:8, 216; and the middle trend, 1:32; unity of, 1:101, 376, 415, 416, 493; 2:274, 289. *See also* historical consciousness, historical processes: and God; monotheism; pantheism, panentheism; religion

Greek culture, 1:331–32, 505; and Chajes, 1:76, 371, 372, 374; and Hildesheimer and Mendelssohn, 1:405; and Hirsch, 1:222, 226, 274, 286–87, 298, 300, 392, 393, 405, 407–12, 431, 444; 2:243; and Luzzatto, 1:456, 331, 511n; and Maharal, 1:348. *See also* philosophy: Aristotelian; philosophy: and Luzzatto and the Atticists; philosophy: Neo-Platonic

H

Halakha, 1:5, 11, 13n9, 14n, 26, 31, 149n, 158, 159–61, 169–70, 178–79, 494n; 2:1, 83, 87, 96, 217, 311, 316; and Chajes, 1:22n, 25, 68, 74, 78–79, 192–205, 375, 391; 2:22, 31, 226, 230, 234, 294, 296, 297, 311, 334, 336; and Chajes, on changes in, 1:182–83, 185–89; and Chajes, and need to defend, 1:103; development in historical process, 1:11, 12; and the Essenes, Pharisees, and Christians, 2:204; and Frankel, 1:246–54; and Graetz, 1:230–46, 248; and Hirsch, 1:8, 16, 98, 153, 159, 186n, 226, 227, 233–53, 258–67, 268, 278n, 279, 295, 424, 429; 2:67n89, 153, 172, 173n63, 187, 188, 199, 238, 300, 301, 311, 322, 342; and Hirsch, on girls' education, 2:463; and Hirsch, on historicism of, 2:163n; and Hirsch, on laws regarding women, 2:153, 164–65, 168–69; and Hirsch, on organ use, 1:186; and the Historical-Positivists, 178–79; and Krochmal, 1:11, 199–200, 234, 248, 325n; 2:297, 311; and Luzzatto, 1:11, 26, 246n, 316–224; 2:187–88, 200, 306, 343, 500, 509; and Luzzatto, on marital, 2:192–97; and Luzzatto, attitudes to Sages', 2:187, 200; and Maimonides, 1:18, 160–63, 165, 166, 192, 193, 194, 200, 203–4, 233, 327, 252; 2:306, 311; and the Middle Way, 1:8; 2:2; to Moses from Sinai, 1:161, 162, 164, 165, 166, 170, 193, 194, 197, 202, 232, 233, 236, 247–48, 249, 250, 252, 255, 259, 264, 442; and Nachmanides, 1:164, 166–69, 236, 251–52; prophetic, 1:494n; and Reform and Haskala extremists, 1:7, 173–75, 183n32, 186n40, 209, 365, 442; 2:138, 222; rejection of, 56, 66; and status of women, 2:44n, 128–32; and Wessely, 1:359. *See also* commandments; Oral Law; philosophy: inference

Ḥasidei Ashkenaz, 2:4, 225

Hasidism, 1:16, 33, 36, 50, 351, 359, 365, 493n; 2:4, 139, 295, 304; and Chajes, 1:37; 2:152, 298, 312; and Hirsch, 1:268, 395; and Luzzatto, 1:455n165;

Middle Way's attitude to, 2:312; Orthodoxy of, 1:35; religiosity of, 2:140, 149; *See also* Orthodoxy

Haskala, Maskilim, 1:4, 67, 334–61, 364, 430; 2:14, 126, 152, 172, 181, 213, 219, 224, 334; and biblical criticism, 1:64, 67; and Chajes, 1:17, 30, 36, 37, 180, 209, 220, 365, 386, 391; 2:15, 99, 126, 140, 143, 181, 198, 293, 297, 298, 331, 335; and counter-enlightenment, 1:462, 463; extreme and Reform, 1:5, 6, 158, 173, 174–75, 180, 232, 277, 345, 364; 2:318; and Hirsch, 1:10, 11, 27, 29, 274, 297, 392, 405, 440, 463, 511; 2:38–43, 79, 96, 126, 152, 153, 171, 181, 293, 301, 331; and Judah Halevi, 1:355; literature, 1:52, 314, 342, 361, 362, 387; 2:297, 304, 306, 502, 505; and Luzzatto, 1:17, 48, 52, 419, 447–49, 462, 474n, 498–99, 508; 2:99–103, 113, 126, 182, 277, 293, 305, 306, 331, 502, 505; and Neo-Orthodox thinkers, 1:9; radical, 1:13, 16, 442, 450, 454; 2:318; spread of, 1:5; and universalism, 2:96; and women's status, 2: 133–35; and Wissenschaft des Judentums, 1:361–62. *See also* Biblical Revolution, influence of; education: Haskala revolution in

hatred and persecution of Jews, 1:129, 363, 410, 426; 2:13–19, 30, 31, 37, 45, 206, 208, 209, 211, 212, 216–17, 220–21, 224, 226–29, 237n, 238, 242, 277, 279–80, 298, 322; and blood libels, 2:213, 229–31, 232, 234

Hebrew, 1:51, 52, 65, 120, 363; 2:437, 449, 478; Frankel writing in, 1: 246, 254; and the Haskala, 1:360, 362, 390, 391, 430, 440, 499, 508; and Hirsch, 1:441; literature, 1:362, 457, 2:181–82, 185, 194, 333; and Luzzatto, 1:314, 336n269, 505, 510; 2:304, 305, 307; and Judaism, 1:83; prayer in, 1:187n, 307, 365, 391; research into, 1:105; sanctity of, 1:113, 388, 441, 472; 2:27, 134; study of, 1:117, 360, 388, 390, 428, 440, 497, 499, 508; 2:83, 133, 134, 138, 139, 153, 171–74, 175, 199; and terms *'am* and *goy*, 2:50; and women, 2:133, 134

hermeneutic principles, the thirteen, 1:74, 102, 171, 180, 234n, 256n, 321, 442; Chajes on, 1:342; 2:311; and Halakha, 1:125, 161–63, 164, 172, 204, 233; and Halakhic innovation, 1:196, 318; Hirsch on, 1:235–53, 240, 251, 255–56, 258, 259; 2:300; Luzzatto on, 1:315n244, 325, 326n; and Oral Law, 1:155; and process of derivation, 1:170; and term for concept of religion, 2:273; and term for faith, 2:272; and written commandments, 1:160, 200. *See also* Sages; seven principles for interpreting the Torah, Hillel's; thirty-two principles of Rabbi Eli'ezer, 1:206

historical consciousness, historical processes, 1:4, 6, 11, 14n, 25, 49n45, 65, 67n11, 79, 89, 92, 93, 95, 135, 174, 196, 199, 345, 497; 2:75, 170, 208n, 272n114, 315, 316; and Chajes, 1:37; 2:35, 77, 105, 126; 293–94,

295–96, 298, 311, 331–36; and God, **1**:200, 346, 393, 400; and Hegelian dialectics, **1**:9, 16n11, 30, 198, 354, 357, 361, 363, 402, 488, 494n; **2**:257, 260, 332, 342; and Hirsch, **1**:42–43, 238, 253, 273, 284, 288, 394, 400, 401, 402, 419, 442–43, 445; **2**:51n, 65, 67n, 77, 79, 88, 89–90, 91–93, 94–95, 105, 126, 163n, 293–94, 299, 301, 331–32, 337–42; and Luzzatto, **1**:497, 499, 503, 512; **2**:103, 105, 110–11, 124, 126–27, 189n, 293–94, 304–5, 308, 331–32, 342–43; and Maimonides, **2**:3, 57; and Mendelssohn, **2**:12–13, 35, 79, 105. *See also* historical positivism and movement; Jewish people, the; philosophy: Hegelian

historical positivism and movement, **1**:6, 11–12, 94n, 177–79, 362, 365, 442; **2**:295, 311; and Chajes, **1**:191; the Conservative movement and, **1**:177n; and Frankel, **1**:192n47; and Hirsch, **1**:44, 90, 94n, 99, 103, 230–35, 442–47; **2**:57–58, 163n, 299, 300, 342; and innovation, **1**:159; and Luzzatto, **1**:13, 179, 305, 311, 324n, 325, 342, 503; **2**:305. *See also* Wissenschaft des Judentums

historiography, **1**:177n, 232
historiosophy, **1**:42, 232
holiness. *See* sanctity
Holy Scriptures. *See* Bible
human rights, **1**:27, 405, 340; **2**:29, 31, 39, 42; **2**:1, 2, 39, 42, 43, 219, 240, 320; and Hirsch, **1**:104, 279, 281, 393, 405, 409, 414n102; the Middle Way and, **1**:29; and status of women, **1**:130, 133–34, 136. *See also* civil rights

humaneness, **1**:416; **2**:315; and Hirsch, **1**:292, 393, 430; **2**:159, 270, 323n

humanism, **1**:53, 56, 59; and Haskala, **1**:65, 345; and Hirsch, **1**:19–20, 226; and Luzzatto, **1**:483n; the Middle Trend and, **1**:29; and prophets, **1**:65, 66; and Reform, **1**:66, 365. *See also* universalism; ethics; pluralism: ethical

humanity, **1**:2, 3, 6, 14, 26–27, 32, 43, 44, 47, 84, 104, 278, 306, 363, 407, 433, 443; **2**:14, 43, 44, 45, 50, 54, 60, 67, 68, 76, 82, 89, 93, 95, 114, 126, 142, 198, 199, 218, 242, 283–84, 285, 286, 291; and Chajes, **1**:384, 385; **2**:126; and Christianity, **1**:32; **2**:202, 212, 214, 237n, 245, 251, 257, 275, 298; and God, **2**:60, 110; and Hirsch, **1**:275, 279, 292, 293, 294, 300, 402, 408, 413n, 415, 416; **2**:38, 39, 47, 54, 55, 68, 80, 86, 91, 126, 177, 320, 342, 512; the Jewish people and, **2**:60, 80, 84, 91; a Jewish state and, **2**:55, 86, 96; and Judah Halevi, **1**:355; **2**:99–103, 104, 115, 116, 118, 119, 126, 307, 312and Luzzatto, **1**:330, 334, 479, 482n, 486, 493, 513; **2**:99–103, 114, 118, 126; and Maimonides, **1**:26, 31, 39, 385; and Mendelssohn, **1**:377; **2**:214, 218; the Middle Trend and, **1**:23, 29, 30; **2**:139, 314; the mission of, **1**:355, 384; new, **1**:433; progress of, **1**:28; 45, 489; **2**:6, 13, 14, 45, 67, 99; and redemption, **1**:8,

179, 199, 300, 487; **2**:2, 59, 70, 75, 76, 124; Reform movement and, 104, 222; reform of, **2**:3; and revelation, **1**:377, 392, 480; **2**:32; and salvation, **1**:27, 28, 30; **2**:35, 96, 302, 342; and Torah, **1**:33, 136, 340; **2**:39, 50, 78, 81, 97, 98, 113, 114, 208, 300, 314, 337; and universalism, **1**:27; **2**:38-43, 99-103; and Wessely, **1**:65, 358; and women, 132, 136, 156, 157, 177. *See also* commandments: Noahide; mission of the Jewish people

I

idealism, **1**:197, 199, 215, 288, 310n238, 361; **2**:75, 116, 126; romantic, **1**:9, 27, 174, 274, 331, 363, 365, 392, 405, 508; **2**:15, 134, 240n, 252
identity: crisis of, **1**:3; separate Jewish, **1**:40
individualism, **1**:27, 345; **2**:38, 39, 41; and romantic idealism, **1**:174
innovation, **1**:6, 174, 179, 181, 195, 239-43, 260, 311, 318; as existing from time immemorial, 246n; as goal, **1**:2, 3; and Graetz, **1**:232, 235; in Halakha, **1**:158, 160, 161, 162, 163, 182, 184, 194, 198, 205, 231; of historical development, **1**:200
integration: reaction against Jews', **1**:5
intellect. *See* reason
Isaiah, Book of, **1**:77, 116; two Isaiahs, **1**:8, 77n33, 111, 115, 141-44, 145, 146, 147; **2**:305
Islam, Muslims, **1**:32; **2**:201, 208, 213; 244, 290; and Chajes, **2**:25, 201n, 226, 226n, 232-33, 235, 237, 238, 277, 291; and Graetz,

50n45; and Hirsch, **2**:77, 273-74, 275, 292, 338; and Ibn Ezra, **1**: 459; **2**:298; and Judah Halevi, **2**:107, 208, 278; and Luzzatto, **1**:107, 121, 454, 467; **2**:107, 116, 201n, 277, 279, 309; and Maimonides, **1**:459, 485n; **2**:208, 237n, 274, 275, 290, 298; and redemption, **2**:292; and women's status, **2**:129

J

Jewish people, the, **1**:364, 217, 218; **2**:2, 13-14, 110; and Chajes, **1**:377; **2**:15-20, 32-35, 75; and choice of Land of Israel, **1**:57-61; divine plan for, **2**:61-62, 332; excellence of, **2**:79, 80, 96, 101, 111-114, 121n; and Hirsch, **1**:412; **2**:41-42, 50-55, 75, 246, 252-53, 303; ingathering of, **1**:323n; and Judah Halevi, **2**:6, 79, 80, 121n, 236, 288; Luzzatto, **1**: 57; **2**:99-103, 111-14, 118-22, 282, 288, 308, 332, 343; and Maimonides, **1**:377; and Mendelssohn, **2**:5, 15, 78, 101; and the Middle Trend, **1**:8; **2**:2; and Revelation, **2**:78-81; and Reform, **1**:32; **2**:298, 322, 334; *See also* chosenness of the Jewish people; dual loyalty; Exile; mission, Jewish; Return to Zion

K

Kabbala, kabbalists, **1**:18, 19, 24, 26, 31, 33, 100, 201n67, 267, 350-51, 352-53, 494n; **2**:4, 149, 164n49, 315; and Chajes, **1**:18, 365; **2**:293, 312; and Essenes and Christians, **2**:205, 291; and Hirsch, **1**:19, 20n20, 42, 83, 98, 257, 258, 268, 297, 395,

416n103; 2:56, 58, 73, 260, 293, 300, 314; and Luzzatto, 1:48, 52, 112, 123, 320, 323n, 324n, 454–55, 459, 460, 470, 487, 491, 496, 505; 2:293, 304, 307, 314, 343, 460; and Nachmanides, 1:163, 166, 167, 169; and Reform, 2:222; rejection of, 1:6, 30, 42, 460; 2:304, 314

Karaites, neo-Karaites, 1:57, 171, 176, 181, 186, 191, 191n45, 229n, 314, 323n, 325n, 326

Kuzari. See Judah Halevi in Index of Names

L

Land of Israel, 1:5, 189, 444, 494n; 2:14, 58, 209; and Chajes, 2: 12n11, 15–32, 36, 38, 126, 298; commandments connected to the, 1:305; 2:2, 59, 71–73, 74, 97, 232; and Hirsch, 2: 12n11, 38–43, 47–98, 125, 126, 303, 337, 342; and Judah Halevi, 2:56; and Luzzatto, 2:12n11, 99, 105–6, 112, 122–26, 127, 308, 343; and Maimonides, 2:57, 302–3; and Mendelssohn, 2:26, 38, 298, 302, 308; Nachmanides, 2:4, 56, 94; neutralization as place of return, 1:2, 31; 2:1–16, 25–32, 41–127, 71n95, 223, 298, 302; Return to Zion, 7. *See also* Redemption; Return to Zion; state: Jewish; Three Oaths, the; Zionism, Hovevei Zion

M

Maimonidean polemic, 1:17–18, 370–76. *See also* Revelation, at Sinai: and Maimonides and Maimonidean polemic

Marxism, 2:260

Maskilim. *See* Haskala, Maskilim

Messiah, Messianism, 1:2, 7, 32, 32, 177, 186, 189, 205, 323n249, 379; 2:1, 2, 5n2, 6, 7, 8, 15, 24, 27, 28, 29, 67n89, 72, 206, 207–8, 217; and Hirsch, 2:89–98, 248; and Luzzatto, 2:105, 113; Maimonides, 2:5n2, 6, 28, 208; Nachmanides, 2:7; and Reform, 2:30, 125, 222; and Zionism, 2:94. *See also* Christianity, Christians: and Jesus as messiah; Redemption; Return to Zion

mission, Jewish, 1:32, 42, 276, 298, 408, 513; 2:40n36, 126; and Chajes, 2:35–38, 235; and Hirsch, 1:86, 157n43, 298; 2:40, 44, 57, 78, 81n, 82–89, 240n, 338, 340, 342; and Judah Halevi, 2:93, 103, 113, 278; and Luzzatto, 1:8, 42, 56, 81n, 108–12, 114–16; 2:108–11, 116, 118–22, 121n, 278, 279, 282; 2:308, 343; and Maimonides, 2:6, 103; and Mendelssohn, 2:13, 78, 84n, 94, 102, 126; and Reform, 1:32; 2:78, 114, 222; and universalism, 2:79. *See also* chosenness of the Jewish people; Jewish people

Modern Orthodox, 1:13, 184, 325n, 427, 440; 2:130, 163n, 170, 178n63, 299, 315. *See also* Neo-Orthodox

modernity, modernism, 1:176, 229n, 262, 276, 325n, 344, 344n; 2:115, 126, 142, 195; accommodation to tradition, 1:2, 8, 13n9, 14n, 23, 25, 179, 345, 358, 359, 363, 393, 406n92, 412, 416, 439, 512; 2:139, 143, 153, 173n63, 178, 189n, 193, 199, 200, 294–95, 297, 310,

312; and Chajes, **1**:34; crisis in Jewish communities, **1**:3–6, 14n, 191, 274, 363; **2**:14, 238, 293; and Luzzatto, **2**:309; and women's status, **2**:130, 133–37, 143–44, 145, 152–53, 176–77, 178–80, 188–89, 198–99. *See also* post-modernism; Reform
monotheism, **1**:176; **2**:92, 103, 112, 113, 116, 118, 121, 178, 223, 224, 233, 234, 255, 277, 288; Christian, **2**:76, 206, 237n56, 243–44, 278, 288, 288n, 309; ethical, **1**:7, 32, 64, 174; **2**:6, 37, 78, 222, 298, 337; humanistic, **2**:222; and Islam, **2**:202n1, 244, 273, 274, 278, 309; and the Middle Trend, **2**:223; pure, **1**:90, 174; **2**:243; transcendental, **1**:101. *See also* Christianity, Christians; ethics; God; Islam; morality; religion
moral qualities. *See* virtues
moral will, freedom of. *See* free will
morality, **1**:9, 29, 32, 65, 204, 345, 349, 360, 386, 410, 423–24, 432; **2**:9, 96n, 198–99, 212, 223, 224, 257, 284, 297, 314, 315; bible as simple message of, **1**:60; and Chajes, **1**:154, 216–17, 374, 376–77, 385, 386; **2**:20, 25, 236, 244, 297; in education program, **1**:429; free-willed, **1**:415, 417; and Hirsch, **1**: 19, 89, 94n, 98, 100, 101, 103, 104, 198–99, 260n155, 300, 306, 340n278, 399, 401, 407, 420, 421, 423, 429, 432, 436, 437; **2**:46, 54, 57, 60, 76, 79, 85, 87, 157, 168, 177, 199, 212n, 239, 244, 246, 248, 250, 251, 252, 256, 258–59, 265–68, 270, 300, 303, 304, 314, 337, 339, 341, 343; and Hirsch, attack on approach of Reform to, **1**:19; and Hirsch, on Torah as ethical doctrine, **1**:100–102; and Hirsch, using Kant, **1**:94n; Judah Halevi, **1**:355; and Luzzatto, **1**:52, 302, 339, 385, 450, 459, 465, 468–69, 473, 477, 481, 484, 492, 509, 510n6; **2**:99, 116, 117, 122, 191–98, 283, 297, 304, 307, 314, 343; and Maimonides, **1**:26, 356; **2**:237n; and Mendelssohn, **1**:274, 283, 358, 377, 423; **2**:215; and mission of man, 395, 399, 420; and moral elevation, **1**:34; and moral philosophy, **1**:33; natural, **1**:33, 275, 284, 330–31, 332, 333, 345, 392, 405, 450, 509; **2**:191, 314; and non-Jewish world, **1**:435; and objectives of Judaism, **1**:421; and polemic over Maimonides, **1**:26, 356, 465; and prophets' universal, **1**:65, 66, 174, 176; and reason, **1**:209, 215–16, 271, 275, 286, 294–94, 336, 345, 350, 362, 392; and Reform, **1**:19, 174; and the situation of the Jews, **1**:209–16; of the Torah, **1**:179; training in, **1**:434, 436; universal, **1**:174, 275, 358; and women, **2**:159, 177, 191
mysticism. *See* Kabbala, kabbalists

N

Neo-Fundamentalism. *See* Fundamentalism
Neo-Orthodoxy, **1**:4, 6, 14n, 90, 94n, 325n, 393, 423n; **2**:299, 311; and biblical criticism, **1**:64; and Chajes, **1**:38, 367n; conceptual world of, **1**:8–10; and dialectical tension, **1**:12; and emancipation, **1**:41, 45; estab-

lishment of, **1**:8; and Hirsch, **1**:12–13, 43; and Middle Trend, **1**:8–9, 43; and Orthodoxy, 227n117; and Reform, **1**:45, 178, 228n; and secularization, **1**:228n, 278n; and Wissenschaft des Judentums, **1**:362. *See also* Orthodoxy, Ultra-Orthodoxy; Orthoprax

Neo-Romanticism (post-Maskilic), **1**:42, 454, 455n165, 458n, 461, 462. *See also* Romanticism

Non-Jews and humanity, **1**:23, 25, 31, 345, 389; **2**:210–13, 214–15, 220–22; and Chajes, **1**:217, 218, 219, 377, 385–86; **2**:16–17, 20–32, 37, 126, 146, 224–238, 241; and Enlightenment, **1**:65, 224; and Hirsch, **1**:156n43, 179, 292, 425; **2**:21n23, 38–43, 45, 76, 77, 79–81, 82, 84, 95, 86, 87, 89, 92, 98, 112, 126, 156n, 239, 240–44, 279, 285n127, 291, 337; and Judah Halevi, **2**:79, 80, 107, 233, 238, 239, 303; Luzzatto, **1**:218, 219, 328, 340, 493; **2**:21n23, 99–103, 107, 111–112, 117, 119–21, 126, 279, 283–91; and Maimonides, **1**:218–20, 327, 340, 377, 402, 463; **2**:21, 22, 34, 49, 80, 100, 101, 215n29, 226, 231, 232, 233, 234, 238, 239, 241n61, 283, 285, 288; and Mendelssohn, **1**:377–78, 508; **2**:12–13, 34, 213–14, 238, 285n127; and progress, **1**:9, 31–32, 44, 278, 331, 345, 405, 409, 417, 418; **2**:35, 37, 75–78, 87, 93, 94, 99, 103, 108, 109–10, 116, 117, 120, 122, 126, 127, 233, 238, 239, 242, 246, 252, 289, 291, 308, 343; and Reform, **1**:174. *See also* Christianity, Christians; dual loyalty; hatred and persecution of Jews; Islam; Redemption: universalist

norm, Halakhic, **1**:170

norms, **1**:358, 376; **2**:31, 219; **2**:283–87, 288, 316; ethical, **1**:285, 286–87, 290, 336, 392, 489; **2**:98, 254, 279, 286–87, 300, 314; moral, **1**:275; social, **1**:232; and status of women, **2**:130. *See also* ethics; morals

O

Oral Law, **1**:24, 26, 57, 66, 149n, 158–61, 169–72, 209, 267, 322n, 351, 364n, 506; **2**:212, 291; and Chajes, **1**:25, 37, 69, 71, 74–79, 154, 155, 179–80, 186, 189, 192–205, 367, 372–83, 392; **2**:17, 20, 27, 142, 147–48, 238, 284n, 296, 297, 311, 336; and Chajes, and Aggadah, **1**:17, 25, 28n, 32, 205–6, 267, 328, 366, 374–75, 376, 378–79; **2**:32, 147, 296, 301; and Chajes, and status of, **1**:68; Frankel, **1**:178, 230, 246–51; ibn Daud, **1**:159–60; and Graetz, **1**:230–46; and Haskala education, **1**:359, 360; and Hildesheimer and Hoffmann, **1**:91n; and Hirsch, **1**:11, 26, 42, 82, 85, 96, 98–99, 102, 104, 154–55, 179, 227–64, 311, 342, 420, 424, 429, 442, 508, 511; **2**:155, 157, 162, 164–71, 172, 174, 243, 284n, 311, 342; and Hirsch, and Aggadah, **1**:25, 103, 260n, 265–73, 328, 419, 422–23; **2**:165, 301; and historical-positivists, **1**:177–79, 230, 442; **2**:14; and Krochmal, **1**:15–16, 199–200, 208, 232–33, 328, 508; and Luzzatto, **1**:21, 25, 56, 105, 118–20, 123, 126, 146, 154, 156, 179, 187n, 307, 311, 313–28,

332, 335, 342–43, 463, 467, 499, 507; 2:123, 179, 187, 188, 190, 191, 192, 200, 283–90, 306, 309, 311, 323; and Luzzatto, and Aggadic Midrash, 1:327–28, 507–8; 2:187; and Luzzatto, attitude to, 2:102, 105, 146, 187, 188–89, 200, 307, 311, 314–26, 305–6, 309, 311, 342–43, 509; and Maimonides, 1:17, 160–64, 165, 166, 168n, 171–72, 195–96, 229n, 236n, 252, 255, 326n, 327, 366, 368, 373–76, 454; 2:145; and Mendelssohn, 1:75, 509, 511; 2:10; and Nachmanides, 1:163–69, 195, 236; and radical Maskilim and Reform Jews, 1:4, 11, 173–77; and Spinoza, 1:60. *See also* Halakha; hermeneutic principles, the thirteen; philosophy: inference; Sages; Written Torah/Law

Original Sin, 1:283, 287, 296; 2:97, 204; and Christianity, 2:128, 209, 216, 255–56, 264, 267, 268, 275, 303; Hirsch on, 2:161–62, 161n48, 249–53, 263, 268–69, 291; *See also* determinism

Orthodox, Modern. *See* Modern Orthodox

Orthodoxy, Ultra-Orthodoxy (Haredim), 1:4, 6, 12, 13n10, 14n, 23, 171n, 181n26, 191, 266n, 325n, 423n; 2:167n53, 198, 315, 318; and biblical criticism, 1:64, 232; central, 1:14n; and Chajes, 1:18, 36, 79, 179, 182, 205, 209, 216, 342, 365, 368; 2:148, 151, 224, 294, 334; and circumcision dispute, 1:312; and the Conservative movement, 1:177n; and education, 1:427; and equal rights in Germany, 1:41; and the Haskala, 1:362, 364n24; 2:219, 335; and Hirsch, 1:97, 248, 268–69, 278n, 325n, 342, 416, 463; 2:163n, 299; and Hirsch and communities right to organization, 2:239; and Hirsch's attitude to evolution, 1:422n113; and Hirsch's criticism of extremist, 1:19, 21, 45, 86, 90, 104, 179; and Hirsch's rejection of Hasidism, 1:268, 395; and Luzzatto, 1:106, 107, 145, 179, 308, 316n245, 317, 320, 325n, 462, 463, 474n, 491; 2:294, 304; and Luzzatto against Hasidism, 1:455n165; and Mendelssohn, 1:364; 2:219; and the Middle Way, 1:5, 13, 179, 183; 2:223; modern development and meaning of, 1:15n; as modern phenomenon, 1:13n10; reaction to Haskala and Reform, 1:13n10; and Reform, 1:7–8, 41–45, 175–76, 177–78, 181–82, 222–29, 361; 2:25, 138, 223, 277n, 298, 299; and Revelation, 1:266n, 267, 325n, 352; and sequestration, 1:41; and status of women, 2:170, 173n63; and traditional Judaism, 1:2, 14; and women's religiosity, 2:135. *See also* fundamentalism; Hasidism; Neo-Orthodoxy

Orthoprax, 1:325n. *See also* Neo-Orthodoxy

P

pantheism, panentheism, 1:26, 61, 125n96, 145, 197n60, 284, 296, 320n246, 335, 470, 471n180, 473, 491; 2:260

particularism, 1:31, 40, 66, 220, 362; 2:2, 42, 103. *See also* universalism

Pharisees, **1**:61, 231; **2**:202, 204, 249, 257

philology, **1**:67, 79, 151, 243, 349, 361, 404–5; and biblical criticism, **1**:7, 21, 63, 90, 243; and Chajes, **2**:299, 336; and Haskala, **1**:346; and Hirsch, **1**:19, 21, 25, 83, 85, 90, 155, 243, 393, 405; **2**:299; and historical research, **1**:25, 67, 91, 154; **2**:299; and Luzzatto, **1**:105, 124, 25, 130, 145, 146, 147, 156, 502; **2**:306, 344; and Mendelssohn, **1**:84, 299, 404; **2**:239; and Middle Trend, **1**:154; **2**:294; and Reform, **1**:7, 173, 174; and Wissenschaft des Judentums, **1**:46

philosophy, **1**:9, 37, 160n3, 274, 353, 358, 360, 363, 364, 393; **2**:312; and Chajes, **1**:198n, 512; **2**:294, 297; and Chajes, and Spinoza, **1**:70; and Hirsch, **1**:28, 83, 84, 89, 90, 94n, 96, 100, 103, 104, 257, 269, 270, 275, 285, 296–302, 429, 437, 441; **2**:89, 178, 239, 260, 299, 302, 314, 337, 393, 399, 403, 416–17; and inference, **1**:147, 162, 164, 166, 170, 200, 201n67, 235, 240, 248, 383, 398, 416, **2**:321, 322; Jewish, **1**:24, 25, 33, 52, 274, 310; and Judah Halevi, **1**:355; and Krochmal, **1**:371n; and Luzzatto, **1**:28, 52, 56, 106, 108–9, 111, 117, 119, 136, 151, 153, 154, 310, 330–32, 335, 385, 447–60, 462, 470, 471n, 474–76, 500; **2**:305, 306, 314, 343; and Luzzatto, and the Atticists, **1**:116n, 118, 120, 125n96, 134, 190n44, 277, 302, 309, 310n238, 311, 324n, 331, 334–35, 456, 458, 464, 466–70, 475, 477, 483, 485, 501, 505, 511n; **2**:103, 116, 120, 196, 307; and Luzzatto, and Spinoza, **1**:53, 115; and Maimonides, **1**:347, 350, 352–53, 355–56, 369–83, 454, 485, 512; **2**:297, 306; materialist, **1**:21, 90, 104, 294, 296, 349, 419, 422n113; **2**: 255, 259–60, 292; and Mendelssohn, **1**:358, 365, 482n; neo-Platonic, **1**:33, 170, 170n16, 196, 274, 355, 494n; **2**:56; and polemic over Maimonides , **1**:217, 463–78; **2**:285n127; and religion, **1**:353, 354; romantic moral, **1**:174; and *"Torah mehashamayim"*, **1**:67n. *See also* determinism; dialectics in Middle Way thought; idealism; pantheism, panentheism; rationalism; reason

philosophy: Aristotelian, **1**:18, 25, 29, 119, 130n2, 142n57, 274, 310n238, 331, 334, 347, 370, 371, 372, 373, 374, 276, 407, 454, 463, 466, 485; **2**: 285, 296, 297, 306; and Chajes, **1**:194, 197, 200, 206n74; and Luzzatto, **1**:458; and Maharal, 163n; and Maimonides, **1**:162, 336, 355, 407; and Ralbag, **2**:130n2

philosophy: Hegelian, **1**:9, 16n11, 27, 28, 174, 198, 208, 296, 329, 361, 363, 365, 402, 485, 488, 494n, 508; **2**:78, 221, 239, 240n59, 257, 315, 332

philosophy: Kantian, **1**:9, 26, 27, 29, 33, 94n, 174, 198, 208, 274, 275, 283, 284, 295, 331, 338, 345, 353–54, 363, 365, 398, 485; **2**:13, 75, 79, 135, 221, 239, 251n, 257, 260, 301, 315

philosophy: of Spinoza, **1**: 73n26, 110, 145, 153, 171, 217, 284, 296, 320n246, 329, 334, 335, 338, 387, 402, 485, 490n;

2:53n58, 119, 122, 190n, 260, 306; and attitude to Jews of rationalist philosophers, 1:136, 174; and Bible criticism, 1:53–54, 62; and Christianity, 2:239; and Exodus from Egypt, 402; linked with Maimonides, 1:385; and Luzzatto, 1:134; and moral value of commandments, 1:297; polemic over, 470–73; and Revelation, 1:25; and search for truth, 1:352; use of Ibn Ezra by, 1:139–41

pluralism, 1:170, 346; 2:1, 220n33, 277, 317, 494n; 2:2; ethical, 1:347–49; values of, 1:346; 2:163n, 277

post-modernism, 1:345n2, 496; 2:130, 153, 163n, 170, 198, 220n33, 316; and Luzzatto, 1:480n191, 512; 2:126, 307; and Orthodoxy, 1:15n, 325n; and pluralism, 1:170n15

prayer, 1:90, 149n131, 184, 187n, 309, 391, 424, 440, 479, 484; 2:27, 48, 49, 70, 106, 228, 262, 336; in German, 1:7, 44, 47, 186, 192n47, 391, 440, 447; 2:136; Hebrew, 1:187n, 365, 391, 444; 2:27; for Return to Zion, 2:398; translations of, 1:44, 52, 187n, 188; and women, 2:132, 148, 170, 173; *See also* Reform: prayer

progress. *See* non-Jews and humanity: progress

prophecy, prophets, 1:6, 7, 31, 62, 65, 66, 69, 164, 170, 353; 2:3, 36, 202, 207, 253; and Chajes, 1:72, 80, 201–2, 206, 213, 215, 374, 377–78, 380, 381–82; 2:21, 26, 27, 31, 142–44, 227, 235; as God's moral commandment, 1:339; and Hirsch, 1:270,

401–2, 424; 2:59, 83, 95, 156, 339; and the holy spirit (in Judaism), 1:78, 144n127, 164, 168n, 169, 171n, 196, 201n67; in Islam and Christianity, 2:202, 204–5, 233, 281; and Judah Halevi, 1:31, 170–71, 449; 2:3, 79, 81, 101; and Krochmal, 1:77, 78, 233, 382; and Luzzatto, 1:52, 53, 105, 106, 110, 111, 113, 116, 117, 120, 121, 122, 123, 124, 126, 132, 134, 135, 142–44, 144n127, 156, 303, 309, 310, 312, 452, 459, 463, 464, 475, 480, 484, 485, 502, 506; 2:99, 105, 106, 107, 108, 115, 119, 120, 125, 281, 282, 289, 290, 304, 307; and Maimonides, 1:161, 172, 347, 366, 374, 381, 382n50; 2:28; and Nachmanides, 1:31; and Reform, 1:32, 394; Spinoza's attitude to, 1:40, 60. *See also* ethics: and prophets

Protestants, 1:59. *See also* Christians

providence. *See* Divine Providence

Q

qualities, good. *See* virtues

R

rabbis, the. *See* Sages

rationalism, 1:5, 9, 26, 27–28, 31, 208, 280, 309, 324n, 342, 361, 364, 371n30, 453, 454; 2:210, 296; and Chajes, 1:37; 39, 201, 220, 365, 380, 382, 384, 392, 483–84, 392, 401, 463, 512; 2:126, 140, 295, 296; and Hirsch, 1:88–89, 94n, 394, 399–400, 402, 407, 463, 469; and Judah Halevi, 1:274; and Luzzatto, 48, 53, 56, 105n73, 106, 329, 407, 463, 469, 502, 512; 2:14, 103, 183, 210, 270,

278, 293, 295, 296, 297, 304, 306, 307, 308, 315; and Maimonides, 1:160–61, 172, 355, 487; 2:7, 141; and Mendelssohn, 1:274, 363, 407, 447; and Reform, 1:5; 2:222; religious, 1:352; universalistic, 1:4, 329, 336, 377; 2:8, 14, 15, 222, 294, 301. *See also* reason; science

reason, 1:4, 5, 9, 9n, 24, 26–30, 39; 2:293, 294, 317; and Chajes, 1:18–19, 29, 38, 207, 209, 212, 213, 214, 216, 220, 365–69, 377; 2:15, 33, 39, 126, 140, 293, 294, 296, 297, 312; and Haskala, 1:5, 345, 346, 358, 360, 508; and Hirsch, 1:8, 11, 29–30, 83, 94n, 97–98, 274–75, 280, 283, 285, 290, 293, 392–402, 404, 406n92, 299, 401–2, 423, 435, 511, 512; 2:75, 126, 262, 293, 299, 300, 301, 309, 313, 340; and Judah Halevi, 1:196, 404; and Kant, 1:26, 27, 33, 274, 283, 295, 353, 363, 476; and Krochmal, 1:16, 198–99; 2:332; and Luzzatto, 1:29–30, 106–8, 145, 153, 154, 314–26, 329, 334, 336, 447–49, 453–59, 462, 465, 471, 474–78, 480, 481, 482, 484, 489, 493, 496, 502, 508–9; 2:102, 110, 114, 116, 126, 182, 294, 297, 306, 309, 313; and Maimonides, 1:163, 196, 297–300, 347, 350, 356, 377, 382, 384; 2: 215n29, 297, 301; and Mendelssohn, 1:274, 283, 363, 364, 404, 405, 423, 462, 489; 2:8, 12, 13, 15, 39, 79, 102, 126, 214, 215, 216, 218, 219, 222; and Neo-Orthodoxy and the Middle Way, 1:8, 9, 23, 32, 403–4, 422n113, 499; 2:223; and Reform, 1:128, 129; 2:222, 269; and revelation, 1:8–9, 16, 26–30; and Spinoza, 1:61; and Wessely, 1:404. *See also* ethics: and reason; morality: and reason; rationalism; revelation, at Sinai: and reason; romanticism: and reason

Redemption, 1:8, 9, 11, 27, 28, 103, 179, 199, 209, 343, 506, 513; 2:2, 3, 39, 72, 73, 91–98, 104, 121; 125, 125n, 161, 208, 215, 240n, 255, 257, 268, 269, 272n114, 282, 292, 300; Chajes, 2:126, 322; Hirsch on, 2:76, 89–90, 126, 270, 275–76, 303, 338, 342; Luzzatto, 1:504; 2:121, 127; 2:104, 106–7, 108–9, 112, 124, 308, 343; of nations, 2:77; political, 2:3, 123; Reform Jews interpretation of, 1:7; and repentance and atonement, doctrine of, 2:249, 254; spiritualization of, 1:31, 346; 2:2, 15, 104, 124, 125n, 135, 275–76; particularist, 1:31, 506; 2:24, 27, 42, 76,107, 108, 220; universal, 1:4, 31, 487n; 2:15, 26, 36, 41, 48, 59–60, 70, 75 , 77, 87, 106, 108–9, 113, 123, 124, 292, 298, 301, 308, 322, 338, 342. *See also* Christianity, Christians: and Jesus as messiah; Land of Israel; Messiah

Reform movement, Reform Jews, 1:4, 6, 7, 13, 15n, 21, 23, 32, 36, 41, 50, 50n45, 185, 232, 253–54, 364, 365, 470; 2:2, 14, 56n66, 152, 154, 171, 209, 238, 242–43, 277n, 318; and assimilation, 1:41; and authorities, 1:40, 44, 45, 185, 189, 222, 224, 313; 2:14, 29–30, 223; and biblical criticism, 1:7, 63, 66; and Chajes, 1:36, 37, 71, 78n35, 79–82, 180–91, 183n32, 187n,

209-11, 213, 313, 369, 391; **2:**16, 29-30, 140, 147, 151, 224, 235, 296, 298; and Christianity, **2:**222-23; and circumcision, **1:**81, 176, 188, 312-13; and commandments, **1:**173, 174, 175, 176, 188-89; and dual loyalty, **2:**25, 29; in Eastern Europe, **1:**4; and education, **2:**136, 137, 138; extreme, **1:**7, 159, 173, 361; **2:**15; and Graetz, **2:**230-31, 254; and Halakhah, **2:**153, 163n49; and *Herev Mitsion*, **1:**43; and Hirsch, **1:**11, 19-20, 43, 83, 88,-89, 90, 99, 187n, 220-21, 254, 263n157, 266, 274, 276, 279, 290, 292, 297, 301, 303, 313, 394, 396, 416, 426, 442-43; **2:**62, 65, 78, 96, 97n139, 152, 153, 163n49 174, 189n, 199, 301; and Hirsch, opposition to, **1:**104; **2:**38, 45, 55-56; and Hirsch, and communities' struggle, **1:**222-29, 238, 299, 412, 414n101, 439; and Luzzatto, **1:**53, 64, 66, 113-15, 179, 187n, 218, 306-14, 329, 446, 454, 473; **2:**103, 114, 116, 125, 200, 277, 289, 306, 308; and marriage and weddings, **2:**137; and Mendelssohn, **1:**364; and the Middle Trend, **1:**12; **2:**223, 311; against Orthodoxy, **1:**41, 224-25; prayers, **1:**7, 173, 177, 188, 309; **2:**15, 29, 30, 121, 136-37, 138, 147-48, 186, 192n47, 222, 227; religious practice in, **1:**14n; and status of women, **2:**135-38, 199, 313; strengthening of, **1:**6; temple, **2:**136; and tradition, **1:**173-77; and Wissenschaft des Judentums, **1:**362. *See also* Society for the Culture and Science of the Jews, The

religion, **1:**9, 28, 34, 50, 274, 404; **2:**294; 318, 531; and Chajes, **1:**17-18, 181, 185, 190, 209, 366, 367, 376, 416; **2:**32, 234, 294; crisis of modernity, **1:**3-6, 361; and Hegel, **1:**9; and Hirsch and Neo-Orthodoxy, **1:**8, 10-11, 19-20, 89, 92-93, 96, 97, 221, 224-25, 250n138, 258, 273, 285, 393-94, 396, 400, 402-3, 404, 410-11, 412-22, 426-27, 433, 511; **2:**252, 255-56, 271, 273, 294; and historical-positivism, **1:**177; and Kant, **1:**9, 274; and Krochmal, **1:**15-16; and Luzzatto, **1:**122-23, 148, 151-53, 305, 226n, 330, 332, 334-35, 336, 338, 339-40, 460, 462-63, 479, 480, 482-86, 488-89; **2:**103, 110, 122, 127, 285, 294, 307, 308; Maimonides, **1:**348, 356, 369; and Mendelssohn, **1:**358; **2:**10, 13, 214-18; of reason, **1:**32, 507; and romaticism, **1:**27; 394; and science, **1:**351-57, 363; and Spinoza, **1:**59-60; and status of women, **2:**128-29. *See also* Christianity, Christians; deism; Divine Providence; faith; fundamentalism; monotheism; Revelation, at Sinai

religious consciousness. *See* faith
religious experience. *See* faith
Return to Zion, **2:**10, 26, 99, 142, 217; and Chajes, **2:**298; and Hirsch, **2:**38, 65, 72-74, 91-92, 97, 302; and Luzzatto, **2:**105, 106, 122, 123, 124, 125, 126, 127, 308, 343; and Mendelssohn, **2:**10-11; and the Middle Trend, **1:**32; and Reform Jews, **1:**7, 177, 186, 365; **2:**15, 222; and Reggio, **1:**323n

Revelation, at Sinai, **1:**4, 8, 9, 24, 26, 64, 67n, 94n, 149n, 150, 154, 167n11, 179, 195–96, 206, 243, 244, 281, 346; **2:**294, 311, 316; and Chajes, **1:**17, 29, 39, 71, 72, 74, 154, 155, 179, 192, 193, 197–98, 342–43, 365, 366, 376–83, 386, 401, 423, 512; **2:**15, 25, 32–35, 79, 102, 232, 294, 295, 296–97, 298, 310–11, 313; and Frankel, **1:**248, 249, 255; and Geonim, **1:**195; and Graetz, **1:**244; and Haskala education, **1:**360; and Hildesheimer, **1:**29; and Hirsch, **1:**8, 29, 77–78, 83, 93, 95, 102, 155, 179, 243, 252, 254, 259, 261, 264, 269, 283–84, 286, 293, 299, 311, 343, 344, 392–93, 400, 401, 403, 409, 412, 414, 419, 421, 423–24, 437, 442, 463, 512; **2:**75, 77, 78–81, 92, 102, 155, 163n, 164–65, 173n63, 241n61, 243, 244, 245, 270, 301, 310, 340, 342; and the historical-positivists, **1:**11, 178, 230; and Judah Halevi, **1:**31, 168n, 170; **2:**279, 311; and Krochmal, **1:**11, 16, 78, 200, 232, 233, 248, 320, 371n30; **2:**311, 332; and Luzzato, **1:**11, 26, 28, 29, 106, 123, 146, 148, 152, 154; 179, 217, 308, 309, 310, 311, 318, 319, 320, 332, 336, 343, 450, 451, 452, 458, 460, 461, 462, 463, 474, 475, 475n183, 479, 480, 483n, 488, 489, 491, 495, 496, 502, 509; **2:**98n140, 99, 101, 111, 122, 279, 293, 306, 311, 344; and Maimonides and Maimonidean polemic, **1:**26, 123, 160–62, 165, 166, 171–72, 182, 195–97, 217, 235n, 256n, 318, 326n, 355–56, 376, 381, 382, 396; **2:**80, 215n, 311; and Mendelssohn, **1:**5, 29, 96, 216, 347, 358, 364, 377–78, 403, 423; **2:**8, 215, 219, 278, 301; and the Middle Way, **1:**19, 23, 29; and Nachmanides, **1:**163–69, 195; **2:**279; radical Maskilim, **1:**17; and reason, **1:**8–9, 16, 26–30, 151, 152, 158–72, 192–205, 215–16, 258–73, 275, 314–326, 364, 376–83, 386–87, 392, 393, 400, 401–3, 409, 414, 437–38, 460, 461, 462–63, 478–82, 488, 496; **2:**15, 301, 307, 309, 313, 447, 511; Reform attitude to, **1:**7, 17, 394; **2:**289; and Spinoza, **1:**25, 351–52; and the Ultra-Orthodox, **1:**266n, 267, 285n, 352. *See also* prophecy, prophets

reward and punishment, **1:**26; and Chajes, **1:**205, 379; **2:**23, 235; and Hirsch, **1:**244, 253–54, 402; **2:**77, 86, 253, 254, 314–15; and Luzzatto, **1:**306, 338, 339, 455, 479, 492; **2:**115, 302, 306, 314–15, 321, 343; and Maimonides, **1:**491n

Romanticism, **1:**5, 26, 39, 41, 49n35, 363; **2:**14, 134, 152n39, 221, 224, 296; and Chajes, **1:**365, 392, 512; **2:**15, 190n44, 293, 295, 296; and Hirsch, **1:**29, 42, 342, 392, 393, 394, 463; **2:**38, 79, 126, 179n, 293, 299–300; idealistic, **2:**134, 274; and Luzzatto, **1:**29, 52, 56, 106, 301, 317n, 329, 342, 453, 455n165, 456, 458n, 461–62, 469, 489, 496, 508, 510n; **2:**99, 126, 189n, 277, 283, 293, 304; Mendelssohn, **2:**179n; particularist, **2:**14; and reason, **1:**29, 208; supernaturalism, **1:**173, 456, 458n, 511; transition from rationalism to,

1:5, 9; and Wessely, 1:361n20. *See also* Haskala: and counter-enlightenment; Idealism: Romantic; Neo-Romanticism

S

Sadducees, 1:126, 171, 176, 231, 315
Sages (the rabbis), 1:59-60, 102, 103, 155, 196, 204-5, 207, 212, 219, 234n, 238-39, 241, 242-43, 244, 245, 246n, 259, 266, 311, 311n241, 321, 375, 463; 2:129, 146, 230, 243, 262; and attitude to non-Jews, 1:218, 219, 220; 2:238; attitude to women, 2:129, 171, 187, 188-90 189n, 191, 199, 200; and Bible text, 1:192, 194, 241, 243, 326; 2:306; and central principle at basis of the Torah, 1:213-14; and Chajes, 1:182, 186, 189, 192-93, 194, 195, 196-97, 200-202, 206, 212, 213, 215, 389-90, 512; 2:18, 230, 238, 296, 332, 334, 336; and commandments, 1:188-91; disputes among, 1:195, 231, 239, 239n131, 240, 305, 322; and Frankel, 1:242, 246, 248, 249; 2:301; and Graetz, 1:230-31, 233, 235, 237, 239, 239n131, 242, 244; 2:301; and Hirsch, 1:237, 240, 242, 243, 244, 248-51, 259, 260n155, 262, 264, 267, 268-70, 273, 298, 420; 2:171, 188, 199, 243, 299-300; and Jost, 1:303, 311; and Krochmal, 1:197-98, 208, 234; and Luzzatto, 1:305, 311, 314-15, 315n244, 316, 317-19, 321, 323, 325, 326n251, 327-28, 343, 464, 468-69, 480, 492, 503-4, 505, 507; 2:106, 187-88, 190, 191, 200, 344; and Mendelssohn's Bible commentary, 1:405. *See also* Halakha; Oral Law; Pharisees

Samaritans, 1:110, 127, 171, 186
sanctity, 1:275, 278, 280, 283, 292, 294, 358, 360, 396, 410; 2:54-56, 101, 270-71, 272n114, 274, 294, 301, 314, 315, 339; of body, sensuality, and property, 1:103, 282, 288-89, 295-96; 2:157n43, 162n, 174, 178, 245, 255, 256, 273-74, 292; ethical, 1:33; 2:300, 301; of Hebrew, 1:113, 388, 441, 472; 2:27, 134; of humanity, 2:82; of the Jewish people, 1:340; 2:82, 100-101, 111; 278, 339, 344; of the Land of Israel, 1:31, 389; 2:3-4, 55-56, 58, 65n82, 68, 71, 303; and Maimonides, 69n92; of marriage, 2:175, 192; moral, 1:275, 279-80, 284, 288-89, 291-92, 295, 358, 392, 425, 431; 2:101, 157n43, 169, 259, 264, 268; of the nazirite in Judaism, 2:265, 266; of places and object, 2:56, 68; and purity, 2:258-59; of the Temple, 2:68-72; of the Torah, 1:62, 103, 126, 149n, 180, 252, 388; 2:24, 236. *See also* Bible: as divine text; biblical criticism; Oral Law; Written Law/Torah
science, 1:4, 33, 35, 37, 171, 346, 348, 352-53, 356, 357, 358, 359, 404; 2:294; 302, 310, 313, 334; achievements of, 1:4; Chajes, 1:37, 373, 383; 512; 2:294, 309, 334; and fundamentalism, 1:149, 150; and Hirsch, 1:10, 83-86, 97-100, 103, 279, 296, 299, 398, 405, 406, 409, 410, 411, 412-22, 426, 429, 434n134, 437, 443, 511, 512; 2:85, 173n63, 294, 301, 309, 313; and historical consciousness, 1:6; and Luzzatto, 1:112, 134, 135,

148, 329, 481, 488, 492–97, 500, 506; **2**:122, 127, 294, 307, 338, 309; and Maimonides, **1**:348, 350, 353; and the Middle Way, **1**:9; and Torah, **1**:351–357, 405. *See also* religion: and science; Wissenschaft des Judentums

secularization, **1**:4–5, 6, 6n3, 15n, 59, 65, 191, 278n, 344n, 346, 361, 363; **2**:1, 14, 119, 135, 144, 171, 187, 238, 294, 315, 318; and biblical criticism, **1**:59; pleasure from, 187n; sanctifying, **2**:157n43; and women, **2**:135

sensuality, **1**:94n, 103, 281–83, 285, 286, 287–88, 293–95, 296, 306, 331, 401, 408, 448, 451, 452, 477, 508; **2**:8, 95, 135, 144, 156, 157n, 263, 266, 270, 274–75, 276, 291, 294, 314; controlling, **1**:356, 392; **2**:301; culture in service of, **1**:436; forces of, **1**:29; hindering reason, **1**:435; **2**:79, 300, 306; overcoming, **1**:33, 424, 425; **2**:251, 264, 337; physical, **1**:33–34; **2**:156, 187n, 256; and Reform, **1**:226; sanctification of, **2**:78, 177n43, 162n; and women, **2**:134

separation, law of (Germany), **1**:41

seven principles for interpreting the Torah, Hillel's, **1**:231, 235, 237, 243, 245, 247, 320

socialism, **1**:104

Society for the Culture and Science of the Jews, The (Verein für die Cultur und die Wissenschaft der Juden), **1**:79, 361–62, 364; **2**:14. *See also* Wissenschaft des Judentums, Die

state, **1**:181, 287; **2**:14, 41, 42, 46–47, 48, 50, 75, 78, 79, 82, 83, 210, 246, 309, 318, 333; absolutist, **1**:3, 40; **2**:117; and civil law, **1**:285; and education to integrate into, **1**:428, 433; **2**:381; Hegelian, **1**:9, 27, 361; **2**:240n; Jewish, **1**:340; **2**:3, 11n10, 39, 40, 72, 85n, 86, 220, 272, 272n111, 272n114, 321; and Jews and Jewish community, **1**:7–8, 34, 40–41, 43, 52, 185, 222–25, 430; **2**:10, 17–20, 29–30, 83, 85n, 130, 206, 208, 210, 217, 223, 225, 229, 233, 234–35, 238, 241, 303; and religion, **1**:45, 285; **2**:12, 85, 86, 130, 136, 210, 217, 219, 220, 233, 271–72, 275; **2**:86; and women, **2**:136. *See also* civil rights; dual loyalty; emancipation; human rights

T

Talmud. *See* Oral Law

Temple (Jerusalem), **1**:77, 115 129, 167, 168, 444; **2**:26, 48, 67, 87, 203, 204, 263, 287; neutralization of, **2**:57, 68–72, 94; Reform attitude to, **1**:7, 32, 177, 189; **2**:15, 29, 30; and redemption, **1**:31; **2**:27, 298; spiritualization of, **2**:68, 71

Temple (Reform), **1**:7, 41, 45, 177, 186, 220, 225, 306, 447; **2**:15, 56, 136, 299; imitation of the church; **2**:138, 138n

thirty-two hermeneutic principles of Rabbi Eli'ezer, **1**:206

Three Oaths, the, **2**:4, 5, 11–12, 11n11, 23, 25–26, 48, 49, 74, 92, 105, 106, 122, 124, 298, 302. *See also* Land of Israel; Redemption

Torah and Derekh Erets, **1**:20n20, 43, 227n117, 430n127, 431, 434n134, 439, 440; **2**:173n63. *See also* Hirsch, Samson Raphael

in Index of Names
Torah min Hashamayim ("Torah from Heaven"), **1:**4, 13n, 67n; **2:**298; and Chajes, **1:**78, 79, 104, 179, 180, 200, 204; **2:**36, 231, 235; and Hirsch, **2:**38, 300, 301, 311; and the historical-positivists, **1:**178; and Luzzatto, **1:**94n, 106, 112, 126, 136, 144, 148, 322n, 504; **2:**129-131; 289, 304, 343. *See also* Revelation, at Sinai
tradition, traditionalism, **1:**4, 9-11, 14n, 62, 155, 358, 363, 439-40; **2:**310-11; and central rabbinical trend, **1:**159-60; and Chajes, **1:**368, 372, 373, 512; **2:**298, 336; combined with general culture, **1:**341, 346, 358-61; and crisis of the Talmud, **1:**66; and Haskala, **1:**345-46; and Hirsch, **1:**32, 227, 265, 278, 300, 406n92, 420, 439, 445, 446; **2:**96, 97, 155, 164, 166, 178-81, 254, 299, 303; and innovation in Halakhah, **1:**158, 179, 245, 246n, 345; and Jewish nation, **2:**118; and Judah Halevi, **1:**170; and Luzzatto, **1:**50, 52-53, 117, 118, 144-49, 154, 156, 157, 318, 321, 457, 474-75; **2:**118, 284, 343, 344; and Maimonides, **1:**26, 160, 167n11; and Mendelssohn, **1:**404; and modernity, **1:**25; post-biblical, **1:**149n; and Reform, **1:**159; **2:**135; and science, **1:**351-52; from Sinai, **1:**162; and source of Halakha, **1:**167n11; and thinkers of the middle trend, **1:**32; **2:**312; and Ultra-Orthodox, 266n; and women, **2:**129, 135. *See also* modernity: accommodation to tradition; Orthodoxy
traits, **1:**209, 464

translations, ancient Bible, **1:**72, 75, 113, 117, 119, 121, 127-28, 505; **2:**336
trends in Judaism, creation of new, **1:**6-13

U

universalism, **1:**27, 31, 346, 363, 365; **2:**8, 14, 133; and Chajes, **1:**220, 386; **2:**15, 20-25, 33, 34, 35, 142-43, 146, 312; and Haskala, **1:**274, 346, 508; **2:**14, 15, 96, 133, 224; and Hirsch, **1:**104, 275, 409-10; **2:**38-40, 67, 79, 87, 95, 96, 98, 301, 303, 312, 319; and idealism, **1:**174; and Luzzatto, **1:**329, 340, 508; **2:**98n140, 99-103, 113, 116, 277, 291, 304, 312, 319; and Maimonides, **2:**21; and Mendelssohn, **2:**215, 219, 222; and the Middle Way, **2:**2, 293, 312, 319; and Reform, **1:**174, 209, 365; **2:**2, 15; and secular studies, **2:**312. *See also* humanism; non-Jews and humanity; particularism; rationalism: universalistic; Redemption: particularist; Redemption: universalist

V

virtues and attributes, **1:**183n32, 215, 217, 219, 330, 333, 334, 336-37, 338, 356n; **2:**115, 131, 212, 212n, 231, 235, 235, 273, 314. *See also* ethics; morality

W

Wissenschaft des Judentums, Die (Jewish science), 21, 64, 232, 255-56, 362, 364; and Chajes, **1:**70, 71, 77, 187n, 387; **2:**297; and Galician Maskilim, **1:**79; and Hirsch, **1:**10, 46n, 85,

88–89, 90–91, 361–62, 427–28, 442–47; **2**:301; and Luzzatto, **1**:304–5, 309, 314, 320, 502–7; **2**:104, 304

women, status of women, **1**:104, 128–200, 316, 317; **2**:159, 313–34; and Chajes, **2**:138–52, 175, 181, 191, 193, 198, 298, 313; **2**:142–45; in Christianity, **2**:128, 129; education of, **1**:351, 429; **2**:132, 133, 134–35, 136, 137, 138, 139, 145–46, 164n49, 167, 171–75, 194, 199, 200, 314; and equality, **1**:104; feminism, 131, 167n53, 198; and Halakha, **2**:44n, 128–32; and Haskala, **1**:133–35, 143–44; and Hirsch, **1**:272; **2**:132, 134, 153–81, 188, 189n, 193, 199, 263n98, 303, 313; **2**:154–66, 163n, 174; and Luzzatto, **2**:182–98, 200, 308, 313–14; Maimonides and education of, **2**:145, 187; and Mendelssohn, 179n73, 187n; and the middle trend, **2**:132, 147–52, 176; the Orthodox attitude to, **2**:138–39; and prayers and worship, **2**:136, 137, 137n18, 186, 307; and Reform, **2**:132, 135–38, 152, 154; response to attitude toward, **2**:135; Torah study by, **2**:146, 199, 200

Written Torah/Law, **1**:12, 24, 26, 30, 33–34, 66, 149n, 154, 158–59, 171, 322n, 348, 354; **2**: 212; and Chajes, **1**:68–69, 71, 72, 74–75, 154, 155, 157, 180, 182, 188, 190, 192, 193, 194–97, 202–3, 205, 311, 342, 366, 368, 372, 374, 376–83, 391; **2**:17–18, 20, 21, 37, 47, 48, 49, 57, 79, 142, 146, 147, 232, 236, 296, 311, 336; and Frankel, **1**:230; and Hildesheimer and Hoffmann, **1**:91n; and Hirsch, **1**:11, 82–91, 93, 98–99, 102–4, 155, 157, 227, 236, 251, 261–64, 279, 342, 395, 404, 405, 406, 410, 412, 419, 421, 422–23, 424, 428, 429, 435–37, 442, 511; **2**:39, 52, 55, 59, 62, 68, 75, 82, 83, 86, 87, 89, 94, 97, 98, 154, 155, 160, 161, 166, 168, 172, 173n, 199, 243, 245, 247, 270, 291, 292, 297, 299, 300–1, 314, 319, 322, 336, 337, 339, 342; and historical-positivists, **1**:178; and ibn Daud, **1**:159; and Krochmal, **1**:78, 232–33; and Luzzatto, **1**:21, 104–5, 110, 112–13, 118, 121–31, 133–44, 146–48, 152–53, 154, 156, 303, 318, 319, 324, 327, 336–42, 467, 469, 480–81, 483–86, 488–89, 492–93, 499, 504; **2**:111–12, 113–14, 115, 116, 123, 186–187, 188, 189n, 190, 191, 196n, 200, 279, 284, 286, 288, 304, 307, 309, 342, 343; and Maimonides, **1**:160–61, 165, 204, 336, 353, 374; **2**:145, 237n; and Mendelssohn, **1**:405; **2**:38–39; **2**:216, 218, 220; and Reform, **1**:7, 173–74, 175, 470; **2**:14, 270; and Spinoza, **1**:60. *See also* Bible: as divine text; Biblical Revolution, influence of; Revelation, at Sinai; translations, ancient Bible

W

Zion. *See* Land of Israel
Zionism, Hovevei Zion, **2**:16, 28n26, 48, 72–74, 94, 98, 125–26. *See also* Land of Israel

INDEX OF NAMES

A

'Amir, Y., **1**:406n92
'Arama, Isaac, **1**:449; **2**:129
Abahu, **1**:242
Abarbanel, Isaac, **1**:448, 466, **2**:227
Abraham, **1**:81, 96, 270, 312, 336, 337n269, 509; **2**:13, 33, 58, 60, 61, 91, 97, 101, 102-3, 108, 111, 115, 202n1, 246, 251, 275, 278, 288, 321, 342, 343
Abraham ben David of Posquières (Rabad), **1**:202n67, 326; **2**:129
Abraham ibn Daud (Rabad), **1**:159, 274, 403
Abulafia, Joseph, **1**:371
Adler, Nathan, **1**:201n67, 267
Akiva, **1**:231, 240-41, 242, 245, 246, 246n, 253, 364n; **2**:21n22, 142
Alashkar, Moses ben Isaac (Maharam), **1**:386; **2**:149
Albalag, Isaac, **1**:348, 355n14, 375
Albo, Joseph (*Sefer Ha'iqarim*), **1**:171, 173n18, 196n57, 449; **2**:140
Alfakhar, Judah, **1**:371
Alfasi, Isaac (Rif), **2**:197
Alḥarizi, Judah, **1**:129n
Alkalai, Judah, **2**:16
Almeda, Joseph, **2**:123
Apion, **2**:227
Artom, M. E., **2**:98n140, 123-24, 124n171, 149n104
Aristotle. *See* philosophy: Aristotelian in Index of Subjects
Ascher, Saul, **1**:173
Asher ben Jehiel, **1**:247, 250, 255; **2**:149, 226
Ashi, **1**:322, 327, 328, 367, 370, 464
Astruc, Jean, **1**:61
Auerbach, Menachem Mendel (*'Ateret Zqenim*), **2**:149
Augustine, **2**:205
Averroes. *See* ibn Rushd
Avicenna, **1**:355
Avtalion, **1**:238

Ayyash, Judah (*Shevet Yehuda*),
    1:338; 2:333
Azariah Dei Rossi, 1:49n45, 76, 348;
    2:336
Azriel (Rabbi), 2:4
Azulai, Ḥayyim Joseph David,
    2:158, 158n44

B

Bachrach, Yair (*Shut Ḥavot Yair*),
    1:248; 2:148
Baḥya ben Asher, 2:129n
Baḥya ibn Paquda, 1:367; 449, 484;
    2:129
Balaban, M., 1:192n47, 387n57
Bamberger, Jacob Koppel, 1:187n,
    439
Bamberger, Seligman Baer (Isaac
    Dov), 1:20n20, 45, 223, 226,
    227n117, 229, 230n118, 412
Bardash, Abraham, 1:498
Baron, S., 1: 461; 2:105n149
Barr, James, 1:149, 149n, 150,
    151-52, 154, 375, 420, 511
Bartel, Israel, 1:344n
Baruch, Joshua Boaz (*Shiltei
    Hagiborim*), 2:149
Barzilay, I., 1:255
Baumgarten, Elisheva, 2:129n
Beer, Bernard, 1:96-97
Beer, Jacob Herz, 2:136
Ben Amozegh, Elijah, 1:50, 261,
    455n165; 2:253n83, 263n98
Ben Azai, 2:21n22, 142
Ben Israel, Menasseh, 2:217, 230
ben Saruq, Menahem, 1:56
Ben Shalom, R., 2:208n
Ben Zeev, Judah Leib, 1:141,
    144n127, 499
Benayahu, M., 1:78n35, 187n
Benet, Naftali, 1:364n24
Ben Shalom, R., 208n16
Ben-Shalom, Ysrael, 1:244

Bentham, Jeremy, 1:4
Bergman, Shmuel Hugo, 1:357,
    471n180, 495
Berkovitz, Dov, 2:318
Berlin, Isaiah, 1:462
Berlin, Saul, 1:173
Bernays, Isaac, 1:8, 42, 42n39, 43,
    274, 402; 2:84n, 299
Bismarck, Otto von, 1:45
Blumenfeld, Dov Ber, 1:305
Blumenfeld, Ignaz (Isaac), 1:113,
    490; 2:195
Blumenfeld, Issachar, 1:501
Bodek, Jacob, 1:19, 198n62
Bonfil, Reuven, 1:49n45
Bonfils, Joseph Ben Samuel, 2:336
Bonnet, Charles, 2:214
Brecher, Gedalia, 1:468
Breuer, E., 1:64n7
Breuer, Isaac, 1:94n, 438n139;
    2:94, 96
Breuer, Joseph, 1:414n102
Breuer, Mordechai, 1:47n41, 228n,
    266n60, 267, 325n, 422n113,
    428; 2:74n99, 81, 94, 132,
    138n22, 163n49, 240n, 246n70,
    247n72, 276n118
Bronznick, N. M., 1:228n

C

Cassirer, S., 1:167n11
Cassutto, M. D., 1:61n6; 2:309,
    315-16
Chajes, Meir, 1:36
Chajes, Zvi Hirsch: and Ḥatam
    Sofer, 1:38, 183; 2:149, 151;
    and Judah Halevi, 1:367; 2:25,
    37, 66n84, 236; and Krochmal,
    1:36, 37, 77n33, 197-200, 208,
    365, 371n30, 382, 382n50, 383,
    387; 2:296, 310, 332, 335; and
    Maimonides, 1:17, 18, 37, 39,
    69, 73, 74, 76n32, 78n35, 79,

181, 182, 189–90, 192–208, 211, 212–13, 215, 216–20, 342, 366–87, 392, 512; **2**:16, 21, 22, 24, 25, 28, 33, 34, 27, 140, 141, 145, 226, 231, 232, 233, 236, 291, 295, 296, 311, 333; and Mendelssohn, **1**:37, 183, 209, 212–13, 215, 220, 379, 383, 387; **2**:15, 17, 26, 28, 34, 35, 126, 232, 297, 298; and Nachmanides, **1**:375; **2**:232
Chajes, Zwi Perez, **1**:39
Charif, Zvi Hirsch, **1**:37
Chertok, S., **2**:152n39, 154n40, 156n43, 157n44, 158n, 164n49, 179n, 189n87, 240n, 321n1, 322n2, 323n
Chorin, Aaron, **1**:21, 173, 305–6; **2**:125, 136
Cohen, Abraham Albert, **2**:123
Cohen, Hermann, **2**:272n114, 309, 315
Cohen, Moses Chaim, **1**:499
Cohen, Moses Leib, **1**:263n158
Cohen, Raphel, **1**:180n26
Cohen, Tova, **2**:133, 135, 139, 152, 181
Condillac, Étienne, **1**:52; 471n180
Copernicus, **1**:100, 419, 421, 422n113, 453, 495
Coronel, Naḥman Nathan, **2**:124
Costantini, David, **1**:309; **2**:110
Crémieux, Adolphe, **1**:229n; **2**:24, 73
Crescas, Ḥasdai, **1**:490n, 510n

D

Daniel, **2**:246
Darwin, Charles, **1**:422
David (king), **2**:246
Davis, Moshe, **1**:177n
De Rossi, Giovanni Bernardo, **1**:128

de Wette, Wilhelm Martin Leberecht, **1**:62–63, 129, 130, 303
Deborah, **2**:148, 173
Delitzsch, Franz, **2**:283
Delmedigo, Elijah, **1**:353, 354n, 357, 427, 487; **2**:307
Delmedigo, Joseph Solomon (Yashar of Candia), **1**:422n113, 487
Disraeli, Benjamin, **2**:73
Dohm, Christian, **2**:9, 216–217, 218
Duran, Ben Tsemah Duran, **2**:213, 290
Duran-Efodi, Isaac, **1**:348

E

Eichel, Isaac, **1**:499, **2**:213
Eichenbaum, Jacob, **1**:116n85
Eichhorn, Johann Gottfried, **1**:61–62, 138, 506; **2**:104
Eiger, Akiba, **1**:364n24
Eilenburg, Issachar Ber (*Beer Sheva'*), **2**:149
Einhorn, David, **2**:136–37
Eisenmenger, Johann Andreas, **2**:220–21, 228
El'azar Ba'al Haroqeah of Worms, **2**:225
El'azar ben 'Azaria, **1**:242
Elbaum, J., **2**:166n52
Eliade, Mircea, **2**:51n56
Eliav, M., **1**: **2**:173n62
Eli'ezer, the son of Yosei Hagalili, **1**:206
Eli'ezer Ben Horkenos, **1**:165, 239–40, 239n131, 245, 249, 250, 253, 374–75, 412–13; **2**:134, 145, 146, 194
Eliezer ben Joel Halevi, **2**:149
Elijah, **1**:45, 46, 46n, 55
Elior, Rachel, **2**:131
Ellenson, D., **1**:95n62, 184n33, 228n117, 229n118, 248n135,

275n166, 278n172
Elon, Menachem, 2:130, 170
Emden, Jacob, 1:180n26, 349, 387, 388, 389; 2:5, 75, 215n, 237n, 285n217, 332; and Chajes, 1:388, 389n; 2:232, 298, 333, 334; and Christianity, 2:210-13, 212n23, 238, 246n70, 290; and Hirsch, 2:241n61, 244, 245; and Mendelssohn, 1:348; on non-Jews, 2:77
Endelman, Todd, 1:344n1
Ephrati, L., 1:476
Epstein, Baruch Halevi (*Torah Tmima*), 2:190n88
Eran, M, 1:61n6
Esau, 1:440n; 2:203; 287
Ettlinger, Jakob, 1:8, 42, 191n45; 2:299
Euchel, Isaac, 1:499
Eve, 2:166
Eybeschutz, Jonathan, 2:4
Ezra (Rabbi), 2:4
Ezra the Scribe, 1:69, 105, 126, 127, 140, 314, 318; and biblical criticism, 1:60, 70, 80, 81, 232; time of, 1:72, 78, 233

F

Farabi, al-, 1:355
Feiner, Shmuel, 1:5, 6n, 22n, 79, 325n, 344n; 2:133n8, 135, 139, 152, 181, 213-14, 215n, 217
Ferdinand (emperor), 2:24, 234
Ferdinand (prince, Braunschweig), 2:216
Fichte, Johann Gottlieb, 2:315
Fischer, Gottlieb, 1:249, 250
Fish, M., 1:246n
Fleckeles, Elazar, 1:180n26; 2:77, 244
Flusser, David, 2:204n, 205
Formstecher, 2:116, 240n
Frankel, David, 1:348

Frankel, M., 1:49n45
Frankel, Zacharias, 1:11, 13n9, 76, 90n, 96-99, 144, 178, 191, 230, 231, 246-57, 242, 243, 244, 304n, 311, 316n, 323n, 326, 362, 387, 502, 503-4; 2:196, 301, 311
Frenkel, Abraham Zeev Wolf, 1:37
Freudenberg, Gideon, 2:202
Friedländer, David, 1:18n15, 173, 186, 303; 2:14, 147, 213, 222
Friedman, M., 2:167n53
Friedrich Wilhelm III, 1:41
Fünn, Samuel Joseph, 1:22n
Fuerst, Julius, 1:70n20, 76, 76n30

G

Gafni, Yeshayahu, 1:244
Galante, Abraham, 2:4
Gamliel, Rabban, 1:239; 2:211
Gans, David, 1:422n113
Gans, Eduard, 1:361
Gasparin, 2:228
Gattinara, Joseph Judah, 316n
Geddes, Alexander, 1:62, 70
Geiger, Abraham, 1:7, 46n41, 70, 78n35, 86n, 87n50, 113-14, 141n125, 145, 173, 174, 254, 309, 311, 317n, 322, 327, 362, 502, 504; 2: 97n39, 116, 125, 125n173, 136, 154n40, 196, 196n93, 240n, 245n; and religious equality between the sexes, 2:136
Gershom Meor Hagola, 2:129n, 169
Gertner, Ḥaim, 2:336
Gesenius, Heinrich Friedrich Wilhelm, 115, 117n, 127, 139, 141, 143, 144, 145, 153n144
Ghazali, al-, 355
Gilat, Yitzhak Dov, 1:244
Ginzburg, Arieh Leib, 2:146
Girondi, Mordecai Samuel, 1:187n
Glicksberg, S., 1:167n11

Goethe, Johann Wolfgang von, **1**:62, 506; **2**:173
Goitein, Menachem, **1**:283n
Goldenberg, Samuel Judah, **1**:55, 497
Goldenberg, Samuel Leib, **1**:130, 371n30, 467, 470n180
Goldenberg, Zvi Hirsch, 50, 302, 307
Goldman, Eliezer, **1**:481n
Goldziher, Ignác, **2**:201
Gombiner, Abraham Abele Halevi (*Magen Avraham*), **2**:149
Goodmann, Micah, **1**:356n; **2**:237n, 318
Gottlieb, L., **2**:213n23
Graetz, Heinrich, **1**:11, 13n9, 22n23, 49n45, 70, 97n65, 99, 191, 230–46, 248, 250n139, 254, 311, 320, 322n, 326, 362, 502, 503–4; **2**:125n, 301, 311
Graf, Karl Heinrich, **1**:63
Grossman, Abraham, **2**:129, 129n
Guggenheim, Frumet, **2**:179n73
Guttmann, Julius, **1**:355, 354n, 356, 356n, 471n180

H

Hacohen [de la Torre], Hillel, **2**:290n
Hacohen, Joseph, **1**:389
Hacohen, R., **1**:64n7
Hacohen, Y., of Lunel, 372
Hagar, 178, 233, 273–75
Hagiz, Moses, **1**:180n26
Halberstam, Shlomo Zalman Chayyim (ShaZHaH), **1**:478; **2**:121n167
Halbertal, Moshe, **1**:158n, 160n3, 162n5, 164n10, 167n11–12, 491n
Halevi, Eliezer, **1**:306
Hanau, Solomon Zalman, **1**:499
Hannah, **2**:173, 246
Harris, J. M., **1**:159n1, 167n11, 175n20, 197n60, 231, 234n123, 256n, 260, 260n155
Hartman, David, **1**:481n; **2**:220n33
Harvey, W. Z., **2**:11n10
Ḥatam Sofer. *See* Sofer, Moses
Ḥayim ben Betsalel, **2**:84n
Hegel, Wilhelm Friedrich. *See* Philosophy: Hegelian in Index of Subjects
Heilprin, Jehiel, **2**:336
Heine, Heinrich, **1**:361; **2**:53n58
Heinemann, I., **2**:66n83
Heller, Zanvil, **1**:37
Herder, Johann Gottfried von, **1**:62, 139, 198, 462
Hershkovitz, M., **1**:70nn17, 20, 78n35, 183n32
Herz, Elkan, **2**:216n30
Herzl, Theodore, **2**:94
Heschel, Abraham Joshua, **1**:244
Hildesheimer, Ezriel, **1**:8, 22n23, 25, 29, 64, 91n, 229n, 241n, 362, 404, 405, 406n9
Hilkiah, **1**:129–30
Hillel, **1**:231, 235, 237, 240, 242, 253, 485; disciples of, **1**:159, 163, 239, 240; disputes with Shammai, **1**:231, 235, 237–38, 303–4; and hermeneutic principles, **1**:231, 235, 237, 238, 243, 245, 247, 320
Hillel ben Samuel, **1**:348
Hillel of Verona, **1**:348
Hirsch, Raphael, **1**:40
Hirsch, S., **2**:116, 240n
Hirsch, Samson Raphael, **1**:2, 3, 8, 10–11, 12–13, 227, 252, 264; and Frankel, **1**:246–57, 229n; and Geiger, **1**:46n, 254; **2**:125n; and Graetz, **1**:230–46; **2**:125n, 154n; and Judah Halevi, **1**:42, 47n41, 94, 273, 274, 284, 292, 342, 393, 402, 403; **2**:66n83, 69n90, 77, 79, 80, 81, 81n113,

93, 96n137; and Maimonides, **1**:44, 47n41, 104, 228–29, 251–52, 254, 269, 267, 268, 271, 274, 275n, 297–300, 393, 403, 407, 412–13, 420, 421n111, 429; **2**:49, 56, 58, 77, 93, 172, 239, 245, 274, 275, 303–4; and Mendelssohn, **1**:84, 96, 100, 274, 280, 283, 288n193, 297, 298, 299, 403, 404, 405, 407, 412, 423, 426, 430; **2**:38–39, 46, 75, 77, 126, 178, 239, 271n110, 301, 302; and Nachmanides, **1**:236, 252, 254, 256, 256n50, 259–60, 268, 271, 275n, 342; **2**:61, 94, 300; and reason, **1**:8, 11, 29–30; and Spinoza, **1**:284, 296, 297
Ḥisda, **2**:163n49
Hezekiah ben Manoah (Ḥizquni), **2**:61; 190n88
Hoffmann, David Zvi, **1**:91n, 244
Holdheim, Samuel, **1**:7; 173, 174, 189, 221, 311, 442; **2**:116, 136
Homer, **1**:144n27
Horkenos Ben Eli'ezer, **2**:145
Horowitz, Abraham, **1**:348
Horowitz, Isaiah (Hashla; Shnei Luḥot Habrit), **2**:3, 66n83
Horwitz, Rivka, **1**:152, 153, 230, 310n238, 461–462, 471n180, 474n, 487n196, 509n223; **2**:85n, 91n129, 94, 96, 96n
Humboldt, Wilhelm von, **2**:152n39, 179n
Hume, David, **1**:4
Huna (Rav), **1**:242
Hupfeld, Hermann, **1**:63
Hutner, Bruria David, **1**:182n34

I

Ibn Ezra, Avraham, **1**:53, 55, 60, 115, 197n60, 465n, 468n, 476, 495n201, 505; **2**:60, 190n, 281n, 287; and Luzzatto, **1**:141, 310n238, 316n, 320, 323n, 449, 458, 459, 467, 468, 476, 485, **2**:287
ibn Gabirol, Solomon, **1**:476
Ibn Kaspi, Joseph, **1**:347–48, 375
ibn Rushd (Averroes), **1**:347, 354n14, 487n196
ibn Tibbon, Moses, **1**:348
ibn Tibbon, Samuel, **1**:347
Ibn Yiḥiye, Gedalia, **2**:164n50
Ilgen, Karl David, **1**:62, 70
Isaac of Acre, **2**:4
Ishmael, **2**:178, 273–74
Ishmael (Rabbi), **1**:194, 231, 237, 240–41, 245, 246, 253
Ish-Shalom, B., **2**:356n16, 357, 494n
Israel Baal Shem Tov (the Besht), **1**:455n165
Isserles, Moses (Rema), **1**:149; **2**:23, 150, 231

J

Jacob, **1**:42; 440n; **2**:13, 107, 203, 246
Jacob (Rabbi), **2**:253
Jacob Ben Asher (Even Ha'ezer; the Tur; Yore De'a), **2**:148, 180, 226, 233, 288, 288n, 290
Jacobson, Israel, **1**:7, 186
Jaffe, Mordecai (the *Levush*), **1**:348; **2**:149
Jeremiah, **2**:25, 46, 49, 106, 121, 122, 124, 298
Jesus, **1**:149n, 151, 333; **2**:7, 9, 202–4, 205, 207, 208n16, 239, 245–49, 271, 271n110, 287, 290; and Chajes, **2**:233, 235, 236, 244, 298; and commandments, **2**:282; Emden on, **2**:210–12; execution of, **2**:6; and Hirsch, **2**:247–49, 291, 303; Jews' rejection of, **2**:204, 209, 281, 287;

and Maimonides, 2:208n16, 236; and Mendelssohn, 2:214, 216, 220; and messiah, 2:202, 209, 233. *See also* Christianity, Christians in Index of Subjects
Joseph, 2:246
Joseph II, 1:3, 34; 2:1
Josephus, 2:84n, 227
Joshua, 1:100, 116, 142
Josiah, 1:62, 63, 130, 142
Jost, Isaac Marcus, 1:53, 55, 70, 112, 145, 311, 456, 475, 478, 511n; 2:103; and Bible criticism, 232; and Chajes, 1:70n20, 76, 78n35, 387; 2:335; and Luzzato, 1:130, 139, 144n127, 153n144, 302–5, 309, 310n238, 320, 499, 502, 504; 2:345; Judah Hanasi, 1:328; 2:163n
Judah Loew ben Bezalel (Maharal), 1:348, 422n113, 494n; 2:4, 163n, 167n53
Judah Halevi (*Kuzari*), 1:24, 30, 42, 47n41, 52, 53, 94, 167n, 201n67, 284, 292, 329, 333, 342, 356n, 367, 373; 2:100, 122, 286; chosenness of the Jewish people, 2:111, 112n; and Christianity, 2:236, 239, 298; and ethics, 1:355; and exile, 2:93, 100, 101; and Islam, 2:238, 298; and the Jewish people, 2:6, 80, 236, 288; and Land of Israel, 2:56, 66n84; and mission of the Jews, 2:93, 100, 101, 113–14, 278; and morality, 1:274; and non-Jews, 1:333; 2:79, 80, 81, 107, 236, 238, 303; and philosophy, 1:274; and prophecy, 1:31, 170–71, 333; 2:3, 79, 81, 101; and rationalism, 1:196, 274, 403; and revelation, 1:31, 168n, 170, 196, 355; 2:101, 302; and tradition, 1:170

Judah the Hasid, 2:225

K

Kahana, M., 1:202n67
Kalischer, 2:16, 72–74
Kaplan, Lawrence, 1:124n, 145, 149–50, 151, 152–53, 266n, 419, 420, 422n113, 423n114, 474n, 496
Kant, Immanuel. *See* philosophy: Kantian in Index of Subjects
Karo, Joseph (Beit Yosef), 1:72; 2:288n
Katz, Jacob, 1:14n, 325n, 344n; 2:213
Katz, Joshua Falk, 2:228n
Kaufman, Yehezkel, 1:61n6
Kellner, M., 2:130n2
Kepler, Johannes, 1:100, 422n113
Kimḥi, David, 1:449, 499; 2:129n
Kirchheim, Raphael, 1:110, 134
Klausner, Joseph, 1:48, 141n125, 197n60–61, 321n, 325n, 336n269, 458n, 459, 460, 460n, 461, 491; 2:104n149, 121n, 125, 125n, 186n, 205, 224n, 253n83, 257n
Klugman, Eliyahu Meir, 1:416n103, 438n139
Kohut, Alexander, 1:177n
Kook Abraham Isaac Hacohen, 1:357; 494n, 495; 2:164, 315
Kranz, August, 2:219
Krochmal, Abraham, 2:28n26
Krochmal, Nachman, 1:25, 35, 48, 70n17, 198–200, 310, 325, 356, 362, 495; 2:311; and Aggada, 1:208; and biblical criticism, 1:65n, 77–78, 79, 111, 115, 141–42, 144; and Chajes, 1:36, 37, 77n33, 197–98, 365, 371n30, 382, 382n50, 383, 387; 2:296,

310, 332, 335; and Halakha,
1:11, 232–33, 239n131, 248,
320, 321, 325n; and the Jewish
nation, 2:75, 334; and Luzzatto,
1:467, 474n, 505; 2:310n238;
and Maskilim, 1:16, 17; and the
middle way, 1:15–17, 22n23;
and reason, 1:16, 198–99; and
revelation, 1:11, 16
Krug, Traugott Wilhelm, 2:18
Kunitz, Moses, 1:173
Kurzweil, B., 2:445n150

L

Landau, Ezekiel, 1:180n26; 2:77, 244
Landau, Moses, 1:466
Landau, Naomi, 1:466
Lasker, Edward, 1:230n118
Lattes, Giuseppe, 1:323n
Lau, Benjamin, 1:244
Lavater, Johann Kaspar, 2:214
Lazarus-Yafeh, Hava, 2:201
Leah, 2:166
Leff, Leopold, 1:506
Lefin, Mendel, 1:35
Lehman, Meir Marcus, 1:22n
Leibniz, Gottfried Wilhelm, 1:485
Leibowitz, Yeshayahu, 1:262n, 481n; 2:67n89, 237n, 262n95, 263n97, 309, 315
Lessing, Gotthold Ephraim, 1:28, 198; 2:18, 35, 75, 110, 214, 220
Letteris, Meir Halevi, 1:53, 471, 472n; 2:283
Levi, Michael, 2:74n99
Levi, Z., 1:460n158; 2:97n139, 122n
Levi ben Gershon (Ralbag), 1:348, 350; 2:129, 130n2
Levin, Joshua Heschel, 2:336
Levinger, J. S., 1:234n
Levinsohn, Isaac Baer, 1:22n
Liberles, Robert, 1:45, 46n1, 277n117

Liebermann, Eliezer, 1:173, 305, 306
Liebman, Charles, 1:177n
Lifschitz, Jacob, 2:74
Locke, John, 1:52, 471n180; 2:210
Lolli, Samuel Chaim, 1:22, 52, 53, 448–49, 448n155
Löw, Leopold, 1:475
Löwe, Joel, 1:499
Luther, Martin, 2:208, 209, 249, 256
Luz, E., 1:200n
Luzzatto, Barukh-Iov, 1:53
Luzzatto, Benjamin, 1:54
Luzzatto, Bilha Batsheba Segré, 1:53
Luzzatto, Hezekiah Raphael, 1:53
Luzzatto, Isaiah, 1:53
Luzzatto, Joseph, 1:53
Luzzatto, Leah, 1:53
Luzzatto, Lolli, 1:448
Luzzatto, Malca, 1:53
Luzzatto, Miriam, 1:54
Luzzatto, Ohev Ger (Filosseno), 1:53
Luzzatto, Samuel David, 1:3, 11, 13; and Abraham ben David of Posquières, 1:326; and Chorin, 1:305; 2:125; and Frankel, 1:320, 326, 502, 503; and Geiger, 1:309, 311, 322, 323n, 327, 502, 504–5; 2:116, 125, 196; and Graetz, 1:320, 326, 502, 503–4; and Ibn Ezra, 1:53, 136, 140, 141, 310n238, 316n, 320, 323n, 449, 458, 459, 467, 468, 476, 485, 2:287; and Jost, 1:302–5, 309, 311, 320, 475, 478, 499, 502, 511n; and Judah Halevi, 1:52, 53, 329, 333, 342, 449, 466, 467, 485, 508, 510; 2:100, 101, 103, 107, 110, 111, 112n59, 113, 114n160, 121n, 278, 279, 282, 285n128, 286, 288; and Krochmal, 1:310n238, 320, 325n, 328, 467, 505, 508;

Index

2:305; and Maimonides, **1**:53, 216–17, 298–99, 310n238, 318, 320, 322, 323n, 324, 326, 327, 334, 336, 340, 365, 370–71, 376, 385, 407, 449, 450, 451, 453, 454, 458, 463–65, 467, 471n180, 474n, 476, 479, 485, 485n, 487, 489, 490n, 505, 508, 510n; **2**:100, 101, 103, 110, 187, 189, 278, 283, 285–86, 291, 304, 306, 309; and Menahem ben Saruq, **1**:56–67; and Mendelssohn, **1**:29, 52, 56, 119, 133, 310n238, 329, 336, 407, 447, 452, 453, 462, 482n, 483, 485, 508–9, 509n, 511; **2**:99, 101, 102, 105, 110, 122, 126, 277, 278, 342; and Rashbam, **1**:57, 110, 476; **2**:281n; and Rashi, **1**:57, 110, 466, 467, 476, 508; **2**:100, 196, 280, 281n, 282, 288; and Spinoza, **1**:53, 110, 115, 134, 136, 140, 145, 153

M

Mahler, R., **1**:304n229
Maimon, Solomon, **1**:173
Maimonides: and Christianity, **2**:100, 213, 236, 238, 245, 249, 290, 291, 298, 309; and ethics, **1**:218, 377; the exile, **2**:93; and faith, **1**:218, 219, 348; **2**:3; and free will, **1**:490n; and God, **1**:355, 375, 377, 381, 491n; **2**:3, 208; and Halakha, **1**:160–63, 165, 182, 193, 194, 196, 200, 203–4, 233, 326; **2**:56–57, 237n, 306, 311; and historical consciousness and processes, **2**:3, 57, 58, 110; and Islam, **2**:237n, 274, 275; and the Jewish people, **1**:377; **2**:80, 93, 100, 103, 110, 236, 278, 288; and the Land of Israel, **2**:57, 58, 69n92, 302–3; and messiah, **2**:6, 28, 208; and morality, **1**:26, 218; **2**:237n, 297; and non-Jews, **1**:218–20, 327, 340, 377, 402, 463; **2**:21, 22, 34, 49, 80, 100, 101, 215n29, 226, 231, 232, 233, 234, 238, 239, 241n61, 283, 285, 288; and Oral Law, **1**:17, 160–64, 165, 166, 168n, 171–72, 195–96, 229n, 236n, 252, 255, 326n, 327, 366, 368, 373–76, 454; **2**:145, 296; and philosophy, **1**:347, 350, 352–53, 355–56, 369–83, 454, 485, 512; **2**:297, 306; and prophecy, **1**:161, 172, 347, 366, 374, 381, 382n50; **2**:28; and Providence, **1**:347, 491n; **2**:6; and rationalism, **1**:163, 220, 274, 296, 297–301, 355, 356, 384, 487; **2**:141; and reason, **1**:9n, 162, 196, 297–300, 347, 350, 356, 377, 382, 384; **2**: 215n29, 297, 301; and religion, **1**:347, 356, 373; and revelation, **1**:26, 161, 165, 171–72, 182, 195, 234n, 256n, 326n, 376, 377, 381, 382, 386–87; **2**:80, 215n, 311; and science, **1**:348, 350, 352; and Spinoza, **1**:60; and status of women, **2**:129, 130n2, 187, 189; and teaching girls, **2**:145; and tradition, **1**:160, 167n11; and Written Torah, **1**:160–61, 166, 172, 182, 204, 336, 352, 374; **2**:145, 237n
Malach, D., **1**:207n77
Manzoni, Alessandro, **1**:52
Margolioth, Ephraim Zalman, **1**: 37; **2**:148
Margulies, Ephraim Zev, **2**:148
Mecklenberg, Yakov Zvi, 364n24
Meir, Moshe, **2**:318

Meir ben Baruch of Rothenburg, 2:3, 66n83
Meir ben Todros, 371
Menachem Meiri, 1:31; 2:5, 24, 210, 249, 290
Mendelssohn, Moses, 1:10–11; attitude towards women, 2:135; and biblical criticism, 1:64, 65n; and Christianity, 2:8, 213–21, 271n110, 290; and ethics, 1:423, 462; and exile, 2:94; and faith, 2:216, 219; and fundamentalism, 1:405; and God, 1:358; 2:216; and Halakha and commandments, 1:509; 2:8, 13; 216, 219, 220; and Haskala, 1:5; historical consciousness and processes, 2:11, 13, 35, 79, 105; and humanism, 2:214, 215; and the Jewish people and their mission, 2:5, 13, 15, 78, 79, 84n, 94, 101, 102, 126; and Jews' rights, 2:217; and the Land of Israel, 2:26, 38; 298, 302, 308; and morality, 1:274, 283, 358, 377; 2:215; and non-Jews/humanity, 1:377, 509; 2:12, 34, 77, 214, 239, 285n127; and Oral Law/Sages, 1:75, 509, 511; 2:10; and Orthodoxy, 1:361, 364; 2:219; Pentateuch translation into German by, 1:65; and philosophy, 1:358, 482n; and Providence, 1:358; 2:9, 12, 13, 102; and rationalism, 1:9, 274, 407, 447; 2:7; and reason, 1:10, 29, 9n4, 274, 283, 363, 364, 377, 403, 404, 423, 462, 489, 508–13; 2:8, 12, 13, 15, 39, 79, 102, 126, 214, 215, 216, 218, 219, 222; and Reform, 1:364; and religion, 1:218, 358; 2:12, 13, 214–20; and revelation, 1:7, 29, 96, 123, 216, 358, 363, 377, 403–4, 423, 509; 2:8, 215, 219, 278–79, 301; and romanticism, 2:468n; and secularization, 1:5; and status of women, 2:135, 178, 187n86; and tradition, 1:10; and universalism, 2:215; and Written Torah, 1:405, 430; 2:39, 216, 218, 219, 220
Meyer, Michael, 1:177n; 2:136; 137n18, 276n
Michaelis, Johann David, 2:9, 10, 11:10, 17, 214, 217, 323
Mints, Judah, 2:149
Mizrachi, Elijah, 2:158n
Modena, Leon (J. A.), 1:171 (Leon Modena) 22n, 332n49; 2:
Montefiore, Moses, 1:24
Morais, Sabato, 1:177n
Mordechai ben Hillel, 2:149
Morino (Catholic priest), 126
Morpurgo, David, 1:308
Morpurgo, Rachel, 2:181–82, 184, 194
Moses, 1:78, 80, 81n, 88, 89, 105, 111, 116, 121–22, 124, 138, 139, 169n13, 242, 243, 270, 334, 381, 458; 2:20, 104, 120, 246, 247, and authorship of the Torah, 1:60, 61–62, 63, 70, 73, 80, 81, 105, 106, 110, 116, 124n, 129, 140–41, 151, 504; 2:32, 305, 310, 344, and commandments, 1:60, 70, 160–61, 356n, 377; 2:34, and Halakha from Sinai–1:161, 162, 164, 165, 166, 170, 193, 194, 197, 202, 232, 233, 236, 247–48, 249, 250, 252, 255, 264, and law, 2:8, 114, 220, and miracles, 1:122, 123; 2:247, and Noahide commandments, 1: 217, 378, 386; 2:23, 24, 34–35, 77, 215, 231, 232, 233, 241, 285, and Oral Law, 1:11, 74, 91n, 102, 155, 159, 261, 308, 367,

442; **2**:300, 310, 311, and prophecy, **1**:62, 80, 81, 122; **2**:36, 119, 235, 290, religion of, **2**:110, 113, and revelation at Sinai, **1**:67n, 69, 80, 81, 106, 123, 154, 159, 160, 162, 164, 178, 180, 194, 197, 205, 246; **2**:23, 25, 37, 77, 101, 232, 233, 241, and Written Torah~**1**:156, 159, 367
Moses Narboni, **1**:347, 375
Motzkin, Arye Leo, **1**:152
Muhammad, **2**:6, 202n1, 208n, 233, 236, 239

N

Nachman of Bratslav, **1**:357, 495
Nachmanides, **1**:252, 268, 271, 275n, 342, 375; **2**:7; and Halakha and Oral Law, **1**:163, 193, 194, 195, 203, 205, 234n, 236, 254, 256, 259, 264; and hermeneutics, **1**:254, 257, 258; and the Land of Israel, **1**:31; **2**:4, 60, 71, 94; and Sages, **1**:175, 196; and women's status, **2**:129n
Naḥman Bar Yitsḥaq, **2**:321
Narboni, Moses, **1**:347, 375
Nathansohn, Naphtali Herz, **1**:480
Nehemia (Rabbi), **2**:280, 281n
Niehoff, M. R., **2**:11n10
Nieto, David, **1**:180n26
Nietzsche, Friedrich, **2**:256n, 260
Nissim of Gerona (Ran), **1**:168n, 169, 169n13, 201n67; **2**:23, 158n44, 197, 231
Noth, Martin, **1**:61n6

O

Orenstein, Meshulam Jacob (*Yeshuot Ya'aqov*), **2**:149

P

Paul, **2**:23, 203–4, 205, 206, 211, 212, 233, 249, 269, 270, 281, 282, 290
Perl, Joseph, **1**:362, 499
Philippson, Ludwig, 173, 506; **2**:118, 119, 125
Philo of Alexandria, **1**:31; **2**:5, 84n114
Phinehas, **1**:45, 46n
Plato, **1**:331, 373, 375; **2**:51n
Prins, Eliezer Liepman Philip, **1**:429n126; **2**:172

R

Rabad. *See* Abraham ben David of Posquières; Abraham ibn Daud
Rabenu Tam, **2**:198, 210
Rabinovich, Samuel Pinehas, **1**:235n124
Rachel, **2**:166, 246
Ralbag. *See* Levi ben Gershon
Randegger, Abraham, **1**:98n140
Rapoport, David, **1**:498
Rapoport, Solomon Judah (Shir), **1**:11, 17, 35, 38, 48, 53, 55, 65n, 70n20, 76, 115, 130, 142, 144n127, 146–47, 192n47, 255–57, 303, 304n, 309, 316n, 323n, 362, 382n50, 387, 458, 465n, 467, 498, 500, 505; **2**:110, 197, 290n, 305
Rashbam. *See* Samuel ben Meir
Rashi, **1**:57, 72, 110, 133, 272, 334, 458, 466, 467, 476, 508; **2**:60, 100, 144, 196, 288n
  Luzzatto citing, **2**:280, 281n, 282, 288, 288n, 290
  and women's status, **2**:129n
Ravina, **1**:327, 367, 370
Ravitsky, Aviezer, **1**:xv, 14n, 19n, 347, 356, 356n, 357, 406n92; **2**:3, 4n2, 11n10–11, 53n58, 66n83, 71n95, 208n16
Rawidovicz, Shimon, **1**:152, 197n60
Rebecca, **1**:440n; **2**:162, 166, 178
Reggio, Isaac Samuel, **1**:52, 53, 70,

78n, 113, 121, 187n, 191n, 321–22, 322n, 323, 362, 371, 387, 447, 453, 456, 458, 463–64, 468n, 486n, 487n, 495n201, 505; **2**:311
Reifman, Jacob, **2**:196n
Resh Lakish, **1**:263n158, 272; **2**:20n
Rema. *See* Isserles, Moses
Rendtorff, Rolf, **1**:61n6
Rivkes, Moses, **2**:210, 228, 249, 290
Rofé, Alexander, **1**:61n6
Rosen, T., **2**:129n
Rosenak, Avinoam, **1**:494n
Rosenak, Michael, **1**:474n
Rosenberg, Shalom, **1**:14n, 67n11, 132n110, 158n1, 160n3, 162n6, 169n13, 171n17, 196n57, 202n67, 351–52, 351n13, 353, 354, 354n14, 356, 356n16, 357, 366, 482, 482n193, 493, 493n200; **2**:81, 81n113, 84n, 121n
Rosenblit, Pinḥas, **2**:94, 96n137
Rosenbloom, N. H., 47n41, 460–61; **2**:240n
Rosenmüller, Ernst Friedrich Karl, **1**:115, 139, 141, 143, 145, 153n144
Rosenthal, Solomon, **1**:48, 308, 501
Rosenzweig, Franz, **1**:67n89, 97n139, 309, 315
Ross, J. J., **1**:487n196
Ross, Tamar, **2**:130–31, 132, 138n, 163n
Rostovsky-Halprin, Sara, **1**:317n, 458n
Rotenberg, M., **1**:198n62; **2**:28n26
Rotenstreich, Natan, **1**:434n134, 458n167, 482n
Roth, Cecil, 49n45
Rothschild, Baron Simon Wolff, **2**:72
Rousseau, Jean-Jacques, **1**:4, 52, 458n167, 462; **2**:135

Rubashov, Z., **1**:61n6
Rubin, Solomon, **1**:476, 478; **2**:190n88
Rubinstein, B., **1**:190n88

S

Sa'adia Gaon, **1**:9n4, 122, 123, 167n11, 274, 352, 355n, 469; **2**:5, 60
Sachs, Michael, **1**:189
Sachs, Shneur, **1**:53, 476, 479
Sagi, Avi, **1**:14n, 474n, 168n, 170, 171n, 196n57, 201n65, 239n131, 262–63, 474n, 481n, 494–95n; **2**:21n23, 220n33, 318
Salanter, Israel, **1**:438n
Salvador, Joseph, **2**:205, 233, 237n, 243, 245, 247n71, 253n83, 256, 257, 290, 291
Samet, Moshe, 13n10
Samson ben Abraham of Sens, **1**:168n, 170
Samuel ben Ḥofni, **1**:367
Samuel Ben Meir (Rashbam), **1**:57, 110, 133, 316, 476; **2**:61, 281n, 288n
Sarah, **1**:96; **2**:160, 162, 166, 176, 178, 179, 246, 273, 274
Sasportas, Jacob, **2**:213, 290
Schelling, Friedrich Wilhelm Joseph, **1**:394, 494n
Schiller, Friedrich, **1**:81n40, 111, 117n, 394, 395n66, 506
Schlegel, August Wilhelm, 152n39
Schleiermacher, Friedrich, **1**:27, 30, 384, 385, 508; 152n39, 221, 239
Schorr, Joshua Heschel, **1**:36, 48, 53, 54, 128, 132, 145, 183n32, 310, 310n238, 311, 321, 325, 362, 466, 468n, 486n, 501, 504, 505
Schorsch, I., **1**:46n45, 249n138, 434n134, 445n150

Schwab, Simon, 1:266n, 416n103
Schwartz, D., 1:494n; 2:5n2, 82n113
Schwartz, M., 1:299n220
Schweid, Eliezer, 1:86n, 367n, 406n92, 474n, 494n; 2:81
Sefer Haḥinukh, 1:167n12
Segal, David Halevi (*Turei Zahav*), 2:145-46, 174
Sforno, Obadaiah, 2:61, 190n88, 278
Shahar, Shulamith, 2:128
Shamai, 1:231, 235, 245, 249, 253, 321; disciples of, 1:159, 163, 239; disputes with Hillel, 1:235, 237-38, 303
Shavit, Y., 1:61n6, 65n9, 474n, 481n
Sheli, Ḥ., 65n, 105n73, 141n125
Shema'ya, 1:238
Shilo, Elḥanan, 2:318
Shimon bar Yoḥai, 2:21n23
Shimon Ben Gamliel, 2:168
Shinan, Avigdor, 207n15
Shlomo ben Aderet (Rashba), 1:207
Shlomo Yitzhaki. *See* Rashi
Shmuel Hanagid, 1:219
Shohat, Azriel, 1:334n
Sherira Gaon, 1:76; 2:336
Silber, Michael, 1:14n, 141n, 266n
Silbermann, Eliezer Liepman, 1:106, 323n249, 506; 2:118
Silman, Y., 1:487n
Silman, Y. D., 1:239n131, 246n133
Simeon the Just, 1:233
Simon, A. E., 1:474n, 481n
Simonsohn, Shlomo, 2:203n6, 205n10, 205n12
Sinkoff, N. B., 1:35n31
Sklare, Marshall, 1:177n
Slymovics, 1:23n24, 324n; 2:150n104
Smolenskin, P., 2:186n
Soave, Francesco, 1:52
Sofer, Moses (Ḥatam Sofer), 1:8, 13n10, 19n6, 176, 183-84, 184n33, 188n, 201n67, 230n118, 278n172; 2:149, 2:149, 151
Soleveitchik, Joseph B., 1:262n, 357, 494n
Solomon, 2:22
Solomon of Montpellier, 1:371
Soloveitchik, M., 1:61n6
Spektor, Isaac Elchanan, 2:74
Spinoza, Benedict de (Baruch), 1:25, 59, 60-61, 139-41, 351-52; and Hirsch, 1:284, 296, 297; and Luzzatto, 1:53, 110, 115, 134, 136, 140, 145, 153. *See also* Philosophy: of Spinoza in Index of Subjects
Stein, Leopold, 1:224
Steinheim, Solomon Ludwig, 2:116, 240n
Steinschneider, Moritz, 1:362, 471
Stern, E., 413n101
Stern, Salman, 2:193n91, 445n150
Stern, Sigismund, 2:136
Stern, Sigismund, 2:136
Stern, Yedidia, 2:318

T

Tanḥuma, 1:242
Tanḥum ben Ḥanilai, 1:242
Tarfon, 2:253n84
Teller, Wilhelm, 2:222
Tevele of Lissa, David, 1:180n26
Tishby, Isaiah, 1:275n
Toland, John, 2:210
Tosafists of France, 2:3
Trier, Salomon Abraham, 1:312

U

Urbach, Ephraim Elimelech, 1:244

V

Vargon, Shmuel, 105n73, 316n
Vater, Johann Severin, 1:62, 70

Verses, S., **1**:54n50, 304n229
Vico, Giambattista, **1**:462
Virgil, **1**:144n127
Voltaire, **1**:4; **2**:221, 227
von Lynar (baron), **2**:10n10
Von Rad, Gerhard, **1**:61n6

W

Wahrman, Judah, **1**:326
Wechsler, Pinḥas Elḥanan (Hila), **1**:252, 266–67, 266n, 271, 415n, 419, 422, 423n
Wein, Max, **1**:145
Weinberg, Y. Y., **1**:438n
Wellhausen, Julius, **1**:63
Westreich, Elimelech, **2**:129n
Wessely, Naftali Hirz, **1**:360n20, 361, 404, 406n; **2**:219; and biblical criticism, **1**:64; and Chajes, **1**:220, 387; and education, **1**:29, 51, 65, 358, 393, 425, 426, 428, 499; **2**:171, 194, 299, 312, 342; and Haskalah, **1**:274, 344, 357–58, 365; **2**:213, 331; and Hirsch, **1**:274, 436n; **2**:171, 299, 312; influence on modern religious thinkers, **1**:36n31; and Jewish tradition, **1**:359; and Luzzatto, **1**:51, 329, 447, 499; and Mendelssohn, **2**:219
Weiner, Max, 145, 124n171
Wise, Isaac Meir, **2**:137
Witter, Hennig Bernhard, **1**:61n6
Wolf, Immanuel, **1**:361
Wolff, Christian, **1**:485
Wolfson, H. A., **1**:355n14, 487n

Y

Yanai (Rabbi), **1**:242; **2**:20n21
Yehoshu'a (Rabbi), **1**:231, 239, 239n131, 242, 245
Yeruḥam Ben Meshullam, **2**:231
Yeruḥam (Rabbenu), **2**:23
Yerushalmi, Yosef Haim, **1**:6n; **2**:332
Yishmael Bar Rav Naḥman, **1**:436
Yitsḥaq (Nappaḥa), **1**:242
Yoḥanan ben Napaha, **1**:263n158, 377; **2**:20n; 79n
Yoḥanan ben Zakai, **1**:240
Yom Tov ben Avraham Al'Ashvili (Ritva), **1**:168n, 170, 201n67
Yose (Rabbi), **2**:336

Z

Zacuto, Abraham, **2**:336
Zadok of Lublin, **1**:494
Zamosc, Israel, **1**:35, 348–49, 387
Zechariah, **1**:143
Zeraḥia Halevi, **2**:195
Zevin, Gili, **2**:136
Zinberg, Israel, 49n45
Zoroaster, **1**:470
Zunz, Yom Tov Lipmann [Leopold], **1**:49n45, 53, 76, 79, 126, 197n60, 361, 362, 387; **2**:136
Zweifel, Eliezer Zvi Hacohen, **1**:13n9, 22n23

www.ingramcontent.com/pod-product-compliance
Lightning Source LLC
Chambersburg PA
CBHW051107230426
43667CB00014B/2479